TAKING A STAND

EDITED BY TIMOTHY J. McGEE

Taking a Stand: Essays in Honour of John Beckwith

UNIVERSITY OF TORONTO PRESS
Toronto Buffalo London

© University of Toronto Press Incorporated 1995
Toronto Buffalo London
Printed in Canada
Reprinted in 2018
ISBN 0-8020-0583-7
ISBN 978-1-4875-7891-6 (paper)

Printed on acid-free paper

Canadian Cataloguing in Publication Data

Main entry under title:

Taking a stand : essays in honour of John Beckwith

ISBN 0-8020-0583-7

1. Music – Canada – History and criticism.
2. Beckwith, John, 1927– . I. McGee, Timothy J.
(Timothy James), 1936– . II. Beckwith, John,
1927– .

ML205.1.T35 1995   780'.971   C95-930485-1

University of Toronto Press acknowledges the financial assistance to its publishing program of the Canada Council and the Ontario Arts Council.

Contents

PREFACE vii
ACKNOWLEDGMENTS ix

I Introduction

TIMOTHY J. McGEE
John Beckwith and Canadian Music 5

JAMES REANEY
Serinette 9

II Studies of Composers

ALAN M. GILLMOR
Echoes of Time and the River 15

DON McLEAN
Of Things Past: John Hawkins's *Remembrances* (1969) 45

GAIL DIXON
Symmetry and Synthesis in Beckwith's *Etudes* (1983) 70

JOHN MAYO
Coming to Terms with the Past: Beckwith's *Keyboard Practice* 94

III Music Education

CARL MOREY
Musical Education in Nineteenth-Century Toronto 113

LEE R. BARTEL AND PATRICIA MARTIN SHAND
Canadian Music in the School Curriculum: Illusion or Reality? 125

IV Comparative Studies: Canada and the United States

MARILYNN J. SMILEY
Across Lake Ontario: Nineteenth-Century Concerts and Connections 149

NICHOLAS TEMPERLEY
Worship Music in English-Speaking North America, 1608–1820 166

ELAINE KEILLOR
Indigenous Music as a Compositional Source: Parallels and Contrasts in Canadian and American Music 185

V Canadian Popular Music, Past and Present

GORDON E. SMITH
The Genesis of Ernest Gagnon's *Chanson populaires du Canada* 221

TIMOTHY RICE WITH TAMMY GUTNIK
What's Canadian about Canadian Popular Music? The Case of Bruce Cockburn 238

VI A Canadian Looking-Glass

GORDANA LAZAREVICH
Aspects of Early Arts Patronage in Canada: From Rockefeller to Massey 259

BEVERLEY DIAMOND
Narratives in Canadian Music History 273

LAWRENCE BECKWITH
John Beckwith's Principal Compositions and Writings to 1994 306

LIST OF CONTRIBUTORS 315

Preface

Perhaps I should explain our title: *Taking a Stand*. It is the title of a quintet written for the Canadian Brass in 1972 by John Beckwith, a composition that is both serious and humorous. The work involves movement of the performers to various stations around the concert hall, which allows the audience to hear the music from a variety of perspectives. The title has been adopted for this book because it symbolically represents how John Beckwith has vigorously 'taken a stand' to promote Canadian music; he has chosen his lifetime mission with care and pursued it unswervingly with missionary fervour. And to take the analogy a step further, he has become personally involved in all aspects of Canadian music, observing it, exposing it, creating it, and celebrating it from numerous perspectives. *Taking a Stand*, therefore, is offered to John in the spirit of so many of his compositions: a bit of a pun, but with seriousness of purpose at it roots.

The scholarly objective of this book is to present learned essays on a wide variety of Canadian musical subjects. The authors were carefully chosen to represent as many different areas of current research as possible, and were asked to contribute essays that would stand as models for future research into the various aspects of the subjects. It is my belief that we have accomplished that goal here; that collectively the essays summarize the current state of research in Canadian musical topics, and at the same time they individually provide standards, patterns, approaches, and directions for future research. It is not surprising that these essays also represent areas of John Beckwith's own interests.

In their responses to the invitation to contribute to the Festschrift, many of those contacted took the opportunity to express in some candid way their esteem for John Beckwith. Those who had been students spoke of his inspiring teaching and his encouragement, others praised his constant championing of the cause of Canadian music, and all expressed pleasure in seeing him honoured in this manner. A natural by-product of Beckwith's promotion of Canadian music and Canadian composers has been that the focus of his writings is on others, with a consequent unfortunate neglect of Beckwith himself. This book is a small step towards shifting the spotlight to cast light on John Beckwith's place at the centre of Canadian music. It is offered to John with the best wishes of all his colleagues in Canadian music on the occasion of his retirement from teaching.

Although it had been planned for many years to honour John Beckwith eventually with a Festschrift, when he announced his intention to take early retirement in 1990, we were caught somewhat off balance. Plans for the volume were begun immediately and invitations to contribute were sent out to John's colleagues active in Canadian music research. The authors included here are to be commended for acting so swiftly. The only problem caused by John's surprise announcement was that several of his friends and colleagues were immersed in projects that would not permit them to respond to the invitation in time for this publication. Therefore, in addition to those who honour John Beckwith here with their essays, dozens of other colleagues are present in spirit.

TJM

Acknowledgments

A project such as this one is rarely the work of a single person, and I wish to thank my colleagues both at the Faculty of Music, University of Toronto, and at other Canadian universities for advice and support over the past several years. In particular I am grateful to Carl Morey who has encouraged, assisted, and advised me in this project from its inception. I am indebted to him also in his role as director of the Institute for Canadian Music for raising the necessary funds to assist with the publication of this volume. Thanks are also due to Robin Elliott for his careful and skilful copy-editing, and to Karen Boersma of the University of Toronto Press for seeing to the production details.

TIMOTHY J. McGEE

It is appropriate that the Institute for Canadian Music should play a part in the publication of these essays in honour of John Beckwith. During his tenure as first director of the Institute for Canadian Music, he was responsible for the organization, editing and publishing of a series of books under the general title of *CanMus Documents*. In a sense, this present volume continues his initiative.

The Institute was able to offer financial support for the publication of these essays through the generosity of several donors. It is a pleasure to acknowledge the assistance of the Erlaine and Gerard Collins Foundation (Mrs G.H. Collins), the Henry White Kinnear Foundation (Mr Arthur R.A. Scace), Mr James Walker, and Mrs E. Wilma Smith.

I want especially to thank Stephen Smith for the personal interest that he took in this project, as well as for his generosity. Lastly, I want to acknowledge the important gift from the Charles Jordan Fund, which continues its earlier subvention of *CanMus Documents*.

CARL MOREY
Jean A. Chalmers Chair in Canadian Music
Institute for Canadian Music
Faculty of Music
University of Toronto

TAKING A STAND

PART ONE

Introduction

TIMOTHY J. McGEE

John Beckwith and Canadian Music

It is not an exaggeration to say that John Beckwith has been the single most important influence on Canadian music over the past forty years. He has been engaged actively and energetically in the forefront and behind the scenes in *all* areas: championing and promoting Canadian music and Canadian composers; encouraging scholarship and serious criticism in the field; and contributing high quality scholarship and creative compositions in overwhelming quantity. This is not to say that he has acted by himself: dozens of people have been extremely influential in various aspects of the field during those years, but much of the energy can be traced back to Beckwith. A forthcoming study of the life and works of John Beckwith by John Mayo will review his accomplishments in detail, but I would like to present here an encapsulated view of how the efforts and vision of one man have changed the history of Canadian music.

The most often cited single contribution by John Beckwith is his article 'About Canadian Music: The PR Failure,'[1] which was the inspiration behind the *Encyclopedia of Music in Canada*. As the story goes, philanthropist Floyd Chalmers was so taken by the article that he organized a team of musicians, scholars, and businessmen to help correct the problem, and the result was the encyclopedia. What had ignited Beckwith and inspired his article was the results of his survey of music encyclopedias and reference books from all over the world. Their concept of music in Canada was appalling. In those books where Canadian music even rated a mention, ignorance and misinformation reigned.

The resultant *Encyclopedia of Music in Canada* (EMC) alone would merit John Beckwith a large mention in the history of Canadian music. But rather than standing by itself, it is typical of his effect on the Canadian music scene. In the case of EMC, Beckwith's writing was the catalyst that caused action by others, but it is far more typical for Beckwith to take the lead himself in solving the problems. And whereas *EMC* might be classified as a fortunate unintended result, countless other benefits to Canadian music were the direct result of long, arduous work on the part of Beckwith, often undertaken in the face of adverse conditions, opposition, and, what is worse, overwhelming apathy on the part of many Canadians.

As Beckwith's seminal article made clear, in the 1950s one of the most serious obstacles to learning about Canadian music was the lack of information about the composers and their music. Some books were available on rather specialized topics, for example Ernest Gagnon's *Chansons Populaires du Canada* (1865), but there was nowhere one could go to read a history of music in Canada. The 1954 edition of *Grove's Dictionary of Music and Musicians*, by far the most comprehensive encyclopedia of music in the English language, contains a six-page article on Australia, but no entry on Canada, and although Healey Willan rates an entry (as 'English organist, conductor, teacher and composer'), Claude Champagne does not.

There was some effort within Canada to support Canadian products: since its inception in 1936, the CBC has broadcast Canadian music and commissioned works from many composers. Canadian orchestras, choruses, and various soloists and ensemble musicians also performed Canadian music, but until recently this was almost exclusively internally generated and directed. Canadian music simply had no international profile, and was not pursued as a legitimate area of historical or critical study either at home or abroad.

It is in that setting that we can appreciate the impact and importance of the many writings of John Beckwith (see 'John Beckwith's Significant Compositions and Writings to 1994' by Lawrence Beckwith). Canadian composers and their works were simply unknown, both to Canadians and to the rest of the world, and someone would have to make an effort to rectify the problem. The titles of some of Beckwith's articles from the 1950s show how clearly he saw that need and how directly he proceeded to satisfy it: 'List of Canadian Recorded Music,' 'Composers in Toronto and Montreal,' and 'Jean Papineau-Couture.' It was the logical first step in the organization of any kind of overview of Canadian composition, and Beckwith was quick not only to perceive the need but to begin to solve the problem. The volume *Contemporary Canadian Composers* that Beckwith co-edited with Keith MacMillan in 1975 provided the first comprehensive list of Canadian composers and their works. It was the logical outcome of such an enterprise and absolutely basic source material for any serious view of Canadian composers. If no one else would promote Canadian composers, he would.

That there is a significant body of critical writing on Canadian music, its composers and its performers, is directly attributable to Beckwith's efforts. His teaching at the University of Toronto has resulted not only in a large number of fine composers, but also in a significant number of scholars whose interest in Canadian topics stems from their exposure to them in Beckwith's classes. His classroom influence alone has resulted in dozens of dissertations, theses, articles, books, and university courses on Canadian music subjects. As director of the Institute for Canadian Music he convened symposia on subjects as diverse as music education, ethnomusicology, and sacred music, and published volumes of research articles in a series he aptly named *CanMus Documents*. The limitless variety and scope of Beckwith's scholarly interests can be understood by simply noting the kinds of subjects he commissioned and published works on in that series. Two of the volumes bear the titles *Hymn Tunes in Canada* and *Hello Out There! Canada's New Music in the World, 1950–85*, and others include historical studies of the Toronto Conservatory and the Arraymusic concert series, essays on Canadian country music, and analyses of the varieties of ethnic music in Canada.

Beckwith's assault on the lack of information has been a many-faceted campaign. He was a member of a small committee led by Keith MacMillan that convinced the Canadian Music Centre and the University of Toronto Press to begin the series 'Canadian Composers/Compositeurs Canadiens,' a continuing set of detailed studies of the life and works of significant Canadian composers. To date four volumes have been published and several more are in preparation.[2] Typically, Beckwith became general editor of the series and, therefore, a *Beckwith* volume was not commissioned until recently, after he had retired from that position. Significantly, although less directly, Beckwith had a hand in both historical studies of Canadian music published in the 1980s, one by Clifford Ford and one by myself.[3] Ford was a long-time composition pupil of Beckwith's, and was one of the students influenced by Beckwith's course on the music of North America. The commissioning of my text was a direct result of Beckwith's series of complaints to the editors of the New York publishing firm W.W. Norton concerning the absence of references to Canadian music and Canadian composers in their reference books and texts.

In his careers as composer and radio broadcaster, John Beckwith has also been an active promoter of Canada; nearly all of his compositions reflect his preoccupation with the country and its history. His radio collage, *Canada Dash – Canada Dot* (1965–7, with a script by James Reaney), criss-crosses the country, pausing to sample the culture and heritage of various places. His operas *Night Blooming Cereus*, *The Shivaree*, and *Crazy to Kill*, (all with Reaney), are based on Canadian subjects. An even more concentrated example of his nationalistic involvement is the series of more than fifty compositions written and arranged between 1981 and 1989 for the Music at Sharon festival, many of them inspired by his interest in the musical history of the Children of Peace, David Willson's nineteenth-century utopian farm community at Sharon, Ontario.

There have been many honours for John Beckwith over the years, including the Canada Council Medal, the Order of Canada, and several honorary doctorates. In 1984 Floyd Chalmers, who was the source of enormous undertakings in the arts for over sixty years, decided to endow a Chair of Canadian Music at the University of Toronto, and to fund the establishment of an Institute for Canadian Music. After a careful search to find the most distinguished person in Canadian music for this position of honour, John Beckwith was chosen. No one was surprised.

NOTES

1 *Musicanada*, July-August 1969, pp. 4–7, 10–13.
2 Published so far are volumes on Harry Somers, Barbara Pentland, R. Murray Schafer, and Jean Papineau-Couture.
3 Clifford Ford, *Canada's Music: An Historical Survey* (Agincourt: GLC Publishers, 1982); Timothy J. McGee, *The Music of Canada* (New York: Norton, 1985).

JAMES REANEY

Serinette

This poem is dedicated to the Chalmers family and to John Beckwith.

Serinette: – petit orgue mécanique, à tuyaux et à cylindre, actionné à l'aide d'une manivelle, et dont on se sert pour instruire les serins. *Par extens.* Personne qui chante de routine et sans aucune expression.'
            (Nouveau Petit Larousse Illustré, 1951)

'Un dictionnaire san examples est un squelette.'

 I
There was a mocking bird in William Faulkner's orchard
Could do anything that his gramophone could & dared
Symphonies, string quartets, Oriental gongs, pianoforte,
Harps and even from nearby Memphis, Elvis Presley.
The mimicry
Drove the author crazy with its instant pickup in a minute
  Of jazz, funeral march...............serviette, minuet.

 II
Serinette, yes, the bird box
The small mechanical organ
Some farmer found in his barn near Sharon
And brought into the museum.

Serinette, yes: what you taught your canary
To sing Donizetti and Meyerbeer with;

More or less a musical saturationer
Played over and over again until the bird replies:

Janis Joplin, Elliott Carter, Ludwig Beethoven,
Petrouchka, Two Part Invention, Firebird.
My own little song which was my soul I've long forgotten.
I'll sing whatever you want, sir, if you'll stop

Turning the the handle handle of that mechanic organ
With pipes and a cylinder specially fitted
To mimic the latest: CBC Stereo trying to teach us
Even the Tintangel Suite, Arnold Bax, Rhapsody Cornish.

Meanwhile CHUM & CKSL grind their serinettes
Of Top Forty, Top Ten over and over again.
A special station in the States does Beatle songs
Over & over again & over & over again,
And eighteenth-century German soldiers
Marched to battle singing four part harmony,
And Muzak in the Atlantic & Pacific stores
Sirens you to reach for Brillo pads and *flocons de riz*.

Serinettes of various sorts we love you,
But we stop you now and listen to the silence.
What did we sing when we were a bird newly arrived
    In this wilderness?

If we could go back and find the Irish fiddler & the Scottish,
The Kentucky & the Acadian, pebbles in our eardrum ponds,
    Old hymn tunes John has found
    Named after of all places – Toronto!

Those I sing this evening encourage and do this,
    Though no doubt belittled in the Star,
    Meeting craggy resistance in the Globe,
Hit with mallets, even hectored by the charlesworth shades,
  Told that 'it is almost a work of genius, but not quite.'
    These I sing
    This evening
    Who unravel
    Who unbaffle

The trail from the forest to the lawn,
   From the bush to the salon,
The buried stream that flows from *then*
   To today when without the bird organ
      We tattle our own rattle,
      Hum our own drum,
      Ding our own gong
      Sing our own song.

15.XI.1984

This poem was written on the occasion of John Beckwith's appointment as the first Jean A. Chalmers Professor of Canadian Music and director of the Institute for Canadian Music. It was read by the poet at 'Musical Chairs,' a ceremony held on 1 December 1984 to honour Floyd S. Chalmers, Jean A. Chalmers, and John Beckwith. The poem has previously been published in James Reaney's *Performance Poems* (Goderich, Ont. 1991).

PART TWO

Studies of Composers

ALAN M. GILLMOR

Echoes of Time and the River

> I know now that people do not die once but many times, and that life of which they were once a part, and which they thought they could never lose, dies too, becomes a ghost, is lost forever. There is nothing to be done about this. We can only love those who are lost, and grieve for their spirits ... I must go on into a new world and a new life, with love and sorrow for what I have lost.
> Thomas Wolfe, in a letter to Mabel Wolfe Wheaton
> 5 January 1930

Even Wagner took a day off now and then from the most grandiose mission ever conceived by the mind of a musician – an *Albumblatt* here and there and, of course, the perennially fresh *Siegfried Idyll* – and if he was not exactly imbued with the comic spirit, *Die Meistersinger* notwithstanding, there are fleeting moments of lightness, of unabashed triviality even, that, if nothing else, serve to tame one of the most monumental and raging egos of the Romantic age. István Anhalt is not a man without humour, without a highly refined sense of the absurd (how else does one survive in the late-twentieth century?), but he did confide in me once, apropos a conversation about Erik Satie and the Gallic muse in the 1920s, that the spirit of comedy does not fit easily and naturally into his particular *Weltanschauung*. As if in verification of this, one searches in vain for the 'album leaf,' the mere bagatelle, among the creative works of Anhalt. *A Little Wedding Music*, written in 1985 for the wedding of his elder daughter Helen, is as close as he has come – at least publicly – to the *pièce d'occasion*. Anhalt's entire life has been an unusually intense and quite conscious search for meaning and identity, which is, perhaps, just another way of saying that he is an artist. And to this quest he brings a mind-set that I would risk calling 'central European,' a particular world-view (one is tempted to say *Weltschmerz*) that he would seem to share to a considerable degree. 'To be simple,' he wrote in 1988, 'is the most difficult act of all, and I haven't mastered it yet.'[1] And so, Anhalt shares the fate of all those who refuse to be anaesthetized by the fatuity and shallowness of much popular culture: they are doomed to join ranks with those who, like Arthur Koestler, suffer acutely from 'chronic indignation' during the perpetual process of mediation between self and external world.

I first met Anhalt in the fall of 1970 when I was a young assistant professor in the Faculty of Music at McGill University. Even now, over twenty years later, I vividly recall the initial intimidation I felt in the presence of a man whose entire being seemed to radiate a dark intellectual energy rendered all the more powerful through its emotional containment, for Anhalt is a person of quiet demeanour and easy grace, what not so long ago used to be called 'old-world charm.' But the appearance of outward calm is deceptive, unable to mask entirely a restlessness mingled with traces of anxiety born, perhaps, of a sense of alienation and displacement, however sublimated.

As my friendship with Anhalt grew in those early months at McGill, I learned a few of the basic biographical facts about my older colleague: a Hungarian Jew born in Budapest in 1919, studies with Kodály in his native city and after the war with Boulanger, Soulima Stravinsky, and Louis Fourestier in Paris, emigration to Canada in 1949. Much later I would learn about the wartime labour brigade in the Hungarian army for Jewish conscripts, the escape in late 1944, the months of fear and concealment in Budapest until the arrival of the Russian armies early in 1945. But even in the early stages of our acquaintanceship, in 1970 and early 1971, at a time when an entire generation was discovering something in the immensely troubled and nostalgic symphonic world of Gustav Mahler that seemed profoundly to match the mood of the agitated, soul-searching sixties, I had sensed in Anhalt something vaguely Mahlerian, a faint echo of the older composer's haunting plaint about being 'thrice homeless.'

> Why did I come?
>   Why then?
>   Why there?
>   Where is my home?
>   Where shall I be going now?
>   For how long?
>   And to what end?[2]

When musicians search through the memory-labyrinth looking for the faintest ripples on the psychic surface that might aid the process of individuation it should not surprise us that fragments of their past should be filtered to a high degree through an aural dreamscape:

> Yes, the bandstand, the music ... all that *was*, and still *is*, part of the music, and the music is part of it all. There is no division ...
> The sounds of Haydn, Mozart, Schubert, some popular marches and operettas, mixed with the cries of the peacocks, the ice-cream vendors' calls, the yells of the children, and the deep tootings of the river barges that plied the Danube from the East to the West and back downstream.
> All of this stuck in the mind, but it was the music that mattered most: that throbbing river of sound, filling, shoving, pulling, lifting the boy ... making him move with the pulse (or against it), making him believe that he controls it all ... (He was about four years old at the time.) Arms thrust forward, he holds a wheel (only he sees it) and with it pretends to steer the flow. He thinks the music is for him alone and he holds it all. Yes, it was also a feeling of power, the illusion of it, over that surging sound-river ... and the urge to be one with it. Yes, it was a mystery, but no questions were asked.[3]

Then there are the recollections of his father Arnold, separated from his mother Katalin when Anhalt was four or five. Arnold Anhalt had wanted to become a musician but had had little chance to study seriously. He played the piano and the violin, but technical limitations seemed, with maddening regularity, to get in the way of complete performances. Fragments of the father's limited violin repertoire – Bach, Kreisler, a few others – short passages endlessly repeated, seemed at times to the boy to be the whole piece. But in the end, frustration and futility, many departures but few arrivals. Could it be that a great deal of Anhalt's creative energy has gone into providing, in some mysterious way, a kind of closure for those halting performances of long ago, fulfilling that thwarted musical ambition? For there is something much deeper here than simple nostalgia, that bittersweet emotion that can so easily degenerate into sentimentality. Here is a more profound fusion of memory and affect that transfigures nostalgia into a form of mourning; catharsis replaces bathos.

Had Anhalt been a gentile living in the Hungarian capital during the 1930s there is little doubt that his musical career would have developed along quite different lines; to appropriate his own Foucauldian expression, he would have carved out for himself a different 'epistemic-affective space.'[4] The early twentieth century was of course a proud time for Hungarian music. By the late 1930s both Bartók and Kodály were at the apex of their powers, acknowledged even beyond the borders of their homeland as among the most original and forceful musical figures of their generation; rarely has the Magyar spirit been so generously served. However, the Second World War, like all cataclysmic events, would once again destroy an old order, in music no less than in so many other areas of human activity, and by the early 1950s any lingering tendencies toward an overt musical nationalism – at least on the western side of the Iron Curtain – were considered by the more progressive thinkers to be anachronistic in the extreme, if not downright politically naïve.

Assuming that the primary function of the great teacher is to provide the resistance necessary for the emergence of anything genuinely new, it seems certain that Anhalt, like any strong creative personality, sooner or later would have exorcized the ghost of Kodály. But the particular form his resistance took has disturbing overtones. Quite early in his career Anhalt realized that Kodály's great mission to ennoble the Hungarian cultural renaissance could not be his mission:

> How could I, I told myself, regarded, as I was at the time, in the country where I was born, as a person not fully acceptable in the political sense (and soon after increasingly also in the social sense), for the sole reason of belonging to a certain minority religious faith, how could I make this goal also mine? I saw clearly that this could not be a valid choice for me.[5]

In 1984, in her eighty-sixth year, Anhalt's good friend, the Anglo-American writer Theresa de Kerpely, published her autobiography, *Of Love and Wars*. Kerpely was the English-born wife of Jenö de Kerpely, co-founder, in 1909, of the Waldbauer-Kerpely Quartet and a distinguished teacher of cello at the Academy of Music during Anhalt's tenure there as a student. In the late 1930s Anhalt was an occasional guest at the Kerpely villa on the Kelenhegyi út on the Buda side of the Danube. Much later, after his dramatic escape in late 1944 from a forced labour battalion, Anhalt, disguised as a seminarian of the Salesian Order, was taken in by the Kerpely family, now living at the northern end of Buda on the Rózsadomb, or Mount of Roses, where they would survive numerous terrifying encounters with the Germans, the equally dreaded Nyilas or Hungarian Nazis, and finally the liberating but highly undisciplined Russians. It is of course a story shared by countless thousands during these darkest years of a troubled century, a story told a thousand times and more but none the less compelling for all that. 'To suffer woes which hope thinks infinite' – even Shelley's immortal words seem inadequate in the face of such unspeakable horror.

Even before the war Anhalt had begun to experience in a quite personal way the pain of social rejection. From the moment he is introduced into the life of Theresa de Kerpely two facts of singular importance emerge which will appear and reappear throughout the narrative with leitmotivic regularity: his deeply romantic attachment to Kerpely's daughter Genevra, one of four children from her first marriage to the British diplomat Edmund Gorst, and his growing awareness of the seemingly unbridgeable gulf between Jew and gentile in a society on the very eve of its surrender, willingly or unwillingly, to the mass psychosis of fascism. With the uncanny precision of the professional writer Kerpely sketches this perceptive portrait of Anhalt. It was an evening at the Kerpely home on the Kelenhegyi út, a first encounter, filtered through the memory of more than forty turbulent years, but those who know Anhalt well will have little difficulty recognizing the subject:

I can still see him sitting up ramrod-straight in his chair; extremely polite, extremely shy, and almost totally silent. It was not, I felt sure, the silence of nothing to say; it was, rather, the emotion-charged silence of someone who is afraid of saying too much. This silence persisted through several subsequent visits ... Aside from that, he gave the impression of being happy to be there with us, even when Genevra was absent.

He was then, I believe, twenty years old; tall, upstanding, and a little armored in his movements and manner. His most striking feature was his high, intellectual forehead ... His heavy-lidded dark eyes held the age-old sadness of the Jewish race, but his smile, a subtle smile that played around his lips even when they were closed, balanced the melancholy strain with a sharp note of ironic humor.[6]

In that surrealistic first winter of the war when this encounter took place, with life in Budapest still seemingly normal, Kerpely saw a shy and quiet young music student in love and, mirrored in his dark eyes, something of the ancient sorrow of his race. But, she concludes, with the special insight of the observant parent, despite the intensity of the relationship between Anhalt and Genevra, it had 'no foreseeable future,' for it was 'fraught from the start with difficulties, obstacles – tangible and intangible and potential danger.'[7] A little later the Kerpelys sensed a distinct change in the relationship between the two young people. 'I don't know exactly what's happened,' Kerpely recalls saying to her husband,' but I think they have given up an impossible dream.'[8] And so they did. When next we meet Anhalt in Kerpely's memoirs he has been sent off to a labour camp in the Carpathian Mountains, not to surface again in the narrative until a late November night in 1944 when he appears at the Kerpely door in the Rózsadomb 'wearing a filthy shirt and stolen army pants and boots,'[9] seeking asylum. From then until the end of the war Anhalt's life will be inextricably bound to those of his protectors, and the story of their survival, their courage and endurance, during the long dark night of fascist terror and Russian bombardment and occupation is one of high drama; once again truth has proven stranger and more powerful than fiction.

We learn of Anhalt's escape from the labour company while it was passing through Esztergom, a small town on the Danube not far upstream from Budapest. While the company was billeted in a stable in the town, Anhalt managed to slip away one starless night and make his way to a nearby monastery. Under the protection of the Salesian Fathers he was provided with false identity papers and a train ticket back to Budapest where, because it was too dangerous to return to his own home in Pozsonyi Street, he sought out the Kerpelys. Feeling that his cover was extremely weak, especially considering that he was a young man of prime military age, the Kerpelys urged him to seek further help from the Salesians so as not to endanger the lives of the entire family. As if to dramatize their concern, within hours of his departure German officers arrived at the Kerpely residence demanding billets. While the retreating armies were in the process of destroying the lovely Danube bridges that linked the two parts of the ancient capital, Anhalt carefully picked his way through the rubble of his native city toward the Salesian monastery in Obuda, a district of Buda north of the Rózsadomb. From here he was directed to the Salesian motherhouse in Rákospalota in the southeast corner of Pest where he met Pater János Antal, the Superior of the Order. After listening to his story, this gentle and courageous priest (to whom, nearly four decades later, Anhalt would dedicate, in memoriam, his *La Tourangelle*) would provide him with temporary shelter and a new, more convincing, set of papers describing him as a refugee priest from the provinces. Thus, robed in the cassock of a seminarian, Anhalt made his way back to the Kerpely villa, which by now housed, in addition to Theresa's younger daughter Nina and a few others including the cook Marcsa, the elder daughter Genevra, now married with two young children. Here on the Mount of Roses, caught between the retreating Germans and the advancing Russians, the little band of refugees lived out the war, the rhythm of their lives attuned to the exigencies of the moment, hunger a constant companion, fear and a barely controlled panic accompanying every knock on the door and every distant burst of artillery fire.

In 1952, under the pseudonym Teresa Kay, Kerpely published her first novel, *A Crown for Ashes*, an exploration of the tensions between the Roman Catholic majority and the persecuted Jewish minority during the Nazi era in Hungary. The primary stimulus for this novel, based to a great extent on the author's wartime experiences in the Hungarian capital, would appear to have been her conversion, in the early 1950s while living in California, to the Roman Catholic faith. In the fictional guise of Andrew Marton, a young Jewish music student conscripted into a forced labour camp, Anhalt plays a leading role in the story, the central episodes of which are based quite closely on his wartime experiences as related above and in much greater detail in Kerpely's autobiography.[10]

Considering that *A Crown for Ashes* appeared just seven years after the war's end, it would not be unreasonable to assume that some of the thoughts and feelings Kerpely places in the mind of Marton reflect to a considerable degree Anhalt's own inner turmoil as a young man torn between his race and his country in the face of rejection and monstrous betrayal. The depth of this psychological burden is clearly revealed in the following passage wherein Kerpely offers the reader a glimpse of the demons battling for supremacy in Marton's troubled soul shortly after he has made his escape from the labour brigade during a forced march not far north of Budapest. It is a tranquil autumn day in 1944, all the more poignantly lovely when contrasted with the pain and brutality that lay in wait all around. Marton is making his way through a densely wooded area to avoid the straggling lines of retreating soldiers. 'The weather was clear and still. The trees had turned color. The whole landscape was a chromatic poem in every tone and quarter tone of the scale, beginning with palest amber and ending up with the deepest cardinal red. I felt free ... and almost happy.' It is clearly a revelatory moment, an epiphany:

> In Hungary, autumn, of all the seasons of the year, is the most beautiful and the most satisfying to the spirit. There is nothing sad about it. The face of nature conveys no impression of age or death, or decay; but rather a sense of victorious culmination, of fulfillment in joy and peace, of repose in triumph before renewed gestation.
>
> Andrew was not immune to the mystic spell of all this tranquil splendor. It had caught and held him, and constrained him to linger. He had thought, with pride, and a feeling which was in part the love of a son, and in part the love of a lover ... To this I belong. With this I am one – both possessor and possessed. This lovely, fertile land is mine and I am hers. This is my country! ... And with this feeling, which was profoundly embedded in the fundaments of his being, went the desire to serve, to give, to enrich through every talent at his command – and be in his turn enriched, both spiritually and materially. This emotion at once intensified and mitigated the hurt and humiliation of his present lot. He felt the double shame of the still loving child who has been disowned; shame both for his own unworthiness and for the cruelty of his mother, coupled with an inability fully to accept the reality of either,

because they strike at the roots of his existence. Thus, the very profundity of Andrew's love for the mother country which had betrayed him drove him, by rendering that betrayal unendurable, to find excuses for it; to put the blame for it on outside pressure, to call it madness, blindness, stupidity – anything but the cold-blooded murder of the heart and soul which it was.

He had tried once to express some of these things to Vágó who, more realistic, had advised him not to take it so hard. 'We are the stepchildren of the world,' he had said, 'and you may as well reconcile yourself to the fact.'[11]

Although Anhalt, particularly after the labour camp experience, did not and could not share the patriotic feelings Kerpely ascribes to Marton, he almost certainly must have shared something of his fictional counterpart's deep sense of rejection and betrayal. Thus one can see, mirrored in the procession of Anhalt's creative works, a psychic journey from fear and doubt and anger towards a reconciliation of the divided self, the only path, for 'the stepchildren of the world,' that leads into the light.

In chronicling her odyssey from the old world to the new, Theresa de Kerpely, who arrived on the North American continent only a short time before Anhalt, records her first impressions of Los Angeles, already in 1948 a sprawling monument to American energy, individualism, and vulgarity:

Looking back, I see that for us, for our particular condition, its faults were, in fact, its virtues. Its rawness, its brashness, its vulgarity (tempered by the unfailing amiability of its citizens) were a drastic but effective cure for an unhealthy attachment to a decadent past, whose values had to be set free from their old forms before they could modify and civilize the new.[12]

Compare this with Anhalt's first impressions of Montreal on a cold day in the first month of 1949:

The city looked so different, so picturesque, unlike any other I had known before. For hours, I just kept walking the streets, hopping over mounds of snow, with an eye on the ever-present mountain, and another on the traffic. The neon lights gave the downtown a festive character that I associated in the old countries only with fairgrounds, public celebrations and the exterior of nightclubs. And there were the many churches, the numerous banks and the cornucopia in the stores.

Shortly after my arrival I was taken to a Friday evening religious service followed by a social in the community hall that was located in the basement of the synagogue. There were food, drinks, a band, dancing, and lots of laughter. What a long way, I thought, from the atmosphere of the austere cavern that was the great synagogue on Dohány Street. (Which of the two is the dream? ... I asked myself.)[13]

Over the next four decades Anhalt would search for the answer; each new work would supply a missing piece of the puzzle: the *Piano Trio* (1953), dedicated to Theresa and Jenö de Kerpely, the *Violin Sonata* (1954), dedicated to his father, the *Fantasia* (1954) for solo piano, written for Glenn Gould, and the *Symphony* (1958), dedicated to the bicentenary of Canadian Jewry – harsh, angular works of great emotional intensity, couched in the 'abstract' language of serialism, which impress through the sheer force and energy of their expression; the four *Electronic Compositions* (1959–61), the third of which, subtitled 'Birds and Bells,' recalls something of the elusive blend of jubilation and tears with which the composer greeted the cessation of hostilities in 1945[14]; the monumental *Symphony of Modules* (1967), a transitional work for large orchestra which employs, in addition to a wide array of percussion instruments and a mixed chorus, pre-taped material and moments of controlled improvisation scored in graphic notation; the mixed-media *Cento* (1967) and *Foci* (1969), the former a kind of phantasmagorical 'deconstruction' of Eldon Grier's long poem 'An Ecstasy' which explores both Anhalt's fascination with the expression and meaning of language and speech and with the psychology of alienation, the latter a dramatic, ritualistic work, rich in a multi-layered symbolism which, like the dream-state itself, suspends a multitude of memory fragments in time, blurring the distinction between past and present, self and other. Taken together, *Cento* and *Foci* are perhaps the most powerful manifestations of an arch Anhaltian theme, what he has called 'the hierophany of the victim,'[15] a disturbing leitmotiv in contemporary Western music which accounts for a high proportion of the towering musical masterpieces of this century, from *Wozzek* and *A Survivor from Warsaw* to *Peter Grimes* and the *War Requiem*, as well as more recent works by Berio, Ligeti, Penderecki, Schafer, and numerous others, from both sides of the cultural divide (Bob Dylan, for example).

To follow Anhalt's intellectual development throughout his four decades in Canada, both through his music and his extensive writings about music, is to stand in admiration of a restless mind which ranges freely through the history of ideas in search of his way in the labyrinth. For – to allude to Bruno Walter's memorable distinction between Bruckner and Mahler – Anhalt is not a finder but rather a seeker, which no doubt explains the high esteem he enjoys among his peers, from John Beckwith, for whom he is 'a musical personality of extraordinary vitality and breadth,'[16] to Udo Kasemets who, in more prosaic language, sees him as 'the heavyweight among Canadian composers.'[17]

What is quite remarkable about Anhalt's achievement is that works from each period of his stylistic development have weathered the vagaries of time remarkably well. Even though Schoenberg, with barely forgivable arrogance, declared in the early 1920s that he had discovered a principle that would assure the supremacy of German music for the next hundred years, not long after his death in 1951 the pendulum began to shift dramatically away from serialism as an organizing principle. We can now see the Schoenbergian language, particularly in its earliest Expressionist phase, as a symptom of a society in crisis – a kind of nervous breakdown in the consciousness of art. Later, in the period between the wars, serialism courted neoclassicism and the resulting union spawned a depressingly large body of works written in what the less charitable critics have dubbed 'the international academic style.' Once again in the long chronicle of Western music manner had triumphed over substance. What has died, of course, is not atonality per se, but rather orthodox serialism in its purest most abstract form, and we can now see atonality, whether free or serialized, as yet another expressive tool, a powerful one to be sure, most effective (as in Berg, for example) when used in conjunction with other gestures, such as tonal stability, to suggest contrasting mental states and varied psychic orientations. It is, in short, a language of instability, and therefore, in psychological terms, of abnormality.

Whether or not Anhalt (like his friend George Rochberg) came to see serialism as a stylistic cul-de-sac, giving rise to a form of musical expression that, arguably, has never taken deep root in North American soil, the period in the 1950s during which he adhered to a fairly orthodox serialism was actually very short, no more than about six years. And yet, there is not one of his serial works that deserves neglect, that can justifiably be relegated to that special purgatory reserved for the drearier specimens of academic cosmopolitanism. And the primary reason for this has been noted by Anhalt's critics: his serial works – like any successful artistic expression – are a superb marriage of technical control and intuitive expressivity. As Beckwith has observed 'The serial works show a distinctive duality – a combination of sophisticated technical calculations and controls ... with a powerful degree of emotional intensity.'[18]

If serialism at its most orthodox has more or less run its course, so, it would appear, has *elektronische Musik* in its purest form. Once again the expressive boundaries of the art were greatly expanded, but all but the most doctrinaire of critics soon came to the realization that, without a referential base or a dramatic context, electronic music at its most nakedly abstract was problematic; what had begun as a search for new sonorities (Schaeffer) became at one extreme (Babbitt) a search for total control, a totalitarian concept as dehumanizing in the artistic as in the political realm.

Given the extraordinary exploratory drive that is such a visible aspect of his nature, it now seems inevitable that Anhalt should have been among the first composers in Canada to realize the potentialities of synthesized music. And even though his four *Electronic Compositions*, like so much else from the halcyon days of the electronic studio, seem like relics from an age long past, they survive on the fringes of experimental music in this country as among the more enduring examples of the genre; one senses that the composer had creative control over his medium (not a commonplace feat in the early years of synthesized composition when the converse more often was the case) and was able to make it serve his expressive purposes without a trace of self-consciousness. Like dodecaphonism, it helped open the doors of perception and extend the range of expressive possibilities, and when he had mastered the new medium, he moved on. By 1961, the composer later recalled, he had felt the need for integration, 'to use electronic sounds only in conjunction with acoustical ones.'[19]

In the early 1970s Anhalt was asked to contribute to a symposium sponsored by the Canadian Ethnic Studies Association. The resulting article, 'About One's Place and Voice,' is Anhalt's most extended statement on the all-consuming question of 'identity' in Canadian society. At the outset, this former student of Kodály rejects, quite rightly, the notion of a simplistic folklorism as being in any way relevant in the Canadian context, suggesting instead that a national musical identity must be sought at a much deeper level of perception. Then Anhalt states his central thesis, namely 'that there is no formula that predictably defines how a man composes by using his place of birth and residence as firm indicators. While there are numerous cases where correlation between country and idiom are demonstrable,' he continues, 'there are also many cases where there seems to be no correlation.'[20] Accordingly, he is able to conclude that the concept of ethnicity may in fact be irrelevant. Although Anhalt demonstrates in this same article his great affection for his adopted country, which more than any other place has given him the opportunity to function freely as a composer, and although one can only agree that it is the whole man that counts most – 'who he is, how he got to be who he is and his secret aspirations for the future'[21] – it seems not unreasonable to suggest that he evades an issue that strikes at the very heart of the Canadian dilemma. It should not be surprising that a man who witnessed, on such a deeply personal level, that very moment in European history when a highly romanticized nationalism was cruelly distorted into a mass psychosis of horrifying dimensions should have deeply ingrained suspicions of cultural chauvinism in any form. Nevertheless, it is arguable that any artistic expression that does not emerge, naturally and spontaneously, out of a community of experience at the deepest, if not necessarily the broadest, level is in effect stillborn.

Thomas Mann, through Leverkühn in *Doctor Faustus*, makes an important distinction between a community that simply *has* a culture and one that *is* a culture. Implicit is the notion that a genuine culture has deep roots, that it emerges – almost literally – from the soil, grows naturally from the ground up; it does not descend upon the land from some distant, airy region, like some ancient god or goddess in a baroque opera; it cannot be bought. If, as seems self-evident, music is inherently social, then it follows that style is ultimately national, for music does not simply reflect personal identity: in a powerful way it creates it by shaping the human experience of time – past, present, and future – and giving us a way, as Simon Frith posits, 'of managing the relationship between our public and private emotional lives.'[22] And when affective memory and critical reflection are dissolved into a single entity, we experience a moment of ecstasy, of complete transcendence, beyond mere sensation, beyond our public and private emotional lives, beyond a sense of self and other; we have reached that point in the dialectic where we become one, emotionally and cognitively, with a non-verbal universe of sounds. In psychological terms, it is that moment when the music simultaneously expresses and discharges the liberated energies of the listener. At such an instant of complete identification the listener has regressed, according to Heinz Kohut and Siegmund Levarie, to an early ego state to which belongs

> ... the most primitive form of mastery by incorporation and identification. At this moment the ecstatic listener does not clearly differentiate between himself and the outside world; he experiences the sounds as being produced by himself, or even as being himself, because emotionally they are what he feels. With the breakdown of the ego boundaries, the 'oceanic feeling' [the term is Freudian] of being one with the world ('*Seid umschlungen, Millionen!*') is reached, and with it a socially acceptable form of magical omnipotence and a repetition of early, primitive kinesthetic pleasures as the listener flies through space with the sounds.[23]

When such a process of identification moves beyond the private into the public domain, that is, from an individual to a collective sphere of aesthetic consciousness, we begin to perceive the outlines of that community of experience through which a cultural identity is ultimately articulated. In the absence of any significant community of experience the primary social function of music – communication – has been subverted, thus eliminating any possibility of the process of mythologization even beginning; and without the myth, as Murray Schafer is constantly reminding us, the nation dies.

Near the end of one of Anhalt's recent articles we find this revealing passage:

We all chart our way in this vast labyrinth of texts, contexts, situations and horizons, and even add a wrinkle, or two, to it. We compare notes with each other. And while we do this, we also hear voices that say that, basically, we might be alone.[24]

Although it is true that we each have our 'unique access to Revelation,' surely we are never really entirely alone, least of all the artist, who, through the very act of self-discovery and self-rediscovery, has transformed a very private ritual into a public one. Anhalt is right when he says in another context that 'we all learn differently from each other,' see 'different "images" of the same "thing,"' that there are 'as many ways of seeing what has been done, or shown, as the number of those who see,' and that, moreover, this is not incompatible 'with the notion of a degree of "sharing."'[25] To be sure, ambiguity is as fundamental to the condition of art as it is to life. Nevertheless, one significant gauge of artistic value, within a particular cultural community, is the extent to which an artistic statement becomes a shared experience on the very deepest levels of perception, however much ambiguity may exist on the personal level of response. The number of dreamers may appear to be nearly infinite, but the number of dreams ...?

In 1986 Anhalt noted:

The process leading to understanding is complex and simple at the same time. Its complexity resides in the inevitability of matching the respective epistemic-affective spaces – those of the composer and the interpreter, and the hearer/questioner – against each other. This can be, and frequently is, one of the noblest games there is, and one's skill in playing it is cumulative.[26]

So it would appear, for Anhalt's skill in playing the noblest of games has never been better. In the two major works that followed *Cento* and *Foci*, he explored a theme deeply embedded in the Canadian psyche. Crudely stated, it is the immigrant experience itself, or rather the tribal memory of 'here' versus 'there.' *La Tourangelle* (1975) and *Winthrop* (1983) form a large-scale diptych through which Anhalt examines the ethical-philosophical roots of the Canadian experience as manifest in the social and spiritual evolution of the two dominant immigrant peoples. The composer himself came to the realization that the 'common *locus*' of these works is 'not a place, ... but rather a "state," both in the physical and psychic sense: "the state" of being in "transit," going from one place to another, propelled by some urge to "move," for one reason or another.' More accurately, he concludes, 'it is rather the memory of being "in transit," that I was composing in these works.'[27]

Through the lives of the two central figures in these historical pageants, the French-born Marie de l'Incarnation, née Marie Guyart (1599–1672), founder of the Ursuline order in Canada, and the English-born John Winthrop (1587–1649), first governor of the Massachusetts Bay Company and founder of Boston, Anhalt probes the very spiritual-psychological core of the 'two solitudes.' The Ursuline nun, intuitive, compassionate, and female, and the New England governor, rational, puritanical, and male, symbolize, with compelling vividness, the archetypal paradigm of French-English relations in the New World.[28] The very quest in the agonizing search for identity has become a key metaphor in contemporary Canadian life, and it is arguable that the dialectic itself embodies the Canadian personality to a very considerable degree; indeed, it would appear that the continued existence of the nation in anything like its present form depends utterly upon its remaining unbroken.

Finally, we come to a trilogy of orchestral works which, I believe, reveal Anhalt at the very peak of his powers – *Simulacrum* (1986–7), *SparkskrapS* (1987), and *Sonance•Resonance (Welche Töne?)* (1988–9) – a very personal triptych wherein the voyage of self-discovery reaches a new plateau. Like many notable composers before him Anhalt has, in later years, turned increasingly inward, become more introspective, delved deeper into the memory-labyrinth, and in the process has at least hinted that some sort of reconciliation is possible.

The three orchestral works share a common aesthetic-conceptual frame. What Anhalt offers here is more than a series of collages assembled from random pages of the scrapbook or the diary, something more akin to a psycho-narrative remembrance of things past, in short, not so much an exploration of memory as an exploration of 'the experience of memory.'[29] As the composer himself said in interview with Jeffrey Reid apropos the world premiere of *Sonance•Resonance:*

> This is what I'm interested in, how one lives with memory, how memories are never the same as the first event. There is transformation, distortion. We grow, we remember, we forget. I'm interested in what we are and what the thing remembered means to us at different stages of our life. This is resonance.[30]

Of the three orchestral works none, it strikes me, resonates on a more deeply personal level than the first, *Simulacrum*, composed in 1986–7 for the National Arts Centre Orchestra and its then newly appointed music director, Gabriel Chmura.

The composition of *Simulacrum* was begun in Kingston on 1 December 1986. It is tempting to speculate that the central idea of this piece was stimulated by two very nearly contiguous events: the release of Theresa de Kerpely's autobiography in 1984 and Anhalt's meeting with Chmura, like himself a central-European Jewish immigrant to Canada. Kerpely's book provides the most detailed published record we have of Anhalt's early years in Budapest, highly dramatic events, as we have seen, that Anhalt in his 1985 autobiographical sketch records with unnerving detachment or ignores altogether. Kerpely's vivid memoirs must have stirred numerous memories that had either been suppressed or had lain dormant in the subconscious, whereas in Chmura, a Polish Jew and fellow musician whose homeland suffered unspeakably at the hands of the Nazis, he must have sensed a kindred spirit.

All of the preliminary sketches for *Simulacrum* are now held by the Music Division of the National Library of Canada. An examination of these sketches affords us an occasional glimpse of Anhalt's *modus operandi* and is especially revealing with respect to the genesis of the piece. Preceding the actual musical sketches for *Simulacrum* are a series of 'memos,' seemingly random jottings that reveal something of the mind in action as the composer searches for a conceptual framework for his piece. For example, on one sheet we find the following list of nouns and short phrases: 'Image, likeness, portrait, effigy; reflection in a mirror, or water; shade, ghost, vision in a dream; recollection of a thing; character picture; a mere [mirror?] image; imitation; a phantom, appearance'; on the bottom half of the same sheet we find these almost Scriabinesque phrases: 'Horror of the abyss; Survival; Renewal; Remembering/Not knowing; The creative urge; The proliferation into the world; The creative urge victorious over the memory of destruction.'[31] On another sheet we find the following short list, a kind of addendum to the above: 'Enigmas (hidden quotes); Dissolves; Juxtapositions; Metamorphoses.' Elsewhere the composer has compiled lists of more technical terms, among them, 'diatonic fields,' 'pentatonic assemblies,' 'microtonal variation,' and 'multiphonics.' Then Anhalt begins playing with the work's prospective title. On one sheet we find, underneath a brief biographical sketch of Chmura, the words 'Simulacrum' and 'Speculum'; on yet another, attempts to translate 'Simulacrum' and 'Chmura' into musical notation (see Example 1).

Example 1

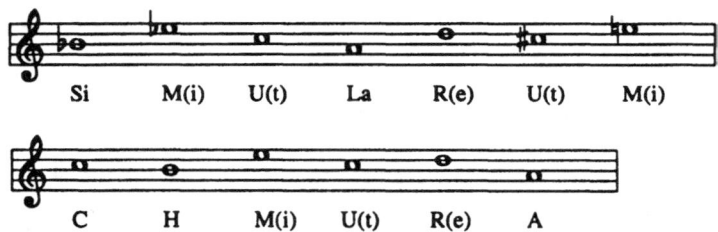

There is even an attempt to tease out the musical pitches in the name of the commissioning organization, the National Arts Centre Orchestra (NACO), and one can only hope that there is no veiled symbolism in the equation that reduces the word 'National' to 'N ≅ naught' (see Example 2).

Example 2

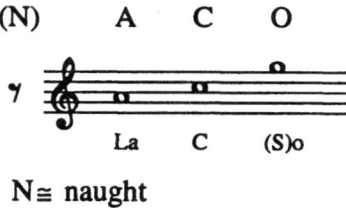

Having worked out possible pitch equivalents of 'Chmura,' 'Simulacrum,' and 'NACO,' Anhalt formulated a fifteen-note row which he organized into three pitch cells (see Example 3).

Example 3

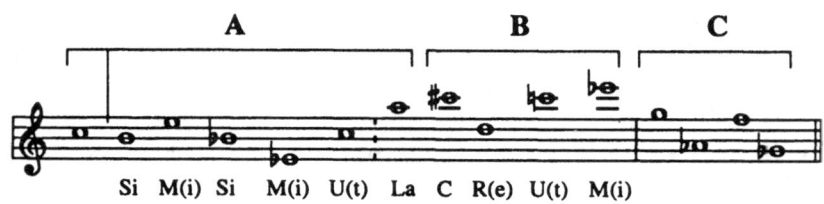

As can be seen in Example 3, the composer has chosen to let 'Si' stand for both B-natural and B-flat, 'Mi' to stand for both E-natural and E-flat, and 'Ut' to stand for both C-natural and C-sharp. Omitting the initial C, the A and B cells taken together – disregarding the 'stuttering' repetition of 'Si M(i)' – spell out SIMULACRUM. The C cell (G, A-flat, F, G-flat) contains the remaining four pitches, thus completing a twelve-tone row. The appearance of E-flat and C in both the A and B cells (albeit with octave displacement) added to the lone initial C completes a fifteen-note pattern. Much of the pitch structure of *Simulacrum* is derived from this material, its transpositions, inversions, retrogrades, and retrograde inversions. Although the work is by no means dodecaphonic in any orthodox sense, the 'atonal' gestures implicit in the pitch cells of the row are affectively congruous with the dreamlike nature of the piece.

A simulacrum is an image, a portrait, an effigy, a reflection, an imitation, a superficial or shadowy likeness, and Anhalt must have been delighted to discover that the last five letters of the word very nearly form an anagram for the dedicatee's surname: 'acrum' equals 'c(h)mura,' hence 'simul-acrum' equals 'simul-cmura' or 'like Chmura' (that is to say, Anhalt is like Chmura). But this slippery word belongs to an even wider semantic field for it can also mean 'illusion,' 'phantom,' 'sham,' 'imposture,' 'deception,' 'fraud,' or 'counterfeit.' It is, in fact, the very ambiguity of the term that seems to have captured the composer's imagination, bringing to the fore fundamental questions concerning the nature of reality. Are dreams real? Is consciousness the only thing we have? What of the preconscious, the collective unconscious? Are these real or imaginary? In short, the perception of reality is deceptive, multifarious, and many-layered and hence we are constantly surrounded by the notion of simulacrum – illusion, semblance – during every moment of our entire existence. Anhalt offers a clue to his philosophical-aesthetic intentions by reproducing an idea attributed to the sixteenth-century rabbinic scholar and mystic Isaac Luria (1534–72) on the flyleaf of the score of *Simulacrum:*

... every word of the Torah has six hundred thousand 'faces,' that is, layers of meaning or entrances, one for each of the children of Israel who stood at the foot of Mount Sinai. Each face is turned toward only one of them; he alone can see it and decipher it.[32]

But we have more than a few tantalizing clues. Fortunately, the composer has left a fairly detailed written account of many of the extramusical ideas embedded in *Simulacrum*. Like John Beckwith and Murray Schafer, Anhalt, had he never composed a note of music, would be assured a distinguished place in Canadian music. His published writings and unpublished lectures reveal an eclectic mind of remarkable vitality. In addition to his penetrating and provocative study of contemporary vocal music, *Alternative Voices*, Anhalt has left a detailed written record of the genesis of nearly every one of his major works beginning with *Cento*. Far from mere program notes, compiled after the fact, these essays probe a variety of 'deep themes' of special concern to the composer. Moreover, there is in some instances a fascinating interplay between the writings and the music. *Simulacrum* is a case in point. Before Anhalt had begun the actual composition of the piece, he was exploring in print a number of ideas that would eventually find their way into the score.

In his 1986 article, subtitled 'Hearing Voices from Yesterday,' Anhalt further developed some of the themes previously explored in *Alternative Voices*. For Anhalt, the human voice, with its 'seemingly limitless capabilities for expressing thought and feeling ... functions as the picture of the mind.'[33] In a pre-Gutenberg (pre-fax!?) world, before the word was frozen into print, rendered mute, and mechanically cloned, human communication was direct and immediate, meaning was undivorceable from sound, and 'sounds,' as Aristotle observed twenty-three centuries ago, 'show the passions in the soul.'[34] In this sense all music might be considered an attempt to rediscover the magic and potency of language as an aural-oral phenomenon, to create a metalanguage that mirrors 'the passions in the soul' in a way denied the unspoken word. Even though *Simulacrum*, like its two companions, is a purely instrumental work, on a kind of subliminal level it incorporates the human voice, or a 'simulacrum' of the human voice, for in all there are six allusions to other music in the piece, all of it vocal. In addition to Anhalt's own 'duo-drama' *Thisness* (1985), these allusions include two Sephardic tunes, the *St Matthew Passion*, *Der Rosenkavalier*, and the two late Verdi operas *Aïda* and *Otello*. Analyses of what we might call the subtexts of three of these excerpts – from *Aïda*, *Otello*, and the *St Matthew Passion* – form a significant part of the 1986 article, completed before the commission for *Simulacrum* had been received.

If there is an overriding 'deep theme' in *Simulacrum* it is that the notion of time as a linear construct is an illusion, a mirage, for past, present, and future are unravelable 'organic tangles' or 'interlocking chains of memory cells.'[35] Anhalt posits that there is a mental space wherein past and future meet, as in the centre of a 'pluri-dimensional maze,' spinning along the trajectory of an endless spiral, facing forward and backward at the same time. That is to say, both past and future are acts of projection situated on either side of that 'terribly narrow sliver of an existential moment to which we give the name "present,"'[36] that fleeting moment suspended between memory and anticipation, for just as the remembered past resonates with projections into the indeterminate future so the anticipated future is informed by events and ideas of the past.

On a less abstract and more intimate plane, *Simulacrum* is a personal odyssey, a search, as the composer himself informs us, 'for connections, correspondences, and the like. And when one does this, one almost inevitably finds a child standing somewhere way down the corridor of memory.'[37] But there is an ineluctable loss of innocence; the image of *this* child, filtered through the nightmarish black mists of the Nazi era, is forever changed, distorted, fractured. So in searching for the child within, Anhalt inescapably comes face to face with two thousand years and more of the Jewish experience.

Simulacrum begins softly and eerily with a questing four-note figure in solo timpani and low strings that builds gradually and tentatively amidst the sheen of muted upper strings, flutter-tongued flute in its lowest register, and the quiet shimmer of soft mallets on suspended cymbal. Anhalt recalls that early on he knew the piece would begin softly in a low register and a 'loose' texture, 'groping, as if listening intently to a faint voice inside, not unlike the psycho-physiological awareness of a beating heart.'[38] For some time the music moves forward hesitantly, with frequent tempo changes and moments of high intensity juxtaposed with sparse, rhythmically broken gestures still dominated by the initial four-note figure. A final dynamic surge, disintegration, and silence: at this point (bars 78–81) Anhalt introduces the first allusion to other music. It is that chillingly dramatic moment in the *St Matthew Passion* when the crowd responds to Pilate's fateful question: 'What then shall I do unto Jesus, whom ye call the King of the Jews?' There is a moment of hesitation before the mob, voices tumbling over one another in a furious fugato, exclaims: 'Let Him be crucified!' Again a pregnant silence. Then, like a cinematic montage, the historical time-frame shifts to Bach's Leipzig and the St Thomas Church. As the last echoes of the howling mob die away a serene chorale emerges, quietly sung by the choir and the congregation, 'a miraculous reverberation spanning the centuries and linking diverse people in a complex and deeply-felt bond.'[39] Thus it is that, beyond the obvious symbolism of the biblical text and the composer's profound spirituality and deep understanding of human behaviour, Anhalt is fascinated by the concept of multidimensional 'historical space' in Bach's monumental masterpiece.

Of course in appropriating a passage from Bach he transfers it to yet another dimension of time and place. Anhalt distances himself from the original by imbuing 'the crowd scene' with something of the serenity of the chorale; the tempo has been considerably reduced, the dynamics never rise above mezzo piano, and the twisting lines of Bach's counterpoint, now drained of their energy, are surrounded by additional contrapuntal lines, a transformation, the composer explains, aimed 'at giving the impression that it is but a "recall of a thing," a memory image, which is being cited here more for its connotative, or symbolic, value, or potential, than for its literal reference to a peak work, to an icon in the repertoire.'[40]

Whereas the Bach quotation could conceivably be missed on a first hearing, even by an informed listener, there is no such possibility that the fleeting reference to *Der Rosenkavalier* could pass unnoticed. For me this moment is the emotional heart of the work, a moment of ineffable sweetness all the more poignant when understood in its extramusical context. The quotation this time is the famous waltz introduced in Act II by Baron Ochs during his clumsy attempts to charm Sophie ('mit mir keine Nacht dir zu lang'), a melody, several Strauss scholars have noted, almost certainly 'borrowed' from Josef Strauss's *Dynamiden*, op. 173 (1865).

The tune, introduced at bar 136 of *Simulacrum* by two solo violins doubled by clarinet and flute, emerges from a quiet ripple of strings, the shimmering vibrato of soft mallets on vibraphone adding to the dreamlike ethereality of the passage. The strong melodic profile of the original (with its distinctive sequence of upward-leaping sixths, fifths, and fourths) is retained. But Anhalt alters the rhythm of the original through a process of augmentation whereby, in quick succession, the opening sixteenths are expanded to eighths, then quarter-notes, with the effect, of course, of slowing the tune until it limps to a halt and, after a last faint echo in muted trumpets (bars 146–9), disappears altogether, absorbed back into the soft haze of strings and woodwinds from whence it materialized.

At first blush the famous Strauss tune, coming as it does not long after the sublime Bach reference, might seem curiously out of place. What is it doing in *Simulacrum*? Is this yet another statement on the nature of time? Perhaps Anhalt has remembered that time is a major theme of the Hofmannsthal-Strauss drama. Certainly Strauss, who was not always to be certain of his collaborator's sometimes cryptic intentions, recognized this, for the most glorious music in the opera belongs to those bittersweet moments of resignation and renunciation where we are reminded of the transience of all things in the stream of time, of the evanescence of youth and beauty and innocence, of the need to impose meaningful patterns on our lives. Such a transcendent moment is the Marschallin's first-act meditation on the passing of time; another – and for Straussians the chief glory of the work – is the soaring last-act trio which brings this most beloved of Strauss operas to a close in a mood of quiet resignation and acceptance. All of this is surely there, at least in the mind of the knowledgeable listener. But Anhalt had a more direct purpose, and it is the very simplicity of the scheme that renders this exquisite moment of *Simulacrum* so unforgettable. In a letter of 2 November 1987, written not long after the Ottawa premiere of *Simulacrum*, Anhalt shared the following, very personal reminiscence with me:

Imagine a boy of about 8 or 10. Parents divorced. Both remarried. Father wanting to make music, but is unskilled. Plays by ear the piano and on the violin parts of a few pieces that he <u>can</u> manage. With his violin, my stepmother relegated him to the bathroom, the only place where his playing (in front of a small mirror) was tolerated. He spent <u>many hours</u> in the evenings, playing his 'repertoire' this way. As a small boy I also remember hearing-seeing him trying to 'find' the notes of this R. Strauss tune on the piano. To me, who did not know where the few notes came from, this tune (or rather its beginning only) meant <u>then</u>, and keeps on meaning, my father's futile efforts, yet his ever resurgent tries, at finding the 'key' to this melody. Not <u>then</u>, but <u>sometime</u>, subsequently, I came to feel an aching sorrow at my father's rather futile (to the outsider, at least) attempts in music. At one moment, and I really did not (do not) know when this has occurred, I began to feel a deep empathy and regret over what I sensed might have been an ongoing sense of frustration on his part. His was a life that knew very few fulfillments; he was smothered by circumstances, yet he continued on fighting with the few means at his disposal. And he was <u>always</u> a good man, a loving father, a generous son and brother to his sisters and brothers. I loved him dearly, although was unable to respond <u>then</u> to his repeated requests to be his 'friend.' I still love him, with the same intensity that I felt when he was alive. (I learned of his death, from a heart attack at the age of 60, in 1955, in a letter ...).[41]

But there is more than what is implied by the actual quotation, as Anhalt further explains:

But the memory recall does not end with the Strauss tune. You will recall that it is 'embedded' in a long 'string line' (it is but a 'phase' of it) that begins at bar 96 in a solo violin, 'gathers' bulk (the other violins come in) splits with different (yet similar) strands, drives on, becoming obsessive in character (it <u>does</u> what I think my father may have <u>imagined</u> performing: a huge virtuoso arabesque of a never-ending violin line); at bar 171 it 'descends' with the violins, furioso, and finally settles in the 'cellos & doublebasses in bar 183 for another stretch of 'mumbling/singing' that peters out at about bar 200–203.'[42]

Elsewhere Anhalt has publicly added to these poignant reminiscences: 'My father and his violin was, and remains, a permanent image in my memory of him, a recollection which includes much sweetness, besides the tenseness and the harshness of the thirty's and forty's we shared in Budapest.'[43]

On the surface we might be dealing with simple nostalgia, a sentimental yearning for an idealized past mingled with an irrecoverable sense of loss. But of course the famous Strauss tune sets off a chain of secondary associations in the listener's mind. And when these are married to Anhalt's very private perceptions we move beyond mere sentimentality closer to the level of tragic irony. First of all there is the tension between the historical time zone of the opera, eighteenth-century Vienna during the early years of the reign of the Empress Maria Theresa, and the actual time of its composition (1909–10), near the end of that strange dreamlike autumn of the Habsburgs. And of course the greatest musical symbol of nineteenth-century Vienna, up until the very eve of war, was the waltz. So it is not the Vienna of Maria Theresa that is evoked by Strauss's gigantic 'operetta' so much as Franz Josef's enchanting capital, itself an outrageous anachronism, the last romantic outpost of a civilization moving rapidly toward the abyss of 1914–18. In this context the waltz becomes not so much a symbol of love and laughter in some improbable fairyland as a symbol of decadence, a macabre dance of death (as Ravel so magnificently depicted in *Wien*, as *La Valse* was originally called). After all, the *fin de siècle* Vienna of popular imagination, the lovely fairy-tale kingdom of Lehár and the other Strausses, is of course a myth, a facade with no more substance than the very operetta plots that created it in the first place. The real Vienna of 1909–10 was the Vienna of Freud and Schnitzler and Klimt, of Karl Kraus and Oskar Kokoschka, of an anti–Semitic mayor called Karl Lueger and an obscure and impoverished artist called Hitler.

Then perhaps the mind leaps forward to 1933 and we recall that Strauss is proclaimed, without consultation, president of the newly created Reichsmusikkammer. At the same time we remember that his daughter-in-law is Jewish, his grandchildren therefore half-Jewish; we recall his courage in defending Jewish friends and colleagues, and the official demand in 1935, on Goebbels's orders, that he resign his position in the Reichsmusikkammer 'on the grounds of ill-health.' But perhaps above all, the listener, during that fleeting moment of recognition, recreates a mind-picture of war's end, the

Echoes of Time and the River   37

Third Reich in flames, and the image of a dignified old man, tall and gaunt, his beloved Germany in ruins all around him, greeting a contingent of American soldiers at his villa in Garmisch with the memorable words, curtly delivered in English, 'I am the composer of *Rosenkavalier*; leave me alone.'

It should not be surprising that memories of the father should in turn evoke memories of the grandfather. For not long after the 'father's violin' is reduced to a vague 'mumbling/singing,' the music moves into a related memory event triggered by two traditional Sephardic tunes, the first of which appears at bar 237 of *Simulacrum*. The tunes may be found as numbers 253 and 246, respectively, in Abraham Idelsohn's *Thesaurus of Hebrew Oriental Melodies* (see Example 4a and Example 4b).[44]

Example 4a

Example 4b

Again through the composer's public and private statements we can piece together a fairly complete picture of his aesthetic intentions. First of all, Anhalt has described the passage in question (bars 237–58) as a passionate 'free-for-all,' rather like two orthodox cantors trying 'to "out-sing" each other, with their individual, independent cantilenas.'[45] The melismatic and ornamented Sephardic melodies clearly relate to the child's vivid impressions of the synagogue in the Jewish quarter of Budapest. It is not long after the Great War. The child is perhaps ten or twelve years old: 'I recall visits, during the High Holidays, to my paternal grandfather, as he, clad in his white death-shroud, was praying, chanting, swaying in the tiny, smelly, orthodox synagogue, with the cantor belting out coloraturas and everyone vocalising individually.'[46] This lively jumble of sights and sounds and smells waited over six decades for its time to resurface in the imagination. Specifically, this quasi-oriental 'free-for-all' is, as Anhalt has stated, 'a much belated message to my grandfather, a kind of reciprocal gesture for his gentle smile, that would say: now, after much delay, I am beginning to understand you.'[47] More generally, as he confided in me, it 'is a part of my search for things Jewish.'[48] And this is true, it would not be unreasonable to conclude, of the entire piece, as well as of its 'twin,' *SparkskrapS*, completed not long afterward, in early December 1987.

As the 'echoes of the synagogue' fade from memory (bar 258) we hear the distant strains of off-stage harp doubled by off-stage pizzicato strings (save first violins and double-basses). Again a temporal dislocation; like time travellers we are transported from one temple to another, back through millennia to the inner sanctum of an Egyptian temple. It is the Temple of Vulcan at Memphis *(Aïda,* act 1, scene 2) and we hear the eerie voice of the High Priestess invoking the great god Phtha, life-giving spirit of the world. The chromatic arabesque of this melody, its exotic flavour reinforced by the solo oboe and the hieratic harp arpeggios, seems but a continuation of the timeless Sephardic tunes. But like the waltz from *Der Rosenkavalier* it is a mere fragment, another tiny island of memory – five bars in all – soon lost in a soft haze of strings and harp. Aside from the ritualistic nature of Verdi's music – the responsorial chanting, the internal repetition and circular melodic construction, the austere dignity of the scene – Anhalt was intrigued by the fact that Verdi's 'Egyptian' tune bears a fairly close family resemblance to the Jewish melodies; thus its appearance in *Simulacrum* effects a symbolic rapprochement between Arab and Jew, a point of particular significance to the composer – as to all people of good will – during these times of deep mistrust, hatred, and strife in the Middle East. Perhaps we can even suggest that the symbolism of the passage stretches far enough to embrace the fact that, as of 1987, Egypt was the only Arab nation to have recognized the legitimacy of the Israeli state.

Perhaps the recollection of *Aïda* brought to mind its great successor, *Otello,* that powerful work of Verdi's old age whose opening scene is surely the most dramatic in all opera. The storm music that opens *Otello* cuts through the silence with the explosive force of a microcosmic big bang. Anhalt seems to have recognized the connection between the two Verdi scenes, namely that the scene in the Egyptian temple and the scene on the storm-tossed Cypriot shore, however different musically, are both invocations to the gods for victory and salvation. Thus is brought into play Anhalt's fascination not only with the psychology of collective behaviour – the imploring crowd ('Dio, fulgor della bufera!') with its incantatory melodic refrains – but also with the connection between art and magic.

Of course in both *Aïda* and *Otello* the prayers of the supplicants are answered: the Egyptian armies go on to defeat the invading Ethiopians and the Moorish general is saved from a watery grave. But in *Simulacrum*, in what must be the most hidden of the 'deep themes' in the work, there is no salvation, the gods are silent. Whereas the great choral interjections in *Otello* are answered with an exultant cry ('È salvo! è salvo!'), the parallel moment in *Simulacrum* (bars 367–71) is followed, after a dramatic pause, by a passage of furious orchestral activity, fortissimo, which the composer himself has described as 'an even more chilling series of sounds, as if another source of danger would have been sighted, with the realization that this time hope for a rescue is non-existent. The passage conveys the impression of piercing shrieks of fear and laments.'[49]

The key to this Dantesque passage is found in Anhalt's *Thisness* (1985), a 'duo-drama,' as he calls it, for mezzo-soprano and accompanist (piano), written for Phyllis Mailing and the Vancouver New Music Society. Significantly, Anhalt dedicated the work 'To My Parents.' Bars 373–88 of *Simulacrum* are based on a slightly modified fragment of the accompaniment in Section 7 of *Thisness*, entitled 'Unreason.' The text, the composer's own, reads as follows:

> Is this the end of your speech, foreigner?
> How strangely you speak.
>
> I hate you for it.
> I hate you, pharmakos.
>
> They claim: you know all
> that I don't understand ...
>
> I fear you, pharmakos,
> wizard and poisoner.
>
> You stir up my life,
> sacred and accursed soul.

You must be exorcised!
And what's the worst;
you dweller upon the boundary line,
you bring what I've come to need.

I hate you the more for it.

Strain, stress, strife ...
the going gets rougher now.

  You, Ishmael, you are at hand to blame.

    'The plague's upon us!
    Bring out the pharmakoi!'

You are handy to strike.

    'Blow, pharma, blow, pharma,
    pharma, blow!'

More yet to come!

    'Attack between the legs!'

    'Aim at the head!'

    'Blow out their lights!'

    'Destroy the forms!'

    'Erase their formulas!'

    'Kill to clear!'

    'Kill to clean!'

    'Kill to cure!'

The boil is lanced ...
the air heavy ...

Trace and retrace ...

... try to forget ...

Peace will now return
with the settling dust ...

And now a warning:

You mustn't ever, ever, bring it up again,
It never even took place.

Then ... perhaps ...
the voice, also, will go away ...
in time ...

A single word unlocks this disturbing poem: the ancient Greek word 'pharmakos,' a person (often already under sentence of death) sacrificed for the purification or atonement of the community. And there can be no doubt that the *pharmakoi* in this instance, like the outcast Ishmael, are the children of Abraham.

There can be but one resolution to this deeply disturbing passage, a mournful dirge, a hymn of sadness, begun softly in three muted trumpets over strings and the soft tread of timpani (bar 395). But it cannot end here. Perhaps, in time, the voice will go away ... in time ... Anhalt's poignant conclusion reveals much:

... life continues for those who are the survivors. Other memories take over; there is time now for other gestures, however fragmentary they might be. Towards the close occurs an attempt to achieve a gesture of apotheosis, but perhaps it is not 'full' enough; it cannot, or doesn't want to, sustain itself, and after which the piece returns to the vicinity of the same affective terrain from which it emerged at the outset.[50]

And so the music comes very nearly full circle; a variant of the initial questing figure returns quietly in the timpani as the sound dissolves into silence – *niente* – over a blur of tam-tam, muted strings, and a great chromatic cluster in the piano.

Of course the Jewish experience is not the whole story. But certainly *Simulacrum* is a singularly powerful reflection of Anhalt's ongoing 'search for things Jewish.' It brings us back to war-torn Hungary through the imagination of Theresa de Kerpely. Anhalt's fictional *doppelgänger*, Andrew Marton, is speaking with great passion to the aristocratic gentile women he loves, and who loves him:

... generations of persecution have gone to make me what I am, and I can never separate myself from them; they are in everything I say and do and feel; they are in my music – they are in all the music of my race, in its poetry, in its prose, in everything that is uttered and created by my people. And I don't even come from the aristocracy of my race.[51]

While the tragic experience of the Jews in this century is an inseparable part of Anhalt's being, his recognition of the immensity of 'time' and the 'world' has allowed his imagination to transcend the boundaries of religious faith, race, and ethnicity. But even though only a part of the fictional Marton can be said to be Anhalt, and even though only a handful of works, notably *Thisness, Simulacrum,* and *SparkskrapS,* speak directly, even unequivocally, of the Jewish experience, Anhalt's lifelong search for meaning has been shaped and coloured by the rich intellectual tradition and the ancient faith of his ancestors to a degree far greater than even he perhaps realizes.

NOTES

1 István Anhalt, 'Thisness: Marks and Remarks,' *Musical Canada: Words and Music Honouring Helmut Kallmann,* ed. John Beckwith and Frederick A. Hall (Toronto: University of Toronto Press, 1988), 212.
2 Anhalt, '2. Thisness (Haecceitas),' from the score of *Thisness* (Toronto: Canadian Music Centre, 1985); quoted in Anhalt, 'Thisness: Marks and Remarks,' 216.
3 Anhalt, 'What Tack to Take? An Autobiographical Sketch (Life in Progress ...),' *Queen's Quarterly,* 92, no. 1 (Spring 1985), 96–7.
4 See Anhalt, 'Pst ... Pst ... Are You Listening? Hearing Voices from Yesterday,' *Queen's Quarterly,* 93, no. 1 (Spring 1986), 71–2.
5 Anhalt, 'What Tack to Take?,' 101.
6 Theresa de Kerpely, *Of Love and Wars* (New York: Stein and Day, 1984), 118.
7 Ibid., 135.
8 Ibid., 143.
9 Ibid., 197.
10 Although it is clear from a comparison of the novel and Kerpely's autobiography that Anhalt is the chief model for Marton, it should be noted that the

character also encompasses some of the features of Anhalt's close friend László Gyopár, a fellow student of composition in the class of Kodály at the Academy of Music, who died under tragic circumstances in 1944 on the Russian front.
11 Teresa Kay, *A Crown for Ashes* (Milwaukee: The Bruce Publishing Company, 1952), 85–6.
12 Kerpely, *Of Love and Wars*, 364.
13 Anhalt, 'What Tack to Take?,' 103.
14 For an account of this programmatic connection see Kerpely, *Of Love and Wars*, 287; Anhalt, 'What Tack to Take?,' 102; and *Anthology of Canadian Music – István Anhalt* (ACM 22), Radio Canada International (1985), 8.
15 Anhalt, *Alternative Voices: Essays on Contemporary Vocal and Choral Compositions* (Toronto: University of Toronto Press, 1984), 199.
16 John Beckwith, 'Vocal Usage Frontier Pushed Back in New Anhalt Works,' *The Music Scene*, No. 281 (January/February 1975), 4.
17 Udo Kasemets, 'Anhalt, István,' *Contemporary Canadian Composers*, ed. Keith MacMillan and John Beckwith (Toronto: Oxford University Press, 1975), 8.
18 Beckwith, 'Vocal Usage Frontiers Pushed Back,' 4–5.
19 Anhalt, 'What Tack to Take?,' 105.
20 Anhalt, 'About One's Place and Voice,' *Identities: The Impact of Ethnicity on Canadian Society*, ed. Wsevolod Isajiw (Canadian Ethnic Studies Association, Vol. V) (Toronto: Peter Martin Associates Limited, 1977), 39.
21 Ibid., 45.
22 Simon Frith, 'Towards an Aesthetic of Popular Music,' *Music and Society: The Politics of Composition, Perfomance and Reception*, ed. Richard Leppert and Susan McClary (Cambridge: Cambridge University Press, 1987), 141.
23 Heinz Kohut and Siegmund Levarie, 'On the Enjoyment of Listening to Music,' *Psychoanalytic Quarterly*, 19 (1950), 84–5; reprinted in *Psychoanalytic Explorations in Music*, ed. Stuart Feder, Richard L. Karmel, and George H. Pollock (Madison, Conn.: International Universities Press, Inc., 1990), 19.
24 Anhalt, 'Text, Context, Music,' *Canadian University Music Review*, 9, no. 2 (1989), 18.
25 Anhalt, 'Music: Context, Text, Counter-Text,' *Contemporary Music Review*, 5 (1989), 132.
26 Anhalt, 'Pst .. Pst ... Are You Listening?,' 72.
27 Anhalt, 'Music: Context, Text, Counter-Text,' 113.
28 Anhalt is certainly not alone in seeing a clear historical connection between New England and Canada inasmuch as the 'New England mind,' as nurtured by the Winthrop colony, was transmitted to Canada in the period surrounding the American Revolutionary War, principally through the United Empire Loyalists,

where it was transformed into the 'English-Canadian mind.' (See Anhalt, *Winthrop:* The Work, the Theme, the Story,' *Canadian University Music Review*, 4 [1983], 185.)
29 Gordon E. Smith, '"Deep Themes, Not So Hidden" in the Music of István Anhalt,' *Queen's Quarterly*, 98, no. 1 (Spring 1991), 114.
30 Jeffrey Reid, 'A Short Conversation with a Composer,' *Toronto Symphony Times*, 2, no. 1 (September 1989), [p. 1].
31 This and the following extracts from the sketches for *Simulacrum* can be found in the National Library of Canada, Music Division, István Anhalt Fonds, 1985-11, Series 1, File 1.10 and File 1.15.
32 Gershom G. Scholem, *On the Kabbalah and its Symbolism*, translated from the German by Ralph Manheim (London: Routledge and Kegan Paul, 1965), 13.
33 Anhalt, 'Pst ... Pst ... Are You Listening?,' 71.
34 Quoted in ibid.
35 Anhalt, 'From "Mirage" to *Simulacrum* and "Afterthought,"' unpublished lecture, Faculty of Music, University of Toronto, 5 January 1988, 5.
36 Ibid., 4.
37 Ibid., 3.
38 Ibid., 5.
39 Anhalt, 'Pst ... Pst ... Are You Listening?,' 82.
40 Anhalt, 'From "Mirage" to *Simulacrum* and "Afterthought,"' 6.
41 Anhalt, letter to the author, 2 November 1987.
42 Ibid.
43 Anhalt, 'From "Mirage" to *Simulacrum* and "Afterthought,"' 6-7.
44 A.Z. Idelsohn, *Thesaurus of Hebrew Oriental Melodies* (Vol. IV, *Songs of the Oriental Sephardim*) (New York: Ktav Publishing House, Inc., 1973), 207, 204. Reproduced with permission.
45 Anhalt, 'From "Mirage" to *Simulacrum* and "Afterthought,"' 7.
46 Anhalt, letter to the author, 2 November 1987.
47 Anhalt, 'From "Mirage" to *Simulacrum* and "Afterthought,"' 8.
48 Anhalt, letter to the author, 2 November 1987.
49 Anhalt, 'From "Mirage" to *Simulacrum* and "Afterthought,"' 9.
50 Ibid., 10-11.
51 Kerpely, *A Crown for Ashes*, 216.

DON McLEAN

Of Things Past: John Hawkins's *Remembrances* (1969)

Remembrances (1969) was commissioned through the first award made by the John Adaskin Memorial Fund in 1968 for performance at the Stratford Festival in July 1969. It was published by Iroquois Press of London, Ontario (a Jaymar publication © 1971), with the assistance of a grant from the Canada Council in collaboration with the Canadian Music Centre. The published score, which is reproduced from the composer's holograph, is dated 'Montréal JAN–APR. 1969 (revisions – NOV. 69).' It consists of a grey-blue cardboard cover, a title page, and 15 sheets (44 x 28 cm). The work is scored for a five-player ensemble, and the instrumentation is piano, harp, trumpet in B-flat and in D, horn in F, and trombone (also doubling on xylophone). The piece has been recorded by the Société de musique contemporaine du Québec (SMCQ) on the Radio Canada International label (Music of Today/ Musique d'aujourd'hui, volume 3, RCI 300).[1]

Remembrances suspends the listener-reader in a delicate balance of memories extrinsic and intrinsic to the work through its incorporation of musical and literary quotations. In the penultimate section, for example, Hawkins quotes a musical gesture which is remembered to be measures 4 to 7 of the second movement of Beethoven's Piano Sonata, op. 111. Other gestures, however – those simultaneously presented, those which have preceded and those which follow – are clearly not from the same sonata. The process of intrinsic connection is, of course, common to all musical perceptions; familiar classical examples include the recognition of motivic continuity at the phrase level and recapitulation at the large-scale formal level. But extrinsic connection involves the bisociation of matrices not normally connected – here, a specific op. 111 matrix and a specified matrix of gestures which are not op. 111.

Danger is involved. The quotations and the non-quotations may not bisociate but bifurcate: they may diverge from an (inadequately articulated) point of intersection.² Every juxtaposition, after all, has the potential to be received as revelation, or as nonsense. This is an aesthetic issue of great contemporary interest, and it is the critical issue to which we will return towards the end of this essay. In examining *Remembrances*, however, we will treat the quotations as an absolute decision of the composer, a decision which is, in itself, beyond musical-structural analysis.³ We will concentrate instead on the analytical challenge of revealing how the quotations are connected to each other, to their contexts, and to the overall design of the work.

To this end, and because the perceived connections in *Remembrances* are necessarily musical, a method of combined musical-graphic and verbal analysis is employed. Naturally it is assumed that readers will wish to obtain access to the score. At the same time, however, it should be noted that all figures in this essay (except those which are themselves analytical reductions of other figures) contain virtually every pitch of the score (though not every reiteration of pitches, or, of course, their rhythmic profiles). The figures, therefore, can serve as a reasonably complete reading/listening guide.

The musical-graphic notation serves to elucidate the author's interpretation of the relationships which obtain among the pitches. In the graphs, conventional note values designate structural levels within the section under discussion – from larger-scale half- and quarter-notes to (occasional) eighth-notes and stemless notes on the more local scale. The relative note values are, thus, qualitative and interpretive rather than quantitative (durational). Slurs denote contextual relationships; dotted slurs denote the return to (the structural retention of) a note or pitch collection (which retention may incorporate a transfer of register). Beams are used to denote certain relationships more emphatically. The direction of stems associates notes which are interpreted to be in the same 'voice.' (Any part can, of course, represent more than one voice and can act on more than one structural level.) Other graphic signs are assumed to be self-explanatory or are explained in context. References in the text to measure numbers pertain to their numbering on the graphs. Pitch-class set designations, where employed, use the standard table of set-class prime forms.⁴

Verbal explanations of the graphs are restricted to particularly interesting or problematic cases and do not function as a detailed transliteration. The main function of the graphs is to demonstrate the musical connections and structural-hierarchical relationships of the composition by representing analytical judgments in a concise musical-graphic format. The broader technical goal of the paper is to demonstrate the efficacy of employing graphic analytical procedures to the analysis of quotation- or collage-based compositions.⁵

Of Things Past: John Hawkins's *Remembrances* 47

Remembrances is in nine sections; these are assigned roman numerals in the score. In performance, there are no breaks between sections (they are not movements). Analytically, I have divided the work into five groups of sections as follows: (1) **I** (which is introductory); (2) **II, III,** (which establish the quotation technique); (3) **IV, V** (both of which are more fragmentary than the preceding, and are also formally subdivided); (4) **VI, VII, VIII** (which represent loud and soft attempts to achieve a tonal ordering only to yield to the op. 111 quotation); and (5) **IX** (which is designated coda). Between the analyses of these groups, I have placed three brief commentaries on more general features of the work as a whole: (1) timbre, (2) the visual aspect of performance, and (3) notation. Readers may prefer to defer these commentaries until after the discussion of section **IX**. Some critiques and conclusions concerning the musical quotation phenomenon follow the analytical comments on the coda.

I. 'All the world's a stage ...'

The section is introductory; there are no musical quotations and the brass are (here only) omitted. Six dramatic ('brusque, wrenched') anacruses for piano are punctuated by five pauses, during which a complex overtone cluster and an evolving four- to seven-note chord for harp are left to resonate. The perceived theatrical quality of these gestures is suggested by the heading (*As You Like It*, II.v). The section is in two parts. (See Figure 1. Figure 1b is a structural simplification of the piano system of figure 1a.)

'A' (measures 1–3): The basic structural pitches of the piano part are its 'outer voices,' A and C, both of which, despite the thick low register, are treated with fairly clear voice-leading motions. The main motions are the neighbour [N] notes around A and the descending bass motions from C to B♭ or B♮. The exchange B♭ⓍB♮ (Figure 1b) foreshadows a continuing conflict between these pitch classes (see **IV**, for example). The N-note motion is similarly accompanied by an exchange of pitches E♮ and E♭ in m. 2. Note the repetition of the braced motive [(] D♭, C, B♮ in mm. 2–3. This will descend to become the bass cluster C♭, B♭, A in m. 4 (square note head). The harp chord arises as a specific selection of pitches from the initial piano overtone cluster and includes the pitch classes of the braced motive. The additional F♯ (m. 2) should be associated with the E♮ (m. 3; see bent-stemmed, beamed notes; however, its anticipation in the piano, mm. 1–2 [?], is more dubious). This dyad becomes an important motive in **IV**.

'B' (measures 4–6): The basic structural feature is an exchange of associated harmonies in the piano part. These harmonies, indicated by the aster-

48 Don McLean

Figure 1. I. 'All the world's a stage ...'

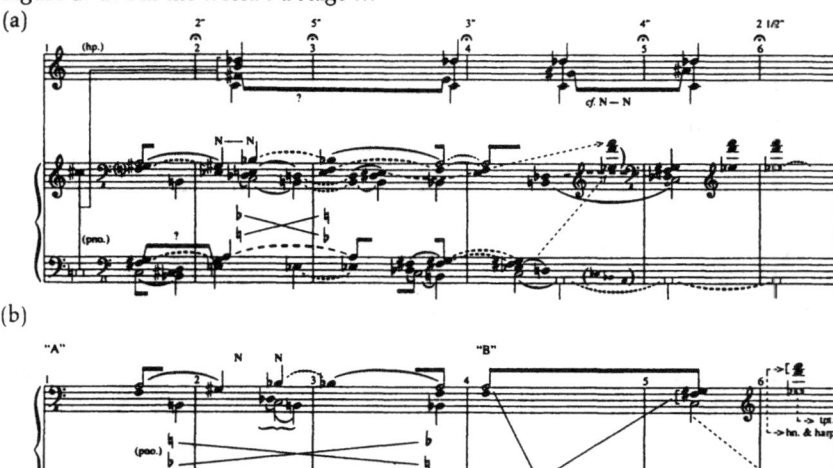

isks (*) in Figure 1b, clearly mark the beginning and end of the binary subdivision. The prominent 013 trichord (E♭, D, F) in the upper register of the piano part is the product of a registral transfer (see arrow markings in Figure 1a, m. 4). The E♭ and the D, as well as the C (in m. 5), are transferred to the indicated instruments at the beginning of section II.

In general, pitch-class and interval-class identities are the chief means of musical connection in this atonal context, whether these function vertically (as in the associated harmonies) or horizontally (as in the various motives). The six phrases of the piano part show a trichordally rich set-class structure: trichords 014 and 016 are particularly prominent either alone or as subsets in the A section; section B continues with 015, the bass cluster 012, and the treble-clef 013.[6] Further analytic details are presented in the graphs. Note, for example, the recurrence of the N-note pitch classes in the harp (mm. 4–5; [cf. N–N]) or the anticipation of the motif A–G (mm. 4–5) in the left hand of measure 3. Throughout section I, however, the density of the writing and the low register make tenuous all but the general quality of anacrusis and the immediate pitch-class connections to section II.

II. 'Veni ... creator spiritus'

The headings of sections II and III refer to the musical quotations these sections feature. In II (see Figure 2a), the trumpet (cup-muted) quotes 'Veni

Figure 2. II. 'Veni ... creator spiritus'

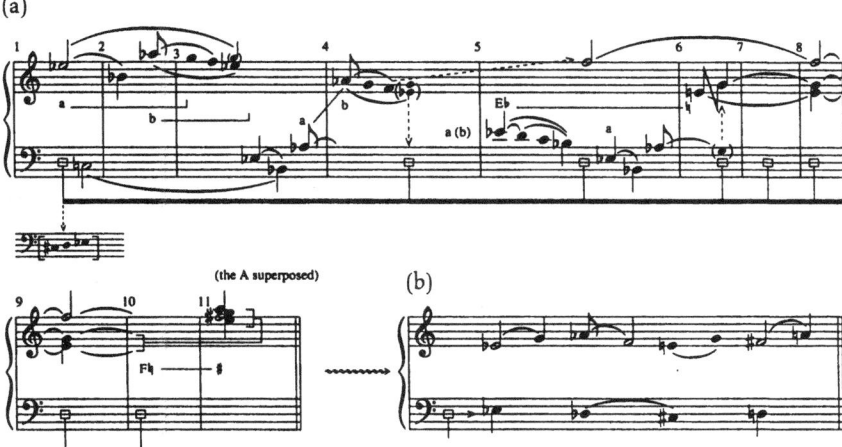

creator spiritus' as found in the first movement of Mahler's Eighth Symphony. Motives marked **a** and **b** are fragmented from the quotation; the A♭ which links them has a strong tendency to descend through the major-scale tetrachord of motive **b**. Motives **a** and **b** are combined in measure 5. The trombone's 'slow vibrato within 1/2 tone limits' connects its C to its B♭ (m. 3), which motion recalls that of section I (Figure 1b), m. 1 bass and m. 3 braced motive. The cluster (C♯, D, E♭) in the bass clouds the clear E♭ major tonality of the trumpet line (mm. 1–3) and permits a gradual shift of tonal focus from E♭ to D (as shown in Figure 2b). The 'unfolding thirds,' which form the structural basis of this section, constitute a projection of the 013 treble-clef trichord (E♭, D, F) from section I, both in the initial brass notes (C, D, E♭) and, more remarkably, in the main upper-voice notes (E♭, F, F♯) of the section as a whole (again, see Figure 2b). A strong condensation of materials is present in m. 11: the chromatic change F♮ to F♯ (harp) is simultaneous with the register transfer of the third E–G (from lower brass to piano harmonics) and with the superposition of A♮. Two additional interlocking 013 trichords are thus formed – E, F♯, G, and F♯, G, A. The harp F♯–A anticipates the third for trumpet and horn which begins section III.

III. 'Grant us peace ...'

The quotation refers to the 'Dona nobis pacem' section of Bach's Mass in B minor (mm. 32–4, trumpets). The musical content of the section is in

Figure 3. III. 'Grant us peace ...'

three instrumental groups (see Figure 3a): (1) trumpet (in D) and horn; (2) trombone; and (3) piano and harp.

(1) The filigree cadential pattern of the quotation is an elaboration of a simple fourth-motion – A to D and back – over F♯ (see Figure 3b). The F♯ is the main structural note (horn, *senza sordino*); the trumpet (straight-muted) is a superposition stemming from the A mentioned at the end of section II.

(2) The trombone ('whisper'-muted) quotes the incipit of Beethoven's choral theme from the finale of the Ninth Symphony. It is important to understand that the main notes of this fragment are F♯ and E. This anticipates the main motive of section IV. The trombone (m. 3) then joins the trumpet and horn to converge on, though not actually to arrive at, the piano's D-major triad. Note again (recall section II) the presence of the major-scale tetrachord (here A–D) as well as the principle of exchange (here between trumpet and trombone, mm. 3–6).

(3) The piano and harp parts are an overt attempt to scumble what would otherwise be clear functional tonality. The 'pizz. clusters' for piano are only approximately pitched. Nevertheless, the tonal clarity of the upper lines and the pizzicato clusters for harp (including a complete dominant thirteenth in

Of Things Past: John Hawkins's *Remembrances* 51

compressed position [end of m. 2]) make the 'quasi V' function ascertainable despite the continuing haziness of bass definition.

Commentary 1 – Timbre

This first of three commentaries concerns the use of timbre in *Remembrances* as a whole. The instrumental groups – piano, harp, and brass – are treated separately. Similarities of timbral usage between piano and harp have been emphasized by adopting a parallel topical organization.

Piano. (1) *Pedals*. The use of pedals is meticulously notated; they are numbered P1 (damper pedal), P2 (sostenuto pedal), and P3 (soft pedal). (2) *Damping*. P1 is used to separate and, complementarily, to meld large sections of the work. It is gradually released to dampen all but the D-major triad which separates sections **III** and **IV**; it is held down *sempre* (i.e., the dampers kept raised), structurally, to sustain the cluster in section **II**. A different technique of damping – muting with the fingertips placed on the strings near the pins – is employed in sections **II, IV, VII,** and **VIII**. (3) *Harmonics*. P2 is employed in the introduction and in the coda to sustain an area of overtones; a similar effect is obtained in section **III** by silently depressing a D-major triad. Harmonics are also played directly: the fifth partial and the first partial in section **II**. (4) *Glissandi*. P3 is employed in section **IV** to isolate *una corda* for the performance of a semitone glissando: an E string is pressured with a tuning crank (2 inches from the pins) to produce F♮. Harp-type glissandi (over several strings) are employed in sections **III** and **VI**. (This is not completely without problems; in **III**, m. 4, the frame of the piano tends to get in the way; the placement of frame members varies with instrument makes and models.) (5) *Other timbral effects* include fingertip pizzicato (or plucking) in **III** and **IV**; striking the strings with the palm of the hand in **III**; and altering the sound quality of a vibrating string by touching it with a paper clip in **V**. A most unusual effect is prominent in section **IV**: the tuning crank is placed on the node of the first harmonic and moved along the string to produce '"whining" glissandi (in contrary motion).' The effect combines judicious use of pedals, harmonics, glissandi, and the timbre alteration.

Harp. Hawkins realizes that the combination of harp and piano makes two 'harps' available. The use of the harp is similar to the specialized use of the inside of the piano as described above. (1) *Pedals*. An interesting effect – *bisbigliando* (whispering) – is obtained in section **IV** by the continuous changing of the G pedal through the three available positions. (2) *Damping*.

Hand damping has been indicated at two points only (see **III** and **IV**). Presumably other dampings are left to the discretion of the performer. Muting with the fingertips placed near the table is employed in sections **II, VI, VII,** and **VIII.** (3) *Harmonics.* Simple harmonics are employed in **II, VI, VII,** and **VIII.** (4) *Glissandi.* The standard harp glissando technique complements the inside-the-piano glissandi in **III** and **VI**. (5) *Other timbral effects* include the use of the fingernail (once, in **VII**); striking the strings with the palm of the hand (in **III** and **VI**); and altering the sound quality of the vibrating string by touching it with a paper clip (in **V**). The latter two effects are exactly parallel to those of the piano discussed above. The effect which complements the piano's tuning-crank glissandi in **IV** is accomplished by moving the harp's tuning key along the specified B string. Playing positions – centre of the string, *à la table* – are also of timbral consequence.

Brass. The only conventional alteration of brass timbres has been the use of mutes. Hawkins employs cup, straight, and whisper varieties for trumpet and trombone; the horn may be muted or stopped. Pitch-timbre variations are employed in sections **II, IV,** and **VIII** by means of wide vibrato, half-valving, and lipped (or slide-produced) glissandi. Flutter-tonguing is employed in **VI**. A variety of multiphonics are created in **IV**: the players sing quarter-tone inflections into their instruments while playing. In **V**, the brass players are required to 'click fingernails against the bell of horn.' This percussive 'finger clicking' is done in sympathy with the 'paper clipping' of the harp and piano. The trombonist actually doubles as a percussionist in this section, playing a descending white-note glissando on xylophone.

Several of the special timbral effects enumerated above recur in the coda. (The first commentary concluded, we return to our discussion of the next group of sections.)

IV. 'I hear lake water lapping with low sounds by the shore'

The headings of sections **IV** and **V** refer to the composer's personal recollections of the natural sound environment. Section **IV** is a large binary structure with an appended link to section **V**.

Figure 4a: The musical quotation recalls Mahler's Ninth Symphony, first movement – the fragmentary idea F♯–E (via sections **III** and **I**) or its conflicting 'minor form,' F♮–E. Other material is freely composed. The tonality of D is well established by measure 2. This is structurally in effect throughout the main divisions of the section. There is strong motion to the dominant in m. 9; and mm. 10–11 clearly imply a D closure. The harp

Of Things Past: John Hawkins's *Remembrances* 53

Figure 4. **IV.** 'I hear lake water lapping with low sounds by the shore'
(a)

(b)

motive (m. 2 and m. 4) is an elaboration of the now familiar F♯–A third. The trumpet motive, mm. 6–8, is more difficult to comprehend. If the prominent E is understood to be a neighbour-note [N] (appoggiatura) to the D – a resolution which, following its Mahlerian model, is significantly *not* granted in the octave below (m. 5) – then the underlying motion (A, D, A) can be understood as an elaboration of its occurrence as the Bach quotation in **III** (with the same cup-muted trumpet timbre). The unfolding thirds, F♯–A and E–G (mm. 7–8), also recall **III**; at the same time, they transfer the register so strongly downward that they imply an A to D descent (shown in square brackets on Figure 4a).

Figure 4b: This descent is not actually allowed to occur. Instead, F♯ is reintroduced to open this second division of section **IV**. The section is underpinned by the peculiar tuning-crank/key glissandi (diamond-shaped notes) for piano (F♯) and harp (B♭). The F♯–A third of the harp motive (m. 1, F♯–A–B–A, on the graph) is given further elaboration (to C♯) on 'whisper'-muted trumpet in m. 6. The core of the same motive is repeated on stopped horn in m. 7, but is transposed to the conflicting F♮ (F♮–B♭–A♭). The 012 cluster which evolves through mm. 8–14 recalls the introduction; furthermore, its bass motion, C–A, returns! At the end of the link (mm. 14–17), the A–C third, elaborated as A–C–D–C (plucked piano and harp), should be compared to the previous, and similarly elaborated, F♯–A third.

V. 'a green hill – August ...'

This section is also binary (see Figure 5). The 'quotations' are atmospheric, Messiaen-like bird-calls: (1) 'white-throated sparrow' – the whistled and played A–C's; and (2) 'veery' – the xylophone descending 'jagged spiralling glissando.' The exchange of A and C again recalls the introduction. In measures 2–4 the quotation (marked 'with utmost nostalgia' and '... still, sad music ...') is from Brahms's *Paganini Variations* (op. 35, part 2, variation 12, mm. 9–11). The main melodic line of the quotation (upper staff of the graph, mm. 2–3) bears a motivic (in addition to the obvious pitch-class) affinity with the bass of m. 1 (bottom staff). The bass returns to D and leads the structural line of this section – a descent, D, C, B♭, to an implied A (inferred from the context, but not realized). (Note that this is Hawkins's context; the quotation originates in F major, to which key Brahms cadences in his measure 12.) The right hand follows in tenths, moving chromatically from F through D and D♭ (=C♯). The accented tones in the piano melody (beamed F–E♭, as well as A–G) work at cross purposes to this prevailing structural motion in order to recall the motive of section **IV** (F♯/F♮–E♮). This motive, as well as the inner-voice neighbouring motions about A and the return of the 013 trichord (B♭, D♭, B♮) which the brass trio plays into the piano, may further recall the introduction. Section **V** is framed by the whistled A–C motive.

Of Things Past: John Hawkins's *Remembrances* 55

Figure 5. **V.** 'a green hill – August ...'

Commentary 2 – The visual aspect of performance

Hawkins has a stated interest in the visual aspect of performance and *Remembrances* supports that statement.[7] Player movements and gestures have a strong theatrical element in any musical performance. Here, the pianist must often reach inside the piano (perhaps armed with tuning crank or paper clip); the harpist employs tuning key or paper clip. For the brass, there are mute changes and a trumpet change; the trombonist prepares to play brief gestures on xylophone; and the brass trio moves to, and plays into, the piano before resuming normal playing positions. Note, too, that the initial gesture of the composition is the pianist's silent preparation of the overtone cluster. When well executed, these various movements enhance, indeed form an integral part of, a concert performance of *Remembrances*.

VI. 'tonality is a complex topic???'

The headings for sections **VI** through **VIII** are puzzling. They are personal, and the interrogative forms of **VI** and **VIII** are not without a satirical bite of humour. There are no quotations in **VI** (compare **I**). Figure 6 presents a general picture of the composite stasis which here prevails. Its subdivisions correspond to pages of score. The component parts of the section, which are superimposed in presentation, are: (1) the continuing 013 trichord (B♭, D♭, B♮); (2) the F♯–A motive on trumpet; (3) an F♯–F♮ conflict (recall **IV**) over two registers (both times as part of 012 trichords: E, F, F♯ and F, F♯, G); (4) the

56 Don McLean

Figure 6. **VI.** 'tonality is a complex topic???'

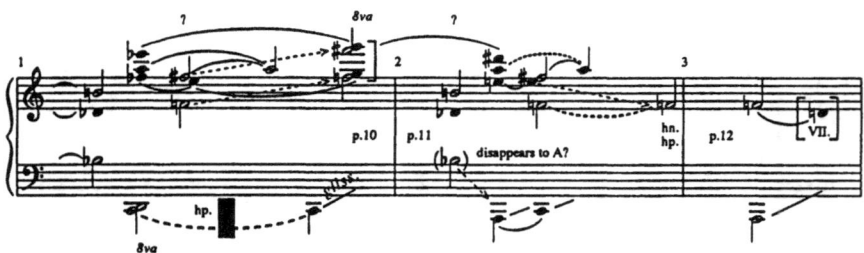

beginnings of a bass descent (D–C elided), which, following the disappearance of B♭ from (1) above, arrives at the A which was abandoned to implication in section **V**; (5) a palmed 'bash' on the lower strings of the harp; and (6) the 016 trichord F♭ (E), A, E♭ (D♯) for harp (later piano). The high E♭ of this trichord, in some ways confusingly abandoned, may be intended to relate to the piano's subsequent F♯–G, thereby conflating the E♭–G from **II** and the A–F♯ and G–E from **III**. All of these components are dissolved to arrive at a (variously timbred) F♮ over the bass A.[8]

VII. 'la rivière ...'
'riverun returns'

The quotations are obscure; it has been suggested that the F–D ostinato (recall the whistled A–C) is based on the final movement of Mahler's *Das Lied von der Erde* and that the motive F, B♭, A♭ (recall **IV**) is from the Adagio of his Tenth Symphony.[9] The heading ('la rivière ...') is intended to be atmospheric;[10] 'riverun returns' alludes, of course, to Joyce's *Finnegans Wake*. The 'return' is perhaps to D, which, played 'normal' by the harp, marks the beginning of the section; however, the superpositions of mm. 2–3 and mm. 4–5 recall section **IV**.

Figure 7. **VII.** 'la rivière ...'
'riverun returns'

Of Things Past: John Hawkins's *Remembrances* 57

VIII. 'Was Beethoven really deaf'?

The quotation from Beethoven's Sonata, op. 111, is perhaps the most easily identifiable excerpt in *Remembrances* (see Figure 8). The 'tonality', though there is no confirming cadential gesture, has fallen to C, the key of the excerpt. The brass once again interrupt with a 013 trichord (m. 4, F♮–A♭–F♯; compare the end of **VII**) and, in m. 7, frame the entire second half of the composition with a recollection of **IV** (recall Figure 4b, m. 7). As a detail, note that the D–F ostinato is not absent from the quotation itself (see *); indeed, there is an outer-voice exchange of those pitches (m. 4). It is important to understand the overall bass motion of this section: the low A which was abandoned at the end of section **VI** and the higher B♮ (section **VII**, Figure 7, m. 3 and m. 5) are here *connected* by the bass line of the quotation.

Commentary 3 – Notation

The notational style of *Remembrances* is conventional musical graphics. It is occasionally approximate with respect to pitch or vertical alignment, but it is invariably controlled in timbre, density, register, dynamics, and structural duration. (The remainder of this commentary is provided as a useful summary; it will, of course, be largely superfluous to those who have examined the score in detail.) In the score, dotted lines are sometimes employed to assist in the vertical alignments; mutings or pitch-approximate pizzicati are x-notated; in general, these and other notations are self-explanatory. Verbal instructions are necessary for the various special effects (discussed under timbre, above) and these instructions are provided with reasonable clarity.

Figure 8. VIII. 'Was Beethoven really deaf'?

58   Don McLean

No peculiarities of notation are unique to the work. The possible exception is the generalized graphic depiction which monitors the progress of the tuning-crank/key glissandi in the second half of section **IV**. The circle-enclosed notation of the final section is a reasonable representation of its controlled aleatoric aspects.

IX. CODA '... a land of grass without memory ...'

The heading is from William S. Burrough's novel *Naked Lunch*, but relates back to the nature-inspired titles of sections **IV** and **V**, to which sections much of the musical materials can be traced. The coda begins with a piano 'cue' gesture from section **I** (compare Figure 1a, m. 2). The graph (Figure 9) isolates common elements from the five 'circles' on page 15 of the score, each of which contains the musical 'segments' for one player: (1) is the beginning of the harp, trumpet, and trombone circles; it recalls the introduction (harp 0127 tetrachord) and conflates the conflicting F♯ or F♮ to E motions; (2) is the beginning of the horn circle (the piano begins its tuning-crank glissandi of harmonics on F♯ at this point); the motive should be compared to section **V**, mm. 1–2. (3) Other elements – marked **a, b, c,** and **d** – are by now familiar; these are the main contents common to all the circles.

Figure 9.   **IX.** '... a land of grass without memory ...'

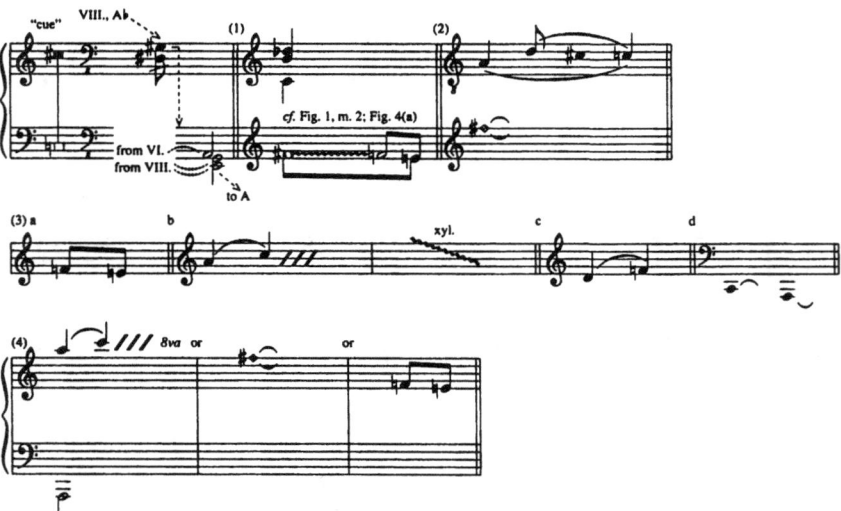

The F♮–E♮ bending which constitutes element **a** is realized by muted glissando on trumpet, horn, and trombone, and also by vocalized multiphonics on trumpet and trombone and by tuning-crank glissando on piano. The bird-calls of element **b** are whistled by the trumpet player, harpist, and pianist; the xylophone glissando is again performed by the trombonist. Element **c**, here on horn, recalls the D–F piano and harp ostinato of sections **VII** and **VIII**. Element **d** is particularly important as the foundational bass pitches, C and A (for harp and piano, respectively; both are *paper-clipped* and are counterpointed by the players' whistled bird-call). The pitches and timbral effects refer back to the central section **V**; the bass functions, however, recall section **I**.

In (4), I show the possible endings of the piece. There is a departure of instruments after about two minutes of 'circling': the conductor stops the brass first; the harp and piano continue with one and two segments, respectively. Thus, the isolated piano segment which concludes the piece will be one of the three shown. With whichever segment of its circle the piano ends the work, the bass A, sustained by pedal (P1), will make its presence felt.[11]

Critiques (mostly by Hawkins) and conclusions ...

Hawkins has been critical of *Remembrances*, which has been called his best-known work.[12] Of his slightly later *Waves* (1971), for soprano and piano, based on fragments from T.S. Eliot's *Four Quartets*, he has said: 'There I feel that I've at least managed to achieve some unified musical language. I know why every note is there. It has a certain meaning for me. Whether it does for the listener is hard to say.'[13] These statements, which are accurately self-critical, point directly or retrospectively to the problems of *Remembrances*. From them, we can extrapolate.

Hawkins has expressed some insecurity concerning the balance of the intuitive and the consciously intellectual aspects of the compositional process in *Remembrances*; he does not, it is implied, 'know why every note is there.' (The issue, of course, is not whether a composer ought to proffer reasons for 'every note,' but whether he or she is completely confident in the correctness of the work – intuitively and/or consciously.)

Hawkins also seems aware of a 'private art' problem; *Remembrances* is 'sort of autobiographical, sad, nostalgic.'[14] He feels personal problems may here intrude upon the musical object, that the composer's 'meaning for me' may not correlate to the listener's response. Verbally, for the composer, the musical quotations and associative meanings of *Remembrances* have a programmatic significance which, even if it were capable of articulation, remains unarticulated. Listeners receive *only* the musical events and those events trigger bundles of associative responses for each individual. The performers, and others who see the score, have the additional layers of meaning which the sectional headings and performance directions communicate. All of this can appear to heap complexities of meaning on what are, otherwise, fairly meagre musical means.

What, then, turning to the larger aesthetic issue, is the motivation for musical quotation in general?

Quotation may be intuitively musical, a type of unbidden mental intrusion, or a triggered free association. The composer may intuit an appropriate juxtaposition of materials, or such materials may simply force themselves upon the creative process.[15] Motivation can also be more conscious and purposive, an act of homage or parody.[16] Stylistic imitations, when they do not fall into neoclassical dissimulation, can combine that angled vision of compositional restraint with a genuinely communicated humour and appreciation for past idioms.[17] Quotations, pre-existent musical materials of any kind, are chosen for their compositional-structural potential, but they are also chosen for the associative meanings they elicit in the composer personally, and, in so far as the composer can determine, for the correlative meanings they elicit in the social group which constitutes the composer's audience.[18]

To the purist, the inclusion of tonal quotations, of 'nice passages,' in an otherwise dissonant, atonal context seems surreptitiously to curry the favour of the naïve or anti-modern listener. It is a rapprochement which borders on capitulation. Hawkins himself has termed the most salient feature of *Remembrances*, its quotations from the classic-romantic period, 'a flimsy device in some ways.'[19]

Nevertheless, quotations present the elitist (or connoisseur) with a fascinatingly complex variety of responses. The more informed listener may experience a given excerpt as vaguely tonal in an atonal context, as a quotation of unremembered identity, or as the specific repertoire item. These experiences involve an inversely variable degree of cognitive dissonance with their surrounding context. Tonalisms in an atonal context are now generally manageable; recognition of a quotation event of unknown origin is thoroughly disruptive only if the listener begins looping for the call number; precise recognition of chapter and verse, self-flattering smugness aside, poses the greatest problem: what is that piece of music doing inside this piece of music?

This is a familiar problem to students of the music of Charles Ives. The listener's sense of formal dissonance is felt, as Peter Burkholder has said, 'not in respect to the musical structure itself but in respect to our expectations for melodic autonomy on the part of the individual work ... [Ives] unexpectedly makes us think of other music while we are trying to concentrate on his.'[20]

This collision of contexts, the bisociation of matrices to which we referred near the opening of this essay, is the occasion of wit. Wit can manifest as just plain silliness, as would seem to be the case, for example, in the surface buffoonery of the Rossini quotation in the first movement of Shostakovich's Fifteenth Symphony. Or, wit can appear in its more profound transformation – as witness. Consider the toy piano fragment of 'Bist du bei mir' in the fourth section of George Crumb's *Ancient Voices of Children* (1970), or the 'witness for a plea of insanity' represented by the *Messiah* foxtrot in the seventh of Peter Maxwell Davies's *Eight Songs for a Mad King* (1969).

Works which employ quotations at a level more extended than the incidental generate the formal typologies of 'collage' and 'chain.' *Remembrances* is an instance of the chain type. The former type features a plethora of musical materials, the latter a paucity. Collage fashions quodlibet and polyparameters; chain fashions subtlety of link.[21]

Certainly one of the most striking examples of the 'collage' type is section III of Luciano Berio's *Sinfonia* (1968), where not only the multifarious musical materials are quotation-based, but the entire scaffolding in which they are enclosed is also borrowed. As the composer has said: 'The result is a kind of "voyage to Cythera" made on board the third movement of Mahler's Second Symphony. The Mahler movement is treated like a container – rather, a generator – within whose framework a large number of *musical references and characters* are proliferated ... actually they are signalling and commenting upon the events and transformations ... the image which comes most spontaneously to my mind is that of a river flowing through a constantly changing landscape ... present either as a fully recognizable form or as small details lost in the surrounding host of musical presences.'[22] We have, then, a kind of staged Moldau of musical memory.

These *musical characters* from the past, called upon to give witness in Berio's work as in Hawkins's, are usually placed in a high mimetic, romantic, perhaps occasionally even mythic, position relative to their modern surroundings. They are granted greater power of action, and speak in a heightened, archaic, and more formal tongue. The prevailing mode of most twentieth-century art is the ironic; the distinguishing feature of much musical quotation technique is the disintegration, the bald juxtaposition, of quotation and context. At the same time, the quotations themselves can manifest an oracular quality. Quotation strives through irony to regain myth.[23]

Quotation and richness of allusion have always been integral to cultured intelligence. But quotation is not normally an act of reading, it is an act of criticism. The moment we recognize a quotation inside another work we seem to transgress, or are transported across, the boundary delimiting critic and reader. The composer appears to engage in a critical act by selecting the quotation; but we are not privy to his criteria of selection. He has no means (outside the program notes!) of making 'the tenor of his arbitrariness transparent.'[24]

In quotation, however, the composer is *not*, in fact, functioning as a critic, attempting to establish a 'syllabus,' or advocating a selection of favourite tunes; rather, he is making manifest a subset of the text of his personal 'canon' of musical experience. This is projected onto a subset of listeners' personal canons. These subsets meet in the piece, though they are not identical with the piece. It is the composer who directs the presentational sequence and integration of materials. If this process of integration, which derives much of its momentum from its position on the potential edge of *dis*integration, does not actually fall apart for the listener, then the experience can be a series of minor epiphanies, each of which spirals a recessive memory process while the piece continues on the arrow of time.

Remembrances lacks a unified musical language. This is the not-surprising result of the amount of quotation; such diverse musical materials cannot be expected to coalesce into some unified, overall shape, without resort to a lowest-common-denominator approach to borrowed genius.[25] A choice of second, or secondary, phrases may adumbrate the identification process – a passage may meld more easily into its new context if its identifying edges have been removed. But the choice of the device leads, on the whole, to a rather different formal principle – that of a chained succession of highly metamorphic variations in which not only the transformational algorithms are attenuated but the 'orginals' arrive as unannounced guests. Responsible to the structural implications of these chosen excerpts, the composer must articulate some point of intersection in their juxtaposition. As the preceding analytical graphs and commentaries have shown, this connective process is often handled by Hawkins with remarkable transformational ingenuity.

This transformational process is not unidirectionally developmental; the piece does not continually grow forward. This quality is analogous to the multivalent memory process. Apart from the borrowed metrical orientation of the quotations, the sections are perceived as arhythmic. Beyond the exigencies of local obfuscation (the scumbling of temporal and tonal focus), the immediate rhythmic profiles of the transformed motives are not of structural consequence. The significant exception is section I, which, as an introductory anacrusis, does this: ⋖! This directionality is accomplished through a general increase in the number of impulses and in the saturation of the basic time unit, by means of a subtle cell-transformation technique (see Figure 10).

Figure 10. Rhythmic design of section I

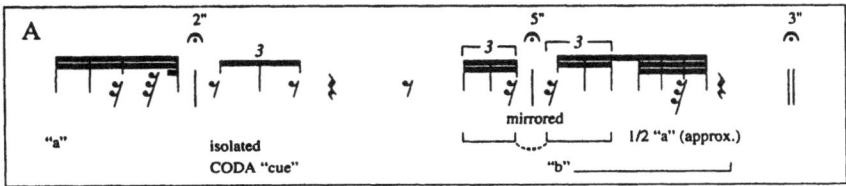

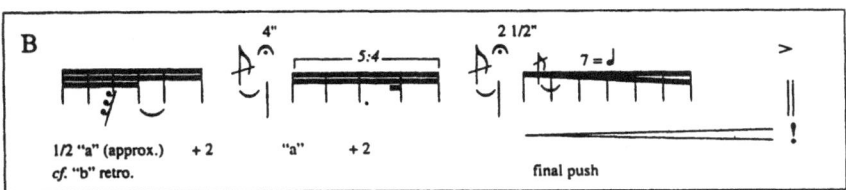

Section I of *Remembrances* has, as we have said, no quotations. Rather it sets the 'stage' for the *musical characters* which follow, beginning, in section II, with the invocation to the muse as 'creator spiritus.' Section III appeals for a spiritual 'peace' containing (literally, in the nested Beethoven quotation) 'joy.' Sections IV and V, in the allusions to Mahler and Brahms and the natural environment headings, are more personal and introspective. Section VI attempts to break out, not with a new quotation, but with a critique of the accrued 'tonality' through cumulative, followed by reductive, stasis. This gives way to (one cannot really speak of resolves to) the 'riverrun' ostinato of section VII (with its obscure late-Mahler allusions). The Beethoven quotation of section VIII is, in several ways, the culminating moment of the work. It regains the 'reverent' mood of section II, not now as invocation but as quiet affirmation. It also reconnects the registrally abandoned bass tones of the preceding sections. And, through common-tone links into the dominant four-two chord which initiates the quotation, it achieves a more satisfyingly elegant fusion of tonal functions – specifically, dominant seventh with enclitic augmented sixth (see Figure 8, mm. 5–6) – than could the 'critique' of section **VI**.

The coda of *Remembrances* also has no quotations; it is 'a land of grass without memory.' As a static and circular reduction of elements, the coda forms an appropriate conclusion to the work. Yet, this effectiveness cannot disguise its reduction to 'special effects' – in its amnesia, the coda approaches a catalogue of remnants.

In bringing this critical essay to a close, we are reminded that one of the functions of criticism is 'economy of syllabus' (we want to know which works are likely to repay our efforts). As George Steiner has said, one of the roles of the critic is 'to consign "inferior" works to non-remembrance (criticism is one of the means of forgetting).'[26] Which, of course, begs a final question: 'Is *Remembrances* worth remembering?'

Hawkins's title, as well as my own, recalls that classic creative representation of the personal memory process – Marcel Proust's *Remembrance of Things Past*. At least, this is the common English title of Proust's encyclopedic *A la recherche du temps perdu*. Hawkins's is *une musique recherchée*. The quotations, personally motivated though they may be, seem 'in search of lost time.' They convey a sense of nostalgia and of introverted loss; they seek community in their displacement, or rather, they ask the listener actively to re-create such community from the fragmentary musical gestures which the composer places at hand. Hawkins demonstrates a remarkably keen ear for a wide variety of timbral and tonal atmospheres, which are engagingly interconnected and artfully composed.[27] The result is the successful realization of the poetic idea of *Remembrances* – an exploration of the personal memory process in the musical domain.

NOTES

1 The score of *Remembrances* is available through the Canadian Music Centre.
  In addition to the RCI recording, a taped performance, with the composer at the piano, is available at the CMC [CMC (Montreal) T585=T612; CBC, 24 July 1969].
  This essay, with fondest remembrances, is dedicated to John Beckwith, whose enthusiasm for contemporary Canadian works proved infectious, to John Weinzweig, for whom a much earlier version of this paper was written, and to John Hawkins.
2 The idea of bisociation (and bifurcation) of matrices is central to Koestler 1964.
3 'Absolute decision' and 'beyond analysis' recall Cone 1972.
4 Much of the pitch-class set content of *Remembrances* beyond the introductory

section is of limited analytical interest. Indeed, it becomes apparent that musical materials (including the quotations) were selected for reasons other than their relatively trivial redundancies of pitch-class set content. It was, in part, the realization of this fact which suggested our alternative analytical approach. The standard table of set-class prime forms is found in appendix one of Morris 1987, as well as in numerous other sources.

5 The superficial similarities between the musical-graphic analytical procedure employed here and that of Schenkerian analysis of tonal music should be readily apparent. The differences in this case perhaps require more fundamental emphasis. I am not arguing that *Remembrances* displays a single referential sonority (triadic or otherwise) of overriding structural consequence, much less that any such sonority is the subject of structural prolongation or composing out. The absence of such features does not, however, completely preclude the interpretation of contextually defined, sectionally significant structural hierarchies (or, better, in view of the aforementioned lack of a highest level – 'heterarchies'; see Hofstadter 1980 133–4). Nor does this absence render illegitimate the disclosure of surface voice leadings and of the musical connections between quotations and their surroundings, for all of which – it is hoped the reader will agree – our musical-graphic analytical procedure is of some heuristic value.

6 The six phrases of the piano part correspond to the six measures on the graph, Figure 1a. The motivically significant set-class structure is as follows: (1) 014, 016, 0134 (as the union of two 014s); (2) 01256 (which combines 014 and 016 trichords), 0236 (which contains an explicit 014), 014; (3) 016, 0146 (which combines 014 and 016), 015 (new), 016, 012456 (which combines two 015s); (4) 015, 0147 (which combines 014 and 016 trichords), 013, 012 bass cluster and the treble-clef 013; (5) 012 cluster, 0167 (which combines two 016s) and again the treble-clef 013; and, finally (6) the 012568 hexachord (which results from the 012 bass cluster and the treble-clef 013). The harp chord evolves from tetrachord to septachord as follows: 0127, 01257, 012579, 0123579; however, the motivic function of the specific pitches (F♯–E and N-notes G♯–A♯) is of greater consequence than any putative cluster-plus-whole-tone derivation.

7 Morgan 1972, 25c.

8 Both the low A for piano and the harp C (which arises from the D–C elision) are treated to upward, cross-string glissandi. In the case of the harp, this twice involves a rather quick pedal change to C♮ and back to the C♭ of the 013 trichord which follows. The complete pedal setting at the beginning of section **VI** is thus: D♭ C♭ B♭ E♭ F♭ G A.

9 See Mather 1971, 102. These attributions seem strained, although Mather was in contact with Hawkins.

10 Personal communication with the composer.
11 The concluding value of the low A is further enhanced in the taped performance of *Remembrances*, which is available from the Canadian Music Centre (Montreal, T585 or T612). In the quietude of the ending, the low A is played, but a live-performance decision is made not to disrupt the moment by continuing with the remainder of the segment (paper-clip, whistle). The composer is at the piano.
12 Morgan 1972, 12c, lists nine performances in the first three years. Also see Schulman 1973, 4b, and Mather 1972. This observation is repeated in the EMC entry [=Ford 1981] for Hawkins.
13 Schulman 1973, 8a.
14 Schulman 1973, 8a.
15 Samuel Dolin, with characteristic humour, told me about the provenance of the 'birdsong quotations' in his piano piece *Queekhoven and A.J.* (1975): 'The bird just wouldn't shut up, so I had to put him in.'
16 Consider, for example, John Rea's chamber work *Jeux de Scène; fantaisie-hommage à Richard Wagner* (1977); Derek Healey's *Lieber Robert* (1974), in homage to Schumann; or, more abstractly, if not to say arcanely, Serge Garant's use of Bach's *Musical Offering* in the series of *Offrandes I–III* (1969–71) and *Circuits I–III* (1972–3).
17 Consider, for example, the style-study variations of Michael Colgrass's *As Quiet As* (1966); or, among John Beckwith's numerous revitalizations of hymnody, *Sharon Fragments* (1966) and *Upper Canadian Hymn Preludes* (1977).
18 Berg's work, for instance, is a labyrinthine layering of subjective and objective meanings, as the 'secret program' of his *Lyric Suite* and *Violin Concerto* – to cite only the best-known examples – demonstrate. In a similar manner, Brian Cherney's solo viola piece *Shekhinah* (1988–9) layers programmatic meanings from Jewish mysticism and from holocaust history – the title is a reference to the feminine aspect of the deity and the piece, written for Rivka Golani, is dedicated to the memory of an anonymous woman in an Auschwitz photograph – with 'quotations' from a composed lullaby, Schubert's *Der Tod und das Mädchen* and a partisan song from the second World War (information supplied by the composer). Of course, any work which quotes music with associated nationalistic or political meanings attempts to elicit a correlative response on a more public scale. Examples would include such disparate works as Stockhausen's electronic *Hymnen* (1969), Rzewski's piano variations *The People United Will Never Be Defeated* (on the Chilean independence song *El pueblo unido jamás será vencido*) (1973), and, in a more impish vein, Godfrey Ridout's

George III, His Lament (1976), an occasional piece honouring the American bicentennial.
19 Schulman 1973, 8a.
20 Burkholder 1985, 26. Also valuable for Ives's use of quotation techniques is Ballantine 1979.
21 An example of such a collage is John Beckwith's *Canada Dash – Canada Dot* (1965–7), where the multiplicity of musical materials is contained in the conceit of two cross-country runs and a final repose. The 'chain' variety of formal type is made explicit in the modular third piece of Brian Cherney's *Dans le crépuscule du souvenir* (1977–80): the circularly disposed boxes, which contain quotations (from Schubert's A-flat major *Impromptu*, op. 142, no. 2, D.935, to Beethoven's D minor Piano Sonata, op. 31, no. 2) as well as emulations of tonal idioms, are linked by a graphic depiction of a chain.
22 From the composer's commentary to the recording, here quoted from Watkins 1988, 649; my emphasis. Berio actually claims that the quotations 'do not constitute a collage but, rather, illustrate an harmonic process.' Watkins 1988, particularly chapters 30 and 31, and Griffiths 1981, particularly chapter 11, are useful surveys of contemporary musical retrospection in general, and of quotation techniques in particular.
23 Aspects of this paragraph are indebted to Northrop Frye's theory of thematic modes (Frye 1957, 33–4, 61–2, also Glossary 365–7).
24 Steiner 1984, 72. The distinctions between critic and reader which Steiner establishes in this essay include 'syllabus' and 'canon' which I employ in my following paragraph.
25 This phrase is an unabashed distortion of Milton Babbitt's assessment of style-imitative compositional pedagogy (Babbitt 1952, 263a).
26 Steiner 1984, 90.
27 It was never the intention of this paper to overview Hawkins's works, despite the lamentable lack of such useful resources for so many contemporary composers and compositions. (Plawutsky 1979 is a survey of Hawkins's output to the mid-1970s.) However, the interested listener may welcome a few observations on the more recent works. Hawkins undertook a thorough review of counterpoint (combined species), of rhythmic techniques (polyrhythms and metric modulation), and of more sophisticated broadway lyric and harmonic idioms (Weill and Sondheim) in the late 1970s and early 1980s. Explorations of the rhythmic techniques are found in *Breaking Through* (1982) for voice, percussion, and piano; the percussion duo *Substance-of-we-feeling [music]* (1985); and the *Dance Variations* (1983; rev. 1986) for percussion quartet. Hawkins wrote his own lyrics for the first of the above, as well as for *Light to*

Dark (1987) for soprano, clarinet, and piano, and for *The Cicada's Song to the Sun* (1988) for soprano, oboe, and guitar. This conscious effort to reach audiences through a more popular musical, as well as a more personal lyrical, idiom is also found in *Two Popular Pieces* (1986; *Romance* and *Calypso*, for the Wilson-McAllister guitar duo) and in *The First Fable* (1988), a children's entertainment with songs and mime (text by Timothy Findley). *Three Archetypes* (1984, rev. 1986) served as the required test piece for the Banff International String Quartet Competition and proved very popular with the performers (it was recorded by the winners of this category of the competition, the Parisii Quartet, on RCI 632). The work shows Hawkins's continuing efforts to regain what we have called the musically mythic – here, the means are not quotation but the genuinely expressive, and quite tonally centred, realization of what the composer has called 'musical archetypes': *Dance – Invocation – Hymn*. Though it actually forms the turning point before Hawkins's more popular, more tonally conventional efforts, *Prelude and Prayer* (1980), for tenor and orchestra (text, 'i thank You God,' by e.e. cummings), successfully combines many of the stylistic developments noted above; it remains one of Canada's finest orchestral compositions.

REFERENCES

Babbitt, Milton. 1952. Review of *Structural Hearing* by Felix Salzer. *Journal of the American Musicological Society* 5: 260–5.
Ballantine, Christopher. 1979. 'Charles Ives and the Meaning of Quotation in Music.' *The Musical Quarterly* 65: 167–84.
Burkholder, J. Peter. 1985. '"Quotation" and Emulation: Charles Ives's Uses of His Models.' *The Musical Quarterly* 71: 1–26.
Cone, Edward T. 1972. 'Beyond Analysis.' In *Perspectives on Contemporary Music Theory*, Benjamin Boretz and Edward T. Cone, 72–90. New York: W.W. Norton. (Orginally published in *Perspectives of New Music* 6 (1967):33–51.)
Ford, Clifford. 1981. 'John Hawkins.' In *Encyclopedia of Music in Canada* [=EMC], ed. Helmut Kallmann, Gilles Potvin, Kenneth Winters, 421a. Toronto: University of Toronto Press. (See also the French language edition, with updated bibliography, *Encyclopédie de la musique au Canada*, 1983, 453c–454a.)
Frye, Northrop. 1957. *Anatomy of Criticism*. Princeton, NJ: Princeton University Press. (Princeton Paperback Edition, third printing, 1973.)
Griffiths, Paul. 1981. *Modern Music: The Avant Garde since 1945*. New York: George Braziller. (Specifically, chapter 11, 'Quotation → Integration,' 188–222.)
Hofstadter, Douglas R. 1980. *Gödel, Escher, Bach: An Eternal Golden Braid*. New

York: Vintage Books. (Reprint of the edition published by Basic Books, New York, 1979.)
Koestler, Arthur. 1964. *The Act of Creation*. New York: Dell Publishing. ('A Laurel Edition.' Reprinted by permission of The Macmillan Company. Third printing, 1975.)
Mather, Bruce. 1971. 'Le collage musical: *Remembrances* de John Hawkins.' *The Canada Music Book* 3: 99–102.
– 1975. 'John Hawkins.' *Contemporary Canadian Composers*, ed. Keith MacMillan and John Beckwith, 92–4. Toronto: Oxford University Press.
Morgan, Kit. 1972. 'Hawkins Believes Performance Integral Part of Composing.' *The Music Scene* 265: 12, 25.
Morris, Robert D. 1987. *Composition with Pitch-Classes*. New Haven and London: Yale University Press.
Plawutsky, Eugene. 1979. 'The Music of John Hawkins.' *Canadian Association of University Schools of Music Journal* 8:112–34.
Schulman, Michael. 1973. 'For John Hawkins, Composing Isn't Easy.' *The Canadian Composer* 83:4–8.
Steiner, George. 1984. '"Critic"/"Reader".' in *George Steiner: A Reader*. New York: Oxford University Press, 67–98. ('First published in 1979 in *New Literary History*, a publication of Johns Hopkins University Press.')
Watkins, Glenn. 1988. *Soundings: Music in the Twentieth Century*. New York: Schirmer Books. (Specifically, Part IX, 'Past Imperfect – Future Subjunctive,' 639–90.)

GAIL DIXON

Symmetry and Synthesis in Beckwith's *Etudes* (1983)

Beckwith describes his *Etudes* for solo piano as both more 'complicated' and more 'single-minded' than many other works which he has written in recent years. Analysis confirms this view, revealing the remarkable ways in which the relationships inherent among the source materials are projected on many levels in the piece.

Commissioned by the Vancouver New Music Society, the work was completed in 1983 and given its première performance by pianist Jane Coop in Vancouver on 8 April 1984.[1] There are six etudes, each with a descriptive title: (1) Opposed sonorities 1; (2) Repeated notes and octaves; (3) Glides; (4) Opposed sonorities 2; (5) Harp; (6) Clusters and chords. This is a substantial work, both in duration and in content.[2]

Despite being a trained pianist himself, Beckwith has written remarkably little (beyond the purely pedagogical) for solo piano. Indeed, this is his first solo concert work for the instrument in over thirty years. The appearance of a major work of the calibre of these etudes has thus been warmly welcomed by Canadian pianists, despite the formidable technical challenges which are posed.

Although the actual composition of the work occupied only four months towards the end of 1983, Beckwith had been thinking about the project for a number of years. An important inspiration for the etudes was provided by the technical possibilities inherent in the piano itself. As Beckwith writes in the liner notes to the *Anthology of Canadian Music* recording of the work:

I have preferred here to look newly at the various physical actions of fingers and hand in piano playing, taking them as departure points for a series of short compositional essays. This could be regarded of course as a parallel approach to that used by

Chopin, Debussy, Scriabin, and others.[3] As with their etudes, so with mine also there is a dual sense of the term 'study' – a study in an aspect of performance skill which becomes at the same time a study in abstract musical design and expression.

Thus, these are not only 'etudes' in the pianistic sense, but in the compositional sense as well. It is this latter aspect of the work which is our primary interest here.

On hearing a good performance of the etudes, the listener may be struck, as I was, by the powerful sense of coherence which is projected. In this article I will suggest several explanations for this coherence. One obvious reason is that all the precompositional materials are generated from a single source, and the operations by which they are generated are themselves interrelated. On a more subtle level, the work is organically integrated by the large-scale application of these materials, and the relationships which exist among them, in the domains of pitch, texture, and form.

Each etude has a number of surface features which serve to distinguish it clearly from the others. At the same time, each relates in a fundamental way to a very limited number of source materials which serve both to unify and to link. The source material for the etudes consists of eight distinct, but closely related, hexachordally all-combinatorial 12-tone Sets, each generated from the inherently symmetrical pc set 6–8.[4] Seven are trichordally derived Sets, while the eighth is a synthesis of trichordal adjacencies featured in the first seven. The relationships which are evident both within and among these eight Sets are manifest in remarkable ways in other levels and dimensions of the work.

Before embarking on a discussion of individual etudes, it would be helpful to investigate the innate properties of the precompositional material. Symmetry[5] and synthesis are inherent in many aspects and dimensions of this material. That Beckwith fully understood the implications of his resources is clear from the systematic manner in which he exploits many of the possibilities described below.

The eight Sets which constitute the precompositional material for the etudes are shown in Example 1.

Beckwith's interest in intervallic adjacencies, as distinct from (but not to the exclusion of) total intervallic content, is made clear in his sketches for the work,[6] in which he carefully notes the succession of intervals in the unique segment which characterizes each Set. (These characteristic intervallic adjacencies are noted in Example 1.)

All eight Sets belong to that class of source sets described by Milton

Example 1

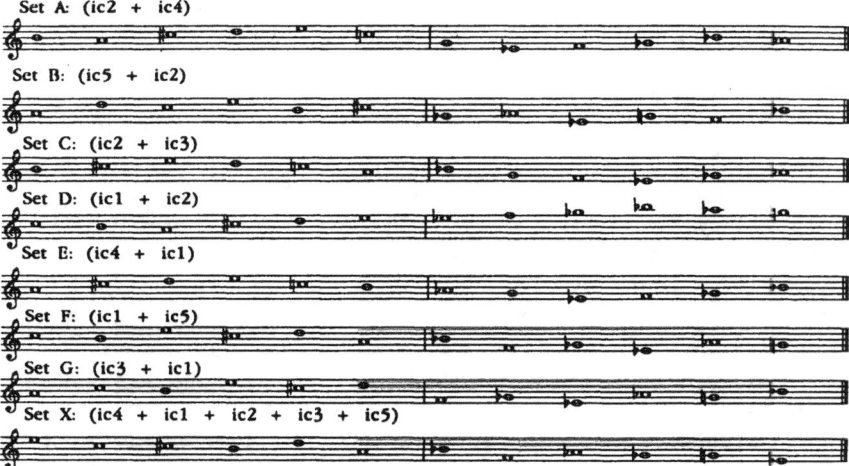

Babbitt as all-combinatorial; each is hexachordally combinatorial with its own P6, R0, I1, and RI7. (Numerous possibilities for trichordal combinatoriality also exist for each Set, though Beckwith does not exploit this aspect of his material.) In each Set, the second hexachord is a transposed retrograde inversion of the first. Since P0 = RI1, only twenty-four unique row forms are available for each Set. Each of their constituent hexachords can be reduced to pc set 6-8 [0,2,3,4,5,7], and the hexachords are related to one another at t=6. In the case of Sets A through G only, each hexachord can be further partitioned into equivalent trichords, the second of which is a transposed inversion of the first. Sets A through G are thus trichordally derived sets.

Several kinds of relationships are evident among the trichords of Sets A to G. The following pairings are based on identical trichordal set classes:

A – (no match)	[0,2,4]
B – C	[0,2,5]
D – G	[0,1,3]
E – F	[0,1,5]

Unlike the trichordal arrangements of Sets A to G, those of Set X relate neither to each other nor to trichords of other Sets, a fact that no doubt accounts for Beckwith's departure from a strict alphabetic labelling. This anomalous Set does, however, function as a kind of intervallic synthesis,[7] since each of its hexachords contains all five of the characteristic trichordal adjacencies from the preceding seven Sets. (See Example 1 above.) The only interval class which is not represented in any of the eight Sets is ic6.

Trichordal segmentation is clearly an important aspect of the structure in most of Beckwith's Sets. In abstract terms, eight unique trichordal subsets are available in pc set 6–8, of which the two most heavily represented are pc set 3–2 [0,1,3] and pc set 3–7 [0,2,5], each of which is embodied four times. The other six trichordal subsets are represented only twice each. Only four of the eight trichord types are capable of generating Sets A to G, and Beckwith has used all of them: pc set 3–6 [0,2,4], realized as the unordered trichords 024/357 (Set A); pc set 3–7 [0,2,5], realized as the unordered trichords 035/247 (Sets B and C); pc set 3–2 [0,1,3], realized as the unordered trichords 023/457 (Sets D and G); pc set 3–4 [0,1,5], realized as the unordered trichords 045/237 (Sets E and F).[8]

A quick review of Example 1 confirms that in ordering Sets A to G Beckwith has ensured, by using an I7 relationship between the trichords, that 0 in one trichord is so placed that it is answered by 7 in the other, 2 by 5 and 3 by 4. (See Example 2.)

In making use of his Sets, Beckwith is highly selective in his choice of transposition levels. One factor in his choice is the number of invariant pitch classes which are available for juxtaposed or superposed hexachords. It may provide a useful perspective to give a complete list of the number of invariant pitch classes which are available between analogous hexachords, under various levels of transposition or inversion:[9]

Example 2

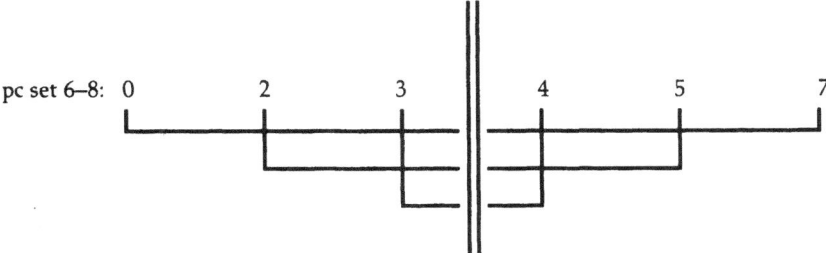

74   Gail Dixon

0 invariant pitches:	P0 with	P6				
		I1				
1 invariant pitch:	No available combinations					
2 invariant pitches:	P0 with	P4	P8			
		I3	I11			
3 invariant pitches:	P0 with	P1	P3	P5	P7	P9 P11
		I0	I2	I4	I6	I8 I10
4 invariant pitches:	P0 with	P2	P10			
		I5	I9			
5 invariant pitches:	No available combinations					
6 invariant pitches:	P0 with I7					

Another factor which influences Beckwith's choice of transposition level is the availability of invariant dyads (or even single pitches) at the beginning or ending of hexachords which he wishes to conjoin. It would be far too cumbersome to list all of these possibilities here. A single example will suffice: in Set A, hexachord 1 of P0 overlaps with hexachord 2 of P9 by virtue of the invariant dyad E–C. (See Example 3.)

Example 3

P0: B A C♯ D E C
P9:   E C D E♭ G F

A final innate characteristic of the material should be mentioned here. Given an appropriate context and arrangement, pc set 6–8 lends itself easily to a tonal interpretation, since it comprises the initial pentachord of the major and minor scales combined.

Having examined the characteristics of the precompositional material, we turn now to the etudes themselves. From the point of view of large-scale form, the six etudes divide naturally into two halves, based on a clear relationship between numbers 1 and 4 as well as between numbers 3 and 6, and a rather more tenuous relationship between numbers 2 and 5.

First half   Second half

(1) Opposed sonorities 1   (4) Opposed sonorities 2[10]
(The Sets occur in almost identical order in each. Also, as the titles suggest, there is a shared focus on sharply opposed sonorities within the texture.)
(2) Repeated notes and octaves   (5) Harp
(The middle section of each features a marked degree of tonal focus.)

Symmetry and Synthesis in Beckwith's *Etudes* 75

(3) Glides (6) Clusters and chords
(There is a common preoccupation with black versus white notes.)

The symmetry inherent in the source material is thus manifest on a large scale in the symmetrical disposition of material on either side of the midpoint of the work. A wealth of other smaller-scale symmetrical properties will be revealed in the discussion of individual etudes which follows.

Etude No. 1: Opposed sonorities 1

This etude is tripartite in design, with the second part (mm. 11–19) being a textural inversion of the first, and the third part (mm. 20–30) a synthesis of the first two. The two elements in the texture are dramatic in their contrast, as the title suggests. One layer consists of a series of cumulatively built chord clusters, the last note of which is extended by repetition. Each cluster takes place within the range of a perfect fifth. The other layer of the texture consists of a series of highly disjunct single lines, each featuring internal repetitions. The range of this layer is wide – between a tenth and a fourteenth. The two layers are superposed, creating a complex stratified texture.[11]

In parts 1 and 2, the cluster layer (which appears in the left hand in the first part, and in the right hand in the second) is organized as shown in Example 4.[12] (Upper-case letters refer to the eight Sets [A, B, C, D, E, F, G, X; see Example 1]; hex. refers to hexachord; P refers to prime form, R to retrograde; RH to right hand, LH to left hand.)

Example 4

Part 1:
LH: P5, hex. 1:   A   B   D   E   G   F   C   D   B
Part 2:
RH: R5, hex. 1:   A   B   D   E   G   F   C   D   B

Note that, for each Set, the twelve pitches proceed in symmetrical fashion from the boundary pitches inward to a central axis marked by the formal division between parts 1 and 2. Note also that the part 1 cluster layer focuses on one transposition of pc set 6–8 (the 'D' transposition), while the part 2 cluster layer focuses on its complement (the 'A-flat' transposition),[13] as shown below:

Part 1: order nos. 1   2   3 4 5 6   (P5, hex. 1, or the 'D'
                                        transposition of pc set 6–8)
Part 2: order nos. 12 11 10 9 8 7   (R5, hex. 1, or the 'A♭'
                                        transposition of pc set 6–8)

76   Gail Dixon

Part 2 is thus the logical sequel to part 1 for this layer of the texture.

The other layer of the texture in parts 1 and 2 is similarly organized, though some of the adjacent hexachords are interlocked by shared single pitches or dyads. Example 5 shows the order of Sets:[14]

Example 5:
Part 1:
RH: P3, hex. 1: B B D E C A F F G / R3, hex. 2: A A E G B C C D

Part 2:
LH: P3, hex. 2: A A E G B C C D / R3, hex. 1: B B D E C A F F G

In this layer, as in the cluster layer, part 1 focuses on one transposition of pc set 6–8, part 2 on its complement. However, the more rapid pace at which the hexachords unfold allows a prime and retrograde statement of both hexachords. Further, the bipartite division which is formed by the change from prime to retrograde ordering is underscored by an exchange of material between the two halves. As we shall see shortly, part 3 both extends and synthesizes these operations.

In part 3 the characteristic texture of the first two sections (i.e., cluster chords and repeated notes in one layer with a rapid, disjunct line in the other) is replaced by a texture in which both layers now feature rapid, disjunct single lines strongly reminiscent of those which had been used as only one component of the texture earlier. The superposition of two such lines, coupled with the destabilization of the earlier rhythmic regularity, creates a heightened intensity. To compensate for the absence of the cluster chords from this section, Beckwith interpolates five brief references to this earlier material. The interchange in the order of Sets which was shown in Example 5 as a characteristic of part 2 is now extended in part 3 to include reciprocity between prime and retrograde forms and between right and left hands. The exchange of material between the two halves is imperfect, although sketches indicate that originally a precise exchange was envisioned. (Underlined Sets deviate from the expected pattern.)

Example 6
Part 3:
RH: P3, hex. 2: G G C A F E E D / R3, hex. 1: F F E B C G D D A

LH: R3, hex. 2: F F D C E G A A B / P3, hex. 1: F F C A F E E D

Symmetry and Synthesis in Beckwith's *Etudes* 77

Yet another connection is apparent: Set A in parts 1 and 2 is normally replaced by Set G in part 3, and vice versa. Set B is similarly affiliated with Set F, and Set C with Set E, while Set D remains unchanged (cf. Examples 5 and 6, remembering the exchange between right and left hands). Once again, the symmetry of the exchange feature is apparent (see Example 7).

Example 7

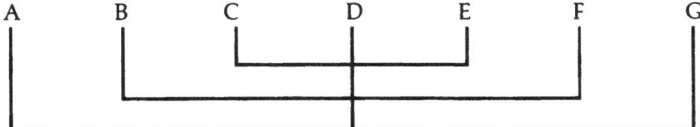

As is the case with the order of Sets in this part, the correlation just described is occasionally imperfect.[15]

It is interesting to note that the order of Sets in the five interpolations of the cluster texture in the third section reinforces the correlation shown in Example 7 (see Example 8).

Example 8

RH: R5,	hex. 2, Set A	⎯⎯⎯⎤		(m. 22)
LH: R11,	hex. 2, Set B	⎯⎯⎯⎤│		(m. 24)
RH: R5,	hex. 2, Set D	⎯⎯⎯┘│		(m. 25)
LH: R11,	hex. 2, Set F	⎯⎯⎯⎯┘		(m. 26)
RH: R5,	hex. 2, Set G			(mm. 27–8)

The only one of the eight Sets which is not overtly presented in this first etude is Set X – that Set which is an intervallic synthesis of the other seven. However, Set X is given covert expression in the repeated notes which culminate each Set in the cluster layer of parts 1 and 2. The trichordal contents of Set X (pc sets 3–3 [0,1,4] and 3–7 [0,2,5] control the order of the first six repeated notes, and thus have a direct impact upon the order of presentation of the Sets. Example 9 illustrates.

Note once again the correlation of 0 with 7, 2 with 5 and 3 with 4, as shown in Example 3.[16]

The climax, which occurs in the last measure of the piece, features the essence of these two repeated note passages, now unfolded, triple forte, in cumulative fashion. Example 10 contains the pitches of the last measure of

78 Gail Dixon

Example 9

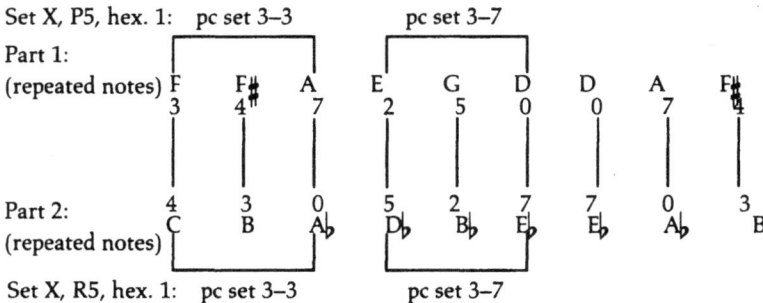

the piece. (The top line shows the upper voice of the texture; the bottom line the lower.)

Example 10

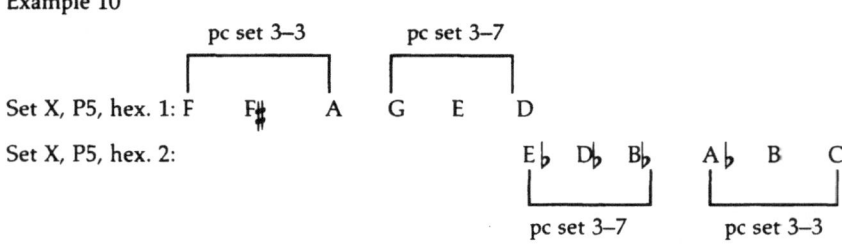

Not only is the lower part a retrograde inversion of the upper part, but segments can be mapped upon one other without the retrograde inversion feature, as shown in Example 11.

Example 11

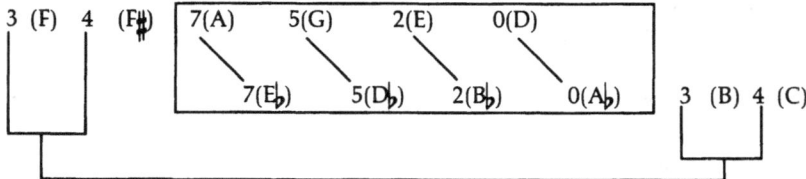

Thus, Set X synthesizes the material of this etude at several levels. Further, the tritone-related hexachords in this last measure combine to form an aggregate which is symmetrical in two dimensions. (Note the inversional registral symmetry in the vertical dimension and the retrograde symmetry in the horizontal dimension, as shown in Example 12.)

Symmetry and Synthesis in Beckwith's *Etudes* 79

Example 12

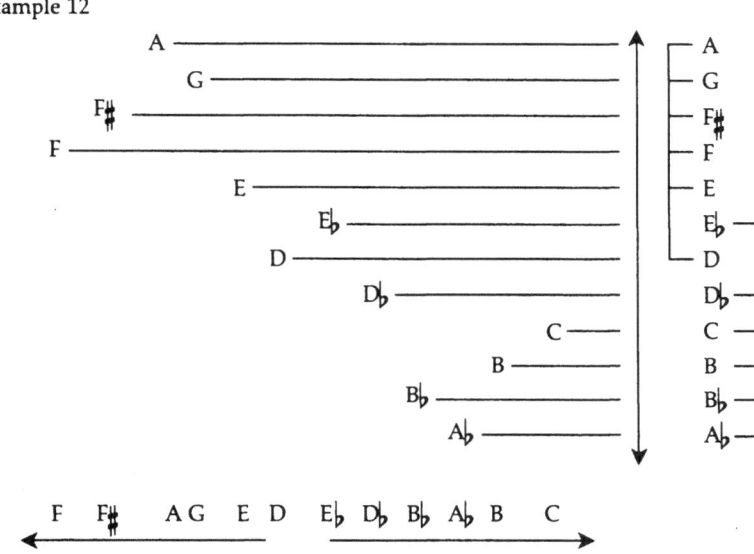

The transpositional relationships which Beckwith has chosen for this etude are both intrinsically interesting and ultimately significant for the work as a whole. Only four transpositions of pc set 6–8 are used in this etude: 'C', 'D', 'F♯', and 'A♭'. In both parts 1 and 2, the superposed layers have four pitches in common. However, the third part features changes in transposition levels, both within and between the layers. Example 13 illustrates the transposition levels used in *Etude No. 1*. The asterisks in part 3 denote interpolations of different materials (derived from the cluster texture of parts 1 and 2), as well as new transposition levels, within the prevailing 'F♯' transposition of the upper layer and the 'C' transposition of the lower. Thus, although when 'C' and 'F♯' transpositions of the hexachord coincide there are no common pitch classes, when interpolated material intrudes, the relationship between the layers reverts to that used in the first two sections (i.e., the layers have four common pitches). Over the course of the entire etude, each layer has an opportunity to use each of the four transposition levels.

Example 13

Part 1 (mm. 1–10):
Upper layer: 'C' transposition (of pc set 6–8)
Lower layer: 'D' transposition

Part 2 (mm. 11–19):
Upper layer: 'A♭' transposition
Lower layer: 'F♯' transposition

Part 3 (mm. 20–30):

Measure no.	20	21	22	23	24	25	26	27	28	29	30
Upper:	F♯		*D	F♯		*D	F♯	*D	F♯		D
Lower:	C				*A♭	C	*A♭	C			A♭

Etude No. 2: Repeated notes and octaves

In the first part of this etude (which is in ternary form) the left hand delivers a fusillade of rapid repeated notes, interspersed with brief rests between changes in pitch. The right hand marks these changes in pitch with a series of chords. On four occasions the prevailing texture is interrupted by fortissimo octave passages which feature cross rhythms (e.g., 3:4, 4:5) between right and left hands. The middle part of the etude (mm. 69–85) provides a dramatic contrast; here, tonal implications abound in the unison octaves arranged in lyrical phrases with widely fluctuating dynamics. An exact repetition of the first part brings the etude to a close.

First part: (mm. 1–68)

The 'A' and 'C' transpositions of pc set 6–8 are used in this first part. For the first time in these etudes, we see evidence of Beckwith's intention, to be more fully exploited in later etudes, of pitting white notes of the piano against black notes. The 'A' and the 'C' transpositions of pc set 6–8 each contain only one black note. A typical procedure in this section of the etude is to initiate each small (3 to 5 measures) subsection with only the white notes of the hexachord in both hands, and to end each by using the missing black note as a particularly extended fortissimo barrage of repeated notes in the left hand, coupled with a single sustained white note in the right. Hence, each subsection culminates either with a repetition of C♯ (the black note of the 'A' transposition of the hexachord) or of E♭ (the black note of the 'C' transposition of the hexachord), along with a single sustained white note. The stability provided by the frequent repetitions of this pattern is shattered on four occasions by the loud staccato octave outbursts.

The left-hand part is based on a series of hexachords which are interlocked by either single pitches or dyads. (Only one hexachord from each Set

Symmetry and Synthesis in Beckwith's *Etudes* 81

is used in part 1; the missing hexachords are supplied in part 2.) This first part of *Etude No. 2* is binary in design, and mirrored about the central axis, with the exception of the two X statements, which function as codettas. Example 14 shows that a symmetrical relationship exists both *between* the two halves (based on Set usage), and *within* each half (based on the organization of prime versus retrograde forms of the Sets).

Example 14

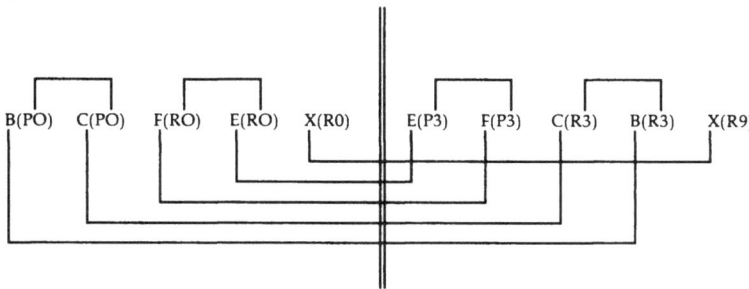

Second part: (mm. 69–85)

The Sets which were initiated in the first part are completed with the other hexachord in the second. Symmetry is also evident between the two halves of this part. This time, however, the relationship *between* the two halves is based on the organization of prime and retrograde forms, while that *within* each half is based on Set types. Both statements of X now appear at the end, as shown in example 15.[17]

Example 15

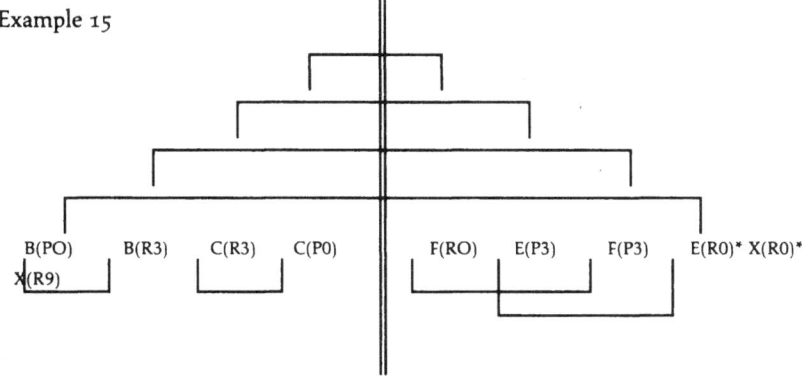

Example 16

Etude no. 2, Part 2, mm. 5 - 8:

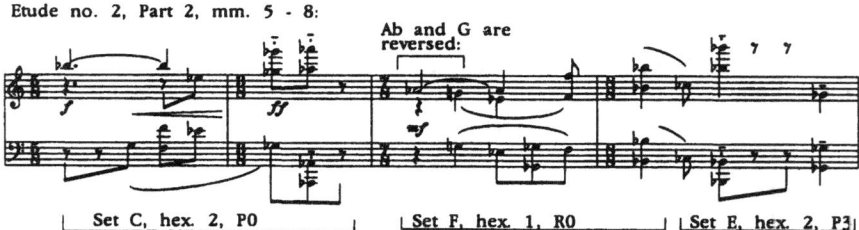

For the first time in these etudes, Beckwith provides his listeners with a clear tonal focus. He accomplishes this by selecting the three pitches which are invariant between the 'E♭' and 'F♯' transpositions of pc set 6–8 for particular prominence in this middle part of *Etude No. 2*. These pitches (G♭, A♭, and B♭) achieve special significance by virtue of their duration and their registral and metrical placement within the texture. In fact, there is an interesting deviation from the expected pitch-class order in the seventh measure, such that A♭, rather than G, appears on the first beat of the measure (see Example 16).

Etude No. 3: Glides

Double and single white-note or black-note glissandos constitute the predominant pianistic device of the piece. Subordinate devices include tremolos and repeated notes which begin rapidly then gradually diminish in speed. The piece is symmetrically laid out in a nested ternary form (the middle part is itself ternary):

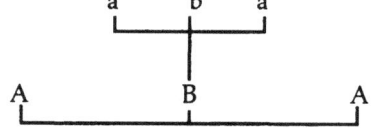

This etude is one of two in which Beckwith departs from his normal practice of extracting hexachords from his Sets for independent presentation; for most of *Etude No. 3* all twelve pitch classes of the Set routinely appear as linear entities. The outer parts of the ternary structure are based exclusively on Set X, and are quite strictly serial. Successive pitches of the Set are connected by white- or black-note glissandi, while successive transpositions of the Set are connected by the overlapping of invariant dyads. The first and last dyads of Set X are ic4 and are related at t=9, yielding a symmetrical relationship between the two outer parts of the etude, as shown in Example 17. A short coda employs a partial restatement of RP3.

Symmetry and Synthesis in Beckwith's *Etudes* 83

Example 17

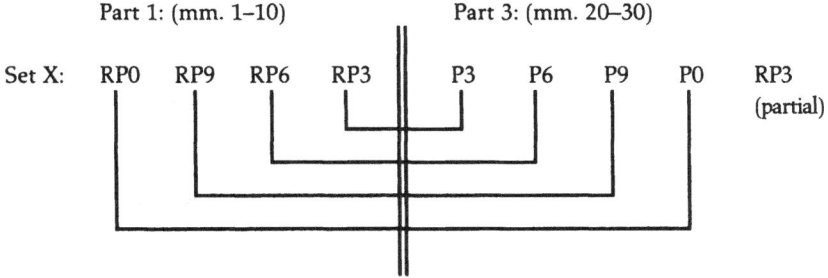

In part 2 of this etude (mm. 11–19) Beckwith exploits fully the polarity between white and black notes of the piano. This polarity is clearly presaged in several ways in part 1. As noted above, white- or black-note glissandi connect the registrally diffuse pitches of Set X. Further, Beckwith's choice of transposition levels for the Set provides the maximum hexachordal contrast between white and black keys. The maximum number of black keys in any form of pc set 6–8 is four, while the maximum number of white keys in any form of that set is five. There are eight transpositions which satisfy the criterion of the maximum number of black keys in one hexachord with maximum number of white keys in the other; Beckwith uses four of these – P0, P3, P6, and P9.

The brief middle part of this etude, itself in ternary form (a: mm. 11–13; b: mm. 14–16; a: mm. 17–19), abandons serialism in favour of a simple complementary relationship between black and white keys. The freedom of the outer portions of this middle part is supplanted at its centre by a more focused opposition between 'F♯' and 'C' hexachords, but serial ordering is absent.

The glissandi in this etude constitute an extensive catalogue of pianistic possibilities for this device. In part 1, Beckwith requires black- or white-note single glissandi at three different speeds, rapid, medium, and slow, as well as fingered scale passages. In part 2, he demands double white-note glissandi as well, in parallel seconds, thirds, fourths, and fifths.

In his sketches Beckwith includes a chart in which he counts the number of occurrences of white notes which begin or end glissandi in part 2. This is one of many clear demonstrations of his interest in maintaining approximately equal representation among whatever elements he is using. At another point in the sketches for this etude, he has a chart which counts the number of occurrences of a given pitch class in each register. Beckwith has

84   Gail Dixon

clearly made a conscious attempt to reduce any perception of hierarchy among his materials in this etude, a clear contrast with the deliberate tonal focus which is evident in the middle part of *Etude No. 2*.

Etude No. 4: Opposed sonorities no. 2

The opposition between sonorities suggested in the title is manifest in three distinct textures which I have labelled 1, 2, and 3, in order of their initial appearance. Formally, this etude combines aspects of binary design and variation technique, since these textures receive varied restatement in the second half of the piece. Thus *Etude No. 4*, which Beckwith probably composed first, and which he considers to be the most weighty, rigorous, and complex of the six, embodies on a small scale the same formal principles as does the work as a whole (cf. formal diagram on pp. 74–5).

Texture No. 1: (mm. 1–10 and mm. 37–46)

Texture 1 embodies two layers, one consisting of three-note chords, the other of rapid, disjunct, single pitches interspersed with rests. The constituent elements conspire to disrupt the underlying metre to a considerable degree. Further disruption is caused by the exchange of elements between the upper and lower layers of the texture. The order of the five Sets used in texture 1 is precisely that of the first five Sets in texture 1 of the first etude: A B D E G. It is clear that Beckwith is thinking in terms of the aggregate in *Etude No. 4*, since only one transposition is used (P0), and its constituent hexachords unfold simultaneously, one in each layer. This contracts sharply with his approach in the analogous position in *Etude No. 1*, where coincident hexachords belong to two different transpositions, and generate four invariant pitches. When texture 1 returns in the second half of *Etude No. 4* (mm. 37–46), the order of Sets is G F D C A. The symmetrical correlation between the Sets in each half is shown in Example 18. Note, once again, the exchange between A and G, B and F, and C and E.

Example 18:

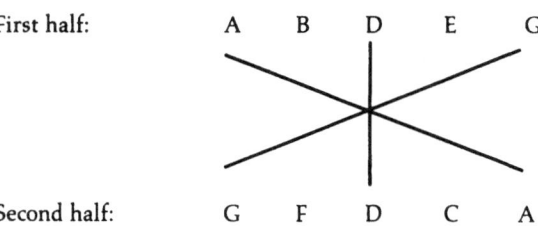

First half: A   B   D   E   G

Second half: G   F   D   C   A

Symmetry and Synthesis in Beckwith's *Etudes* 85

The three ordered tones of each trichord in the single line are repeatedly cycled, although each iteration is unique owing to registral changes of one or more of the tones. The first hexachord of each Set is identified with the chords, the other with the single disjunct lines. (This allocation is reversed when this texture returns later in the piece, further evidence of textural involvement in aspects of symmetry.)

The three-note chords of texture 1 are disposed in as many different arrangements as practicable, given the limitations of a hand span, and they are symmetrically arrayed, based on the type of third (major or minor) within the prevailing hexachord. For example, within the 'A' transposition, if the chord contains a C♯, Beckwith labels it major (+) in his sketches, while if it contains a C♮, he labels it minor (-). Example 19 shows the number of occurrences of each type (major or minor). The hexachord types are given in order of their appearance. Note the symmetrical relationships among successive Sets and between the first and second halves of the etude.

Example 19

Texture 1: (The letters refer to Sets, the figures to the number of occurrences of each constituent trichord, while the plus or minus signs denote the kind of third contained therein.)

First statement: A: 7+ 6– B: 6– 7+
                  D: 8– 7+ E: 7+ 8–
                  G: 6– 8+
Second statement: G: 8– 6+
                  F: 7– 8+ D: 8– 7+
                  C: 6+ 7– A: 7+ 6–

The trichords which are unfolded as successive single pitches in the other layer of texture 1 are cycled repeatedly. A similar kind of symmetry governs the number of cycles for each trichord (see Example 20).

Example 20

First statement: A: 5 3 B: 3 5
                  D: 6 4 E: 4 6
                  G: 3 4
Second statement: 6 5
                  F: 4 6 D: 6 4
                  C: 3 5 A: 5 3

Texture No. 2: (mm. 11–19 and mm. 47–50)

This texture is based entirely on Set X, in four t=3-related transpositions, as shown below. Note once again the reciprocal relationship between Sets in the two layers: retrograde of the Set in one layer is answered by prime in the other, while the transposition levels are reversed.

Upper layer of texture: R6   R3   R0   R9
Lower layer of texture: P9   P0   P3   P6

Successive transpositions are connected by overlapping dyads whose constituent pitches may be reordered. Further, three of the four vertical combinations feature common dyads:

R6, hex. 1 and P9, hex. 1, both begin with the dyad A–C♯
R0, hex. 1 and P3, hex. 1, both end with the dyad E♭–G
R9, hex. 2 and P6, hex. 2, both end with the dyad A–C♯

Beckwith underlines the importance of these pitches by placing them at the beginning or end of sections, and by assigning them long durations. In particular, the 'A' appears as an unaccompanied half note to initiate the section, while the 'E♭' also an unaccompanied half note, bisects the section. Thus, the tritonal polarity which was expressed on the vertical plane in texture 1 (as superposed 'A' and 'E♭' hexachords) achieves form-defining status in texture 2. A similar focus upon these two pitches occurs later in the piece, since the second iteration of texture 2 provides a repetition, in reverse order, of the middle portion of the first occurrence.

Texture No. 3: (mm. 20–36 and mm. 51–7)

One element of this texture is a rapid trill or tremolando, coupled with a single sustained pitch. The other element is a triplet figure in a light contrapuntal setting. In the first appearance of texture no. 3, Sets A to G are presented in alphabetical order in the triplet figures. The second iteration of this texture is a varied compression of the first. Since, for each element of the texture, the first six pitches of a Set are presented in one layer, while the last six move to the other, the two elements alternate in each layer. Thus, the layers are out of phase with one another, and at any given time both musical ideas coexist. The result of the textural exchange, of course, is that the upper layer focuses exclusively on the 'A' transposition, the lower on

Symmetry and Synthesis in Beckwith's *Etudes* 87

the 'E♭' transposition. In the model for this process, shown in Example 21, the prime form of Set A is presented by the trill element, the retrograde form by the triplet element.

Example 21

Upper layer: Set A, P0, hex. 1 R0 hex. 2
Lower layer: Set A, R0, hex. 1 P0 hex. 2

Etude No. 5: Harp

This etude consists of one main section (mm. 10–82), preceded and followed by a short prelude (mm. 1–9) and postlude (mm. 83-91) which are identical. The prelude begins with two unaccompanied full statements of Set D: P6 hex. 2 (i.e., the 'A' transposition of pc set 6–8), R6 hex. 2 (= 'E♭' transposition), P3 hex. 1 (= 'C' transposition), and R3 hex. 1 (= 'F♯' transposition). The line is then attenuated to successive tetrachords drawn from t=3-related hexachords and accompanied in the left hand by invariant dyads drawn from adjacent upper-layer tetrachords. In a further manifestation of abstract symmetry, these invariant dyads succeed one another in such a way as to form an ordered octatonic scale (see Example 22).

Example 22

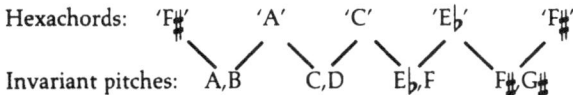

The prelude ends with a statement of the A-major/minor scale which includes all of the pitches of that scale except its 'tonic' A, an omission that is redressed in the middle portion of the piece, which provides that missing pitch as a kind of drone.

The large central section of *Etude No. 5* is based exclusively on the 'A' transposition of pc set 6–8. The title of this etude is an apt description of the graceful accompaniment figure of this section, which consists of steady sixteenth notes arranged in a continuous series of short undulating ostinati, each embodying the first hexachord only of one of the Sets. The sequence of these Sets is the same, initially, as that seen at the opening of the first and fourth etudes.

Above and below the accompaniment figure are prominent isolated pitches

88 Gail Dixon

which are also drawn from the 'A' transposition of pc set 6–8, and which mirror one another in a manner already familiar to us: 0 (= A) in the lower stave is paired with 7 (= E) in the higher, and so on. In this central portion of the piece the three 0/7 pairings are marked by tempo changes at each appearance, and serve to delineate the form (Example 23 illustrates). Note that this pivotal 0/7 pairing is the only one which does not occur in inverted form. The vertical compound fifth at critical junctures contributes to a perception of A as a tonal centre, a perception which is reinforced by the *beginnings* of both the prelude and postlude (the notes of which are A B C E D C♯), but weakened by the *endings* (the notes of which are B C C♯ D E F♯ G♯, i.e., every pitch of an A-major/minor scale *except* A).[18]

Example 23

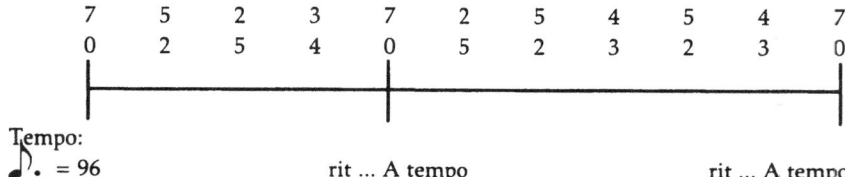

Etude No. 6: Clusters and Chords

As the title suggests, this piece pits clusters against chords, either by superposition or juxtaposition. The clusters, which consist of either black or white keys, range in intensity from those played with flat fingers parallel to the keys, to those which call for the use of palms, fists, and even forearms. The other important element is three-note chords, most of which reduce to pc set 3–7 [0,2,5], and are paired with other three-note chords to form pc set 6–8.[19] A subsidiary element, introduced toward the end of the piece, is a pianissimo cascade of rapid single pitches.

The etude is divided by changes of texture, rhythm, and figuration into sections A (mm. 1–11), B (mm. 12–51), C (mm. 52–62), and A¹ (mm. 63–85). Section A begins with percussive black-note clusters in the left hand, matched with sustained white-note chords in the right. This section pits the white-note collection (pc set 7–35) against its complement, the black-note collection (pc set 5–35), with the distinctive articulation assigned to each l ayer helping to distinguish the two, aurally. The chords of the right hand part include every possible [0,2,5] trichordal subset of the white-note collection, while each of the clusters of the left hand part contains the entire black-note collection.

Section B features a number of iterations of the following pattern: alternating black- and white-note clusters, in alternate hands, which function as an anacrusis to pairs of three-note chords which follow, one in each hand. Section B is itself partitioned into a miniature ternary form by short links (mm. 22–3 and mm. 36–8) which use material from the opening. The resultant 'aba' is not characterized by a change in material in the middle portion, but by a change in the transposition level of pc set 6–8.

The paired trichords which form the termination of each pattern are all of the [0,2,5] type.[20] Unlike section A, section B features 'synthesized' [0,2,5] trichords – that is, trichords which consist of a mixture of black and white pitches. All possible [0,2,5] trichords within the twelve-note collection are utilized within section B. In virtually every case, these paired trichords together form the pc set 6–8.

Section C comprises the climax and the material which leads up to it. A thunderous cascade of black- and white-note clusters erupts, played by the right and left fists in alternation, and culminating in a double cluster – a black-note forearm cluster in the left hand, and a white-note one in the right. Since this climactic *sfffz* chord encompasses every black and white note within the span of both forearms, and since its resonance is enhanced and prolonged by use of the sustaining pedal, it is certainly the ultimate synthesis of *Etude no. 6*, and, arguably, of the work itself. Section A^1 begins immediately following this climax, with a pianissimo filigree of blurred rapid figuration in one hand complemented in the other by the three-note chords of the opening, this time played as delicate arpeggiations. The ethereal quality of this section is enhanced by a generous use of the sustaining pedal.

The final measures of the piece present an interesting anomaly. Pc set 6–8 in its 'E' transposition (m. 81) is followed by what 'should' have been its 'F' transposition, according to the sketches. However, in the score the 'F' transposition contains an intrusive B♭, left over from the previous 'E' transposition, instead of the expected B♮. As a result, a tritonal figure B♮, G♯, F (rather than the expected B♭, G♯, F) is clearly exposed in the boundary pitches of the left hand as the final linear statement of the piece. Given that ic6 is the only ic which is absent in pc set 6–8 – the source hexachord for the entire work – its prominence at this crucial point requires some explanation. When queried on this point, Beckwith speculated that he had changed the B♭ to a B♮ so that the line would be (in his words) 'more interesting' and leave 'a more up-in-the-air feeling at the end.' I wonder if there is not also something more subtle here; perhaps this striking and entirely unprecedented linear expression of the tritone as the conclusive gesture in the work is a reflection – obviously purely intuitive on Beckwith's part – of the structural role of the tritone in the work as a whole. Recall that the unordered hexachords of all eight twelve-tone rows are related to one another at t=6. Because of the identity between the two halves of each row engendered by the symmetrical order relationship between them, this tritonal link will have been readily sensed by the perceptive listener. Consider also the frequency with which Beckwith uses the tritone on a larger scale, as the preferred intervallic relationship between juxtaposed and successive elements of the texture. His instinctive choice for the final gesture, and our ready acceptance of its aptness, should thus hardly be surprising.

Perceptive listeners will be intuitively aware, even at first hearing, of both great complexity and an underlying powerful sense of coherence in Beckwith's *Etudes* for solo piano. Analysis has revealed the scope and nature of that complexity as well as the innate simplicity from which it springs. Pc set 6–8, along with its trichordal subsets, provides virtually all of the source material for the work. The symmetrical and synthetic processes by which these components interact on a small scale are replicated in various dimensions on a larger scale. The result is a work which is both lucid and subtle; it is one of the twentieth-century masterpieces of the genre.

NOTES

1 The reader is strongly encouraged to refer to a copy of the score when reading this article. A score can be purchased or borrowed from any branch of the Canadian Music Centre. A commercial recording is available in Radio Canada International's *Anthology of Canadian Music* series (ACM 26), and several other performances are available on tape at the Canadian Music Centre.
2 The work is approximately seventeen minutes in duration. Beckwith actually wrote two other movements based on the same material, but, because they did not conform to the 'etude' idea, and because the work was long enough without these two, he decided to omit them from the final version.
3 Besides studying the etudes of Chopin, Debussy, and (to a lesser degree) Scriabin in preparation for writing his own etudes, Beckwith told me that he also used certain works of Bartók and Kalkbrenner as models. (Here, and elsewhere in this article, I draw upon remarks made by Beckwith in an interview which he granted me on 17 August 1990.)
4 In order to distinguish between 'sets' as in unordered pitch-class sets and 'sets' as in ordered twelve-tone sets, I shall label the former as 'pc sets' and I shall capitalize the latter – 'Sets.' Pitch-class sets are labelled according to Allen

Forte's tables in his *The Structure of Atonal Music* (New York and London: Yale University Press, 1973), 179–81.

5 The Funk and Wagnalls Standard Desk Dictionary (1977) defines symmetry as '[a]n exact correspondence between the opposite halves of a figure, form, line, pattern, etc., on either side of an axis or center.' I take this definition to include both reflexion and congruence on either side of an axis, which itself may be on any plane.

6 Beckwith has kindly allowed me access to his sketches for these etudes. He has also given me his permission to reproduce excerpts, both from the sketches and from the score, in this article.

7 Indeed, Beckwith is explicit about the synthetic properties of Set X in his sketches, labelling it an 'all-interval' Set. (Clearly, Set X is not an all-interval Set in the normal sense, since ic6 is not represented. Beckwith has used the term to show that all the ics used in Sets A to G have been absorbed and synthesized in Set X.)

8 The two trichords of Set X are not equivalent, as explained earlier; one of its constituent trichords is pc set 3–3 [0,1,4], the other is pc set 3–7 [0,2,5].

9 With retrograde forms of any of the above, of course, the number of invariant pitches is the reciprocal of 6 (e.g., P0 and I3 have two invariant pitches; P0 and RI3 have four).

10 By virtue of the tautness and density of its structure, the diversity of its material, and its sheer length, the fourth etude could be regarded as the 'centre of gravity' of the work as a whole. Beckwith is not absolutely sure which of the six etudes he actually wrote first, but he suspects that it was the fourth. Certainly, this one is the most dense and rigorous in its construction.

11 Beckwith considers this etude to be a kind of condensation of the first two Chopin etudes from the point of view of texture (i.e., wide spacing versus narrow, now appearing simultaneously, rather than consecutively). For this reason, he acknowledges this as the most difficult of his etudes to perform.

12 While the order of cluster layer Set types in the first part is unequivocal, that of the second part is difficult to verify, since the order of the first five pitches in some of the hexachords is obscure. However, the probability is high that there is a restatement of the original ordering of Sets, now at R5 and using the opposite hexachord. The repeated notes which end each hexachord statement always conform to the expected pattern, lending credence to the hypothesis. The complementary relationships between hexachords and between prime and retrograde forms elsewhere in the piece are further evidence.

13 Because so often in this work Beckwith is dealing with single hexachords, independent of the twelve-tone set, and in order to avoid the cumbersome

necessity of making clear each time to which hexachord of a set I refer, I shall label the transposition levels of hexachords according to their lowest pitch class in prime form. For example, the collection of pitches E D F♯ G A F, when reduced to prime form (pc set 6–8 [0,2,3,4,5,7]: D E F F♯ G A), has D as its lowest pitch. Thus such a collection will be labelled as a 'D' transposition of pc set 6–8.

14 Beckwith's sketches for this movement show that on page 2, line 2, measure 2, Row E (hexachord 2 of R3) is 'due' in the left hand, and the fifth and sixth left-hand notes of this measure 'ought' to be F♯ and A♯, respectively, rather than the A♯ and C♯ which appear in the score. When I asked Beckwith about this, he conceded that, while he might simply have made an error, it is more likely that he made the change deliberately, to avoid too many closely proximate F♯s, with resulting unwanted tonal associations.

In the course of analysing these etudes, I detected a number of other discrepancies, either between the sketches and the score, or between the 'expected' pattern and the score. In discussing these with Beckwith, it became clear that, while some of the discrepancies were deliberate (and these are all discussed in the article), most were genuine errors or oversights. It is therefore important for readers to ensure that their scores are updated with the December 1990 errata sheet, available through the Canadian Music Centre.

15 Beckwith asserts that, while he begins with a strict model, he does not hesitate to deviate from it should the musical results not prove satisfactory to him. When questioned about specific discrepancies, he was usually able to explain them in quite specific terms. Occasionally, as in this case, he was unable to reconstruct his reasoning, stating only that the changes seemed to make the passage work better, musically.

16 The import of the last three sets of repeated notes in each part is not clear. Perhaps the triadic outlining presages a similar effect in *Etude No. 5*, where tonal focus is clearly intended.

17 Note the asterisks in the example. I have labelled these Sets as Beckwith has in his sketches. However, he has actually mislabelled them; what he marks in the sketches as E(R0) and X(R0) are, in fact, E(P0) and X(P0), respectively. The symmetry for which he was evidently striving has thus been compromised, as has the clearly intended relationship of forms used for Set X with that seen in part 1 (see Example 15).

18 Beckwith states that his destabilization of the tonal centre at the end of *Etude No. 5* was done quite deliberately, as a needed antidote to the all-pervasive A drone of the central portion of the piece.

19 One notable exception appears on page 22, system 1, measures 2–3. Each trichord of the pair represents pc set 3–3 [0,1,4]. The resultant hexachord (pc set

6–Z42 [0,1,2,3,6,9]) is anomalous, indeed unique in the work. When I queried Beckwith on this point, he admitted that he himself was surprised at this unexpected departure, but that he could not recall exactly why he had made the change. However, my colleague Don McLean pointed out to me that if the RH E and the LH E♭ were interchanged, two [0,2,5] pc sets would be obtained. McLean further conjectured that the C and G of the 'expected' pc set 6–8 (C, D, E♭, E, F, G) might have been semitonally displaced, yielding the B, D, E♭, E, F, A♭ of the pc set 6–Z42, a procedure which Beckwith might have used to underscore the articulating formal function of those measures. I am grateful to Don McLean for these insights.

20 Clearly, Beckwith is interested in the juxtaposition of black and white notes. The all-black and all-white trichords which permeate much of this etude are shown in the sketches as being derived from the hexachords of Set C, each of which consists of two [0,2,5] trichords. Beckwith selects those trichords from any transposition of the hexachord which conforms to this requirement. By the end of the second system of the piece, Beckwith has used every possible [0,2,5] trichord which consists of all-white or all-black notes. In the middle portion of the piece, he focuses on trichords of mixed black and white notes, in fact using every possible combination of pitches which form the trichord 3–7 [0,2,5]. *Etude No. 6* is thus a comprehensive exploration of the trichord 3–7.

JOHN MAYO

Coming to Terms with the Past: Beckwith's *Keyboard Practice*

This essay is about understanding music, more precisely about understanding one particular kind of music, and even more precisely one particular composition. On one level it may be read as a piece of criticism. On another, it is an enquiry into the nature and limits of criticism itself, and a logical place to begin such an enquiry is by considering what we mean by 'understanding' a piece of music. Monroe Beardsley usefully distinguishes three different categories of understanding – causal understanding, configurational understanding, and semantic understanding.[1] The first is concerned with how something or other came to be the way it is, the second with the way in which the various subordinate parts of something hang together to form the whole, and the last 'consists in knowing what something signifies'. In practice, as we attempt to come to grips with a particular composition or group of compositions, we can find ourselves using all three approaches, although our professional inclinations as historians, as analysts, or as critics will lead us to favour one of these three modes. It is the last approach that is the most problematic, and it is one that has received a great deal of attention recently from, among others, Jean-Jacques Nattiez. In ascribing meaning or significance to a work of art we are, according to the classic or commonsense view, uncovering something that has been put there by the artist. The work of art becomes a middle term in some form of communication, which we might represent in strictly musical terms as follows: Composer → Message [i.e. the composition] → Listener. The measure of our success in interpreting the work is then, presumably, how close we can come to matching the intentions of the composer. Nattiez rejects this straightforward, linear interpretation in favour of a more controversial one in which 'a symbolic form [in our case the composition] is not some "intermediary" in a process of "communication" that transmits the meaning intended by an author (composer) to an audience' but rather 'the result of a complex *process* of creation' that is also 'the point of departure for a complex process of reception ... that *reconstructs* a message.'² A simple but telling example from outside the world of music may help to clarify this idea.

If you are driving in Quebec you will frequently encounter red, octagonal signs with the word 'Arrêt' on them. The 'meaning' of this is clear enough, and if you want to keep on the right side of the Quebec police you would be well advised to obey the instruction. In a more reflective mood, however, you might wonder why the signs do not say 'Stop,' as they do in France (and in the rest of Canada). If you have any knowledge whatsoever of French–English relations in Canada you will soon be able to reconstruct a number of additional meanings for the sign. These meanings will depend very much on your particular point of view, but they might include some reference to the Quebec government's obvious desire to impress the Frenchness (or Quebec Frenchness) of the province on all drivers. But the reconstruction need not stop there. You might, for example, go on to speculate about what the use of an obviously French word, rather than a more usual but linguistically ambivalent work, tells us about Quebeckers' self-image; or how the use of 'Arrêt' says something not only about French–English relations within Canada, but also about relations between French Quebec and France. And so on. My analogy is not perfect. In this case there is a clear, intended meaning in the sign: the meaning intended by the sign's makers, and which, in most circumstances, we ought to accept. But if we subject it to some elementary analysis, the sign can tell us much more than how to avoid accidents and keep out of Quebec lawcourts. And so it is with music, although a composer's meaning may be much less clear than that of the Quebec government. For Nattiez any ambiguity in this regard is of little consequence, since he seems to reject the composer's intentions entirely. This, I think, is unwise, but I would say that they represent only part of what understanding a piece of music involves.

These thoughts are provoked by my recent attempts to understand the complete compositional output of John Beckwith. In dealing with so many of his works one quickly comes to the conclusion that conventional methods of analysis leave much that is of significance completely untouched. At the same time one is frequently encouraged by the composer himself to search for meaning in his works, not necessarily by anything that he has said or written about his own compositions but by the very nature of the compositions themselves. In the end, after subjecting his works to close interpretive scrutiny, we may decide that we are no nearer to their core. Indeed we may conclude that the composer has simply provided the stimulation and the material for a complex interpretive game with no right or wrong answers. Nonetheless, participating in this game is, I think, part of the aesthetic enjoyment of his music. In what follows I am primarily concerned with putting forward an interpretation of one particular composition, the 1979 chamber work *Keyboard Practice*. At the same time I am interested in the methods by which one arrives at such an interpretation. Thus *Keyboard Practice* will be the focus, but the implications of the method stretch out well beyond Beckwith's music to embrace all instrumental music that is referential in some way or other. The task is not to uncover the 'one true meaning' of the composition, placed there by the composer, but rather to enter into a dialogue with the various levels of meaning to be found in the symbolic form. The danger, of course, is that there seem to be few, if any, logical grounds for limiting the critic's (or the audience's) reconstruction of the 'meaning' of a composition. Without some sort of limits the critic could soon be writing Humpty Dumpty criticism, making compositions mean exactly what he or she says they mean. Lawrence Kramer has tried to grasp this particular nettle and suggests that the apparent lack of unbiased criteria may not matter, or to be more accurate he says that the objection is based on a misconception both of what the critic is attempting to do, and of how we judge whether the results are true or false. Interpretations of this kind may be false when bad, he says, but when good, 'can never be manifestly true' but only persuasive.[3] In this he comes very close to Nattiez who likens the task of the critic to that of the performer.[4] Both critic and performer, in their own way, are involved in exegesis of a symbolic form. Both aim to discover meanings in that form and to persuade others to their viewpoint.

Although the constraints upon interpretation of a composition, from the critic's point of view, are far from clear, they do exist. In arriving at an interpretation of a work we do not work in a vacuum. Nor do we simply allow our imaginations to wander in free association around the composition. Rather we make use of whatever concrete clues we can uncover, whether they form part of Beardsley's category of causal understanding, or are to be found in the physical material of the composition. We search, in Kramer's term, for the 'hermeneutical windows' in the work: those places which seem to pose questions, the gritty, uncomfortable spots, the discontinuities, the aspects of the work that disturb.[5] And we take nothing for granted. In spite of this a useful starting point is at least to pretend an innocent ear.

Keyboard Practice, written to a commission from New Music Concerts in Toronto, is for four performers playing ten different keyboard instruments: regal, harmonium, harpsichord, clavichord, celeste, grand piano, upright piano, electronic piano, electronic practice keyboard, and dummy keyboard. It brings together most of the features of Beckwith's mature instrumental style and in addition makes very prominent use of quotation. For me, and I suspect for the majority of listeners, the most obvious element of a first hearing of this work is the juxtaposition of clearly contemporary textures with substantial quotations from pre-existent music. Quotations of this kind are not uncommon in twentieth-century music. Paul Griffiths complains that they have become something of a cliché, but cliché or not, their presence calls for, even if it does not always receive, explanation, either in accompanying notes or within the syntax of the music itself.[6] Even the first hearing of *Keyboard Practice* suggests that the quotations are of fundamental importance to the meaning of the whole composition; the presence of the quoted material presents an interpretive puzzle, the solution of which may or may not be forthcoming.

The original concept for the piece came from an important course that Beckwith taught on the history of keyboard instruments and the music written for them.

I used to enjoy that course very much because it gave me a chance to keep practising piano and keep looking at new pieces of music of all different ages. And I learned also a good deal about keyboard literature – was always looking at different aspects of keyboard literature for that reason.[7]

The idea was given further impetus in 1972 by a CBC commission to write music to accompany a broadcast reading of Margaret Atwood's *Journals of Susanna Moodie*.

In the background music for that cycle I used six different keyboard instruments and some percussion instruments ... played by two players and ... it was sort of fun to contrast the different timbres of the different instruments all using that very handy mechanism of the keyboard.[8]

In these two quotations we have the surface meaning of the composition – a composer's view of the literature for the keyboard, and an examination of the variety of timbres to be found among keyboard instruments, not forgetting of course the 'fun' of doing it. The way in which these origins are translated into artistic terms is interesting. We soon notice, for example, that the quoted works, each played by an appropriate instrument, and with each of the performers being allotted one quotation each, form a miniature history of keyboard styles, beginning with an anonymous Alman from the *Fitzwilliam Virginal Book*, moving through part of a Couperin *Ordre* and the

Liszt 'Au bord d'une source,' to Charles L. Johnson's 'Cum Bac' Rag.[9] I have said that these quotations present a history of keyboard styles, but that is not quite accurate – the four quotations are simply a collage of keyboard styles in chronological order. They present historical data rather than history. The visual appearance of the score also suggests a collage, using that term in the way that a visual artist would. Like the scraps of found material in a Picasso collage, the four quotations from the pre-existent works are literally stuck on to the score. What turns these scraps into history is the fact that the borrowed compositions are subjected to a process of examination and interaction. It was the historian E.H. Carr who supplied a now familiar definition of history when he called it 'an unending dialogue between the present and the past.'[10] The interactions which take place in *Keyboard Practice* are a musical equivalent of Carr's dialogue. The composer in Beckwith looks at the material in the way that composers have always looked at borrowed material: as a springboard for his own creative activity. The historian in Beckwith sees the borrowed music on its own terms, and allows it room to speak for itself. The mere presence of the historical material as a part of the body of the work might lead us to this interpretation. In fleshing it out we have made use of the composer's own words about the genesis of the work. We have, in effect, practised Beardsley's first two modes of understanding.

What I have described so far, however, differs little from many other contemporary works that make use of quotations. With *Keyboard Practice* we have to take into consideration another, and typically Beckwithian, dimension – the theatrical. This, if you like, is another window into the meaning of the composition. In a number of works prior to *Keyboard Practice*, notably in *Taking a Stand* and in *Musical Chairs*, Beckwith demands that the players perform extensive theatrical moves and gestures as a part of the performance. Such moves are always carefully calculated, grow out of the nature of the music being played, and are often comic in effect. At the same time they sometimes have another rather curious effect in that they can make us question our commonsense idea of the relationship of instrument and performer. This sounds rather fanciful, but some examples may make this clearer.

Keyboard Practice opens with the clattering, percussive sound of a dummy keyboard – all articulation and no voice – soon joined by a simple diatonic theme for the regal with answering two-part phrases for the harpsichord. The dummy keyboard is played by the same performer who gives out the regal melody; the performer of the harpsichord phrases meanwhile operates the bellows of the regal. This division of labour points up the sheer mechanical nature of the instruments and gives the impression of the performer as servant of the instrument, rather than the other way round. We get in effect a musical analogy to the sculpture already residing in the block of stone – here the music resides in the instrument and simply requires the mechanisms to be set in motion to realize the sound. The idea that the music resides in the instruments rather than being put there by the performers is enhanced by a number of gestures which take place later in the work. All of these impress on us that the instruments remain constant, while the performers are interchangeable. The instruments retain their individual character; the players have none, at least none that is separate from a particular instrument. On page 12 of the score the grand piano has a passage based on scale patterns in the lower range and a chordal pattern in the upper range. These two elements, played by two different performers, gradually exchange pitch ranges without a break in the sound. This is engineered by an actual exchange of performers, player no. IV (the scale pattern) sliding to the right on the piano bench, forcing player no. III to move off of the bench and move round the back to take up position at the lower end of the keyboard. At the close of page 29 a chordal passage for electric keyboard continues unbroken despite a complex change of performers part-way through. We can view these manoeuvres as a comic heightening of the to-ing and fro-ing that takes place in the percussion section during any complicated symphonic work. More seriously, they all tend to reinforce the sense of the performer as servant of the instrument. This division is even emphasized by the fact that keyboard players normally have their instruments waiting mutely on stage before the performance begins and simply enter to set them in motion. When there are ten instruments and only four performers, this particular effect is magnified since no player can become exclusively associated with any one instrument.

One interesting result of this theatrical element is that the listener hears the historical dialogue, the primary meaning of the work, less as one between Beckwith and his sources than as a series of dialogues among the instruments. In this way the composer manages to keep an ironic distance from his borrowed material at the same time that he presents a reconciliation between it and the contemporary sounds.

If the central idea of *Keyboard Practice* is dialogue between past and present, and a coming to terms with the music of the past, we should turn our attention now to the contexts of the four quotations. In each case we find something in the music that I can only describe as gestural – musical passages which seem to mimic human physical and vocal gestures and which give the music an immediately dramatic, almost choreographic, impact. The very opening of the work provides some sanction for this kind of interpretation. The composer directs that the regal's theme shall be presented 'like a slow announcement,' while the harpsichord's two-part counterpoint is to be 'quicker ... like a nervous comment.'[11] There are numerous other examples, although they may not have the explicit instructions associated with this opening. This gestural quality seems particularly noticeable in those sections that contain the quotations, and is at the root of that feeling of dialogue that is presented. Listen, for example, to the presentation of the anonymous Alman. The comments come very gently, almost reflectively, from the celeste as an outgrowth of the quoted material, with no sense of disruption. Later in the work the remarks from the grand piano which accompany the harpsichord's Couperin quotations begin in much the same mood as the celeste's comments on the Fitzwilliam Alman. The piano makes use of a motive from the left-hand pattern of the Couperin, and this becomes a unifying element throughout. In this Couperin section, however, the commenting instruments digress from the quoted material to a far greater extent. The harpsichord quotation is also set off from its surroundings much more clearly. The Alman had been placed at the centre of an arch-shaped section. The Couperin quotation has no introduction and ends rather abruptly.

The much more flamboyant Liszt quotation causes far more disturbance. It is introduced by full-scale flourishes in a quasi-Lisztian manner from the practice keyboard, the upright piano, and the celeste. The piano also reacts to the other instruments, something neither the clavichord nor the harpsichord had done in their quotations. At one point, as though reacting to the foreign, contemporary style, the grand piano bursts out with a brief and dissonant non-Lisztian flourish. Eventually, by sheer force of rhetoric, the Liszt music forces the other three instruments into a climactic final section and the grand piano finishes with some pastiche Liszt gestures.

It is worth comparing this with the appearance of the Johnson rag. This, like the Liszt, is introduced by a pastiche, in this case a pastiche rag from the harpsichord. The comments throughout are almost all in keeping with the spirit of the rag. Of all of the quotations this is the one that seems to generate the most agreement among the other instruments. This culminates, as the Liszt quotation had, in a climactic section for all four instruments, but in this case with the whole ensemble of one mind. The conclusion of this section suggests, however, that this momentary sense of agreement is quite fragile. The instruments drop out one by one in a rather pathetic way.

Having looked at the four quotations we can sum up the relationships that are set up in each case. In the Alman, the clavichord presents the borrowed material a phrase at a time, apparently quite oblivious of the comments. The comments, in their turn, are tentative, interrupting the clavichord as little as possible. In visual terms, there is a sense of distance between the clavichord and the celeste, and this emphasizes the historical distance of the clavichord sound. The harpsichord presentation of the Couperin, like the Alman, is unaltered by the comments, continuing in its motoric fashion into oblivion. The comments, on the other hand, are more strident, make use of ideas from the quoted material, and develop them in a much more complex manner; that is, they draw attention to themselves much more. The Lisztian quotation is the most disturbing of the four: the quoting instrument itself is drawn into the comments, and all the instruments are used in a not entirely harmonious climax, with the grand piano providing a modern, non-Lisztian postlude. Lastly, the rag provides the most social material of all the quotations with a climax in which all four instruments are playing, however briefly, in a ragtime style. Is there some overall message in this? At the very least, as we progress through the four quotations, we are made aware that we are approaching more familiar territory as the accompanying instruments have less and less difficulty conversing with the quotation. The sense of historical distance is emphasized by the chronological order of the quotations, and this provides one more thread of time to play off against the other temporal levels on which the piece works. At the same time, these four sections provide four dramatic vignettes with the instruments as characters, which almost need the hand of a stage director or choreographer to do them justice. But in the end it is not so much whether or not we have interpreted these meanings correctly that is important. What is of more interest is the simple fact that Beckwith chooses this ironic, dramatized game as a vehicle for the historical dialogue. I will return to this idea in a moment because there is meaning, and very important meaning, in this very act of choice.

I have spent considerable space discussing the four historical quotations because of their relevance to the meaning of the composition as a whole, but they are not the whole of the composition. How do these sections fit into the fabric of the rest of the piece? In some notes accompanying a recording of the work, Beckwith points out that *Keyboard Practice* is a set of fifteen variations on an initial theme.[12] This information, too, provides a window into the work, but one that leads to few important insights. One can, it is true, hear the work in this way. It certainly provides all the context that is required for the listener to be able to accommodate the changing textures of the piece, since each new texture is a new variation. And, since each variation is as much an exploration of keyboard textures and timbres as it is a conventional thematic variation, listeners can even accommodate the slightly incongruous quotations within this formal scheme without too much difficulty. The quotations form variations 2, 4, 8, and 13. But if that was all that had happened, if indeed the quotations had been introduced simply in the collage fashion that the score seems to suggest they were, then they ought to sound a good deal more foreign than they do. The truth is that the dialogue of past and present that is at the root of this composition works not only in a very overt way in the flamboyant, theatrical vignettes that I have discussed already but also, more subtly, in the contrast of an outer, slightly chaotic, playful, apparently spontaneous, contemporary world, and an inner, carefully controlled, logical one. The main integrative element of this inner world, which manages to transcend historical quotations, heterogeneous textures, and a multitude of different timbres, is Beckwith's own particular style of serialism.

In most of his serial works Beckwith uses the row as a source of motivic and thematic material; linked with this is a predilection for rows which contain the potential for tonal reference. For example, one of the earliest serial works, *The Trumpets of Summer*, uses two rows, one scalar, one chordal, each of which is divisible into two diatonic hexachords. More interesting from the point of view of *Keyboard Practice* is his method of unfolding the row. It is rare for this to happen without internal repetition. The general rule is that notes of the row which have already been exposed may be repeated at will with successive pitches added bit by bit. The complete exposition of one form of the row may therefore be extended over a considerable period of time, and if necessary any diatonic elements contained in the row can be emphasized for momentary effect. This method, which he had used in a number of works, helps to explain the derivation of the row in *Keyboard Practice*. The original ordering of this runs as follows:

D G F♯ A E C B♭ F B E♭ G♯ C♯

Beckwith obtained this from the anonymous Alman (the first quotation), using the reverse of the unfolding technique described above. The notes of this clavichord piece provide the first ten pitches of the row. The two missing pitches (G♯ and C♯) are then added, and added in this particular order so that pitches 10, 11, 12 of Po are equivalent to pitches 1, 2, 3 of RIo. This allows for the frequent overlap of appropriate row forms within the course of the piece. Thus the 'initial theme' on which the variations are built is itself derived from melodic material that appears in its original form in variation 2.

It might be thought that by having derived the pitch material from one of the quoted compositions, the other three quotations would tend to be isolated from their surroundings, since clearly these other borrowings will not have

Coming to Terms with the Past 103

this same relationship to the row material. This is not so. Beckwith goes to considerable pains to integrate these other quotations into the whole using the row material. For example, all of the comments which the grand piano adds to the Couperin music are based on one or other form of the row, with some of the comments even related motivically. Beckwith also manages to produce parodies or pastiches of both the Liszt and Johnson quotations using versions of the row, although the order of the pitches is not always strictly adhered to. These pastiches help to cement the quoted material into the body of the work. Let us look briefly at each of the quotations in turn. The celeste's comments to the phrases of the original Alman melody are based on four versions of the row, P0, R7, R5, and RI11. The choice of these rows, and some internal reordering that takes place with these rows, seems motivated by the need to integrate the Alman and the derived row material (see Example 1). In using R7, for example, to bridge the second and third phrases of the clavichord piece, Beckwith alters the pitch order to 1, 2, 9, 10, 3, 4, 5, 6, 7, 8, 11, 12, mainly so that the celeste's phrase flows almost tonally onto the opening D-major harmony of the Alman. A typical piece of keyboard figuration that had appeared first in variation 1 is shown on page 4 to be derived (non-serially) from a measure of the Alman; shown, that is, by the two passages being heard in quick succession, so that the connection is clearly audible. Given the derivation of the row material, it is obviously fairly easy to suggest connections between old and new material in the Alman section. The connections in the case of the Couperin quotation are rather different. There is no real connection between the row material derived from the anonymous Alman and the Couperin piece, but Beckwith suggests otherwise. He does this mostly by internal reordering of the row material, and with two apparent aims – to provide some conventional cadential gestures in the serial material (as he did with the first quotation), and to

Example 1

produce motifs which echo motifs in the Couperin original (see Example 2).

The Liszt quotation is introduced by pastiche textures from the other instruments. These pastiches are derived with some ingenuity from the spirit of the row material, if not always its exact letter (see Example 3). The same is true of the comments which accompany the Liszt quotation – most notably the brief out-of-character gesture which the grand piano interjects on page 23 of the score as comment on one of the pastiches. This is derived from P4. The most stylistically integrated of the quotations is, as we have seen, the Johnson rag. Nevertheless, most of the new music in this section is also derived from the twelve-tone row – the opening harpsichord pastiche, for example, is derived from P8 followed by I7, although later comments are more loosely derived.

Enough has been said to show the way in which a foreign, contemporary technique is instrumental in integrating a series of heterogeneous quotations into a unified composition. The serial techniques, not surprisingly, are also a strong unifying element in the remainder of the work. A complete serial analysis demonstrates that individual variations often make systematic use of a limited choice of rows. In these 'free' variations the use of the row can be, and often is, much more rigorous than it is in the quotation sections, and in many cases the row is unfolded with all the strictness of an intellectual puzzle or game. A single example will suffice to demonstrate this. The uncoordinated bursts of sound in variation 7 (page 18 of the score) are the result of strict permutation of row forms – the I3, P3, R3, and RI3 versions in keyboard I, the P6, I6, R6, and RI6 transpositions in keyboard II,

Example 2

Example 3

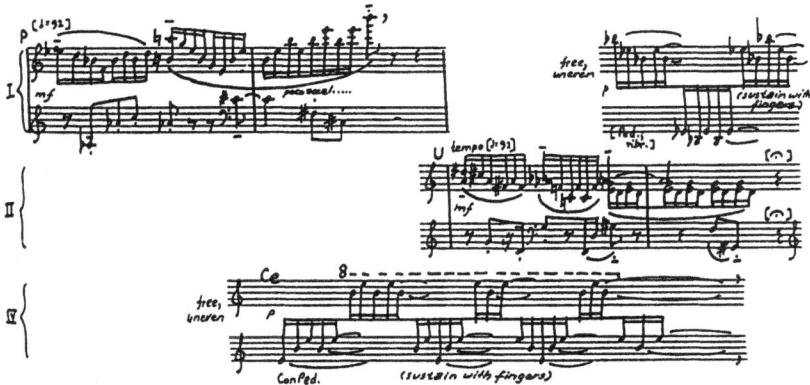

the P9, I9, R9, and RI9 transpositions in III, and the original versions of the row in keyboard IV.

Having looked in some detail at certain aspects of *Keyboard Practice*, it is necessary to draw the various threads together. On the surface this work is a complete fricassee of styles. The composer likes to emphasize this aspect of the work by drawing attention to the heterogeneous nature of the ensemble and the elements of contrast, interruption, collage, and juxtaposition by which the composition proceeds.¹³ But close analysis reveals that the work is a tightly controlled and subtly integrated work with multiple layers of meaning. There is, in other words, a nice balance between the naturally centrifugal effects of the incongruous styles, which have a tendency to fly apart just as easily as they have been put together, and those elements of the music which serve to integrate and unite. It is clear, I think, that the composer had a number of ideas, 'messages' if you like, that he wanted to convey to an audience in this work. There might be argument about what some of these could be, but we could probably draw up a list which most listeners would be prepared to subscribe to – at the very least I think we could agree that the composer does not want us to hear this work as simply an abstract 'symbolic form.' But this is to see the work only according to the scheme of communication that Nattiez rejects; that is, we attempt to discover those meanings that the composer intended us to hear. To uncover these limited meanings is not, however, to exhaust all the legitimate meanings of this work.

Beckwith's intentions – to produce a set of variations which explore keyboard sonorities, to provide a historical perspective by including extensive quotations from known compositions, to suggest that both composition and performance are complex, fun games – all of these are relatively clear. But I have gone beyond this to suggest that the work invites us to hear the quoted works in new ways, in ways that sound as though these historical works must justify their continued presence in the twentieth century. They are taken out of the privileged surroundings of a conventional recital, where they can be held in awe, and also easily ignored, and placed in the rough and tumble of a complicated game of charades. Audiences will vary in their assessment of how well they think the historical music comes out of the encounters – in a sense Beckwith simply sets up the game plan. He encourages us in fact to hear the encounters how we will.

It is at this point that we must pick up one last loose end. There are meanings, and meanings within meanings, to be unravelled in this work, and all the critic can do is be as persuasive as possible about particular interpretations. But there is one undeniable fact about *Keyboard Practice*. A conflict of musical styles, some historical, some contemporary, is presented by the composer in a partly joking, playfully ironic dramatic form. We can explain this by just saying that Beckwith likes a good joke. This is undoubtedly true, but at the same time, the ironic distancing which this tongue-in-cheek approach allows is there precisely because Beckwith feels the need to keep his distance from the dialogue which is taking place. And he needs to do this, I think, because he is dealing with something which is of particular personal significance. There is a certain amount of evidence from other Beckwith works to suggest that he sometimes uses the comic, playful mode to protect the vulnerability of personal expression. In *The Trumpets of Summer*, Beckwith could not realistically match the words of Shakespeare, and devised a wonderful way around that particular dilemma.[14] In *Keyboard Practice*, he does the same for the music of the past. It is immaterial whether these four quoted works are in themselves of overwhelming importance to him; the idea of dialogue with the past clearly is. We might say that every composer has to come to terms with the past. Beckwith chooses to do it publicly in an actual composition, using repertoire which represents important facets of his personal history.

An eclectic composer like Beckwith makes use of whatever material comes to hand. The man who, in the words of one of his contemporaries, could have been a first-class professional character actor delights in donning musical disguises.[15] A romantic in an age that is suspicious of romantics, he is often most clearly himself when using such a stylistic disguise – I have written elsewhere of the particularly moving examples in *Mating Time* – but *Keyboard Practice* is slightly different.[16] Here Beckwith does not enter into the quoted musical styles, he stands ironically apart from them. He places barriers in our way if we try to hear this music as a personal expression. But perhaps he protests too much. This work, as no other work of Beckwith's, faces up to the dilemma of the twentieth-century musician – the obsession with history and the insatiable appetite of the public for music of earlier periods. The performer, the teacher, the historian, all of which Beckwith is, can hide behind a mask of objectivity in dealing with the historical repertoire. If they wish, their dialogue with the past can be presented as an attempt simply to understand things as they really were. But for the contemporary composer this historical repertoire *is* the music of the present. It has to be confronted, or at least its all-pervading presence has to be confronted. It is typical of Beckwith that he should present this confrontation as a theatrical game in which the outcome is far from clear, while at the same time, behind the scenes as it were, a reconciliation takes place through the mediation of the most obviously contemporary compositional technique of all – twelve-tone serialism.

Having analysed *Keyboard Practice* from a number of points of view, it is necessary to go back over this material and summarize briefly the methods I have used. The primary purpose of this essay is to present an interpretation of one Beckwith work. The reasons for choosing this work are many. It made an immediate impact, and continues to make an impact, upon me as a piece of music (ultimately the only worthwhile reason for studying a piece), and on reflection it seemed an important work within Beckwith's oeuvre. As an object of analysis it presents certain challenges, challenges which are common to almost all of Beckwith's mature works and, I suspect, to a great deal of postmodern music. It is therefore an ideal composition to use for an exercise in interpretation. The particular qualities of the work that invite interpretation are its multifaceted eclecticism of style, its use of quotation, its dramatic qualities (but with no text), and its generally referential and autobiographical air; in short, a piece of music that has a multitude of meanings. Interpreting those meanings calls for some kind of theoretical underpinning and I have found this in the work of Beardsley, Nattiez, and Kramer. Beardsley's categorization of modes of understanding provides a useful starting point by isolating very clearly the semantic nature of the quest, while Nattiez and Kramer, in their different ways, encourage investigation of this semantic mode of understanding. Kramer, especially, suggests ways of penetrating this level of a composition, and I have followed his example in looking for 'windows' into the meaning of the music. This has entailed looking at the context and history of the composition – Beardsley's first category of understanding – as well as at the internal structure of the work, including both its formal and its serial structure – Beardsley's configurational understanding. Conventional analyses tend to stop at this point. To do so with a clearly referential work like *Keyboard Practice*, with its ironic, dramatic, eclectic collage of materials, is to ignore the most important aspects of the work. But interpretation of the semantic aspects of a work is far less clear cut, and for this reason we need to emphasize Kramer's injunction that such interpretations can never be manifestly true but only persuasive. I am fascinated by Beckwith's methods in this and other works. I am convinced that his use of humour, irony, and elements of game playing is an attempt to have the best of two worlds: to write, in the nineteenth-century romantic tradition, a music that is personally expressive, but at the same time protect the fragile privacy of his expressive life. By projecting his musical thoughts in forms which invite the listener to participate in the construction of meaning he is able to achieve this delicate balancing act. Whether we penetrate his innermost thoughts or whether we completely misunderstand his intentions, the composer remains invulnerable – for in either case he can retort that the whole thing is, after all, only a game!

NOTES

1 Monroe Beardsley, 'Understanding Music,' in *On Criticizing Music*, ed. Kingsley Price (Baltimore: Johns Hopkins University Press, 1981), 55–6.
2 Jean-Jacques Nattiez, *Music and Discourse: Toward a Semiology of Music* (Princeton, NJ: Princeton University Press, 1990), 17.
3 Lawrence Kramer, *Music as Cultural Practice, 1800–1900* (Berkeley: University of California Press, 1990), 15.
4 Nattiez, *Music and Discourse*, 72.
5 Lawrence Kramer, *Music as Cultural Practice*, 6. Joseph Kerman is talking about a similar idea when he says of a particular analysis of Schumann's 'Aus meiner Thranen fliessen,' 'Ambiguities such as those set up by Schumann's cadences are likely to strike a critic as a good place to focus his investigation. The analyst's instinct is to reduce them out of existence.' 'Academic Music Criticism,' in *On Criticizing Music*, 49.
6 Paul Griffiths, *Modern Music: The Avant Garde since 1945* (New York: George Braziller, 1981), 200.
7 John Beckwith, in conversation with Keith MacMillan. Interview included in *Anthology of Canadian Music – John Beckwith* (ACM 26) (Radio Canada International, 1986).

8 Ibid.
9 The sources of all four quotations are meticulously recorded in footnotes in the score.
10 E.H. Carr, *What Is History?* (Harmondsworth: Penguin Books, 1964), 30.
11 These directions are written into the score.
12 John Beckwith, notes accompanying ACM 26.
13 Ibid.
14 In that work, Beckwith's librettist, Margaret Atwood, provides, in a gently ironic tone, a series of pictures of Canadian reactions to and relationships with the works of Shakespeare. Beckwith's music matches the tone of the text precisely.
15 The comment comes from Donald Davis in conversation with Norma Beecroft. CBC documentary 'Two New Hours.'
16 The discussion of *Mating Time* is contained in 'John Beckwith and the Expressive Power of Magical Eclecticism,' a paper read at the CUMS conference, Victoria, 1990.

PART THREE

Music Education

CARL MOREY

Musical Education in Nineteenth-Century Toronto

Although Toronto was founded in the summer of 1793 as a temporary capital of Upper Canada, the cluster of hastily erected buildings proved more durable a foundation for settlement than had been intended, and despite its vacillating fortunes as a capital, the town prospered politically and economically through the nineteenth century. The town of York, as the settlement was called, reverted to the original local name of Toronto when it was incorporated as a city in 1834. At the time the population was about 9250.[1] Dramatic presentations date from 1810, when performances were given in Mr Miller's Assembly Room (the former Coffee-House),[2] and a theatrical space was available in the ballroom of Frank's Hotel in the 1820s.[3] In 1833 the Theatre Royal opened in a converted church.[4] By the middle of the century there were the Lyceum Theatre, which began twenty-five years of plays and operas in 1848,[5] and the splendid St Lawrence Hall, which opened in 1850 and is still in use. The population, with its mixture of puritan and frontier outlooks, often viewed the arts suspiciously, but, despite that, visiting musicians had been coming to the town since the 1820s, ranging from unknown entrepreneurs to John Braham, the first Huon in Weber's *Oberon*. With the growth of the railways after 1855, Toronto was eventually joined to a circuit that connected into the eastern United States and ranged through Canada from Windsor in the west to Montreal in the east. The great performers of the nineteenth century were regular callers, and Torontonians heard such figures as Jenny Lind, Henrietta Sontag, Louis Moreau Gottschalk, Henri Vieuxtemps, Sigismund Thalberg, and Pablo de Sarasate, among many others, as well as operatic performances by intrepid travelling companies or, after 1867, by its resident group, the Holman Company.

The visitors set standards and performed repertoire that might not otherwise have been available in the city, but the intellectual and artistic life of a society, while it might be spurred on by such glamorous encounters, cannot thrive entirely on the brief appearances of outsiders. Crucial to the development of a sophisticated cultural life in any community is education, in which music must play a part, and musical training of various kinds and at various levels was an important element in the social and artistic growth of Toronto, even if to some extent it was separate from other subjects of instruction. General education apparently began when William Cooper opened a school in 1798,[6] and although a government school was set up in 1807,[7] education remained essentially in private hands. The University of King's College was chartered in 1827 and an important boys' school, Upper Canada College, opened at the beginning of 1830. Musical education had an occasional place in these formal educational institutions, but in general, especially at a serious professional level, it developed parallel with general education, not within it.

The introduction of organized musical training into York occurred in 1810 and its promotion required some justification and explanation. In February 1810 Joseph B. Abbott announced that he proposed opening a school 'in the principles of Church Music.' He explained why:

Music Vocal or Instrumental is universally considered as an elegant accomplishment, not more interesting than useful to the profession. The said Abbott flatters himself he will be able to give satisfaction to all those who may be inclined to encourage him, by teaching it in the most expeditious manner according to the most approved standards of modern time.[8]

Apparently the offer was premature: the town was not yet ready for so elegant an accomplishment and nothing more is heard of Joseph B. Abbott's Music School, although in 1812 Abbott did obtain a licence to keep a tavern, thereby becoming the first Toronto musician to decide his true calling lay elsewhere.[9] Private music teaching was also among the many activities of one of York's most intriguing citizens, Richard Coates. As is well known, Coates was the builder of the first local organs, and two of his barrel organs are still at the Sharon Temple, north of Toronto.[10] In 1818 Coates the painter advertised 'that he intends to continue his occupation in all its various branches, viz: – Portrait Painting, Land and Marine Scenery, Sign Painting, Rooms and Furniture, etc. painted in an elegant style.' Coates the musician went on in the same notice to say that 'He also begs leave to inform the young Gentlemen of the place, that he has long been in the habit of teaching MUSIC, both in theory and practice; and intends to give lessons to those who may feel disposed to be instructed in that science. – Musical instruments tuned, etc.'[11] However long he had been in the habit of teaching music, he had not been doing it at York, where he had only just arrived, and there is no further evidence that Coates was active as a teacher.

Music was also available in York in at least one school, education then being the private enterprise of individuals. Mrs Goodman, in 1820, announced a reduction in rates at her school for girls. The 'general education' course, consisting of English, history, geography, and needlework, was to cost two pounds, five shillings, and music was available as an extra course, but at a cost of two pounds, ten shillings.[12] Presumably Mrs Goodman taught everything herself since she advertised no special teacher for music. By 1828, Miss Purcell and Miss Rose, the operators of another girls' school, advertised that Madame Harris had arrived to teach dancing,[13] and two years later they announced that a 'Music Master' will attend, although he was not identified.[14]

Mrs Goodman, Coates, and Abbott were the first on record to have offered musical instruction in York and they represented three important categories of study respectively – as part of general education in school, private lessons, and group vocal music.

Joseph Abbott's early idea of offering instruction in church music was basically sound; his lack of success is easily attributable to the town's having had only about six hundred inhabitants, many of whom were transitory and attached to the military or government services.[15] The religious interest worked better when, with a larger population (by 1845 there were 19,706 inhabitants),[16] Toronto the Good, as the city somewhat facetiously came to be known because of the number of churches, spawned large choral societies and innumerable church choirs of considerable ambition. Preparation of choristers for these organizations flourished as a kind of musical adult education activity throughout the century. In 1842 the Philharmonic Society (basically a choral organization) announced that Mr Hyde would form private singing classes for those who wished to become members of the society.[17] The notice was addressed only to 'Gentlemen' and offered separate instruction for treble voices, counter-tenors, tenors, and basses. A more equitable and more usual attitude towards 'instruction in sacred vocal music' was offered in 1848 in the basement of the Congregational Church on Wednesdays at half-past seven, and included twenty-four lessons for five shillings.[18]

After mid-century, vocal class became very popular. The connection between singing and some kind of group activity, especially activity with a moral element, is evident in the 1858 courses given by Mr S.S. Hickok for the Early Closing Association, which, moreover, met in the rooms of the Mechanics' Institute, one of the great nineteenth-century organizations created for the moral and intellectual uplift of the working classes.[19] The interest was strong enough to make the giving of such instruction attractive even to private teachers. Mr Sugden, a voice teacher in the 1850s, in 1859 offered at his home 'Choral Classes for the practice of Glees, Psalmody, easy Anthems, etc.'[20] In the same year Henry Sefton, music master at the Normal School (the teacher training school) offered 'Adult Singing Classes' at the school.[21] Sefton offered his services as a kind of choral consultant in 1860 when he announced that he 'will be happy to give elementary instruction in Vocal Music in Classes, to Choirs, Choral Societies, Boarding Schools or Private Circles.'[22] In the 1860s at least five musicians offered classes in choral singing, either privately, in a church, or in a public institution. The practical dimension of this choral interest was in the choral societies that flourished in Toronto in the second half of the century. With the founding of the Philharmonic Society in 1846, Toronto was never without two or three major organizations and often several smaller ones, as well as the choirs that sang in the city's numerous churches. In the 1850s the major ensembles were the Vocal Music Society, the Sacred Harmonic Choir, and the Metropolitan Choral Society. During the 1870s and 1880s there were the Philharmonic Society, the Toronto Choral Society, the Toronto Vocal Society, and the Toronto Glee and Madrigal Union. All of them except the last gave performances of the great oratorios of Handel and nineteenth-century composers, with schedules of rehearsals and performances that appear to have eliminated the possibility of choristers singing in more than one group. One only wonders how they found time to attend the various vocal classes.

As Toronto's community of professional musicians grew, there became available a variety of teachers, many of them claiming distinguished European backgrounds, who could renew the offer of private instruction first made by Richard Coates. Madam Walther, 'Vocalist, and Professor of the Piano and Guitar, from the City of Ulm' was available in 1836 to give lessons on her two instruments to 'the Ladies of Toronto,' although the lack of a similar offer in subsequent years suggests that she was no more successful than Coates had been eighteen years before.[23] Lessons on flute and harp as well as on guitar and in singing were available in 1841 from Mr Ransome, who published his own music for solo flute and for harp or piano with flute.[24] *The Examiner* in the same year accepted at its office enquiries for piano lessons that would be given at the pupil's residence, by a teacher who remained anonymous.[25] One of the more versatile music teachers was H.T. Dickinson, who taught 'instrumental music' (otherwise undefined) and advertised his teaching at the end of the advertisements for his business, which was a dyeing establishment on Queen Street.[26] The first private teacher of unquestioned talent, and who had a lasting reputation in the city, was George Strathy. His Scottish family had settled on a large property near London, Ontario, and by 1847 George had moved to Toronto, where he taught piano, organ, and theory. His advertisements associate him with Mendelssohn, and family papers confirm a German phase of his otherwise unknown training. Certainly his occasional concert appearances, his later appointment to Trinity College, and the several compositions published locally by Nordheimer attest to more than average training and ability.[27] Henry Schallehn, a clarinettist and for a few years director of the Band of the Rifle Brigade, was another musician with a professional background who was available as a teacher. He announced in 1849 his 'intention to open classes during the Winter, when he will teach on a simple and cheap system, all the different Instruments and Singing.'[28]

Other musicians of experience in the mid-nineteenth century offered their services as teachers. The singing teacher Jules Hecht had studied at the Brussels Conservatoire and been a member of the Sacred Music Society at Frankfurt. Henry Haycroft had studied at the Royal Academy in London with Sterndale Bennett and with Mendelssohn. The famous Belgian pianist and composer Martin Lazare performed in Toronto during his American tours and finally settled in the city, where he was active as a conductor and pianist as well as a teacher. From the Prague Conservatory there was Wilhelm Labitzky. Anton Gunther, a student of Liszt and a member of a local family of jewellers, offered the usual instruction in piano and organ, but in 1856 he also specifically taught 'the knowledge of composition.'[29] Henry Sefton added to his singing classes a course of twenty weeks at the Mechanics' Institute in 1862 in 'the theory and practise of music, which will embrace Thorough Bass, Composition, and all the higher branches of the Science.'[30] Keyboard, wind instruments, and the violin were well accommodated but instruction in other string instruments was rare, so that even as late as 1863 it was a matter of some importance that the cellist Haig was available for lessons. Haig announced his intention of forming a viola class for beginners, and he also offered a particularly sophisticated level of training when he proposed giving instruction in violoncello accompanying to advanced piano students.[31] In the period 1845–60 at least twenty-five people declared themselves available for private musical instruction. *Caverhill's Toronto City Directory* for 1859–60 designated twenty-one people in the general address list as musicians or teachers, apart from those in the music trades.

Institutional instruction in music paralleled the general development of musical life in Toronto. In the first half of the nineteenth century, schools were privately operated and students were taught what the operators and the pupils' parents deemed necessary for advancement in the colonial world. For boys, music was seldom considered a necessity, although when music later became part of the curriculum in the public schools, the remaining private boys' schools also often included music. As has already been noted, in the early days music was most often included in girls' schools where it was offered as a refined adjunct to other studies, at an additional charge, in company with other subjects thought appropriate to the education of a young lady, such as dancing, sewing, and flower arranging. The whole school system changed, however, with the appointment in 1844 of Egerton Ryerson as chief superintendent of education in Upper Canada.

In his lengthy 'Report on a System of Public Elementary Instruction for Upper Canada' of 1846, Ryerson stated clearly that 'Music is another department of instruction which I think ought to find a place in every Common School.'[32] His view that music should be a regular part of the new public school curriculum was given substance by the appointment of a music master at the Normal School, which opened in 1847 for the training of teachers. One of the most respectable musicians then in Toronto, J.P. Clarke, was the first of Ryerson's musical appointments, but presumably he did not meet the superintendent's pedagogical requirements, for three years later William Townsend was appointed, with far-reaching effects. Townsend was a local musician and manufacturer of melodeons and it was he who introduced 'Hullah's System' of music education to Canada.[33]

John Pyke Hullah was an English musician who had devoted himself to the idea of educating large masses musically through the use of a fixed-doh system, using staff notation and an unchanging pitch centre. In 1857 Ryerson sought out someone specifically trained in the method and brought Henry Sefton from England in 1858 to teach the Hullah system at the Normal School. Sefton remained in his post until 1883. In 1869 he published the first educational songbook in Ontario, *Three Part Songs*. The general philosophy of the time was that the classroom teacher should teach everything, including music, and there was even a feeling expressed by one inspector in 1886 that 'no person should be licensed who cannot teach music (vocal), and that person who is not gifted with the necessary vocal powers was not born for a teacher and will not be missed from the profession.'[34] In actual practice this led to an attempt to make music teachers out of all teachers, and Sefton's 1869 songbook exemplifies the problems that follow from this. A preliminary section of 'Hints to Teachers' contains the simplest kind of information and suggestions, while the songs that follow in three parts, and some in four parts with a bass, are too difficult to be managed by anyone in need of the elementary introduction.

The Hullah system had its supporters, but it also had its detractors, who rallied around the banner of tonic sol-fa and a system largely devised by John Curwen which used the solfège names and a relative relationship of pitches. This did away with the need to read music in conventional notation and so seemed a far preferable method for the inexpert classroom teacher. Ryerson had retired as superintendent of education in 1876 and died in 1882. When a teacher was appointed in 1885 to teach music in the Toronto public school system it was A.T. Cringan, a graduate in music from the University of Toronto, but more significantly from the Tonic Sol-Fa College in England. Some years before, in 1872, an association had been formally set up in Toronto to promote the rival to the Hullah system, and over the years battles flared up, manifested in demonstration concerts and letters to the editor.[35] In 1887 Cringan participated in a lecture given in Toronto by John Curwen himself, with illustrations of Curwen's method performed by Cringan's class from Victoria Street Public School.[36]

To confound the matter further, Sefton's successor in the Normal School, in 1883, was S.H. Preston, who subscribed to yet a third system. Preston's model was the American educator H.E. Holt, director of music in the public schools of Boston. In 1883 Preston published *The Normal Music Course*, and in 1885 Holt visited Toronto to address the first conference of the Ontario Music Teachers' Association, an event that in itself indicated the growing importance of music education.[37] Preston adapted two books by Holt and John Tufts for use in Canadian schools – *The Public School Music Reader* and *The High School Music Reader* (Canada Publishing Co., 1885). The first volume began with sixteen pages of rudiments for such things as breathing, rests, pitches, intervals, and keys. There is a chart for hand movements for scale degree numbers (not sol-fa syllables as with Curwen), but the fifty-eight tunes given in staff notation are to be learned by rote, which seems to defeat the avowed purpose of making children into fluent readers of music. The Department of Education considered authorizing the Holt method for use in the province but Cringan campaigned so strongly against it that the department ended by authorizing neither Holt nor Curwen.

Discussion, often heated, continued over the years as to the relative merits of the two systems in terms of mass educational purposes. As has been already noted above, from about 1850 until the early years of the twentieth century, Toronto was never without two or three major choral ensembles, and sometimes had more. Singing was a serious business in the community and proportionately meant far more to more people than it does today. How it was taught in the public schools was a concern more immediate and public than it could be now.

The development of higher-level training in the formal surroundings of conservatory and university becomes a story of considerable complexity in the twentieth century, but as with other categories of musical instruction, the foundations and first structures of conservatory and university teaching were set out in the nineteenth century.

During the mid nineteenth century a few of the private teachers made occasional attempts to enlarge the scope of their private instruction, in emulation, if not in realization, of the model of the great conservatory schools of Europe. In 1856 the popular violinist Ferdinand Griebel ran announcements concerning instruction at his Academy of Music, on Church Street opposite St Michael's Cathedral. he was the sole teacher in his academy, but in a modest way it was a genuine centre for musical activity, since Griebel proposed not only to give instruction there but also to have 'quintette parties' for anyone who wanted to join, and to give chamber concerts on his premises. In 1862 John Carter, the organist at St James' Cathedral, opened at his house a

Musical Academy on the plans of the Conservatories and Academies of Music in Europe. Each pupil will receive instruction upon the Piano-forte, in Singing, and in Harmony and Composition, separate classes for the study of which will also be found.[38]

Carter's academy was notable in that it offered an integrated course of study rather than simply a series of separate lessons.

Not until 1878, when Davenport Kerrison opened his Royal Canadian Conservatory of Music in rooms in the Grand Opera House Building, was there a school of some stability. The name and location changed several times, but the school remained in operation for a decade. It may well have been that Kerrison, when he closed his school and retired to Florida, saw a better-financed rival about to eclipse him, for in 1886 the Toronto Conservatory of Music was incorporated. There was now a recognized need for a large-scale, fully financed professional music school, and on 20 July 1882 the *Globe* published a lengthy editorial that called for the establishment of a provincial conservatory along the lines of the Ontario College of Art, which had been set up in 1877. A provincial conservatory never materialized, but the Toronto Conservatory became something like one in prominence and influence. It was set up as a business proposition and was financed as a joint stock company with capital of fifty thousand dollars in five hundred shares of one hundred dollars each. The stock was held by about sixty leading citizens, and there is every indication that the buyers were not motivated only by charity and a love of music, but that they expected eventually to get at least some return on their investment. In the first year of the conservatory's operation there were about thirty-five faculty members, and there were courses in piano and organ tuning. Pupils of the conservatory could also attend lectures in physics at University College in the University of Toronto on the principles of musical acoustics.

The most serious rival to the Toronto Conservatory for pre-eminence in the city was the Toronto College of Music, which had been founded in 1880 by Frederick Torrington, the energetic conductor of the Philharmonic Society and the most prominent figure in the city's professional musical life in the latter part of the century. The college was incorporated in 1890 and although never as large as the conservatory, it nevertheless had a complete faculty and offered regular courses of instruction. On Torrington's death in 1917 the college was absorbed by yet another institution, the Canadian Academy of Music, which was smaller but also of some distinction. The academy was also a private company, belonging to Albert Gooderham. In 1924 the University of Toronto, which had acquired the conservatory in 1919, bought the academy from Gooderham. There was a fourth institution, the Metropolitan School of Music, which the famous piano teacher and composer W.O. Forsyth set up in 1895. Each of the four schools, although varying a good deal in size, had a list of distinguished teachers of a complete range of instruments, voice, and theory, and the conservatory and the college, in particular, also offered planned courses of study as well as individual lessons, lectures, and a wide variety of concerts. The conservatories appear to have enrolled about two thousand students at the turn of the century, when the city's population was a little under three hundred thousand.

Around the world music in the university was quite a different thing in the nineteenth century than it is in the twentieth, but this was especially true on the North American continent. So far as music was studied in university in Europe, it tended to be in theory and academic modes of composition, with the recent study of musicology beginning to appear in German-speaking universities. The first bachelor of music degree was granted by the University of King's College (the nucleus of the University of Toronto) in 1846 to James Paton Clarke.[39] Clarke and George Strathy were competitors for the first university chair of music at Trinity College in 1853.[40] (Trinity was then an independent university and became affiliated with the University of Toronto only in 1904.) Strathy won it and held it until 1883, but it was virtually an honorary position. Strathy gave no lectures, nor were there any examinations or graduates. In 1884 Trinity drew up a music syllabus and candidates for the bachelor of music degree had to pass an annual examination over three years. Trinity, however, did not offer any instruction in music and in order to prepare candidates the college in 1888 accepted into affiliation the new Toronto Conservatory. A similar situation obtained at the University of Toronto, which took the College of Music into affiliation in 1890 and the Conservatory in 1896. For a few years it even embraced the Hamilton Conservatory. There was obviously a good deal of interest in giving music a place in the university, but equal uncertainty as to how to manage it. The Senate of the University of Toronto had been considering music degrees as early as 1856,[41] but the matter was never objectively examined until it came under the scrutiny of a royal commission on the university fifty years later. The commission's report in 1906 clearly stated that the affiliation system of independent conservatories was unsatisfactory and called for a school of music within the university system: 'We think the University should look forward to a time when it will have connected with it a school of music over the management and teaching of which it has complete control, and through the medium of which it may be able greatly to advance the future of music in Canada.'[42] This was realized in 1918 with the establishment of the Faculty of Music at the University of Toronto, with Augustus Vogt as dean.

The first, and for many years the primary, consideration of the citizens of York and Toronto was the clearing of land, the building of houses, and the establishment of the commerce. It is easy to forget that until at least the third decade of the nineteenth century, Toronto was very much a frontier society, and such a society must have had little of the romance that popular fiction often suggests. It is all the more remarkable that so early in the growth of the town there was interest in any kind of formal musical study, and that the interest grew to something of substance by mid-century. Throughout the latter part of the century there was sophisticated musical training at all levels, which provided the foundation for musical life then and in the future. In 1897 H.H. Godfrey began his *Souvenir of Musical Toronto* with the observation that 'although the importance of Toronto as a centre of education is generally admitted, few stop to think how great is the role which musical institutions play in the general educational scheme.'[43] He placed musical education at the head of his *Souvenir*, and after following with sketches of the city's chief musicians, he could, with some justification, conclude 'that by our humble efforts we have fully established the claim of Toronto as being pre-eminently a musical centre, and the home *par excellence* (in Canada) of the Art Divine.'[44]

NOTES

1 *Toronto City Directory, 1837,* 41.
2 Edith G. Firth, *The Town of York 1793–1815* (Toronto: University of Toronto Press in association with the Champlain Society for the Government of Ontario, 1962), 274.
3 Edith G. Firth, *The Town of York 1815–1834* (Toronto: University of Toronto Press in association with the Champlain Society for the Government of Ontario, 1966), 99.
4 Ibid., 341.
5 The theatre opened on 28 December 1848, and burned down the night of 30 January 1874.
6 Firth, *The Town of York 1793–1815*, lxxiii, 192.
7 Ibid., lxxiv.
8 Ibid., 208–9.
9 Ibid., 208.
10 The tunes recorded on the barrels have provided John Beckwith with material used in the composition of his *Sharon Fragments* and *Canada Dash – Canada Dot.*
11 *Upper Canada Gazette,* Thursday, 26 November 1818. Advertisements generally appear in more than one issue of a newspaper, and frequently in more than one paper. Where a newspaper source is cited, it is a basic reference and may not be the unique appearance of this information.
12 *Upper Canada Gazette,* Thursday, 20 January 1820.
13 *Loyalist,* Saturday, 30 August 1828.
14 *Colonial Advocate,* Thursday, 12 August 1830.
15 Firth, *The Town of York 1793–1815,* lxxvii.
16 *Brown's Toronto City and Home District Directory 1846–7,* George Brown (Toronto 1846), 41.
17 *Examiner,* Wednesday, 25 May 1842.
18 *Globe,* Wednesday, 22 November 1848.
19 *Globe,* Tuesday, 13 April 1858.
20 *Globe,* Monday, 10 January 1859.
21 *Globe,* Wednesday, 23 November 1859.
22 *Globe,* Wednesday, 19 September 1860.
23 *Correspondent and Advocate,* Wednesday, 7 September 1836.
24 *Examiner,* Wednesday, 23 August 1841; Wednesday, 29 September 1841.
25 *Examiner,* Wednesday, 3 February 1841.
26 *Globe,* Tuesday, 10 December 1844.
27 'George Strathy' in *Encyclopedia of Music in Canada,* 2d ed. (Toronto: Univer-

sity of Toronto Press, 1992), 1256–7. Strathy advertised his availability as a teacher frequently in Toronto newspapers in the 1840s, 1850s, and 1860s.
28 *Globe*, Saturday, 15 September 1849.
29 *Globe*, Wednesday, 19 November 1856.
30 *Globe*, Friday, 24 October 1862.
31 *Globe*, Thursday, 23 April 1863.
32 J. George Hodgins, *Documentary History of Education in Upper Canada*, vol. 6 (Toronto: Warwick Bros. and Rutter 1894–1910), 186.
33 For an extensive discussion, see George Campbell Trowsdale, 'A History of Public School Music in Ontario,' 2 vols., Ed.D. thesis, University of Toronto, 1962.
34 Archives of the Province of Ontario: Music Education – Ontario 1886 – Inspectors' Reports on Vocal Music. The report quoted is by W.H.G. Colles.
35 *Globe*, Thursday, 30 May 1872. Notice regarding a 'Tonic Sol-fa Concert' to illustrate a method 'which is something of a novelty in Canada.'
36 *Mail*, Thursday, 6 October 1887.
37 Trowsdale, 'A History of Public School Music in Ontario,' vol. 2, pp. 518–19. Holt returned to direct a summer school.
38 *Globe*, Tuesday, 23 September 1862.
39 *University of Toronto Fasti from 1850 to 1887* (Toronto: Williamson and Co., 1887), 5.
40 Archives of Trinity College, University of Toronto. Entries in Corporation Minute Book of Trinity College for 7, 14, and 28 April 1853.
41 Hodgins, *Documentary History ...*, vol. 12, p. 264.
42 *Report of the Royal Commission on the University of Toronto*, 1906, p. xxxviii.
43 H.H. Godfrey, *A Souvenir of Musical Toronto* (Toronto: Mason and Risch Piano Co., 1897), 5.
44 Ibid., 29.

LEE R. BARTEL AND PATRICIA MARTIN SHAND

Canadian Music in the School Curriculum: Illusion or Reality?

Introduction

In recent years there have been systematic attempts to measure and enforce Canadian content in cultural areas under federal control in Canada. For example, the CRTC has regulated Canadian content in broadcasting, and the Canada Council has made grants to performers dependent on meeting Canadian content quotas. However, in the field of education, which is under provincial jurisdiction, there have been no comparable national efforts to control Canadian content. The national organizations which have promoted Canadian content in music education have been non-governmental agencies with no power or authority to *force* educators to teach Canadian music. These organizations have sought to *influence* teachers and music education administrators concerning the value of teaching Canadian compositions, and have developed projects to guide educators in their efforts and to provide opportunities for students to hear and perform Canadian music. It is encouraging to note the various promotional efforts which have been made on behalf of Canadian content in music education, and in Part One of this paper we describe some of these efforts. But the question remains: Is Canadian music in the school curriculum an illusion or reality? In Part Two we address this question as we report the results of an objective analysis of the Canadian content of music curriculum documents published by provincial ministries and departments of education, since these are the bodies with the ultimate responsibility for music education in Canada.

Part One: Historical Review of Efforts to Promote the Use of Canadian Music in Education

During the past thirty years, there have been a variety of efforts made to promote the use of Canadian music in education, efforts designed to make students aware of their national musical heritage and to develop future audiences for Canadian music. Promotional work has been undertaken to acquaint educators with published Canadian music suitable for student performers, to promote publication of additional Canadian music for student use, to encourage Canadian composers to add to the repertoire of music for student performers, to provide teachers with resource materials to assist them in teaching Canadian music, and to provide opportunities for students to perform and listen to Canadian music.

Among those involved in these promotional efforts have been the Canadian Music Centre, the Canadian Music Educators' Association, the Canadian League of Composers, the Canadian Federation of Music Teachers' Associations, the composers' performing rights societies, the Alliance for Canadian New Music Projects, provincial music educators' associations, boards of education, individual educational institutions and teachers, and performing organizations.

The first systematic efforts to promote Canadian music in education were made by the Canadian Music Centre (CMC), which in 1961 began to develop the Graded Educational Music Plan. This plan, initially conceived and developed by John Adaskin, CMC executive secretary, sought to achieve 25 per cent Canadian content in music education.[1] In 1965 the plan was renamed the John Adaskin Project, and in 1973 the Canadian Music Educators' Association (CMEA) joined CMC to co-sponsor the project. Throughout its thirty-year history, the John Adaskin Project has focused on Canadian music for student performers. In 1962, A Graded Educational Music Plan committee began grading and evaluating published and unpublished Canadian repertoire in terms of its suitability for student performers, and the selection and evaluation of repertoire continued through the 1970s and 1980s as the central activity of the Adaskin Project. By 1992, a total of eleven resource guides had been published by the Adaskin Project to assist educators in locating and teaching Canadian music suitable for student performers.

The Adaskin Project has also sought to increase the student repertoire of Canadian music through a variety of commissioning ventures. The first such venture was the 1963 Seminar for Graded Educational Music, during which fifteen Canadian composers visited schools in the Toronto area to observe student performers for the purpose of preparing to write music for their use. 'Seminar II' in 1965 featured concert demonstrations of music written by ten of the composers who had been involved with the 1963 'Seminar I.' By 1992, fourteen works commissioned directly by the Adaskin Project had been published, while a number of others remained unpublished. The Adaskin Project has also assisted teachers and educational organizations interested in undertaking commissioning projects, and has produced guidelines to assist composers writing for student performers. In addition to the commissioning ventures and the publication of resource materials for teachers, the Adaskin Project has sought to promote Canadian music in education through articles and through policy conferences, seminars, workshops, demonstrations, displays of materials, and lectures for teachers. The project has been funded by CMC, CMEA, the Canada Council, the Ontario Arts Council, the Ontario Ministry of Education, private foundations, and individual donors.

Although CMC and CMEA have no other ongoing national projects to promote Canadian music in education, CMC regional offices and provincial music educators' associations affiliated with CMEA have been involved in educational projects designed to influence teachers in particular areas of the country. For example, the Ontario regional office's Creating Music in the Classroom project has, since the 1983–4 academic year, sent composers into Ontario elementary and secondary schools to work with students on creative projects. This project grew out of the Composers-in-Schools project developed during the late 1970s and early 1980s by the Canadian League of Composers to introduce students to Canadian composers and their music. During the period from 1983–4 to 1990–1, 22 composers were involved in 73 residencies in 67 Ontario schools through the Creating Music in the Classroom project. In some cases, students created pieces which were performed by visiting professional performers, while in other cases composers collaborated with students to create pieces which the pupils could perform. In still other cases, the composers themselves wrote pieces for the students to perform, or the composers guided the students in exploring sound through listening activities.

The Quebec regional office of CMC, working in cooperation with the Quebec Ministry of Education, has put considerable effort into producing resource materials to guide teachers and students in analysing music written by Quebec composers. The Prairie regional office has since the mid-1980s worked to provide additional repertoire for student performers through its McCurdy commissioning program, supported financially by Alberta Culture and the Alberta Music Festival Association. Commissioning projects have also been undertaken by provincial music educators' associations, with the resulting pieces being premiered at teachers' workshops and conferences.[2]

While CMEA and the provincial MEAs are associations of school and university music educators, the private music teachers of Canada have their own national association – the Canadian Federation of Music Teachers' Associations, with affiliated provincial associations. CFMTA began Canada Music Week in 1960 to promote Canadian music and performers. Since 1960, there have been Canada Music Week programs in centres across the country annually, often involving other organizations and individuals in addition to the registered music teachers and their students.

Composers obviously have a vested interest in developing audiences for their music, so it is not surprising that composers' performing rights organizations have undertaken promotional efforts. The free biographical brochures about Canadian composers and the sample recordings of Canadian musical excerpts produced by PROCAN and CAPAC,[3] while not aimed solely at the educational market, have proved valuable to teachers and students.

One of the most ambitious and interesting of the projects to promote Canadian music in education has been Contemporary Showcase, a noncompetitive festival which has provided opportunities for student soloists and ensembles to perform for one another and to receive guidance from knowledgeable adjudicators in a workshop environment. From its inception in 1970, the Showcase festival has been held in Toronto, with an extension of its operation in later years to other Ontario centres (London, Kitchener, Ottawa). In 1990, the first Contemporary Showcase festival outside Ontario was held in Calgary. Although Toronto-based, the Contemporary Music Showcase Association (changed in name to the Alliance for Canadian New Music Projects in 1978) has been influential across the country because of its ongoing program of commissioning Canadian composers to write for student performers, and because of its graded syllabus of Canadian music, which is a valuable reference guide for teachers seeking suitable repertoire.

It is beyond the scope of this survey to describe the many other promotional projects which have been local in nature – commissioning projects and residencies of composers organized by local boards of education or individual schools or teachers, or educational programs presented by provincial composers' associations or local performing organizations to introduce teachers and students to Canadian compositions. Suffice it to say that much time and energy have gone into the promotion of Canadian music in education. But to what extent have such promotional efforts been successful? The seeds have been planted, but has there been a harvest? Has John Adaskin's aim of 25 per cent Canadian content been achieved? Is Canadian music in the school curriculum an illusion or reality? In seeking answers to these questions, we undertook to analyse music curriculum documents published by provincial ministries of education in Canada from 1980 to 1990.

Part Two: Content Analysis of Provincial Music Curriculum Documents

Our study focused on the following research question: What priority is given to Canadian music in the published music curriculum documents for Canadian schools?

More specifically, the study addressed the following subquestions: (1) What proportion of music and musical materials recommended for study and performance by published curriculum documents in Canada is of Canadian origin? (2) Are there differences in the priority given to Canadian music in Canadian school curricula related to region? (3) Are there differences in priority related to music of Canadian origin with French texts vs. music with English texts? (4) Are there curricular differences in priority related to traditional folk music vs. composed music of Canadian origin? (5) What proportion of music curricula in Canada identifies a specific priority for Canadian music with a policy statement, and what effect does this appear to have on references?

Research Procedures

Music curriculum documents published during the period from 1980 to 1990 were obtained from all provincial ministries of education. Forty-one publications met the criteria for inclusion in the study, but since one document was not available for analysis, forty publications were included. One document was designated as an 'omnibus' publication and was therefore analysed as three separate curricula, resulting in a total of 42 curricula in our final content analysis.[4]

Before the content analysis began, research questions and the classification system were formulated and circulated to all research associates of the Canadian Music Education Research Centre (CMERC)[5] for comment and criticism. The initial classification system was employed in a pilot analysis of three documents by the two principal researchers and a graduate student. On the basis of the response from the CMERC research associates and the pilot study, the classification system employed in the study was established. Details of this system are described below. Initial analysis of all documents was done by selected graduate and undergraduate students at the Faculty of Music, University of Toronto.[6] As the principal researchers, we checked the analyses of all documents to achieve reliable classification according to the established criteria.

Classification Categories

Two types of classification were necessary. First, each curriculum document was classified in terms of aspects such as grade level and policy concerning Canadian content. Following this, all the recommended pieces of music and the related resource materials in each document were itemized and classified.

(1) Classification of Documents
Grade Level: The complexity and nonuniformity of Canadian educational organization are reflected in curriculum documents. For that reason, classification of curricula by grade level is less than neat and tidy. We established four general categories: grades K–6, 7–9, 10–13, and combined 7–13. Documents that did not coincide precisely with the established categories were classified in the nearest category.
Policy Statement: Some curriculum documents contain statements of policy or priority regarding certain kinds of music. For example, a curriculum could include a statement that each ensemble preparing music for public performance should perform a piece composed by a Canadian. Such a statement would be classified as a policy on Canadian music. If a document listed an objective that indicated official encouragement for the inclusion of Canadian or multicultural music, that document was classified as having a policy regarding that music.

(2) Classification of Recommended Music and other Materials
This research study undertook to identify and categorize each piece of music and each book, recording, film/video, kit, or computer software package listed in each curriculum guide. Two broad categories structured the analysis: (i) individual pieces of music; (ii) larger collections: books, recordings with multiple pieces, films/videos, kits, software packages. Each item to be classified was given an item number. All individual pieces were then classified, whether excerpts (e.g., Bach's Fugue in G Minor, exposition only) or whole works, and whether recommended to be performed or to be heard. When an individual piece was recommended for study but was identified as part of a particular collection, the individual piece and not the collection was listed. Similarly, if an excerpt from a larger work was listed, it was classified as the excerpt and not as the larger work (e.g., a movement from a sonata). The collection or complete work was listed only if it was recommended in its entirety or if at least a substantial portion of it was recommended.

(i) Analysis of Individual Pieces: The first major classification of an individual piece was whether or not it was Canadian in origin. This classification was made according to the music itself and not the performance. (For example, Bach's Fugue in G Minor performed by the Canadian Brass would be classified as 'other' rather than as Canadian.) If the piece was of Canadian origin, it was classified next as traditional folk (no known composer or specific date of origin) or as composed (composer known). In the case of a substantial arrangement of a folk-song (e.g., 'She's Like the Swallow' arranged for SATB by Harry Somers), it was classified as composed. Composed pieces were next judged to be either 'long' or 'short.' The guideline employed was that a work with a duration of ten or more minutes was considered 'long,' while a work less than ten minutes in duration was 'short.' Canadian choral and vocal works with text were classified by language: English, French, Native, and 'Different' for any other language. All non-Canadian works were classified as 'other,' and further as 'traditional folk' or 'composed long' or 'composed short.' If the origin of a piece could not be determined after exhausting the resources of the University of Toronto, it was classified as 'Unknown.'

Individual pieces were classified into the following categories:
Instrumental Canadian Folk
Instrumental Canadian Composed Long/Short
English-Canadian Folk
English-Canadian Composed Long/Short
French-Canadian Folk
French-Canadian Composed Long/Short
Native-Canadian Folk
Native-Canadian Composed Short
Different Canadian Folk (non-English, French, or Native)
Different Canadian Composed Long/Short
Other Folk
Other Composed Long/Short
Unknown

(ii) Analysis of Books, Recordings, Films, Etc.: Any item other than an individual piece of music was listed in this general category. A book of songs with commentary was classified as a music book (e.g., *Canada's Story in Song* by Edith Fowke and Alan Mills, which contains songs and historical commentary). Instruction books were classified as music books. Books containing historical, pedagogical, or psychological information pertinent to music teaching or the music taught, and not consisting primarily of performance music, were classified as reference books. Such books could also, for example, include descriptions of musical activities or instrument-making instructions. All sound recordings on disc or tape were classified together. Kits were taken to be combinations of books, recordings, videos, charts, cards, etc. (Music books with accompanying recordings were classified as kits.) The 'miscellaneous' category included items such as computer software, wall charts, activity cards and transparencies. General types of materials recommended without specific titles (e.g., 'Books on Pop Stars, Rock Music, and Careers in Music') were not listed.

After appropriate categorization, an item was further classified as Canadian, other than Canadian, or of unknown origin. In the case of music books, reference books, kits, and most miscellaneous items, the classification was made on the basis of the origin of the material (where the author lives rather than whether the publisher has a branch in Canada) and not the music content. In the case of sound recordings and films/videos, the origin and the content were considered. Of primary importance was the music, and therefore Canadian music performed by non-Canadians would be classified as Canadian. (Thus *The Mennonite Piano Concerto*, featuring music by Victor Davies, recorded by a British orchestra, would be considered Canadian, while a record featuring the Canadian Brass performing works by Bach and Gabrieli would *not* be considered Canadian.) However, if the intent of the recording was a pedagogical project, the origin determined classification despite content. (For example, tapes of accompaniments created by Canadian school board personnel to be used in conjunction with curricular material were considered Canadian even if some song material was non-Canadian.) The following categories were used for classification of books, films, videos, recordings, and kits:

Canadian/Other Music Book
Canadian/Other Film or Video
Canadian/Other Recording
Canadian/Other Kit
Canadian/Other Reference Book
Unknown Book, Film, Record, Kit
Canadian Miscellaneous
Other Miscellaneous

Results and Discussion

In seeking to determine the priority given to Canadian content in the published music curriculum documents for Canadian schools, the following

Table 1 Individual Pieces of Music

Province	Canadian		Other	
	Number	Per cent	Number	Percent
British Columbia	80	16.3	411	83.7
Alberta	7	4.7	143	95.3
Saskatchewan	33	2.9	1,097	97.1
Manitoba	84	9.9	762	90.1
Ontario	60	24.6	184	75.4
Quebec	185	19.6	759	80.4
New Brunswick	6	1.2	485	98.8
Nova Scotia	12	6.1	183	93.9
Prince Edward Island	0	0	0	0
Newfoundland	151	18.5	666	81.5
Totals	618	11.6	4,690	88.4

question must first be addressed: What proportion of music and musical materials recommended for study and performance by published curriculum documents in Canada is of Canadian origin? The second question about regional differences will be considered as part of the discussion of results.

An examination of individual pieces recommended in the 42 curricula reveals that, for the nation as a whole, 11.6 per cent are Canadian (Table 1). Regional differences are, however, apparent. Canadian content is highest in Ontario (24.6 per cent), Quebec (19.6 per cent) and British Columbia (16.3 per cent). Individual pieces of Canadian origin are notably low in the curricula of the Prairies provinces and the mainland Maritime provinces.

Canadian content is higher in the categories of recommended music books and reference books (Table 2) than in the category of individual selections (Table 1). There are 201 recommended Canadian music books and 263 reference books, for a total of 21.3 per cent Canadian content. Analysis by province again shows Ontario to have the highest percentage (57.7 per cent), but no clear pattern of regional difference emerges. The Atlantic provinces vary from 18.2 (New Brunswick) to 39.0 per cent (Newfoundland), with a four-province average of 29.7 per cent. The western provinces range from 8.3 per cent (Manitoba) to 25.8 per cent (Alberta), with a four-province average of 15.2 per cent.

The film/video, recording, kit, and miscellaneous categories combine to reveal the highest Canadian content percentage (30.7) of the materials described (Table 3). Quebec lists the most Canadian materials in this category

Table 2 Music Books and Reference Books

	Canadian			Other		
Province	Music Books	Ref. Books	Total	Music Books	Ref. Books	Total
British Columbia	18	23	41 (11.6%)	104	208	312 (88.4%)
Alberta	21	3	24 (25.8%)	47	22	69 (74.2%)
Saskatchewan	11	7	18 (15.0%)	23	79	102 (85.0%)
Manitoba	4	33	37 (8.3%)	177	233	410 (91.7%)
Ontario	15	26	41 (57.7%)	13	17	30 (42.3%)
Quebec	36	124	160 (24.4%)	98	397	495 (75.6%)
New Brunswick	11	3	14 (18.2%)	5	58	63 (81.8%)
Nova Scotia	9	26	35 (36.1%)	13	49	62 (63.9%)
Prince Edward Island	15	3	18 (25.4%)	53	0	53 (74.6%)
Newfoundland	61	15	76 (39.0%)	40	79	119 (61.0%)
Totals	201	263	464 (21.3%)	573	1,142	1,715 (78.7%)

(60.4 per cent) and Alberta the least (6.9 per cent). Although Saskatchewan lists relatively few individual pieces and books of Canadian origin, it lists 32.9 per cent Canadian films and recordings.

The priority given by ministries of education to Canadian music content can be inferred from an examination of the total references to individual pieces and collections (Table 4). For the nation as a whole, material of Canadian origin constitutes 16.1 per cent of all references in the 42 music curricula produced since 1980. Although this is a substantial number (1362 references), it falls considerably short of the 25 per cent set as a target by John Adaskin. Specific regions, however, do approach or meet the 25 per cent target. Ontario (27.4 per cent) and Quebec (25.2 per cent) narrowly exceed that point, while Newfoundland (23.8 per cent), Prince Edward Island (22.9 per cent), and Nova Scotia (21.1 per cent) are just under the mark. The western provinces (10.8 mean percentage) are considerably under the 25 per cent point, as is the one New Brunswick document.

A second question concerning the proportion of Canadian music in curricular references involved consideration of the length of the compositions listed: What is the proportion of short and long pieces recommended for study? Table 5 presents a regional analysis by length of recommended pieces. On a national basis, there were very similar proportions of Canadian content when we compared short and long pieces (12 per cent of the recommended short pieces and 10.6 per cent of the long pieces were Canadian). At the

Table 3 Film/Video, Recordings, Kits, and Miscellaneous

	Canadian					Other				
Province	Film	Recording	Kits	Miscellaneous	Total	Film	Recording	Kits	Miscellaneous	Total
British Columbia	7	8	13	3	31 (14.8%)	25	92	47	15	179 (85.2%)
Alberta	0	1	1	0	2 (6.9%)	1	0	15	11	27 (93.1%)
Saskatchewan	24	22	0	0	46 (32.9%)	34	27	31	2	94 (67.1%)
Manitoba	3	8	2	0	13 (11.4%)	0	62	39	0	101 (88.6%)
Ontario	2	10	0	0	12 (26.1%)	2	32	0	0	34 (73.9%)
Quebec	12	29	61	0	102 (60.4%)	16	30	19	2	67 (39.6%)
New Brunswick	0	5	1	0	6 (20.7%)	0	0	9	14	23 (79.3%)
Nova Scotia	18	7	3	1	29 (42.0%)	6	24	10	0	40 (58.0%)
Prince Edward Island	0	0	6	0	6 (17.6%)	0	0	28	0	28 (82.4%)
Newfoundland	0	13	20	0	33 (45.8%)	2	18	18	1	39 (54.2%)
Totals	66	103	107	4	280 (30.7%)	86	285	216	45	632 (69.3%)

Table 4 Total References to Individual Pieces and Collections

Province	Number of Documents	Canadian Material	Non-Canadian Material	Unknown
British Columbia	2	152 (14.4%)	902 (85.3%)	3 (.3%)
Alberta	3	33 (12.1%)	239 (87.2%)	2 (.7%)
Saskatchewan	2	97 (7.0%)	1,293 (93.0%)	0
Manitoba	5	134 (9.5%)	1,273 (90.5%)	0
Ontario	3	113 (27.4%)	248 (60.2%)	51 (12.4%)
Quebec	10	447 (25.2%)	1,321 (74.7%)	1 (.1%)
New Brunswick	1	26 (4.4%)	571 (95.6%)	0
Nova Scotia	1	76 (21.1%)	285 (78.9%)	0
Prince Edward Island	3	24 (22.9%)	81 (77.1%)	0
Newfoundland	12	260 (23.8%)	824 (75.5%)	7 (.7%)
Totals	42	1,362 (16.1%)	7,037 (83.2%)	64 (.7%)

provincial level, there was considerable variation, and no regional pattern was evident.

The third question investigated was: Are there differences in priority related to music of Canadian origin with French texts vs. music with English texts? To answer this question, we classified individual choral and vocal pieces of Canadian origin according to the principal language employed. It must first be noted that some of the provincial documents listed very few

Table 5 Individual Pieces by Length

Province	Short (100%)		Long (100%)	
	Canadian	Other	Canadian	Other
British Columbia	37 (11.8%)	276 (88.2%)	43 (24.2%)	135 (75.8%)
Alberta	7 (4.6%)	143 (95.3%)	0	0
Saskatchewan	33 (3.3%)	978 (96.7%)	0	119 (100.0%)
Manitoba	81 (11.3%)	633 (88.7%)	3 (2.3%)	129 (97.7%)
Ontario	31 (20.0%)	124 (80.0%)	29 (32.6%)	60 (67.4%)
Quebec	147 (27.8%)	382 (72.2%)	38 (9.2%)	377 (90.8%)
New Brunswick	6 (1.3%)	455 (98.7%)	0	30 (100.0%)
Nova Scotia	7 (7.1%)	91 (92.9%)	5 (5.2%)	92 (94.8%)
Prince Edward Island	0	0	0	0
Newfoundland	150 (19.9%)	604 (80.1%)	1 (1.6%)	62 (98.4%)
Totals	499 (12.0%)	3,686 (88.1%)	119 (10.6%)	1,004 (89.4%)

Canadian Music in the School Curriculum 137

individual pieces (see Table 1) and that the percentage of Canadian pieces among those listed was low. Consequently, the percentage from certain provinces may not truly represent the language priority of the ministry of education (e.g., 100 per cent English references in Alberta).

Table 6 reveals that 60.2 per cent of Canadian pieces referenced in curriculum documents since 1980 across Canada were English, 35.3 per cent were French, 1.5 per cent were in Native languages, and 3.0 per cent were in other languages, including Latin. The overall figures, however, do not accurately portray the strong regional differences that exist. Quebec lists 99.1 per cent French material while Ontario lists only 6.5 per cent French – the same percentage as Native songs. New Brunswick lists only English material.[7] The recommended songs in documents from the provinces not including Quebec include 84.0 per cent English, 9.6 per cent French, 2.1 per cent Native languages, and 4.3 per cent in different languages.

The fourth question considered in this study was: Are there curricular differences in priority related to traditional folk music vs. composed music of Canadian origin? It may not be easy to determine the appropriate balance of composed to folk material. One way of assessing the situation is to compare the balance within the material of Canadian origin to the total list of recommended material. Table 8 presents an analysis of all individual pieces referenced. Folk music constitutes 28 per cent of the total number of pieces. In comparison, Table 7 shows that 40.5 per cent of the Canadian repertoire

Table 6 References to Individual Canadian Choral/Vocal Pieces

Province	English	French	Native	Other
British Columbia	24 (75.0%)	2 (6.3%)	1 (3.1%)	5 (15.6%)
Alberta	5 (100.0%)	0	0	0
Saskatchewan	27 (81.8%)	6 (18.2%)	0	0
Manitoba	45 (78.9%)	6 (10.5%)	1 (1.8%)	5 (8.8%)
Ontario	25 (80.6%)	2 (6.5%)	2 (6.5%)	2 (6.4%)
Quebec	1 (.9%)	112 (99.1%)	0	0
New Brunswick	6 (100.0%)	0	0	0
Nova Scotia	3 (75.0%)	0	1 (25.0%)	0
Prince Edward Island	0	0	0	
Newfoundland	137 (91.9%)	11 (7.4%)	1 (.7%)	0
Totals without Quebec	236 (84.0%)	27 (9.6%)	6 (2.1%)	12 (4.3%)
Totals	237 (60.2%)	139 (35.3%)	6 (1.5%)	12 (3.0%)

Table 7 Individual Canadian Pieces: Folk and Composed

Province	Folk		Composed	
British Columbia	9	(11.3%)	71	(88.7%)
Alberta	0		7	(100.0%)
Saskatchewan	27	(81.8%)	6	(18.2%)
Manitoba	5	(6.0%)	79	(94.0%)
Ontario	13	(21.7%)	47	(78.3%)
Quebec	67	(36.2%)	118	(63.8%)
New Brunswick	4	(66.7%)	2	(33.3%)
Nova Scotia	0		12	(100.0%)
Prince Edward Island	0		0	
Newfoundland	125	(82.8%)	26	(17.2%)
Totals	250	(40.5%)	368	(59.5%)

consists of folk music. Major differences exist among provinces in this balance. Newfoundland, for example, lists 82.8 per cent folk material, including Newfoundland songs, while Manitoba lists only 6.0 per cent. This may in part be explained by the fact that Newfoundland has a long history and a rich heritage of folk material while Manitoba is a 'younger' region with fewer of its own folk-songs. The apparent differences between provinces may also be related to the grade level of the majority of curriculum documents analysed from a particular province. It is significant to note that the Manitoba documents, in which only 6 per cent of the Canadian music was

Table 8 Individual Pieces: Total Folk and Composed

Province	Folk		Composed	
British Columbia	43	(8.8%)	448	(91.2%)
Alberta	0		150	(100.0%)
Saskatchewan	564	(49.9%)	566	(50.1%)
Manitoba	10	(1.2%)	836	(90.7%)
Ontario	72	(29.5%)	172	(70.5%)
Quebec	88	(9.3%)	856	(90.7%)
New Brunswick	216	(44.0%)	275	(56.0%)
Nova Scotia	25	(12.8%)	170	(87.2%)
Prince Edward Island	0		0	
Newfoundland	466	(57.0%)	351	(43.0%)
Totals	1,483	(28.0%)	3,824	(72.0%)

Canadian Music in the School Curriculum 139

folk material, were all high school curricula. In contrast, the Saskatchewan documents, which we analysed as including 81.8 per cent folk material, were for elementary grades. An examination of differences in the overall folk/composed balance by document grade level (Table 9) reveals that Kindergarten to Grade 6 documents include 46.5 per cent folk material whereas high school documents list only 1.1. per cent folk material. A clear pattern seems evident in the figures: there is a decrease in folk material toward the upper grades. When comparing all Canadian material with all other material (Table 9), no pattern of differences by grade level seems evident.

The final question addressed in this study was: What proportion of music curricula in Canada identifies a specific priority for Canadian music with a policy statement, and what effect does this appear to have on references? Table 10 presents a comparison between documents which have a statement regarding Canadian music (40.5 per cent) and documents which do *not* have such a statement (59.5 per cent). Documents with a statement of policy regarding Canadian music have almost 4 per cent more Canadian references than do those documents without such a policy. Documents with a Canadian music policy also have almost 7 per cent more references to folk material. Multicultural policy statements were found in 21.4 per cent of the curriculum documents. A multicultural statement might lead one to expect a greater emphasis on folk material, but this was not evident in the results (Table 10). Those documents with a multicultural statement did, however, include a greater number of Canadian references (almost 5 per cent more). The analysis data seem to indicate that ministries of education which consciously state a policy regarding Canadian music or multicultural music include more Canadian references.

Table 9 Document Grade Level

Grade Level	Number of Documents	Selections (100%)		All References (100%)	
		Folk	Composed	Canadian	Other
K–6	15	1,113 (46.5%)	1,278 (53.5%)	526 (15.2%)	2,940 (53.3%)
7–9	6	294 (42.1%)	405 (57.9%)	264 (23.4%)	862 (76.6%)
Combined Jr & Sr High	6	66 (5.6%)	1,112 (94.4%)	398 (19.3%)	1,666 (80.7%)
10–13	15	11 (1.1%)	1,029 (98.9%)	174 (10.0%)	1,569 (90.0%)

Table 10 Policy Statement

Policy Stated	Number of Documents	Selections (100%)		All References (100%)	
		Folk	Composed	Canadian	Other
Canadian Music Specified	17	849 (31.2%)	1,870 (68.8%)	790 (18.0%)	3,611 (82.0%)
Canadian Music Not Specified	25	635 (24.5%)	1,954 (75.5%)	572 (14.3%)	3,426 (85.7%)
Multicultural Music Specified	9	104 (7.4%)	1,305 (92.6%)	484 (19.6%)	1,989 (80.4%)
Multicultural Not Specified	33	1,375 (35.3%)	2,519 (64.7%)	878 (14.8%)	5,048 (85.2%)

Conclusion

Having addressed our specific research questions regarding Canadian content in provincial music documents, we return now to our initial question: Is Canadian music in the school curriculum an illusion or reality? Our answer, based on the analysis of music curriculum documents, is that the presence of Canadian content in the schools *is* a reality, but that the *amount and type* of Canadian content varies widely from one province to another and from one grade level to another.

But this answer must be qualified, since there is frequently a gap between curriculum as prescription and curriculum as instructional reality. We cannot assume that a province's music curriculum documents actually reflect educational practice in all the schools of that province. Although each ministry of education publishes documents to guide the province's music teachers, it would be naïve to assume that all teachers *follow* the recommendations of the ministry. A more accurate answer to our question would require follow-up studies of the Canadian content of music curriculum documents published by local boards of education in each province, plus detailed case studies of music programs in specific schools. Nevertheless, our current research does provide an initial indication of the extent of Canadian content in music education across the country. In addition, it provides a baseline for further investigation. A comparable analysis of provincial music curriculum documents published during the 1990s would certainly be useful in tracking increases or decreases in Canadian content.

There are obviously many factors to consider when interpreting our findings concerning the Canadian content of provincial music curriculum documents. For example, our findings should be considered in the light of the political situation in the country. Thus the 25.2 per cent overall Canadian content in the Quebec documents may be seen not as a measure of support for Canadian unity but rather as a reflection of the province's emphasis on *Quebec* culture. The fact that 99.1 per cent of the Canadian vocal and choral pieces recommended in Quebec's music curriculum documents have French texts seems a clear indication of the province's concern with preserving the French language. The high proportion of folk material in Newfoundland's documents seems to reflect the province's strong sense of regional identity (82.8 per cent of Newfoundland's recommended individual Canadian selections are folk-songs, with emphasis on the province's folk heritage). The relatively low overall Canadian content in the Manitoba, Saskatchewan, and Alberta documents (9.5 per cent, 7 per cent, and 12.1 per cent respectively) may in part reflect the alienation from central Canada in those provinces. The low proportion of Native music recommended in the provincial curriculum documents seems significant in light of the ongoing problems between Natives and other residents of Canada, and the increasing dissatisfaction of Canada's aboriginal people with their treatment by national and provincial governments. It is simplistic to suggest that adding more Native music to school curricula would solve the problems of Canada's aboriginal people, but at the same time the low representation of Native music in the curriculum documents seems symptomatic of the unwillingness of the dominant culture to respect aboriginal cultures. So too, the lack of Canadian music in languages other than Canada's official English and French seems symptomatic of the marginalization of Canada's growing multicultural population. It may be that a study of the curricula of local boards of education and individual schools would reveal that there is more sensitivity at the local level to the special needs and interests of various ethnocultural groups, and that local documents contain a higher proportion of Canadian content reflecting the non-English and non-French backgrounds of students.

Our study revealed that in only two provinces, Ontario and Quebec, did the Canadian content of the curriculum documents exceed John Adaskin's target of 25 per cent. Much of Canada's cultural activity is centered in those two provinces, and the majority of CMC associate composers live there (47 per cent in Ontario, 22 per cent in Quebec). Canadian content is highest in the documents of Ontario, which has had a Canadian Music Centre office since 1959. Canadian content is next highest in the documents of Quebec, which has had a CMC office since 1973. Canadian content is considerably lower in the documents produced by the western provinces, where CMC offices were established more recently (the Vancouver office in 1977, the Calgary prairie regional office in 1980). The John Adaskin Project, although sponsored by two national organizations, CMC and CMEA, has since its inception in 1961 had its headquarters in Toronto and has been most active in southern Ontario. Contemporary Showcase has also been Toronto-based. It is impossible to demonstrate conclusively that the various promotional projects described in Part One of this essay have born fruit in the Canadian content of the music curriculum documents analysed in Part Two. Nevertheless, we do suggest that those promotional efforts have made a contribution by producing a variety of educational materials and by exerting influence on at least some teachers and music education administrators to include Canadian music in their curricula. And although we cannot establish a clear causal link, we can point to the fact that the proportion of Canadian content is highest in the documents produced in central Canada, where the greatest promotional efforts on behalf of Canadian music have been made over the longest period of time.

It would therefore seem advisable not only to continue national promotional efforts in central Canada but also to increase such efforts in the other provinces and territories. In addition, local initiatives are needed – especially in smaller communities across the country. The seeds of creative and cultural activity are sown by individuals – composers, teachers, and students creating, sharing, and growing wherever they may be. Such individual creativity and growth can be nurtured by national promotional projects and by provincial ministry of education guidelines and curriculum resource books, but ultimately, change is effected by each individual wherever he or she lives, works, listens, performs, and creates. At a time when political, economic, linguistic, and geographic factors are dividing Canadians from one another, the arts can help to bring us together. But as Murray Schafer wrote about John Adaskin's original plan to promote increased Canadian content in music education: 'This is not a one-time job. It is a "forever" piece of work.'[8] Continued efforts are necessary to ensure that in the future, Canadian content in music education will be a classroom reality, not a curricular illusion.

NOTES

1 John Adaskin, 'CMC Has a Story,' *Music across Canada*, vol. 1, no. 1 (Feb. 1963), 10.
2 The MEAs of Nova Scotia, New Brunswick, Ontario, Saskatchewan, and British Columbia have all undertaken commissioning projects.
3 The Performing Rights Organization of Canada (PROCAN) and the Composers,

Authors and Publishers Association of Canada (CAPAC), prior to their amalgamation into the Society of Composers, Authors and Music Publishers of Canada (SOCAN), each produced promotional material.
4 Curriculum documents at times are issued in publications that include all the program guidelines for a certain grade level or even several grade levels. The document then may be designed so that each section is complete in itself as a description of objectives, instructional techniques, and resources for a specific subject area. Such a publication can be described as an omnibus curriculum document. Prince Edward Island's *A Style for Every Child* is an example of an omnibus document. We analysed each of the three music sections of this document as a distinct curriculum, and enumerated each section separately in our analysis.
5 CMERC is a network of music education researchers from across Canada. Established in 1989, it is located at the University of Toronto Faculty of Music. The Music Education Data Project was begun by Lee Bartel and Patricia Shand in 1988 with financial support from the Institute for Canadian Music at the University of Toronto. The music curriculum document content analysis research described in this article is one of the main investigations of the Music Education Data Project, now under the auspices of CMERC.
6 We gratefully acknowledge the contributions made by David Melhorn-Boe, Angela Jones, Esther Leung, Bram Abramson, and students in the undergraduate and graduate classes in music education research during the 1990 fall term.
7 This number must be qualified by the fact that this document was issued for the province's anglophone school boards.
8 'Canadian Music for Education,' *Music across Canada*, vol. 1, no. 4 (May 1963), 12.

BIBLIOGRAPHY

1. Music Curriculum Documents Published by Provincial Ministries and Departments of Education

Alberta Department of Education
Junior High School Curriculum Guide: Choral Music, 1988.
Junior High School Curriculum Guide: General Music, 1988.
Junior High School Curriculum Guide: Instrumental Music, 1988.

British Columbia Ministry of Education
Elementary Fine Arts: Curriculum Guide/Resource Book, 1985.
Secondary Music (8–12): A Guide/Resource Book for Teachers, 1980.

Manitoba Department of Education
High School Choral Repertoire List: Supplement to the Music 105, 205, 305 (Choral) Interim Guide, 1984.
Music 105, 205, 305 (Band) Interim Guide, 1983.
Music 105, 205, 305 (Choral) Interim Guide, 1983.
Music 105, 205, 305 (Guitar) Interim Guide, 1983.
Music 105, 205, 305 (Strings/Orchestra) Interim Guide, 1983.

New Brunswick Department of Education
Music for All: A Curriculum Guide for Elementary Music Education, Grades I–VI, 1984.

Newfoundland Department of Education
Choral Performance 1103, 2103, 3103, 1983.
Choral Performance 1103, 2103, 3103 Appendix D: Evaluation Guidelines, 1984.
Elementary Music: Curriculum and Teaching Guide, 1985.
Games and Movement for Newfoundland Primary Schools: A Supplement to the Primary Music Guide, 1983.
A Guide for Aural Training: The Exploration of Rhythm, Intervals, Melody and Harmony, 1982.
Instrumental Performance 1104, 2104, 3104, 1983.
Intermediate Music: Curriculum and Teaching Guide, 1988.
Music 1200, 1982.
Music 2100: Theory and Aural Training, 1982.
Music History 2101, 1982.
Music History 3101, 1982.
Primary Music: A Teaching Guide, 1983.

Nova Scotia Department of Education
Music 5 to 9, 1980.

Ontario Ministry of Education
Curriculum Guideline – Music – Intermediate and Senior Divisions, 1990.
Music is Special, Children are Special, 1981.
Music, Senior Division: Curriculum Ideas for Teachers, 1983.

Prince Edward Island Department of Education
A Style for Every Child: Program of Studies and Related Information for Schools of PEI, 1986.

Quebec Department of Education
Curriculum Guide – Secondary School Music, 1986.
Elementary School Curriculum: Art (Drama, Visual Art, Dance, Music), 1985.
Elementary School Curriculum Guide: Music, First Cycle, 1985.
Elementary School Curriculum Guide: Music, Second Cycle, 1985.
Guide pédagogique, Primaire: Musique, 1er cycle, 1982.
Guide pédagogique, Primaire: Musique, 2e cycle, 1982.
Guide pédagogique, Secondaire: Musique, 1983.
Programme d'études, Primaire: Art (Art dramatique, arts plastiques, danse, musique), 1981.
Programme d'études, Secondaire: Musique, 1981.
Secondary School Curriculum: Music, 1984.

Saskatchewan Department of Education
Curriculum Guide for Division II, Year 1 (Grade 4), 1981.
Curriculum Guide for Division II, Year 2 (Grade 5), 1981.

2. Other Books and Articles

Adaskin, John. 'CMC Has a Story,' *Music across Canada*, vol. 1, no. 1 (Feb. 1963), 8–10.
Brown, Glen. 'The John Adaskin Project – A History,' *The Recorder*, vol. 29, no. 4 (June 1987), 151–160.
Canadian Music Centre. *Report on the John Adaskin Project Policy Conference.* Toronto, 1968.
'The John Adaskin Project: Towards New Music in Education,' *Canadian Composer*, 23 (Nov. 1967).
Orr, Colleen. 'John Adaskin Project: A History and Evaluation,' unpublished thesis, U of Western Ontario, 1977.
[Schafer, R. Murray], 'Canadian Music for Education,' *Music across Canada*, vol. 1, no. 4 (May 1963), 10–12.
Shand, Patricia. 'The Composer in the Classroom,' *Musicanada*, no. 39 (June 1979), 18–19.
Shand, Patricia. 'In Search of Our Own Music,' *The Canadian Music Educator*, vol. 17 (Winter 1976), 7 ff.
Shand, Patricia. 'The John Adaskin Project (Canadian Music for Schools),' *The Canadian Music Educator*, vol. 27, no. 3 (March 1986), 33–9.

PART FOUR

Comparative Studies: Canada and the United States

MARILYNN J. SMILEY

Across Lake Ontario: Nineteenth-Century Concerts and Connections

Most major studies of nineteenth-century North American music have dealt with the large urban centres. What, however, was happening in the middle-sized cities, towns, and villages which served as regional centres for a predominantly rural America? Were they devoid of culture? Did the people make all their own music, or did they have the opportunity of hearing touring artists? If artists visited, were they the great ones, the mediocre ones, or both? These questions are at the heart of this detailed study of all aspects of music in one town – Oswego, New York – which may help to paint a more accurate picture of musical life in nineteenth-century America.

A glance at a map shows that Oswego is 'just across Lake Ontario' from Kingston and Toronto, and not very far from other major eastern Canadian cities; hence the title of this article. Oswego was on a major transportation route which touring artists used, and its history is probably similar to that of other cities on both sides of the Great Lakes. It is located at a strategic position on the southeastern shore of Lake Ontario, where the Oswego River leads to the interior of the United States. This made it an important military site during the eighteenth century, and a major port for trade and transportation during the nineteenth century, when most travel was done on the waterways. In 1828, the Oswego Canal linked the city to the Erie Canal, and in 1830 the Welland Canal in Buffalo connected Lake Ontario to Lake Erie,[1] giving Oswego access to ports on both of these lakes both in the United States and Canada. Regularly scheduled passenger routes were established shortly afterwards.

Touring artists followed this passageway from New York City or Boston up to Albany and along the Erie Canal and the Great Lakes west to Chicago, and even down the Mississippi to New Orleans. By 1848, the first railroad linked Oswego with other rail lines, many of which paralleled the water routes.² Canada could also be reached by going around the eastern shore of Lake Ontario through the Thousand Islands, and then heading west towards Kingston, or north and east to Montreal and Quebec. Nineteenth-century steamboat and railroad schedules reveal that cities such as Toronto could have been reached by public transportation more easily a century ago than they can be today.

Remarkable similarities exist between the early histories of cities on both sides of the Great Lakes. For example, Oswego and Toronto both originated as fur-trading posts, and then, during the French and Indian War, became British military forts. Neither town attracted many settlers until the 1790s; Oswego was not settled until after Fort Ontario was relinquished by the British, who chose not to leave until 1796, thirteen years after the American Revolution ended![3] During the War of 1812, Fort Ontario in Oswego was attacked by the British and Fort Toronto was raided by the United States.[4] After the conflicts ended, both towns grew rapidly into major ports in their respective countries. Kingston, on the other hand, had a different history since it began as a French stronghold known as Fort Frontenac. In 1756, Montcalm, sailing from there, launched his attack on the British at Fort Ontario, Fort Oswego, and Fort George at Oswego, which he destroyed, and then continued on to victory at Quebec.[5] Other cities along Lake Ontario and the St Lawrence River were similarly affected by the events of the time.

During the eighteenth century, the main link with European music at these British frontier forts was band music. There were fife and drum bands, and later regimental ones, which played for both military (drills, parades, etc.) and recreational (dances, banquets, etc.) purposes. Although records are sketchy, it can be surmised that the functions and repertoire of these bands were similar in all British forts surrounding the Great Lakes, with larger bands stationed at the forts located in garrison towns.[6]

By the mid-nineteenth century, however, things had changed considerably, for it was peacetime, and there were many different types of bands on both sides of the lake. Some were national guard or gunnery bands, others were city bands, while still others were funded by local industries. It was common for bands of different cities to hold contests, and there was a friendly rivalry between Oswego and Kingston.[7] One such contest was held in July 1873 at Alexandria Bay. The Kingston School of Gunnery Band (seventeen pieces) won first place, while the Forty-Eighth (national guard) Band of Oswego (fifteen pieces) placed second, with other contestants coming from Watertown, Adams Center, and Syracuse, all in New York.[8] A more suspicious occasion was the birthday celebration for Queen Victoria in Kingston on 24 May 1899, when the Third Battalion Band from Oswego participated in a grand parade of Canadian and U.S. troops.[9] Throughout the century, it was a popular practice to have bands accompany steamboat excursion groups travelling on Lake Ontario to the Thousand Islands.

Of special interest is the development of concerts by touring artists in these communities along Lake Ontario. Remarkable similarities exist between the musical life of Canada, especially the English-speaking segment, and the United States. Before the visiting artists started to arrive, there were singing-schools and concerts by local performers in churches and schools,[10] which kept interest in music alive and helped prepare residents for an appreciation of touring professional musicians.

Concert artists began to travel west of the Atlantic coastal cities, especially New York City and Boston, as various transportation routes opened for stagecoaches and boats (and later the railroads), and as the population of the villages and towns grew sufficiently for concert halls or rooms to be constructed. The history of concert halls in Oswego may be fairly typical. During the 1830s and 1840s, concerts were held in large rooms found in city government buildings, schools, and hotels, or above business establishments. By 1853, two concert halls were completed, one on each side of the Oswego River, which divided the city. One of these halls was completely remodelled several times and served the community well for many years. Eventually it became unsafe, and a new theatre was constructed in 1895.

Very early in the century, the newspaper advertisements for concerts in Oswego gave reviews from places where the artist had already performed. Some of these included cities in New York State – Albany, Schenectady, Rome, Utica, Syracuse, Rochester, Buffalo, Auburn, Geneva, and New York City – as well as other cities farther away – Boston, Philadelphia, Erie, Detroit, Cleveland, Chicago, St Louis – and even some Canadian ones – Toronto, Kingston, and Montreal. Although most artists came on tours which originated in New York City or Boston, with a few from Philadelphia, a number also came from Canada. The same advance agents and booking companies appear to have served both the United States and Canada. (In this essay, information about Oswego concerts comes mainly from the local newspapers,[11] while that about Canadian concerts comes from several recent books on Canadian music[12] and from remarks in the Oswego newspapers.) At first, concerts were held sporadically, with several performances in close succession, followed by a couple of months with no cultural events at all, but by the 1870s regular concert seasons were established. Nineteenth-century concerts were invariably quite long and included several performers – the featured artist, an accompanist, and other vocalists and/or instrumentalists. A survey of representative concerts reveals that each decade had a distinctive flavour.

Among the earlier touring artists to visit Oswego were the ballad singers. These were English vocalists who had come to North America after the waning of the ballad opera tradition in their native land and the fading of their own vocal powers. Best known is Henry Russell, who, in 1834 or 1835, sailed from England to Canada, where he planned to tour as a vocal soloist. Finding Toronto winters too severe, he migrated south in search of a warmer climate and ended up across Lake Ontario in Rochester, where the winters were just as harsh.[13] After holding positions as organist, choirmaster, and teacher, he made a successful debut in New York City and then toured extensively. He was one of the first major singers to present concerts alone, without an entourage. His Oswego concert was held in 1838.[14]

Several more ballad singers followed in the period up to 1848, some with their wives, which appears to be the earliest evidence of professional women musicians visiting Oswego. According to the Oswego newspaper, Mr and Mrs White, after performing in Oswego in 1842, planned to visit Niagara Falls and then present a concert in Kingston.[15] Other ballad singers, such as John Braham, are also known to have performed in both Oswego and Canada.[16]

Singing families flourished from 1840 to 1865 and were the next category of musicians to visit Oswego. Some groups were actual families, while others were simply troupes of musicians with varying numbers of performers. Best known of the twenty or so families who sang in Oswego were the Bakers, Barkers, Gibsons, Alleghanians, Amphions, and Peaks. Most prominent of all was the Hutchinson family, which consisted of three brothers – John, Judson, and Asa – and their younger sister, Abby. The Hutchinsons gave eight concerts in Oswego from 1848 to 1865: four by the original quartet, one by the three brothers, two later by Asa and his family, and one by John and his family. Of the other families, it is known that the Barker family performed throughout Lower Canada.[17] Another musical family was that of John St Luke, which consisted of himself, a son (a violinist), and a daughter (a vocalist), who presented concerts of art music and appeared in Oswego in 1839. They moved to Saint John, NB, in 1841 and to Halifax in 1842.[18]

By the middle of the century, concert artists with established reputations in Europe and/or America began to appear regularly in Oswego,[19] introducing the cultivated tradition of art music. Since most of them were solo singers, particularly sopranos, the 1850s may indeed be called the decade of the prima donna. This may be partly due to the influence of Jenny Lind, who toured the United States and Canada in 1850 and 1851.[20] Because of her stature as an artist and her fine moral character, it became socially acceptable for a young woman to enter the music profession as a singer. Lind did not perform in Oswego, probably because no concert halls existed there until 1852, though she did appear in neighbouring cities and there was an attempt made to book her to appear in Oswego. She did, however, stop in Oswego on 4 August 1851, on her way from Niagara Falls to Syracuse, when she transferred from a steamer on Lake Ontario to a train bound for Syracuse.[21] Later that year, Lind presented two concerts at St Lawrence Hall in Toronto on 21 and 22 October.[22]

A glance at the listing of concerts in the 1850s provides background on various types of performances at mid-century. The leading singers received top billing, even though they were accompanied by several other artists, both instrumental and vocal. Representative featured singers were Emma Gillingham Bostwick, an American prima donna; Adelaide Phillips, an English contralto; Caroline Richings, the star of a troupe which presented an English translation of Donizetti's *Daughter of the Regiment;* and Anna Vail, one of the 'principal artistes of the Italian Opera Company.' The director of Vail's concert was (Charles) Wugk Sabatier, a pianist, composer, and teacher, of French and German descent, who was educated in France. In 1848 Sabatier settled in Montreal.[23]

Some of the vocalists came with a troupe which featured an instrumentalist. Mademoiselle R.A. Durand was such a singer; she appeared twice in 1854, once with Paul Julien, violinist, and August Gockel, pianist, and again with the Mollenhauer brothers, who were string players. The immortal Adelina Patti appeared with Paul Julien in 1855, when she was only a child of eleven, and Anna de Lagrange, the French coloratura, appeared with Gottschalk in 1856. Patti, Gottschalk, and Mollenhauer also appeared in Canada[24]; as Kallmann explains,

These visits were made easier by the invention of the railway and the steamship, but the chief factor was the country's proximity to the United States, which had long since surpassed Canada in population as well as commercial and cultural development. It is in this period that we can find the roots of the star-worship characteristic of North American audiences. The belief that a foreign artist is necessarily greater than a native one was often justified at that time.[25]

The 1860s showed continued adulation of the prima donna, with numerous concerts by female vocalists. It is often difficult to ascertain whether some of these performances were really concerts or scenes from operas. For example, in 1861 Madame Anna Bishop gave two grand concerts and presented one scene of the last act of Bellini's *La Sonnambula* in opera costume. One of the most popular English singers of her generation, Bishop had been successful in Europe and the United States, and in 1860 began a long tour of the United States and Canada.[26] Other major singers were Charlotte Varian, who performed with her husband, Edward Hoffman, a distinguished pianist; Madame Parepa Rosa, an English soprano of Hungarian parentage who gave a grand concert in 1867; and Emma Albani. Albani, whose real name was Marie Louise Cécile Lajeunesse, was probably the most prominent Canadian artist of the nineteenth century. She visited Oswego in 1864,[27] the same year she took a position as singer at St Joseph's Catholic Church in Albany. Born near Montreal in 1847, she studied with her father and then moved to the United States with her family until enough money could be raised for her to study in Europe. For her 1870 operatic debut in Italy she changed her name to Emma Albani at the suggestion of her vocal teacher. Most of her subsequent career was spent in Europe, though she did return to Montreal to present concerts on three occasions – in 1883, 1887, and 1903.[28]

Some of the great instrumentalists, such as Louis Moreau Gottschalk and Ole Bull, usually included a female vocalist in their troupes. Gottschalk brought Carlotta Patti in 1863, Amalia Patti Strakosch (contralto) in 1864, and Lucy Simons in 1865. Ole Bull in 1868 performed with Miss Barton of Boston, plus Gustavus Hall, baritone, and Egbert Lansing, pianist and accompanist. Even Camilla Urso, a violinist who was the first noted female instrumentalist to present a concert in Oswego, appeared with a soprano, as well as a pianist, cornetist, and bugler in her 1869 concert. Gottschalk, Bull, Urso, and Amalia Patti also visited Canada.[29]

Concerts increased dramatically in number with each passing decade of the nineteenth century. During the 1870s several important events occurred. There were musical conventions in Oswego in 1871, 1872, and 1873, which were modelled after the Boston Peace Jubilees of 1869 and 1872 and were outgrowths of a great interest in choral associations. During these conventions, which lasted about four days, several hundred singers from central and northern New York performed. They were conducted by such notables as John Zundel of Brooklyn and Carl Zerrahn of Boston, who had directed the Boston jubilees. The Mendelssohn Quintette Club of Boston, and other artists such as the famed Madame Rudersdorf, performed on various musical programs throughout the festival. The organizational work was done by local musicians, mainly John G. Parkhurst. A talented Oswego musician,

Parkhurst in 1873–4 was director of William Batchelder Bradbury's oratorio *Esther*, produced by Professor Seager in several U.S. cities. In 1874, Parkhurst directed a production of *Esther* in Toronto, with a chorus of sixty or seventy of the city's best amateurs.[30] The concept of music festivals was also transmitted to Canada. In 1869, Arthur Lavigne[31] and three other Montreal musicians participated in the two peace jubilees in Boston, and by 1883 had organized their own great festival in Quebec.[32]

Other features of the 1870s were a concert by Patrick Gilmore's band of forty pieces, which gave its first performance in Oswego in 1878, and the founding of the Kingsford Band of Oswego the same year by Thomas Kingsford, a local industrialist who owned the largest cornstarch factory in the United States. The Theodore Thomas Orchestra performed for the opening of the Academy of Music, a remodelled concert hall in 1875. The first full orchestra to play in Oswego, it also presented concerts in Canada.[33] Instrumentalists visited in increasing numbers, including Camilla Urso (1875 and 1876), the Mendelssohn Quintette Club, and the Boston Philharmonic Club in return performances. Although female vocalists no longer dominated the concert scene, there were still a few featured singers with their own troupes, namely Emma Abbott, Caroline Richings, and Rosa d'Erina, and nearly all the instrumental ensembles featured a female vocalist. More opera troupes than ever stopped in Oswego and performed works such as Flotow's *Martha*, Balfe's *Bohemian Girl*, and Verdi's *Il Trovatore*, as well as lighter fare, such as Planquette's *Chimes of Normandy*. It was in 1879 that *HMS Pinafore* introduced Oswegonians to Gilbert and Sullivan. The Holman Opera Troupe, consisting of George Holman, his wife Harriet, and their children Sallie, Julia, and Alfred, presented several operas during the 1870s. At that time, the Holmans had recently taken up residency in Toronto (1867–73) and then in London, Ontario (1873–88).[34]

The 1880s may be considered to be the decade of operetta and comic opera, for in Oswego there were at least forty-three visits by various companies, some of which performed for several nights, giving a different opera on each. Much of this activity had been sparked by the Gilbert and Sullivan craze, which continued with productions of *The Pirates of Penzance* in 1880, *Patience* in 1882, *Iolanthe* in 1884, *The Mikado* in 1885 and 1886, and *Yeoman of the Guard* in 1889. *Pirates* was presented by the D'Oyly Carte Opera Co., which later entertained Canadian audiences, who were also experiencing the popularity of Gilbert and Sullivan.[35] Amateur groups in both countries gave their own renditions of these operettas.

Other operas which figured prominently were light ones – *The Beggar Student* and *The Black Hussar* by Millöcker, *Fatinitza* by Suppé. *The Queen's*

Lace Handkerchief by Johann Strauss, and many others. Troupes which performed in Oswego included Stetson's Opera Company, the Bostonians from the Ideal English Opera Company, Mr J.C. Duff's Comic Opera Company, the Oates English Comic Opera Company, and a host of others. Local groups, not to be outdone, gave their own productions of *Chimes of Normandy*, the *Sorcerer*, and other works.

Helmut Kallmann has noted the following connection between Canada and the United States:

Canada benefited from its nearness to the United States, for many troupes would not have come, had it not been easy to extend their U.S. visit to Canada. The majority of the singers were of Italian, French, or English origin, frequently recruited in North America. The troupes ranged from minstrel-show companies with brass bands to genuine opera companies, such as the Strakosch Italian Opera, the Kellogg troupe, or the Hess English Opera Company.[36]

Sopranos still toured, but less often as head of a troupe. Best known were Clara Louise Kellogg, Emma Thursby, and Minnie Hauk. During the 1880s virtuoso instrumentalists took on new importance. Eduard Remenyi, the Hungarian violinist, performed several times in Oswego (1880 and 1882), and also performed frequently in Canada.[37] Other visiting instrumentalists included Donald Levy, trumpeter, William Sherwood and Charles Dennée, pianists, and Maude Morgan, harpist.

The 1890s brought distinct musical changes in Oswego due to the opening of the Richardon Theater, which could seat up to 1400 people. From then on, the character of musical events by touring artists changed, for many productions booked for the Richardson were large, staged events, such as operas, operettas, and other theatrical performances. There were also large musical ensembles, such as Sousa's Band in 1896, which also toured parts of Canada.[38] and Gilmore's Band. The theatre management also offered a classical music series which featured solo, chamber, and orchestral concerts. Instrumental music predominated, with three women's orchestras, several chamber ensembles, and soloists such as Victor Herbert, cellist, Blind Tom, pianist, and violinists Frank Wilczek (an Austrian), Ovide Musin (a Belgian), and François Boucher (a Canadian). Boucher was a member of a musical family from Montreal, and he performed and taught in Ottawa and Toronto before moving to the United States in 1894.[39] The interchange of U.S. and Canadian performers, as well as the sharing of the talents of foreign musicians on tours, proved to be an important influence on the cultural life of both countries.

The strongest nineteenth-century connection between Oswego and Canada, however, appears to be the influx of outstanding French Catholic organists from Montreal into the Oswego churches for a period of nearly forty years. This tradition was established when Dean J. Michael Barry was appointed pastor at St Paul's Catholic Church in Oswego in 1869 and possibly brought Professor George D. Mailloux as organist with him the same year.[40] From that time until 1902, Father Barry hired eight musicians, of whom at least four can be verified as being from Montreal; the other four have French names which indicate possible French-Canadian origins. After 1902, Father Barry hired two renowned Belgian organists, Auguste Weigand (served 1902–4) and Charles Courboin (served 1905–15). See pages 158–61 for a list of organists active in Oswego.

During his forty-five years (1869–1914) at St Paul's, Father Barry was a powerful spiritual force and one of the most influential figures in the community. Besides initiating many civic and moral reforms, he crusaded for good education, beautiful art, and exquisite music. He pursued music as zealously as he did everything else and would accept only the best. Born in 1831 in Ireland and educated in Irish schools, he later moved to Plattsburgh, New York, with his family, and studied for the priesthood at the Grand Séminaire in Montreal. After graduation in 1861, he served at churches in Saratoga and Carthage, New York, before moving to Oswego.[41]

One of his first projects at Oswego was to construct a new St Paul's Church,[42] an impressive edifice which seated 2500 and housed an excellent organ. The main musical contribution of that church was its fine organ music, played by outstanding resident organists (mainly Canadian) and famed guest artists. In 1892–3, the organ was rebuilt by the Detroit firm of Farrand & Votey, with an increased number of stops, an electric action, and an echo organ, and it was reputed to be one of the twelve finest organs in the United States.[43] The inaugural recital was presented on 1 October 1893 by Alexandre Guilmant (1837–1911), one of the world's most eminent organists of that time.[44] Holding the prestigious post as organist at the church of the Trinité in Paris, he had come to the United States that year to play at the Festival Hall of the Chicago World's Fair and to perform in some of the larger cities.[45] His Oswego program was a duplicate of the one given in Chicago, and he expressed amazement that a city the size of Oswego had such a fine organ. After the installation of the organ, St Paul's attracted other nationally and internationally known organists as guest soloists.

Father Barry kept in contact with his alma mater in Montreal and made frequent trips there,[46] which may account for the long line of French-Canadian organists and music directors which he recruited. They not only played

158 Marilynn J. Smiley

for the church services, but also handled other musical responsibilities in the church, participated in numerous community activities as directors or participants in grand concerts, and brought a number of other excellent musicians to the city to present recitals.

The following is a list of organists and music directors at St Paul's during Father Barry's pastorate.[47] Those with an asterisk beside their names are known to be Canadian. Since the names of the others are also French and it is known that Father Barry never hired local organists, it is quite possible that these unidentified ones are also from French Canada. In the Oswego newspapers, all were referred to as 'Professor,' an appellation used for most foreign musicians in the city throughout the nineteenth century.

*1869–?   **Professor George D. Mailloux**

A singer, organist, and teacher in Oswego from 1869 to 1894, he stated he had been organist and teacher at Chambly College and claimed he had been acquainted with Father Barry when he was pursuing theological studies, accompanying him to Carthage and Oswego in 1869. After presiding over the organ at St Paul's until an undetermined date, he played at St Peter's and St John's churches. He also sang in those and other Catholic churches and taught music privately. In 1894, he returned to his native Montreal.[48]

*1873–6   **Professor (Léandre) Arthur Dumouchel**
(B. 1 March 1841, Rigaud, near Montreal; d. 10 January 1919, Albany, NY.)

An organist, teacher, composer, pianist, and choirmaster, he, like his twin brother, Édouard, studied at the Collège Bourget, and with his aunt, Esther Fournier of Rigaud. In September 1866, he made his debut at Carthage, New York, during Father Barry's tenure there, and the same year performed again with his brother and Emma Lajeunesse (later known as Emma Albani). After European study (as a result of which he may have become, in 1872, the first Canadian to receive a doctorate in music) he returned to America in 1872,[49] and became organist at St Paul's in Oswego sometime soon afterwards, in either 1872 or 1873.[50] From 1876 to 1919, he served at the Cathedral of the Immaculate Conception in Albany, and on at least one occasion returned to Oswego to give a recital at St Paul's after the initial improvements of the organ in 1890.[51] According to Kallmann, Dumouchel and Calixa Lavallée (1842–1891) were the first Canadian composers credited with composing symphonies.[52]

1876–80   **Professor J.A. DesRochers**

Little information exists about DesRochers, but by 25 July 1876 he was advertising in the local newspapers that he would give lessons on the organ and piano and would also teach solfeggio. Various documents mention him as organist at St Paul's, one being the program of a grand sacred concert for the fiftieth anniversary of the episcopate of Pope Pius IX on 21 May 1877. It is unknown if he was Canadian, though there are good reasons to believe that he was. First, his name is French; second, he was preceded by French Canadians at St Paul's; and third, on 18 June 1880 he was director of a sacred concert at St Paul's for the benefit of St Louis Church, Oswego's French Catholic church, and the guest organists (Émery Lavigne, then organist at St John's in Oswego, and C.P. Renaud, organist at St John's in Syracuse) were originally from Montreal.[53]

1880–91   **Professor Ernst E. Favreau**

After eleven years as organist at St Paul's, he took a position as orchestra director at the Congregational Church. A highly respected organist, conductor, and teacher, he was best known for his Parlor Orchestra, which played for nearly every reception, commencement, bazaar, and entertainment in the city from the mid-1880s onwards. By 1905, he was engaged to direct the orchestra and teach instrumental music at the Oswego Normal School.[54]

1891–2   **Professor Jas. Lalor**

Succeeding Professor Favreau, he served at St Paul's for only a year, but performed in several benefit concerts. The initial newspaper article announcing his appointment states that he was recently of London and that he was an artist of rare merit.[55]

*1892–6   **Professor Joseph-Daniel Dussault**

(B. 6 January 1864, Charlesbourg, near Quebec City; d. 1 April 1921, Montreal.)

After study in Quebec and in Paris, (1889–91), he became organist at the St Hyacinthe Cathedral in Canada (1891–2) before moving to serve for four years at St Paul's in Oswego.[56] According to the Oswego newspapers, these four years were marked by many concerts, recitals, and a music store partnership with Ernst E. Favreau, in addition to his regular duties. He left in late June 1896, to succeed Alcibiade Béique at Notre Dame Church in Montreal, and held that position until his death.[57] It has been said that he and Birtz laid the foundations for St Paul's musical pre-eminence,[58] even though St Paul's had already established a solid musical tradition nearly thirty years earlier.

*1892–6   **Professor P. Joseph Birtz**

A native of Montreal, he took the position of choirmaster at St Paul's when Dussault became organist.[59] The two of them brought music to new heights and presented many grand concerts. His tenor voice was heard on numerous other occasions during his tenure in Oswego.

1896–1902   **Professor H.C. Racicot**
After becoming organist and director of music at St Paul's in December 1896, he and his wife, a singer, were active participants in the city's musical life. If he was Canadian, he was the last, for Father Barry had not been entirely satisfied with his service, and, while travelling in Europe in 1902, Barry engaged Auguste Weigand, a Belgian virtuoso, who had been municipal organist of Sydney, Australia.[60]

Other Oswego Catholic churches also benefited from the talents of French-Canadian organists, and it is possible that contacts were made through the musicians at St Paul's. St John the Evangelist Church, founded in 1869 with a predominantly Irish congregation, had at least two, and perhaps three, organists from Montreal.

*1878–83   **Professor Émery Lavigne**
(B. 27 January 1859, Montreal; d. 2 July 1902, Montreal.)
Pianist, organist, and teacher, he studied organ with the eminent Canadian musician, Romain-Octave Pelletier. After a brief stay in Paris in 1877, he went to St John's Church in Oswego, New York, in August 1878 at age nineteen.[61] Oswego newspapers recount some of his musical activities during his five years there, but a better account is given in an interview with him printed in an 1890 issue of *Le Canada artistique*. In this article he explained that he taught, directed a philharmonic society, played piano accompaniments at the theatre during some evenings, and played the organ and directed the choir for church services.[62] Finding himself homesick for Montreal, he returned in 1883, demonstrated pianos for awhile, and then served as organist at the Church of the Messiah from 1887 until his death in 1902. Known as an exceptional sight-reader, he accompanied numerous touring musicians and participated in several Montreal musical associations. On at least two occasions he visited Oswego again to present concerts at Trinity Methodist Church (June 1888 and September 1890), and to demonstrate pianos at the county fair.[63]

His two older brothers were pioneers in Canadian musical activities. Arthur Lavigne (1845–1925) was a violinist, publisher, music dealer, and critic who spent most of his career in Quebec City, where he helped organize the orchestra and several large festivals. Ernest Lavigne (1851–1909), composer, businessman, and cornet virtuoso, was instrumental in the organization of bands in Quebec and Montreal, and recruited many young highly trained Belgian and Italian musicians.[64]

1884–6   **Professor A.O. Malard**
   The successor to Lavigne, he may or may not have been Canadian.
*1896–7   **Professor Émiliano Renaud**
(B. 26 June 1875, near Montreal; d. 3 October 1932, Montreal.)
   After studying piano with Dominique Ducharme and holding the post of organist at the Collège de Montréal and Ste-Marie College at age twelve, he took a position in Nova Scotia in 1892. In October 1896, he was appointed organist at St John's Church in Oswego, but returned to Montreal the following May.[65] While in Oswego he presented a series of piano recitals.[66] Next he studied in Vienna and Berlin, and after returning to North America he became such an outstanding piano virtuoso in the United States and Canada that he was referred to as the Canadian Paderewski. The remainder of his life was spent composing nearly two hundred works, performing, and teaching in various conservatories.[67]

   St Louis Church, built in 1871 to serve the French and French-Canadian population of Oswego, did not import Canadian organists, but did have an organ built by the Casavant Frères Organ Company in St-Hyacinthe, Quebec, in 1896.[68] Since the first Casavant organ delivered to the United States was in 1896, to Holyoke, Massachusetts, the one in Oswego was certainly among the earliest.[69] The initial recital was played by Professor Romain-Octave Pelletier (1843–1927), of Montreal, one of Canada's most respected and influential organists, who was then organist of Notre Dame Cathedral of Montreal.[70] At this time he was often asked to inaugurate Casavant organs throughout Canada and the United States.[71] Two of his former students had held posts in Oswego Catholic churches. One was Emery Lavigne, who served at St John's from 1878 to 1883, and the other was Joseph-Daniel Dussault, who was at St Paul's from 1892 to 1896, and who also presided at the organ for a portion of this concert, but who was listed as 'recently of this city.'
   Canadian organists enriched the musical life of Oswego, not only in the churches, but also in the community. Although all churches in the city had music, some excelled only during certain years. St Paul's, however, was consistent in promoting a variety of high-quality musical activities, especially for the organ, throughout the century. The story of these French-Canadian organists deserves more study, for the principal U.S. cities where they held positions were Albany, Oswego, and a few others in upstate New York. These musicians were fine representatives of a strong tradition of organ playing which had originated in Montreal under the leadership of such musicians as Calixa Lavallée, Guillaume Couture (1851–1915), Romain-

Octave Pelletier, and Alexis Contant (1858–1918), all of whom were organists or pianists, teachers, and composers whose compositions stemmed from the Roman Catholic Church service.[72]

Although Canada and the United States have unique musical backgrounds. they also have numerous, interesting connections between communities located 'across Lake Ontario.' Music does indeed transcend national boundaries.

NOTES

1 John C. Churchill, *Landmarks of Oswego County* (Syracuse, NY: D. Mason and Co., 1895), 158.
2 Charles M. Snyder, *Oswego: From Buckskin to Bustles* (Port Washington, NY: Ira J. Friedman, 1968), 113.
3 Ibid., 33.
4 J.M.S. Careless, 'Toronto,' in *The Canadian Encyclopedia* (Edmonton: Hurtig, 1985), 3: 1831.
5 A.A. Kennedy, 'Kingston,' in *The Encyclopedia Americana* (New York, Chicago: Americana Corporation, 1951), 16: 448–9.
6 Helmut Kallmann, 'Historical Background,' in *Aspects of Music in Canada*, ed. Arnold Walter (Toronto: University of Toronto Press, 1969), 35–6. Records of music at Fort Ontario in Oswego are sparse, with only a few references to musical instruments and drills in the eighteenth century while it was under British control. There are accounts of balls during the War of 1812, when it was an American fort, for by this time there were enough settlers to have a village nearby.
7 This was quite a reversal, for in the eighteenth century the French had used Kingston as the base from which to launch attacks on the British at Oswego.
8 *Oswego Daily Palladium*, 25 July 1873.
9 *Oswego Daily Times*, 20, 23, and 25 May 1899. This was the largest body of armed soldiers that ever visited Canada from the United States up to that time.
10 Clifford Ford, *Canada's Music: An Historical Survey* (Agincourt, Ont.: GLC Publishers, 1982), 29, 53–4; Gilbert Chase, *America's Music: From the Pilgrims to the Present*, rev. 3rd ed. (Urbana and Chicago: University of Illinois Press, 1987), 31–4. Information on singing schools in Oswego is available in 'Diary: July 30, 1832–November 1, 1834,' by Joel B. Penfield, now available in Special Collections, Penfield Library, State University of New York at Oswego. Information on local concerts is available in the Oswego newspapers, starting with the first documented concert, held in 1832.
11 *Oswego County Whig., Oswego Daily Palladium, Oswego Daily Times*, and others from 1819 to 1900, with entries too numerous to be listed individually.

Other materials used were scrapbooks, diaries, and other archival documents, as well as published biographies, diaries, and books of the concert artists.
12 Ford, *Canada's Music*; Helmut Kallmann, *A History of Music in Canada 1534–1914* (Toronto: University of Toronto Press, 1960); Timothy J. McGee *The Music of Canada* (New York, London: W.W. Norton, 1985); Arnold Walter, ed. *Aspects of Music in Canada* (Toronto: University of Toronto Press, 1969); Helmut Kallmann, Gilles Potvin, and Kenneth Winters, eds., *Encyclopedia of Music in Canada* (Toronto: University of Toronto Press, 1981), hereafter *EMC*. It would be an impossible task for this writer to examine all nineteenth-century newspapers from Canadian cities.
13 Henry Russell, *Cheer! Boys, Cheer!* (London: John Macqueen, 1895), 50–8.
14 *Oswego County Whig.*, 27 June 1838.
15 *Oswego County Whig.*, 1 and 15 June 1842.
16 Kallmann, 'Historical Background,' *Aspects of Music in Canada*, 46.
17 *Oswego Daily Times*, 9 May 1853.
18 Kallmann, *History of Music in Canada*, 86, 88.
19 By this time transportation routes, including railroads, were open, and Oswego had two concert halls. Canadian cities began to welcome concert artists about the same time. Kallmann, *A History of Music in Canada*, 102–12.
20 Kallmann, *History of Music in Canada*, 102–3.
21 *Oswego Daily Commercial Times*, 4 August 1851.
22 W. Porter Ware and Thaddeus C. Lockard, Jr, *P.T. Barnum Presents Jenny Lind: The American Tour of the Swedish Nightingale* (Baton Rouge: Louisiana State University Press, 1980), 113–14.
23 Kallmann, *History of Music in Canada*, 95–6.
24 Ibid., 102–3, 108.
25 Ibid., 103.
26 Nicholas Temperley, 'Anna Bishop,' in *New Grove Dictionary of Music and Musicians* (London: Macmillan, 1980), 2: 741.
27 Emma Albani, *Forty Years of Song* (London: Mills & Boon, 1911), 23–4. *Oswego Daily Palladium*, 15 September 1864.
28 Ford, *Canada's Music*, 93.
29 Kallmann, *History of Music in Canada*, 108.
30 *Oswego Daily Palladium*, 17 and 30 January and 11 March 1874. *Esther* was presented there four nights for charity under the patronage of Lieutenant-Governor and Mrs Crawford.
31 Arthur was the brother of Emery Lavigne, who served as organist at St John's Catholic Church in Oswego from 1878 to 1883.
32 Kallmann, *History of Music in Canada*, 125.
33 Ibid., 209.

34 McGee, *The Music of Canada*, 68, and Ford, 90–1.
35 Ford, *Canada's Music*, 91, and Kallmann, *History of Music in Canada*, 208.
36 Kallmann, *History of Music in Canada*, 174.
37 McGee, *The Music of Canada*, 70.
38 Kallmann, *History of Music in Canada*, 209.
39 Gilles Potvin, 'François Boucher,' in *EMC*, 102.
40 Since St Paul's nineteenth-century records are lost, the main sources of information are the Oswego newspapers and local history books and materials. It is unclear exactly how long Professor Mailloux served at St Paul's after 1869, but it is known that he remained in Oswego until 1894, and in the interim held positions as organist in other Catholic churches (St Peter's and St John's) and taught music privately. In a newspaper interview of 1894, just prior to his return to Montreal, he stated that he had accompanied Father Barry to Oswego, but in an article the following day, Father Barry denied this. *Oswego Daily Times*, 27 and 28 August 1894.
41 *St. Paul's Church* (South Hackensack, NJ: The Custombook, Ecclesiastical Color Publishers, 1969), 8–13.
42 St Paul's is called the Mother of Churches, because all other Oswego Catholic churches were formed from this parish. The first building was erected between 1830 and 1836 and the second from 1840 to 1844. John M. Hurley, *A Brief History of St. Paul's Roman Catholic Church of Oswego, New York* (Oswego, NY: Palladium Times, 1940), 2–3.
43 *Oswego Daily Palladium*, 2 October 1894, quoted from the Syracuse *Courier*.
44 *Oswego Daily Palladium*, 9, 20, 25, 27, and 29 September and 2 October 1893.
45 *Oswego Daily Palladium*, 9 and 29 September 1893. After that Barry and Guilmant corresponded, and Guilmant returned in 1904.
46 Interview with Miss Frances Barry, great-niece of Father Barry, October 1990 in Oswego.
47 Most information was obtained from the *Oswego Daily Palladium* and the *Oswego Daily Times* from 1869 to 1900, and in many cases there are too many articles about these organists to list each one as a separate source.
48 *Oswego Daily Times*, 27 August 1894.
49 Hélène Plouffe, 'Arthur Dumouchel, in *EMC*, 287.
50 The first newspaper documentation of his arrival in Oswego is the announcement of a series of recitals in June and July 1873 in the *Oswego Daily Times*.
51 *Oswego Daily Times*, 8–10 October 1890.
52 Kallmann, *History of Music in Canada*, 224. Kallmann on p. 133 lists him as one of a first generation of native Canadian musicians, all of whom were born between 1841 and 1851.
53 *Oswego Daily Times*, 17 and 19 June 1880.

54 Dorothy Rogers, *Oswego: Fountainhead of Teacher Education* (New York: Appleton-Century-Crofts, 1961), 128–9. Oswego Normal School, founded in 1861, was the forerunner of the current institution, the State University of New York College at Oswego.
55 *Oswego Daily Times*, 12 August 1891.
56 *Oswego Daily Times*, 27 August 1892.
57 Cécile Huot, 'Joseph-Daniel Dussault,' in *EMC*, 289–90.
58 Hurley, *A Brief History of St. Paul's Roman Catholic Church*, 6.
59 *Oswego Daily Times*, 27 August 1892.
60 Hurley, *A Brief History of St. Paul's Roman Catholic Church*, 6.
61 Gilles Potvin, 'Émery Lavigne,' in *EMC*, 531. He was described in the 19 August 1878 edition of the *Oswego Daily Palladium* as being formerly of St James Church of Montreal.
62 Guillaume Couture, 'Émery Lavigne,' in *Le Canada artistique*, vol. 1, no. 10 (October 1890), 161–3. To get some idea of Lavigne's reputation, it should be noted that Couture, the author of this article, was one of Montreal's foremost musicians.
63 *Oswego Daily Times*, 25 June 1888: 4 and 6 September 1890.
64 Gilles Potvin, 'Arthur Lavigne,' 'Ernest Lavigne,' in *EMC*, 530–1.
65 Gilles Potvin, 'Emiliano Renaud, ' in *EMC*, 804. Although this article states that Renaud served at St Mary's Church in Oswego, all the information in the Oswego newspapers place him at St John's.
66 *Oswego Daily Times*, 3, 8, and 10 April 1897, stated that this talented pianist recently from Montreal would give piano recitals at Normal Hall and then review them.
67 Kallmann, *History of Music in Canada*, 247, lists Renaud as one of three important Montreal composers who began their careers about the turn of the twentieth century.
68 This organ was restored in the 1980s and recognized as an organ 'of exceptional historical merit worthy of preservation' by the Organ Historical Society in 1987. *Oswego Palladium Times*, 1 September 1987.
69 Antoine Bouchard, 'Casavant Frères, Limitée,' in *EMC*, 162–3.
70 *Oswego Daily Times*, 15, 21, and 23 July 1896.
71 Gilles Potvin, 'Romain-Octave Pelletier,' in *EMC*, 734–5.
72 Kallmann, *History of Music in Canada*, 239–46. On p. 133 Kallmann states that from 1841 to 1851 an unprecedented number of musicians were born in Canada. Many became prominent musicians and established reputations in Canada and other countries. Two of those listed are Romain-Octave Pelletier and Arthur Dumouchel.

NICHOLAS TEMPERLEY

Worship Music in English-Speaking North America, 1608–1820

Those of us who study early North American music tend to focus on the large body of music that was printed and published there. We note that after 1770 in the (future) United States and after 1820 in Canada, there was a rapid growth in the printing of music, especially of church music,[1] and that it was numerically dominated for many decades by works published in New England. We concentrate our studies on this music simply because it is there, and in the most convenient form: print. Printed music can generally be dated; it can often be studied in any one of a number of libraries; it tends to exist in a complete and explicit form, while manuscript music may be fragmentary; it generally has a stated purpose that may be lacking in manuscript music, let alone orally transmitted music. Furthermore, one can hope to gain bibliographical control of printed music; one can index it to produce statistics and trace the popularity and varying treatment of individual tunes; and one can ultimately draw general conclusions about it, always qualifying them with the phrase 'in printed sources.'

We have examined this music for a variety of reasons: to study the work of American and Canadian composers, perhaps with a view to reviving their music in performance, and to trace specific tunes to their origins. I admit to all these interests myself. In this paper, however, I am pursuing a different goal.[2] Instead of asking what can be discovered *from* the surviving body of printed music, I want to ask what can be discovered or inferred *about* worship music in English-speaking North America. My question is 'What sort of music was performed in worship?'

In many cases, the answer is not to be found in published collections of sacred music. The great bulk of such music was intended for use in singing schools, not in church; the singing school was, indeed, at the centre of musical culture in New England, where most of the music was published.[3]

Only a relatively small proportion of these published books were clearly for church use.

I propose to approach the question by looking at each of the main Protestant denominations to see where it came from musically: what kinds of music were likely to be favoured by its theology, religious traditions, and social standing. Then, in light of those considerations, I will look at surviving musical sources clearly associated with the worship of that denomination. This is only a preliminary study. Most of the questions I will raise remain just that: questions; some could be answered only after extensive research, others perhaps can never be answered.

Anglican/Episcopal

An Anglican church was founded as early as 1608 in Virginia,[4] and the church was established there by law in 1624, and also in Maryland in 1702, South Carolina in 1706, North Carolina in 1715, Georgia in 1733, and Nova Scotia in 1758.[5] In addition, the Church of England had taken root by the early eighteenth century in the middle colonies of Pennsylvania, New Jersey, Delaware, and New York, where there was relative freedom of religion, and even in the New England colonies, where Congregational or Baptist churches were established by law, and in Quebec after 1763. During the revolutionary period the Church of England naturally tended to be associated with Toryism: a large number of Anglican loyalists migrated north, and the church was established by law in New Brunswick in 1786 and in Upper Canada in 1791. There was also the Protestant Episcopal Church of the United States, established in 1785, for those who remained loyal to the English church but not to the British state.

The Anglican church in the mother country had inherited a divided musical tradition: in cathedrals the liturgy and anthems were chanted and sung by professional choirs with organ; in parish churches there was a spoken liturgy, plus metrical psalms with the fullest accompaniment that resources allowed. In the eighteenth century, the parochial tradition was in turn subdivided between town and country. Urban Anglicans sought to beautify the music, as they beautified the fabric, of their churches.[6] The parish clerk was supposed to lead the congregation in singing metrical psalms, but he was now seldom chosen for his musical abilities and could no longer perform this function adequately. In the absence of an organ, voluntary choirs were formed out of religious societies of young men meeting, ideally, under the guidance of the parish priest. Such Anglican societies were promoted in Maryland by Dr Thomas Bray during his visit of 1700, and there is evidence of their formation in Boston in 1704 and in Philadelphia in 1707.[7] Bray introduced the *New Version of Psalms* (first published 1696) by Nahum Tate and Nicholas Brady, and from that time on this version was associated with reform and progress in church music. In 1713, the vestry of Queen's Chapel, Boston (later King's Chapel), voted 'the psalms of Tate and Brady to be sung in the Church':[8] presumably they had been using the psalms of Sternhold and Hopkins up to that time. In the same year Nicholas Boone, a Boston publisher, brought out an edition of Tate and Brady's *Psalms* 'for the Use of Her Majesty's Chappels in America,'[9] with a 1713 imprint and a supplement of monophonic tunes. We do not know whether vocal harmony was used at this stage. There was certainly a desire for harmony and regularity, but the ideal way to achieve both was by means of an organ.

As it was usually held that an organ could not properly be paid for out of church funds,[10] it had to be presented, bequeathed, or purchased by voluntary subscription. As is well known, the first organ in a Protestant North American church was the one left by Thomas Brattle to the King's Chapel in 1714, after the Brattle Street Congregational Church had turned it down.[11] Anglican churches in other major cities acquired organs in the eighteenth century, for instance Christ Church, Philadelphia, and St Philip, Charleston in 1728; Trinity, Newport, Rhode Island, in 1733; Trinity, New York in 1741; St Paul, Halifax in 1766; and so on. In most cases the organ was acquired by subscription.[12]

The primary function of an organ was to accompany congregational singing of metrical psalms, and we can get some idea of the way this might have been done from various London publications of organ settings, usually with elaborate 'givings-out' of the tune in a highly embellished form and with interludes between lines.[13] As choirs and organists became more ambitious, there is little doubt that anthems and voluntaries were also introduced, with the approval of the clergy. Francis Hopkinson in 1763 brought out *A Collection of Psalm Tunes with a Few Anthems and Hymns, for the Use of the United Churches of Christ Church and St. Peter's Church in Philadelphia*. The music is in three vocal parts, which implies that there was a mixed choir; St Peter's had no organ until the following year.[14] A 1770 vestry minute of St Paul's Church, Halifax, reads:

Voted that whereas, the Anthems Sung by the Clerk and the others in the Gallery, during Divine Service, have not Answered the intention of raising the Devotion of the congregation to the Honour and Glory of [God], in as much as the Major Part of the Congregation do not understand either the Words or the Musick and cannot join therein,

Therefore for the future the clerk have express orders not to Sing any such Anthems ...

Voted that whereas: also the Organist discovers [i.e., reveals] a light mind in the several tunes he plays, called Voluntaries, to the great offence of the Congregation, and tending to disturb, rather than promote true Devotion.

Therefore he be directed for the Future to make a [more appropriate] choice of such his Voluntaries, and that he also for the future be directed to play the Psalm Tunes in a plain Familiar Manner without unnecessary graces.[15]

In 1782 Bela Hubbard, rector of New Haven, wrote to a clergyman in London asking him to procure an organ 'with such a number of stops as will make it proper for excellent church musick from the common Psalm tune to the Anthem – Voluntary &c.'[16]

The typical set-up in English town parish churches in the eighteenth century was to have the psalm tunes led by a choir of children, who learned to sing them at their charity schools. A few times a year there was a special charity sermon in which the preacher enlarged on the virtues of giving, and asked for support for the poor children; on these occasions special hymns or anthems were often sung. This might be called the necessary condition for art music: affluent persons, instead of making their own music, paying to have it provided for them. A few North American cities had choirs of charity children. One was New York, where Trinity and later St Paul's Church had broadsheets printed, headed 'An Hymn to be sung by the charity scholars ... after the charity sermon for the benefit of the school.'[17] The charity school had been established in 1709, and the children appear to have been taught psalmody from 1739, shortly before the organ was installed.[18]

After the revolution some urban churches became ambitious to chant the prose psalms and the liturgy, as in the cathedrals of the mother country. Early evidence of this is found in the chants added to Andrew Law's *Rudiments of Music* in 1783, which Richard Crawford has associated with Law's efforts to establish himself as choirmaster of St Peter's Church, Philadelphia, in that year.[19] The leaders of the Protestant Episcopal Church, most notably William Smith, actively promoted the introduction of chanting. From 1800 to 1820 books were published in Philadelphia, Baltimore, New Haven, New York, and Charleston that contain chants for the psalms, canticles, and other parts of the liturgy, as well as anthems and psalm or hymn tunes with organ accompaniment.[20] Very few of these have any fuging tunes; the tunes are a mixture of old psalm tunes with recent ones of a more elaborately melodious type, some of them adapted from oratorios or secular music. We learn from the preface of Samuel and John Cole's *Sacred Music* that in

Baltimore a Cecilian Society had been formed in 1803 for the practice of church music, combining the choirs of two Episcopal churches, and that the choir of St Paul's had fifteen women and eleven men, that of Christ Church had twelve of each sex.

We must not be misled by these printed sources into imagining that the music in them was typical of the average Anglican church. In rural areas, the absence of financial resources left music entirely in the hands of the parish clerk and people. In the Anglican colonies of the south and in the Maritimes, rural communities were lucky if they had even a parson. Often for years on end the services were conducted by the clerk or another layman. Celebration of communion was impossible and congregations dwindled away. If there was a clergyman, music was the least of his concerns. But there are indications that metrical psalms were sung nonetheless, and that the singing was one of the great magnets attracting Indians to the colonists' churches. Psalms were sung in missions in Virginia from the earliest times.[21] In 1772 a Connecticut clergyman wrote to the Society for Promoting the Gospel in Foreign Parts, acknowledging the receipt of various books, including bibles and prayer books, but declining to distribute fifty copies of Tate and Brady's *Psalms* 'lest these People [that is, the Iroquois Indians], who are more fond of psalm singing than of any other part of Divine Worship ... might be induced to neglect providing themselves with Prayer Books.'[22]

We have to infer that in the absence of printed or even written musical documents, the psalms were sung, as in England, to the traditional psalm tunes (there are twelve or fifteen of them) that were the common heritage of Anglicanism, and that they were sung in the 'old way,' that is, extremely slow drawling with heterophonic embellishments between the notes.[23] It was almost impossible to introduce new music or innovations of any sort. The changes would come only later, with greater affluence and improved urban conditions within the society.

Congregationalists

From the time of the Pilgrims' arrival in 1620, the Congregational churches of New England had sung unaccompanied metrical psalms.[24] Their lack of organs and choirs was due not merely to lack of money but also to disapproval, as when the Brattle Street Church in Boston declined to accept Thomas Brattle's organ in 1713. In 1730 a master's thesis at Harvard College was expounded on the topic 'Do organs excite a devotional spirit in divine worship?' and the conclusion was 'Negative.'[25]

As is well known, the first music printed in English-speaking North

America was the two-voice tune supplement to the ninth edition of the Bay Psalm Book, in 1698.[26] In subsequent editions the tunes were monophonic. I presume that they were sung without harmony, and that these early tunebooks represent an attempt to have the psalms sung more correctly and regularly. Samuel Sewall's diary, among other sources, shows that psalms were lined out and that there was sometimes uncertainty over the tunes.[27] The controversy that arose over regular singing around 1720 has been described many times.[28] It resulted in the formation of voluntary choirs, on the Anglican model, whose primary task was to lead the singing of the congregation. The instruction books of Tufts and Walter show how they were taught, and what they sang: plain tunes in three-part harmony.

In time these choirs developed into semi-independent singing schools, and to keep up their interest they gradually learned new tunes, anthems, set pieces, and fuging tunes, first brought over from England and later printed in America. Undoubtedly, many such choirs wished to introduce this more accomplished music into worship. But they met with stiffer resistance than their Anglican counterparts. Ordinary conservatism was reinforced by theological objections to instruments, and to anything that excluded the congregation from the singing.[29]

There were both progressives and conservatives, of course. Another Harvard thesis, in 1767, asked 'Does the recent reformation in vocal music contribute greatly toward promoting the perfection of divine worship?' (The conclusion was 'Affirmative.')[30] Obviously the compilers of psalmody books tended to encourage choir singing. But Simeon Jocelyn and Amos Doolittle in the preface to *The Chorister's Companion* (1782) said there was 'a danger of erring, by introducing, in public worship, light and trifling airs,' and continued: 'As our principal aim was to serve the interest of social Worship, we were under the necessity of filling our Book, in a great measure, with Psalm-tunes and Hymns, for which reason, we could include but few Anthems.' The book begins with a large collection of plain tunes, and ends with some fuging tunes, elaborate hymns, and anthems, presumably for use in singing schools. Similar views are echoed by Daniel Bayley in his *Essex Harmony & Musical Miscellany* (1785). Collections of plain tunes continued to appear as tune supplements to Watts's *Psalms and Hymns* and Tate and Brady's *Psalms*, such as *The New England Harmony* of 1771. As late as 1816, a book called *David's Harp*, published 'for the use of worshipping assemblies,' contained psalms, mostly Tate and Brady's, and a few hymns, set to plain tunes only.

But by the end of the eighteenth century it would seem that the plain congregational tunes were losing out in settled cities and towns. A collection originally compiled for First Church, Salem, Massachusetts, was published in 1805. Quoting Dr Edward Miller, the organist of Doncaster parish church, England, its anonymous preface asserts that psalm tunes should be simple. It goes on to say:

> It never could have been intended (as might be erroneously inferred from the *general practice* in our own country) that the *choir of singers alone* should perform this part of divine service. Their province originally was ... *to lead the congregation* ... And yet how few societies [i.e., churches][31] do we find, where any but a professed singer is able to follow the choir through the rambling tunes that are now in common use.

This book includes many tunes with elaborately ornate melodies, but no fuging tunes. At the end there are a few set pieces for special occasions. John Hubbard declared that the 'chaos of words' produced by the 'common fuge,' together with the adaptation of secular tunes to religious use, had by 1808 led 'many respectable clergymen in New England ... almost ... to omit music in public worship.'[32]

How did these musical trends relate to the two main movements that affected Congregationalism in the eighteenth century, liberalism and evangelicalism? Both movements diverged from orthodox Calvinism, but on the whole, they were mutually antagonistic. Liberal religion, influenced by the Enlightenment, grew with the spread of wealth and education. It emphasized intellectual rather than emotional aspects of religion and encouraged varying degrees of Arian, Unitarian, or deistic theology. By 1800 all the old Congregational churches in Boston except one had gone over to Unitarianism. The old Puritan distrust of music, especially instrumental music, eventually disappeared along with belief in the concepts of predestination, eternal damnation, and the Holy Ghost, and there was no longer much reason to object to organ, choirs, or bands. Hence Liberal and Unitarian churches relaxed restrictions on worship music; they also promoted rising standards of artistic value, and the imitation of European art music. They were likely to back what has been called the 'reform' of psalmody after the turn of the century. This is clearly true of books specifically designed for Unitarian churches, such as *LXXX Psalm and Hymn Tunes* (1810), designed for the Brattle Street Church (the tunes selected by a church committee), and books that provided tunes for the 1795 book *Sacred Poetry* by the Unitarian Jeremy Belknap (such as Elias Mann's *Northampton Collection* [1797] and Amos Albee's *Norfolk Collection* [1805]).

The Evangelical wing of the Congregational church, known for a time as the 'New Light,' arose from the Great Awakening of the 1740s. The leaders, George Whitefield and Jonathan Edwards, were strict Calvinists, but they now sought to rescue religion from coldness and formality by an infusion of feeling. The hymns of Isaac Watts and his more ardent successors expressed, better than any version of the psalms, the personal emotions put into each singer's mouth. Congregational singing, with simple, inspiring tunes sung with fire and spirit, best suited the mood of the New Lights. Not surprisingly, there is little written record of their music, since organs, choirs, and rehearsals had no place in the scheme. For the same reason, they must have used tunes already known to the people, either the old Congregational psalm tunes or folk-songs and secular tunes. In England there are a number of Methodist tunes of secular origin that were used at outdoor revival meetings and were then printed in hymn books. I do not know of any direct evidence of such in North America from the eighteenth century. But we may infer their existence by the fact that after 1800, when the tunes of the second Great Awakening came to be written down and printed, they proved to be, in many cases, adaptations of Anglo-Celtic folk-songs.

The heights and excesses of the Great Awakening died down before the revolution; by that time, many groups had split off from the Congregational church as 'Separates,' and joined forces with the Baptists. A later offshoot was the awakening in Nova Scotia, begun by Henry Alline at Newport in 1776; but again, little is known of its music.[33]

A few New England collections can be positively identified with Evangelical Congregationalism. Abraham Wood's *Divine Songs* (1789) has texts 'extracted from Mr J. Hart's hymns and set to musick in three and four parts,' but it is choir music, 'suitable to be sung in churches immediately before or after divine worship.' Jonathan Benjamin's *Harmonia Coelestis* (1799) has tunes designed to cater to 'the particular metres, in the Hartford Collection,' that is, the *Hartford Selection* of hymns compiled by the Calvinist-Evangelical Nathan Strong, who was pastor of First Church, Hartford. The tunes are of the elegant Methodist variety described below.

Presbyterians

The Presbyterians clung to congregational metrical psalm singing more tenaciously than the Congregationalists. They, too, were divided by the Great Awakening: the 'New Side' or Evangelical wing was influenced by Whitefield's preaching, and, like the Congregational 'New Lights,' they tended to merge with the Baptists. A major issue here was the introduction of Watts's *Psalms of David Imitated in the Language of the New Testament;* Old-Siders, who were supported by many Scottish and Scots-Irish immigrants, wanted to continue the old Scottish version of 1650 based on the literal paraphrases of Francis Rous, together with the handful of plain tunes that went with it, sung unaccompanied. As John Adams described the psalmody of the Old Presbyterian Society of New York in 1774, it was 'in the *old way,* as we call it – all the drawling, quavering discord in the world.'[34]

The College of New Jersey (now Princeton University), founded in 1747, was strongly New Side in its theology, and progressive in its outlook. James Lyon, the compiler of *Urania* (published in Philadelphia in 1761), was a graduate of Princeton who later became a Presbyterian minister. Several other ministers were subscribers to the book, including the president of the college. This was the first American publication to include elaborate psalm tunes and anthems. It is difficult to associate it with Presbyterian worship of the time. Perhaps it was meant partly for sacred entertainments at the college, while at the same time catering in part to Anglicans (they, too, appear in the list of subscribers). A more likely representative of New Side Presbyterian worship is *Tunes in Three Parts,* published in Philadelphia in 1763 as a supplement to be bound in with Watts's *Psalms.* It has some of the old tunes, and some of the simpler modern ones from *Urania,* one of which it calls 'Lyon.' All are in three-part harmony. Later, Andrew Adgate opened a successful singing school in Philadelphia, the 'Uranian Society,' with the object of improving singing in Presbyterian churches. But its printed productions are quite evidently intended for the society's meetings, not for use in worship. Thus progressive Presbyterians had followed the same route as Congregationalists.

Interestingly enough, Lyon was sent to Nova Scotia in 1764 for a seven-year itinerant ministry.[35] The Presbyterian groups there, and also in Quebec and Upper Canada, were predominantly composed of conservative Scots who had seceded from the Presbyterian Church of Scotland.[36] Musically speaking, they would have rejected the reforms of psalm singing that began in Scotland in the 1760s, and preferred to continue with the old psalm tunes sung in the old way.

Baptists

The Baptist sect also arose in England and in the seventeenth century was engaged in controversy over the propriety of any singing in worship at all. The Particular or Calvinist wing of the Baptist Church eventually accepted both psalm and hymn singing, and in their tradition hymns were chosen for their relevance to the sermon. In America the Baptists had their own colony, Rhode Island, but in the First Church of Providence no singing at all was permitted until 1771. A 'choristers seat' existed there in 1791, occupied by women; in 1807 the singers moved to the gallery, which was enlarged to accommodate them, and a singing school was opened in 1808.[37]

By the mid-eighteenth century the most populous area for Baptists was the mid-Atlantic region, where they had benefited from the religious freedom offered by Pennsylvania and New Jersey. The Philadelphia Baptist Association, founded in 1707, grew to become the central institution of American Baptists. The Great Awakening resulted in a large increase in the number of Baptists, which included many converts from other sects. They gained most of their recruits from the lower socio-economic strata, and they became very active on the frontier.

A unique Baptist publication, *The Customs of Primitive Churches*, appeared in Philadelphia in 1768. It is an anonymous treatise on Baptist practice and polity; its author is known to have been Morgan Edwards, a Welshman who was minister of a Baptist church in Philadelphia. It includes fifteen hymn texts, each set in a particular liturgical or occasional context, and eleven tunes.[38]

Edwards states unequivocally that singing is a part of public worship in which all should join; in this he follows the London Confession of 1689, which was the basic document of Particular Baptists. It is evident that in Baptist meetings a clerk led the singing. By the 1760s, Watts's hymns had become accepted and widely used in Baptist communities, and they account for ten of the fifteen texts in Edwards's collection; the other five have not been traced to any earlier source. The tunes are monophonic, somewhat archaic in notation, and unnamed, but most of them are attributed to composers – generally incorrectly. Of those that had appeared in an earlier printed source, most – six out of eight – come from the 1763 *Tunes in Three Parts* already mentioned, which shows the close ties between New Side Presbyterians and Baptists. The three new tunes are of particular interest. Two of them, found in no other hymnbook, appear to be secular folk-songs, while the third has the sound of a popular theatre tune. Their source has not been found, but they provide evidence, however indirect, that the music of the Great Awakening did indeed borrow popular tunes from secular sources.

Edwards's book is an isolated one, and until further research is done it will not be possible to say much more about the worship music of Baptists in the eighteenth century. By 1800 they had been greatly influenced by the *Selection of Hymns* of the English Baptist minister John Rippon (1786), with its companion volume of tunes in three parts (1792), conceived as a supplement to Watts. Nearly every subsequent American collection for Baptists is heavily dominated by Watts and Rippon. An example is the anonymous *Boston Collection of Sacred and Devotional Hymns* (1808), 'compiled principally with a view to accommodate the Baptist Churches of Boston and its Vicinity.' As with other Baptist books its most important contents are hymns for baptism and communion; they are supplemented by hymns for other specified purposes. The tune supplement, in contrast to the typical singing-school book of the time, is in two-part harmony (air and bass), and has no fuging tunes. This, taken in conjunction with a few other Baptist tunebooks of the time, shows that Baptists at this period used neither organs nor choirs in their worship.

Methodists

Methodism was surprisingly slow to take root in the New World, despite the visits of John Wesley and George Whitefield to the colonies in the 1730s and 1740s. As in England, Methodist societies operated at first within the framework of the Church of England, and therefore had greater success in the southern and mid-Atlantic colonies and Nova Scotia than in New England. The Revolutionary War imposed a check on the growth of Methodism, for Wesley was an outspoken Tory; after the war the Methodist Episcopal Church was established with Wesley's blessing, and it quickly grew, especially in the second Great Awakening, beginning in 1800. The Methodists were the first organizers of camp meetings, and so were well suited to the religious needs of the expanding frontier. Methodism in the Maritimes and in Upper and Lower Canada in the 1790s was an offshoot of the American church, and only later returned to the English fold. In 1798 there were only 850 members of Methodist societies in what is now Canada. The first camp meeting recorded in Upper Canada took place in 1805.[39]

John Wesley, despite his authoritarian and, in some ways, aristocratic direction of his movement, was uncompromisingly committed to the spiritual needs of the individual believer, regardless of social level, and therefore his movement appealed strongly to lower-class people, including many who belonged to dissenting churches or to no church at all. Wesleyan hymn texts express strong personal feeling, and the tunes Wesley introduced came from a variety of sources – Anglican psalms, Moravian hymns, theatre tunes, folk-songs. Thus Methodist music was often quite close to contemporary art music. But the hymns were all designed to be sung heartily and meaningfully by every member of the congregation. For this reason Wesley set himself firmly against 'complex tunes which it is scarce possible to sing with devotion,' and maintained that 'repeating the same word so often (but especially while another repeats different words, the horrid abuse which runs through the modern Church musick), as it shocks all common sense, so it necessarily brings in dead formality, and has no more religion in it than a Lancashire hornpipe.'[40] Thus fuging tunes were outlawed. But repeating tunes, where a single phrase like 'Alleluia' or 'Remember me' was sung two or three times for meaningful emphasis, were allowed, and indeed became characteristic of Methodist music.

These precepts were evidently followed by American Methodists in the early years. The Baltimore conference of the Methodist Episcopal Church in 1784 noted, 'We do not think that fuge-tunes are sinful, or improper to be used in private companies: but do not approve of their being used in our public congregations.'[41] 'Private companies' might well include singing schools. But the first North American book specifically for use in Methodist worship, Part the Second of John Cole's *Sacred Harmony* (Baltimore, 1799), contained no fuging tunes, but only three-part tunes of the type found in English Methodist circles by the likes of Martin Madan and James Leach, which are also prominent in several later American Methodist tunebooks.

These have elegant melodies, harmonized mostly in parallel thirds with cadences of the galant type. They are like the popular theatre or parlour music of the previous generation. Thus they would have caught on well with the British public. But Methodist leaders in North American may well have found that tunes of this type had limited appeal in the rural camp meeting, and so instead they used tunes already known to their flock, generally Anglo-Celtic folk-songs. The principle was the same as Wesley's, but the musical idiom was different. Although folk hymns, properly speaking, do not appear in printed books until after 1800, they may have been used long before.

Stephen Humbert's *Union Harmony*, as I have mentioned, was primarily for singing-school use. But Humbert was a Methodist, and the second and earliest surviving edition of his book, published at Saint John, New Brunswick, in 1816, does contain a group of English Methodist-type tunes of the Madan/Leach variety, taken, as I have shown elsewhere, from a specific English printed source.[42] These may well have been used in worship at the Methodist church in Saint John of which Humbert was a leading member.

Other Denominations

For the sake of completeness I will add a few words about the music of other English-speaking denominations. The Moravians, Mennonites, Dunkers, and German Reformed churches were still on the whole using the German language, as were many Lutheran groups. When in 1756 a volume of Lutheran hymns in English was first published in New York,[43] it was designed to be sung with the traditional German melodies, which were also used by Jacob Eckhard in the Lutheran church at Charleston, South Carolina.[44] Thus the full Germanic tradition could be continued, with organ and choir where available.

The Dutch Reformed Church also kept its music intact when it had Tate and Brady's *Psalms* adapted to fit the Franco-Dutch metrical psalm tunes, a task carried out by Francis Hopkinson in 1767. These English texts were used again in 1774, when some of the tunes were reprinted in Claude Goudimel's four-part settings. Two post-1800 collections for the Dutch church add other psalm versions and some hymns, and a good many 'Anglo' tunes, but unlike most American books they are always arranged with the tune in the top voice.

John Aitken, in 1787, compiled the first Roman Catholic music book printed in English-speaking America. Along with Latin liturgical music it includes a few English-language hymns. Another publication providing English hymns for Catholic use was Benjamin Carr's *Masses, Vespers...*, published about 1805, which specifically mentions the churches of St Augustine and St Mary in Baltimore. Despite the general custom in the Catholic church of using only Latin in worship, these English pieces may have been sung by choirs in place of Latin office hymns. Such a practice was sanctioned in 1791 by the first Catholic synod in the United States, presided over by John Carroll, first Bishop of Baltimore, in these words (after mentioning the antiphons of the Virgin): 'It is desirable during the Office that some hymns or prayers be sung in the vernacular tongue.' The synod also allowed that in smaller parishes where there was a single priest, vernacular hymns might be substituted for the recitation of the Litany if those attending wished to do so.[45] However, the same decree warned priests not to admit music in a popular idiom (*carmina vernaculo idiomate*), and the concession to the vernacular was revoked altogether in 1837.

For music in worship, each denomination tended to continue the traditions brought from Europe, with more or less modification to suit the conditions prevailing in North America. Most of the sacred music published was probably not used very much in worship services. It was intended primarily for singing schools, and was often unwelcome in church.

The basic style for worship music in country churches was probably much the same across Protestant denominations: well-known, traditional psalm or hymn tunes sung congregationally in the 'old way.' On the frontier and in revival meetings, the tunes of popular entertainment and rural folk-songs were adapted to new texts. Though there is little direct evidence, it is quite probable that this practice was already in place during the first Great Awakening in the American colonies, and in the Nova Scotia revivals of the last three decades of the eighteenth century.

Even in more settled communities it seems that worship music was still restricted in the main to the simpler, homophonic tunes, and was typically sung in two- or three-part harmony led by a choir, but without accompaniment. Anthems and set-pieces were used on special occasions, or as a 'sacred entertainment' after service. After 1800 a few affluent urban churches saw further developments: Unitarians and some others joined Episcopalians in the use of organs or instrumental bands, and some Episcopal churches introduced chanting and liturgical music. More exact conclusions must await further research in such sources as church records, local newspapers, and personal letters and diaries.

APPENDIX

Printed collections of music, in the order referred to in the essay

Anglican/Episcopal
A New Version of the Psalms of David by Dr. Brady and Mr. Tate ...London: Printed in the Year 1704. Boston, 1713.
[Francis Hopkinson]. *A Collection of Psalm Tunes with a Few Anthems and Hymns ... For the Use of the United Churches of Christ Church and St. Peter's Church in Philadelphia.* [Philadelphia], 1763.
Andrew Law. *The Rudiments of Music.* [Cheshire], 1783.
Samuel and John Cole. *Sacred Music Published for the Use of the Cecilian Society. Established under the Patronage of the Clergy and Vestry of St. Paul's Church, Baltimore.* Baltimore, 1803.
Israel Terrill. *The Episcopal Harmony.* New Haven, [1803?].
John Cole. *The Beauties of Psalmody.* 2nd ed., Baltimore, 1805.
John Aitken. *Aitken's Collection of Divine Music.* Philadelphia, 1806.
Peter Erben. *Sacred Music ... [for] the Protestant Episcopal Church.* [New York], 1808.
Benjamin Carr. *A Collection of Chants and Tunes for the Use of Episcopal Churches.* Philadelphia, 1816.
Jacob Eckhard. *Choral-Book ... Used in the Episcopal Churches of Charleston, South Carolina.* Charleston, [1816].

Congregational
The Psalms, Hymns and Spiritual Songs, of the Old & New-Testament: Faithfully Translated into English Meetre. 9th ed. Boston, 1698. [Pt. 2:] *The Tunes of the Psalms.*
Thomas Walter. *The Grounds and Rules of Musick Explained.* Boston, 1721.
[John] Tufts. *An Introduction to the Art of Singing Psalm-Tunes.* 3rd ed. Boston, 1723.
[Simeon Jocelin and Amos Doolittle.] *The Chorister's Companion.* New Haven, 1782.
Daniel Bayley. *The Essex Harmony, or Musical Miscellany.* Newburyport (Massachusetts), 1785.
The New-England Harmony. Boston. 1771.
David's Harp: Being a Choice Collection of the Songs of Zion for the Use of Worshipping Assemblies. New London (Connecticut), 1816.
The Salem Collection of Classical Sacred Musick. Salem (Massachusetts), 1805.
[Bryant P. Tilden et al.] *LXXX Psalm and Hymn Tunes.* Boston, 1810.
Elias Mann. *The Northampton Collection of Sacred Harmony.* Northampton (Massachusetts), 1797.
Amos Albee. *The Norfolk Collection of Sacred Harmony.* Dedham (Massachusetts), 1805.
Abraham Wood. *Divine Songs.* Boston, 1789.
Jonathan Benjamin. *Harmonia Coelestis.* Northampton (Massachusetts), 1799.

Presbyterian
James Lyon. *Urania.* Philadelphia, 1761. (Reprinted 1974 with a preface by Richard Crawford.)
Tunes in Three Parts for the Several Metres in Dr. Watts's Version of the Psalms. Philadelphia, 1763.
[Andrew Adgate?] *Introductory Lessons, Practised by the Uranian Society ... Philadelphia.* [Philadelphia], 1785.
Andrew Adgate. *Philadelphia Harmony.* Philadelphia, 1789.

Baptist
[Morgan Edwards.] *Customs of Primitive Churches.* [Philadelphia, 1768?].
John Rippon. *A Selection of Psalm and Hymn Tunes.* [London, c.1792].
The Boston Collection of Sacred & Devotional Hymns: Intended to Accommodate Christians on Special and Stated Occasions. Boston, 1808.

Methodist
John Cole. *Sacred Harmony. Part the Second, Containing Tunes in Three Parts, Adapted to All the Peculiar Metres in the Methodist Pocket Hymn Book.* Baltimore, 1799.

Stephen Humbert. *Union Harmony: or British America's Sacred Vocal Music.*
2nd ed. Saint John (New Brunswick), 1816.

Dutch Reformed Church
[Francis Hopkinson, arr.] *The Psalms of David ... for the Use of the Reformed Protestant Dutch Church.* New York, 1767.
A Collection of the Psalm and Hymn Tunes, Used by the Reformed Protestant Dutch Church. New York, 1774.
Peter Erben. *A Selection of Psalm and Hymn Tunes, for the Use of the Dutch Reformed Church.* New York, 1806.
F.D. Allen. *The New-York Selection of Sacred Music.* 4th ed. [New York], 1820.

Roman Catholic Church
John Aitken. *A Compilation of the Litanies Vespers Hymns and Anthems.* Philadelphia, 1787.
Benjamin Carr. *Masses, Vespers, Litanies, Hymns, Psalms, Anthems & Motets.* [Baltimore, c.1805].

NOTES

1 See Allen P. Britton, Irving Lowens, and Richard Crawford, *American Sacred Imprints 1698–1810: A Bibliography* (Worcester, Mass. 1990); Barclay McMillan, 'Tune-Book Imprints in Canada to 1867: A Descriptive Bibliography,' *Papers of the Bibliographical Society of Canada* 16 (1977), 31–57.
2 A preliminary version of this paper was delivered at Toronto on 21 April 1990, to a joint meeting of the Sonneck Society, the College Music Society, and L'Association pour l'avancement de la recherche en musique du Québec.
3 See, for instance, H. Wiley Hitchcock, *Music in the United States: A Historical Introduction,* 3rd ed. (Englewood Cliffs 1988), 7–9; Karl Kroeger, 'Introduction,' *The Complete Works of William Billings,* vol. 1 ([Charlottesville] 1981), xv. I have argued elsewhere that the one English-speaking Canadian collection of sacred music published before 1820 was also primarily designed for singing-school use: see Nicholas Temperley, 'Stephen Humbert's *Union Harmony,* 1816,' in *Sing Out the Glad News: Hymn Tunes in Canada,* ed. John Beckwith, CanMus Documents, 1 (Toronto 1987), 57–89, especially 74–7.
4 William S. Perry, *The History of the American Episcopal Church,* 2 vols. (Boston 1885), 1, 48.
5 Except where otherwise stated, most of the factual information about the histories of the various denominations is taken from Robert T. Handy, *A*

History of the Churches in the United States and Canada (Oxford 1976; New York 1977).

6 For detailed discussion see Nicholas Temperley, *The Music of the English Parish Church*, 2 vols. (Cambridge 1979), vol. 1, 100–38.
7 See Nicholas Temperley, 'The Old Way of Singing: Its Origins and Development,' *Journal of the American Musicological Society* 34 (1981), 511–44, especially 538–9.
8 Henry W. Foote, *Annals of King's Chapel*, 2 vols. (Boston 1882), vol. 1, 204.
9 *Boston Weekly News Letter*, 13–20 April 1713. I am grateful to Barbara Lambert for drawing my attention to this advertisement, and also to one by James Ivers, who offered to teach 'singing psalm tunes' at his boarding school in Cambridge Street, Boston (*Boston Weekly News Letter*, 12–19 April 1714).
10 For English legal decisions on the point see Temperley, *Parish Church*, vol. 1, 106–7.
11 Foote, *Annals of King's Chapel*, vol. 1, 209.
12 The organ at Halifax was paid for by subscription, despite a story found in several older histories that it was seized from a Spanish ship. See Timothy McGee, 'Music in Halifax, 1749–1799,' *Dalhousie Review* (1969), 377-87.
13 See Temperley, *Parish Church*, vol. 1, 129–30; Nicholas Temperley, 'Organ Music in Parish Churches, 1660–1730,' *Journal of the British Institute of Organ Studies* 5 (1981), 33–45.
14 C.P.B. Jefferys, 'Music and Singing at St. Peter's, 1761–1783' ('The Provincial and Revolutionary History of St. Peter's Church, Philadelphia, 1753–1783,' vol. 10), *The Pennsylvania Magazine of History and Biography* 18 (1924), 181–6.
15 McGee, 'Music in Halifax,' 379–80, citing 'St. Paul's Church Records, vol. 1.'
16 Kenneth Walter Cameron, ed., *The Church of England in Pre-Revolutionary Connecticut* (Hartford 1976), 276.
17 A number of these have survived, the earliest dated 1775. In some cases the music and the composer can be identified from the text.
18 Arthur H. Messiter, *A History of the Choir and Music of Trinity Church, New York from its Organization, to the Year 1897* (New York 1906, rprt. 1970), 17–23.
19 Richard A. Crawford, *Andrew Law, American Psalmodist* (Evanston 1968), 37.
20 See the Appendix for a list of these books. For a discussion of the introduction of chanting in America, see Ruth Mack Wilson, 'Anglican Chant and Chanting in England and America, 1600–1811,' PhD dissertation, University of Illinois, 1988.
21 Perry, *History*, vol. 1, 48.
22 Cameron, *Church of England*, 181.

23 For a description see Temperley, 'Old Way.'
24 For details see Nicholas Temperley, 'Psalms, Metrical: V. North America,' in *The New Grove Dictionary of Music and Musicians*, ed. Stanley Sadie (London 1980), vol. 15, 376–82.
25 Foote, *Annals of King's Chapel*, vol. 1, 210.
26 It has tunes and basses, but it is doubtful if the printer realized he was dealing with music in two parts, because in two places he printed the tune on the last stave of a page and the bass on the top of the next page! Subsequent editions until 1737 printed the tunes without basses. For the music of the ninth edition see Richard G. Appel, ed., *The Music of the Bay Psalm Book 9th ed.* (1698), Institute for Studies in American Music, Monographs, 5 (Brooklyn 1975).
27 For a full discussion see David W. Music, 'The Diary of Samuel Sewall and Congregational Singing in Early New England,' *The Hymn* 41 (1990), 7–15.
28 See, for instance, Allen P. Britton, *Theoretical Introductions in American Tunebooks to 1800* (Ann Arbor 1949); Gilbert Chase, *America's Music from the Pilgrims to the Present*, 3rd ed. (Urbana and Chicago 1987), 19–37.
29 The first organ heard in an American Congregational church was played in First Congregational Church of Providence, Rhode Island, in 1770, according to the diary of Ezra Stiles, but it seems to have fallen into disuse soon after; see Joyce E. Mangler, 'Early Music in Rhode Island Churches. I. Music in the First Congregational Church, Providence, 1770–1850,' *Rhode Island History* 17 (1958), 1–9.
30 Foote, *Annals of King's Chapel*, vol. 1, 210.
31 A frequent problem in judging the designed use of tune collections in this period is that the word 'society' could mean either a singing society or a worshipping community in the sense now generally designated as a 'church.' The context usually, but not always, distinguishes the two meanings. For further evidence of performance practice in American psalmody of the later eighteenth century see Karl Kroeger, ed., *The Complete Works of William Billings*, vol. 4 (Boston 1990), Introduction.
32 John Hubbard, *An Essay on Music* (Boston 1808), 17–19.
33 Maurice W. Armstrong, *The Great Awakening in Nova Scotia* (Hartford 1948).
34 John Adams, *Works*, 6 vols. (Boston 1850), vol. 2, 348.
35 See Timothy J. McGee, 'Lyon, James,' in *Dictionary of Canadian Biography* 4 (Toronto 1979), 490.
36 Handy, *History of the Churches*, 230–2.
37 William Dinneen, *Music at the Meeting House 1775–1958* (Providence 1958), 1–3.
38 Discussed by Margo Chaney in an unpublished paper, 'Morgan Edwards' *Customs of Primitive Churches*: A Clue to Baptist Hymnody of the 1760s.'

39 Arthur E. Kewley, 'The Beginning of the Camp Meeting Movement in Upper Canada,' *Canadian Journal of Theology* 10 (1964), 192–202.
40 James T. Lightwood, *Methodist Music of the Eighteenth Century* (London 1927), 35–6.
41 *The Doctrines and Discipline of the Methodist Episcopal Church*, 8th ed. (Philadelphia 1792), cited in Robert Stevenson, *Protestant Church Music in America: A Short Survey of Men and Movements from 1564 to the Present* (New York 1966), 69–70.
42 Temperley, 'Stephen Humbert's *Union Harmony*,' 80–1.
43 John Christian Jacobi, *Psalmodia Germanica* ... 3rd ed. London, printed: New York, reprinted ... 1756. See also Louis F. Benson, *The English Hymn: Its Development in Use and Worship* (London 1915), 411.
44 George W. Williams, ed., *Jacob Eckhard's Choirmaster's Book of 1809* (Columbia South Carolina 1971).
45 'Optandum est ut inter officia hymni aliqui aut preces linguâ vernaculâ cantentur ... Ubi verò unicus est Sacerdos qui solus omnia peragat ... recitet primò, nisi assistentes cantare velint linguâ vernaculâ, Litanias vel SS. nominis Jesu, vel Lauretanas ...' Statuta synodo Baltimorensis anno 1791 celebratæ, sessio V, die 10 Novembris: *Concilia provincialia, Baltimori habita ab anno 1829 usque ad annum 1849* (editio altera, Baltimore, 1851), 19–20. I am grateful to Ann Silverberg for drawing attention to this decree. See also Peter Guilday, *A History of the Councils of Baltimore 1791–1884* (New York 1932), 64–5.

ELAINE KEILLOR

Indigenous Music as a Compositional Source: Parallels and Contrasts in Canadian and American Music[1]

Settlers on both sides of the Canadian-American border found the indigenous music of the First Nations (Amerindians and Inuit) so far removed from their concept of music that it was only noise to their ears. Anna Jameson's *Winter Studies and Summer Rambles in Canada*, published in 1838, described the music of an Amerindian group in present-day southwestern Ontario as follows:

The orchestra was composed of two drums and two rattles, and a chorus of voices. The song was without melody – a perpetual repetition of three or four notes, melancholy, harsh and monotonous. (144)

This was a typical reaction of North American travellers and settlers, so it is not surprising that few composers have turned to these musics as inspirational sources. Nevertheless, when the question of establishing a music that was truly American or Canadian arose, an obvious way of doing it was to be part of the 'Red Indian School,' as John Powell labelled it in his 'Lectures on Music' in 1923 (Hamm 1983: 421). The Canadian composer Ernest Gagnon wrote in a letter to the ethnologist Marius Barbeau in 1911:

It has always been my belief that the 'discovery' of our roots would help establish a sense of national identity. With particular reference to music, I intended my work on our folksongs and the music of our native Indians to lay a foundation for a musical language based on these repertoires. Perhaps you will continue to encourage Canadian composers to seek out these sources in their musical works. (Smith 1989: 32)

In this essay I will briefly outline the history of this movement on both sides of the Great Divide, highlighting publications and individuals that seem to be crucial to its development and then underline what seems to me to be parallels and contrasts in its American and Canadian manifestations. The American historical overview will precede the Canadian one, while a more detailed examination of various usages of indigenous music in actual compositions will follow.

Historical Overview of American Compositions and Influences

Although references to Amerindian topics occur in American musical theatre and single pieces from the late eighteenth century – for example, James Hewitt's *Tammany* (1794) and John Bray's *The Indian Princess* (1808) – the composers do not appear to have made any attempt to use actual Amerindian melodies in their music. Hans Gram's *The Death Song of an Indian Chief* (1791) has a tune with a descending contour to open, but little else to even suggest that he might have been trying to use an Amerindian model (Marrocco/Gleason 1964: 225). Thus all of these works written by European-born emigrants to America appear to be using the Amerindian theme as exoticism in a fashion similar to that of European composers such as Louis Emmanuel Jadin (1768–1853), who wrote, in 1797, an opera called *Candos ou les sauvages du Canada*.

Hitchcock suggests that the *Symphony The Pioneer* ('Arcadian'), Op. 49 (1874), by George Frederick Bristow (1825–1898) may have the first quotation of an Amerindian tune in an American art-music composition (1988: 96). Bristow's biographer has not confirmed this (Rogers 1967: 180). In 1856 a columnist in the *Criterion* called attention to the American composer, Anthony Philip Heinrich, by writing:

Father Heinrich passed several years of his life among the Indians that once inhabited Kentucky, and many of his compositions refer to these aboriginal companions. He is a species of musical Catlin, painting his dusky friends on the music staff instead of the canvas, and composing laments, symphonies, dirges, and war-songs, on the most intensely Indian subjects. He would be the very one to set Hiawatha to music. (Maust 1981: 309)

In spite of this contemporary of his deliberately calling attention to Heinrich's use of actual Amerindian music, and the fact that eight of his orchestral works completed between 1831 and 1859 clearly denote inspiration from Native material in their titles, little evidence can be found of indigenous sounds in these compositions. An authority on Heinrich's symphonic works, Wilber Maust, specifies the sixth section of *Der Felsen von Plymouth*, entitled *'Baletto indico nazionale: Freudentanze der Squaws nach erhaltenen Geschenken'* (1859), as being the closest 'he comes to the employment of native Indian music' (Maust 1981: 315). In this section there is the use of a harmonic minor scale with the first, third, fourth, and fifth degrees emphasized plus occasional use of the second and sixth degrees, while an ostinato-like rhythm is reinforced by a static and repetitive type of orchestration. In fact, Maust discovered that the actual melodic material used in this section came from two earlier orchestral works, namely *The Columbiad, Grand American National Chivalrous Symphony* (1837) and *The Jubilee, A Grand National Song of Triumph* (1841). Heinrich made no references to an Amerindian theme in the titles of these earlier orchestral works. That makes the likelihood of Native influences in the melodies negligible.

Maust concludes that Heinrich's treatment of the Amerindian is in the mould of the romanticized 'Noble Savage' to be found in American literature of this era. Apart from that widespread approach to Native Americans in the nineteenth century, Heinrich and other composers probably were not using actual Amerindian melodic material. They had little contact with the traditional music, and even if they had a chance to hear it, there were the additional problems of trying to transcribe what Mrs Jameson called 'song without melody' into Western notation. This situation quickly began to change towards the end of the century.

The first serious study of North American Indian music was Theodore Baker's *Über die Musik der nordamerikanischen Wilden*, a doctoral thesis at the University of Leipzig in 1882.[2] Edward MacDowell has been credited with truly initiating the movement in the United States to use indigenous material as a compositional source. In 1887 he had sketched plans for a symphonic poem called *Hiawatha and Minnehaha* (Lowens 1971: 55). Four years later Henry Gilbert provided MacDowell with a copy of Baker's thesis, from which he took melodies to use in the orchestral *Indian Suite* (1891–5) and the later piano pieces, *From an Indian Lodge* op. 51, no. 5 (1896), *Midwinter* op. 62, no. 1, and *Indian Idyl* (1901). States Lowens, 'To MacDowell, the way toward establishing an American music lay not in any common body of American musical resources but in each composer's personal expression of individuality through his music' (1971: 102). In an interview published in the *San Francisco Chronicle*, 3 January 1907, MacDowell is quoted as saying:

Of all my music the dirge in the 'Indian Suite' pleases me most ... The 'Indian Suite' is the result of my studies of the Indians, their dances and their songs. (Lowens 1971: 278)

The 'dirge' motive taken from Baker XXIII, 'Kiowa Song of a Mother to Her Absent Son,' was particularly appealing to MacDowell. A recent article by Francis Brancaleone documents the use of that material in three of the piano sonatas, and in some compositions in the *Sea Pieces*, op. 55, *Fireside Tales*, op. 61, and the *New England Sketches* (Brancaleone 1989: 360–1). Obviously MacDowell took a keen academic interest in Amerindian music through available printed collections, but it is questionable whether he actually had heard any Native traditional music. Hamlin Garland reported that he found MacDowell in 1894 perusing Alice C. Fletcher's *A Study of Omaha Indian Music*, published the previous year. Apparently MacDowell asked Garland for his opinion on the transcriptions. To back up his reply that the songs had been 'robbed of their stone-age tones and rhythm' in the transcriptions, Garland proceeded to sing a song as he had heard it in his travels. Garland's report of MacDowell's response to this rendition was that 'you make these things of mine [compositions based on Native material] seem like milk and water' (Garland 1930: 46).

Possibly this was the only opportunity that MacDowell had to actually hear any Amerindian traditional music, even if it was not sung by a Native. For composers, that situation changed in the 1890s. J. Walter Fewkes recorded Passamaquoddy music in 1890 and soon there was a spate of recordings and publications to feed the 'Indianist' movement in American music. Most notable among these were the efforts of Frances Densmore, Alice Fletcher, and Edward S. Curtis, who began publishing the series of twenty volumes of *The North American Indian* in 1907. The transcriptions of Amerindian melodies for volumes 6, 7, and 8 in this series were done by Henry F. Gilbert. In volume 6, Gilbert included an appendix that not only relays his great difficulties in trying to transcribe Amerindian melodies into 'our ordinary musical notation' but is also revealing in its ethnocentric approach to this music.

It is more than likely that the Indian is somewhat blindly groping for the diatonic intervals which form the basis of civilized music ... All the rhythmic schemes which have come under my observation seem to be very simple, and the complexities which have arisen seem to me to have been purely accidental. (Curtis 6 1911: 165)

On the other hand, he wrote:

Of course the yells practically defy accurate expression in musical notation ... I nevertheless consider these yells to be more interesting, and certainly more significant from an ethnological point of view, than many of the melodies themselves. (Curtis 6 1911: 166)

Gilbert, in his efforts to repudiate the German hegemony in America, proceeded to write some compositions based on Amerindian material but had more success with his compositions based on African-American sources.

Undoubtedly Gilbert's involvement with Amerindian music influenced his friend Arthur Farwell, who with his other varied interests deliberately learned the ceremonies, dances, and melodies of Amerindian tribes, particularly the Omaha. Farwell wrote a considerable amount of 'Indianist' music for piano or piano and voice, from 1897 to 1937.

After Farwell could not find a publisher for his *American Indian Melodies*, he discussed with Gilbert and other composers the difficulties young American composers were having in this area. They concluded that since there did not seem to be anyone that would do it, they would have to print it themselves. As a result, Farwell established the Wa-Wan Press at his family home of Newton Center in December 1901 (Chase 1987: 67). The name came from an Omaha ceremony, and during the years 1901 to 1912, in which Farwell operated the press, compositions, often based on folklore, written by thirty-seven different musicians were published.

Among the composers using Amerindian material that Farwell encouraged in this publishing venture were, in addition to Gilbert, Carlos Troyer, who worked among tribes of the Southwest, and Harvey Worthington Loomis, who used Fletcher's transcriptions. After approximately a decade of Farwell's publishing efforts, other publishers began to accept Amerindian-inspired compositions. Of these publications the most successful were those by Charles Wakefield Cadman, who visited an Omaha reservation as a child and subsequently made recordings of Omaha, Pima, and Isleta peoples before lecturing on Amerindian music, in London and Paris in 1910, and the works of Charles Sanford Skilton, who had direct contact with Amerindian music while teaching from 1915 on at the Haskell Institute for Natives in Kansas.

Cadman became the most visible exponent of the use of Amerindian music, and his lecture demonstrator, Tsianina Blackstone, a Cherokee-Creek, claimed to feel in his music 'kinship with the heartbeat of the Indian' (Blackstone 1970: 112). His song 'From the Land of the Sky Blue Water,' based on a fragment of a Native flute piece (Perlson 1978: 69), became one of the most popular American songs ever. Skilton's *Indian Dances*, along with MacDowell's *Indian Suite*, were among the twenty-seven compositions of twelve American composers which had the greatest number of performances in the United States during the seven years following the First World War (Hallowell 1965: 252). Chase has written that the 'Indianist' movement in American musical composition essentially came to an end in the 1920s (Chase 1977: n.p.).

A glance at Table 1, (see Appendix) a representative listing of works based on indigenous material by American composers, confirms this statement. A relatively limited number of composers were involved in the Indianist movement even at its peak. Of the 458 living composers listed in Claire Reis's *Composers in America*, first published in pamphlet form in 1930–2, 'only thirteen have concerned themselves at all with Indian music' (Skilton 1938/1964: 48). After 1925 only infrequent noteworthy compositions, such as Frederick Jacobi's *String Quartet on Indian Themes*, selected for the International Festival of Contemporary Music at Zurich in 1926, and Elliott Carter's ballet *Pocohontas*, winner of the Juilliard Publication Award in 1940, appeared. The *Theme and Variations No. 1* (1932) by Elie Siegmeister may be based on a Native American theme (Salvatore 1990).

Unlike the most active composers of the early 'Indianist' period, few after 1920 were actively involved in collecting and transcribing Amerindian music. The important exception was Harry Partch, who was hired by the Southwest Museum in Los Angeles to transcribe wax cylinders recorded by Charles F. Lummis around 1900. Among his twenty-four subsequent transcriptions was the *Cahuilla Bird Dance Song*, previously used by Farwell for his setting in 1905 (Kassel 1991: 12). Although Partch befriended the author and ethnologist Jaime de Angulo in the 1940s, he borrowed only Amerindian melodies for use in two works, *Cloud Chamber Music* and *The Bewitched*, both written in the 1950s.

The more recent works that I have been able to verify as being based on Amerindian material, with the exception of those by Louis W. Ballard and Judith Zaimont, are by non-American-born composers. Jerzy Bojanowski used Pueblo tunes taught to him by an Oklahoma chief for his *Indian Sketches*, while the Canadian-born Ruth Loman used Yeibichai night chants which she had heard in Navajo ceremonies. North American Indian influences can be found in other works by Loman, and in this regard she seems to be more representative of Canadian composers. Colin McPhee, who was born in Canada but obtained his American citizenship in 1939, turned to Amerindian material for an orchestral work in 1944. The historical outline of Canadian composers' interest in indigenous music needs to be examined next.

Historical Overview of the Canadian 'Indianist' Movement

Although Marc Lescarbot struggled with trying to transcribe what were possibly Mi'kmaq melodies while at Port Royal on the Canadian East Coast in the early 1600s, there is no evidence of Canadian composers attempting to use indigenous material until the mid-nineteenth century (Kallmann 1960:

9). Ernest Gagnon, whose views on the possibilities of using First Nations' music as a foundation for a truly nationalistic music were given at the beginning of this essay, published a piano piece entitled *Stadaconé: Danse sauvage pour piano* in 1858. Stadaconé was the name of an Iroquois settlement and Gagnon had made an effort to learn about the music of Amerindian tribes in the Quebec City area. In 1983 I selected this work for inclusion in the first volume of the Canadian Musical Heritage series, and at the time I pointed out characteristics which I contended were deliberately based on Native music. Since then, Gordon Smith has tracked down a letter written in 1864 by Gagnon to Thomas-Étienne Hamel that states:

In *Stadaconé* I have incorporated certain stylistic aspects of native music. These include melodic and rhythmic repetition, open fifths, and marked accentuation patterns (Smith 1989: 36).

Moreover, Smith has discovered a contemporary account by Beaurival which describes a band arrangement by the Regiment of Quebec that was performed for a group of Iroquois. According to the writer, in 1862 the 'Indians were suitably impressed by the performance, and ... they recognized familiar elements of their own music in Gagnon's composition' (Smith 1989: 37).

Gagnon's piece remains a unique case, as he apparently did not write any more works based on Amerindian material. He, like Gilbert, had great difficulty with transcription. In a paper that includes his rendition of an Amerindian song that he attempted to learn from an informant in 1859, Gagnon admits that 'he has left out the song's ornamental motives which caused him difficulty when he tried to sing the piece' (Smith 1989: 38).

Like their American counterparts, Canadian composers selected the theme of the 'Noble Savage' for some of their works. Cases in point are Calixa Lavallée's *TIQ: The Indian Question Settled at Last* (1865–6) – 'a melodramatic musical satire in two acts' – and Arthur Clappé's *Canada's Welcome*, a masque written in 1879.[3] Although the *Marche Indienne* from *TIQ* has infrequent references to Amerindian materials, Lavallée seemingly does make an attempt to create some Amerindian-like material in the 'Indian Chorus: "We Never Tell a Lie,"' where the maidens' recurring phrase on 'Ah' has a descending contour to begin, although its closing portion outlining a modal scale is not Amerindian. Clappé uses repeated notes in his 'Recitative of the Indian Chief' even though the melodic contour is more often ascending than descending. Even if Canadian composers had wanted to use authentic material, there was the problem of a lack of published resources.

Baker's study had included some references to other Canadian Amerindian nations, and Carl Stumpf published nine transcriptions of Bella Coola material in 1885. In 1888 Franz Boas's *The Central Eskimo* appeared with transcriptions. In the 1890s, James A. Teit and Franz Boas were the first to record in Canada, and were closely followed by Alexander T. Cringan, who recorded some one hundred Iroquois songs between 1897 and 1902. Any published results of the study of these songs occurred largely in obscure publications: for example, 'Iroquois Music' in the appendix of the *Report of the Minister of Education of Ontario* (Toronto 1898). Accordingly any subsequent compositions with supposedly Amerindian themes in the early twentieth century rarely reveal actual use of Native material. For instance, 'Sleep, my little papoose' from the *Canadian Song Cycle* (1911) by Laura Lemon, with words by Austin Fleming, has a melody that is clearly in the key of E major and generally tends to rise. Its falling intervals of octaves, minor sevenths, and fifths are seldom, if ever, found in a traditional Amerindian melody of North America. Joseph Vézina may have had an opportunity to hear traditional Native music in the Quebec City area because the *Chanson du scalpe* from his operetta *Le Fétiche* (1912) is recognizably Amerindian.[4] Even the text 'Ou-he, Ou-he' consists of vocables used by the Iroquois and the melodic contours and rhythms bear resemblance to the music of this particular Native culture.

The ethnologist who first began to publish articles on Canadian Amerindian music in widely recognized publications was Marius Barbeau. He took Gagnon's admonition, referred to earlier, very seriously as he organized concerts of francophone, anglophone, and First Nations songs from 1919 on. In order to arrange these he was in contact with various Canadian composers, requesting their cooperation in making accompaniments for these songs or by basing larger works on these materials. In 1927 he invited Ernest MacMillan to accompany him on his field trip to northern British Columbia to research Amerindian cultures there. MacMillan did a number of transcriptions into Western notation of songs that he heard on this trip. MacMillan subsequently made effective voice and piano arrangements of some of these. Figure 1 reproduces a program given by Juliette Gaultier de la Verendrye, one of the singers that Barbeau recruited for these concerts. It reveals the input of Barbeau himself, the inclusion of transcriptions done by MacMillan, and the use of the publication of Inuit songs by Helen Roberts.

The year 1925 produced a publication which I view as crucial to the history of indigenously inspired music of Canada: *Copper Eskimo Songs*. Helen Roberts prepared the transcriptions in *Copper Eskimo Songs* from the recordings done for Diamond Jenness's *Report of the Canadian Arctic Expedition 1913–18*, vol. 14. Only two years later, in 1927, the Montreal com-

Figure 1 Program of Juliette Gaultier given in 1928 (Courtesy of the National Library of Canada: Music Division, MacMillan Fonds)

FOLK SONGS of CANADA

FRENCH
INDIAN and ESKIMO

RECITAL BY
JULIETTE GAULTIER DE LA VERENDRYE

FRIDAY EVENING
FEBRUARY TENTH
EIGHT-THIRTY O'CLOCK
AT THE
LITTLE THEATRE, OTTAWA

11. AN INCANTATION FOR HEALING THE SICK
"For thou madest me shiver with fear, (repeated)
It made me return home.
Me thou didst make me shiver with fear.
When thou didst pass on me, (bis)
Me thou didst cast thine eyes on me."

12. WEATHER INCANTATION (to allay a storm)
"My great companion, my great guardian spirit, (bis)
Our fine incantations, our fine cries.
There is no snow hut; it is empty of people,
He is not a real man; it is empty of people.
Underneath it down there let us search.

MOTION PICTURES ILLUSTRATING NATIVE DANCES AND SONGS AMONG
THE NASS RIVER INDIANS. BY DR. J. S. WATSON OF ROCHESTER, N.Y.
WITH THE ASSISTANCE OF MARIUS BARBEAU. (By courtesy of the National
Museum of Canada.)

INDIAN SONGS OF BRITISH COLUMBIA
ALBERTA AND ONTARIO

Recorded for the National Museum of Canada by Marius Barbeau, James
Teit and Edward Sapir, and D. Jenness. Transcribed by Marius Barbeau.
Dr. Ernest MacMillan and Helen Roberts. Stage setting by W. Langdon
Kihn.

1. BLACK BEAR CHANT (Carrier, Northern B.C.)
Among the Carrier Indians of northern British Columbia the hunter
who has mortally wounded a black bear should incant, slowly and
very solemnly, this song. Thus will he please the spirit of the
dying bear and gain power to shoot many others thereafter. (Recorded by D. Jenness).

2. TAMA SONG (Red-headed Woodpecker and the Thunderbird) (Neotka)
"Do not be afraid.
I shall be green salmonberry shoots and look again for you.
I shall be a salmonberry and look again for you.
I shall be a blueberry and look again for you."

3. "I WILL BE A SEAL-HUNTER" (Lullaby) (Nootka)
"I, little one, will be a seal-hunting person, because I am a little
Tsisheeth person, because I am a little Tsisheeth person. Ihi, oho."
(Nos. 2 & 3 recorded by E. Sapir and transcribed by Helen Roberts.)

4. DANCE SONG (Kwakiutl—North West Coast, B.C.)
(Collected by Juliette Gaultier at Beaver Harbour.)

5. NADUDU (Lullaby—Nass River, Northern B.C.)
"Darling, O my son, so small, darling.
(The child is supposed to sing to his mother:)
Sit up at night, O sister, sit up with me, my dear, to raise me, to
make me grow, that I may be a big man, that I may resort to the
wide streams of my forefathers, that I may catch the large spring
salmon, that I may fish at Echo-cliffs. This is where I will get fish
backbones for Thunder-woman, she who now nurses, me when they
has grown too old to work."

Northern Alaskan and Copper Eskimo Songs
Collected on the Stefansson Canadian Arctic Expedition for
the National Museum of Canada, by Diamond Jenness. Transcribed by Helen Roberts. Stage Setting by W. Langdon Kihn.

SONGS OF NORTHERN ALASKA ESKIMOS

1. AKSIATAK AI YAYANGA (Sleeping Song)

2. THE SEAL-POKE (Cat's cradle chant)
"The seal-poke down there,   The sea is tossing it about down
The seal-poke down there,   there,
Down there, down there,   The sea is bringing it to shore
                                        down there."

3. SPARROW SONG (Children's game song)
"Her little nest break it up   Take the nest away,
Her little children rend them,   Take the children away,
Her little nest break it up,   Let us take her little children away
Her little children rend them,   Break them, break them, break
                                         them."

4. SONG OF ASETSAK (Homesick song)
"How many winters, how many
Will you forsake your home here in Tikierark?
How many winters are you return in the big ship?
Yonder in the east, alas, three winters must I linger."

SONGS OF THE COPPER ESKIMOS

5. DANCE SONG (Ancient)
Translation: The Spirit of the Ghost.
"Let me go and watch it vanishing,
Let me go and watch it vanishing."

6. DANCE SONG
"A clod of earth it tripped me,
It laid me flat on my face. He turned to look at me.
On slippery ground it made me slip."

7. DANCE SONG
"What the eastern people are accustomed to expect,
They are accustomed to expect both Kuaktok and Ingalukyak.
His comrade in summer, his comrade in spring.
I am going to spend the summer with them and with Torakaugyuak also."

8. LULLABY
"Falling tears, (bis)
The old knee down there, (bis)
They splash on it." (bis)

9. OLD WEATHER INCANTATION (against evil spirits)
"He made it flee, he made it flee, he made it flee.
To the little sun, to the place where it re-emerges, he made it flee."

10. WEATHER INCANTATION
"The people they worked hard, the people they worked hard,
Sealskin objects, fillets for the head."

6. DIRGE SONG OF THE SKATEEN (Nass River)
"Haro hiye. . . . They proclaim him the head-chief." Sung after
the death of Skateen, head-chief of the Wolf clan, at Gitlarhdamks,
on the upper Nass River.
(Nos. 5, 6 recorded by Marius Barbeau in 1927 and transcribed by
Dr. Ernest MacMillan.)

7. LOVE SONG OF THE SEKANAIS (Telegraph Creek, Yukon)
"O my sweetheart, sweetheart of mine."
(Recorded by James Teit and transcribed by Marius Barbeau.)

8. GAME SONG (Kootenay—South-eastern B.C.)
Redhorn tells his listeners that he obtained this song in a dream
for good luck at the lahal game (a gambling game with sticks.)

9. PARTING SONG (Kootenay)
"He has done an evil thing to me because he has forsaken me. Poor
and to be pitied am I. I will follow him till I see him again."
(Nos. 8, 9 recorded by James Teit and transcribed by Marius Barbeau.)

10. SONGS OF THE STONY INDIANS (Alberta)
(a) Lullaby
(b) Deer dance.
(Collected by Juliette Gaultier, on the Morley Reserve.)

11. OJIBWAY SONG (Of North-western Ontario)
Corn Dance.
(Collected by Juliette Gaultier, near Sault-Ste-Marie.)

12. THE WHITE DOG SACRIFICE (Cayuga Iroquois)
A native white dog was sacrificed in mid-winter, among the Iroquois. It was the most important form of worship to "the Father".
The first and second of the three songs were used when the dog
was sacrificed and burnt, the third, when the people gathered the
ashes with paddles and scattered them to the winds for a blessing.
(Recorded and translated by Marius Barbeau.)

MOTION PICTURES

FOLK SONGS OF FRENCH CANADA
From the collections of Ernest Gagnon, Marius Barbeau and E.-Z.
Massicotte. Cello accompaniment by Marion Bauer, performed by
Carl Lund. Stage setting by Arthur Lismer.

1. Sainte Marguerite (Lullaby).
2. Au bois rossignolet (dance song).
3. J'ai cueilli la belle rose (English translation by John Murray Gibbon.)
4. Isabeau s'y promène (rowing song).
5. Sept ans sur mer (song of the sea).
6. A la claire fontaine..
7. Je's mène bien mon dévidoir (spinning song).
8. Avoine, avoine (round dance).
9. Lève ton pied!.
10. V'là l'bon vent.
(Nos. 7, 8, 9, 10 with table-harp accompaniment.)

poser and pianist Léo-Pol Morin performed his *Three Eskimos*. Recently, one part of this work, 'Weather Incantation', was discovered, and it is based on song 90 of the Roberts/Jenness collection. John Weinzweig also drew material from this collection for the scores of the drama series 'The White Empire,' broadcast by the CBC in 1945-6, and for his contemporaneous compositions, the choral work *To the Lands Over Yonder*, based on song 73, and the orchestral piece *Edge of the World*. Earlier, Weinzweig had used Dogrib Amerindian material in the score for the film *North West Frontier* (1941), one melody of which was used for the organ piece *Improvisation on an Indian Tune* (1942), and Iroquois material appeared in his ballet score *Red Ear of Corn* (1949).

Many Canadian composers, down to the present day, have followed Weinzweig's lead in using Inuit and Amerindian musical materials for various genres. A representative list of these can be found in Table 2 in the Appendix, and some of the works named there will be referred to in more detail in the next section, which will examine the usage of indigenous musical materials by American and Canadian composers.

Compositional Approaches for Usage of Indigenous Materials

At the beginning of this essay the difficulties that the Europeans and European-born settlers had in comprehending Native American musics were exemplified in the comments of Anna Jameson. These monophonic musics not only used scale patterns other than the diatonic major-minor system to which Europeans were accustomed, but also used different melodic contours. In traditional Native musics across North America the descending contour is predominant, although there may be stretches of reiteration of the same pitch or microtonal movement around a certain sound. In addition to significant pitch and contour contrasts, and a tense vocal timbre decidedly different from European norms, rhythms were generally not those to which the non-Natives were accustomed. When the Native music had a drum giving a steady recurring pulse, trained musicians interpreted it as a duple beat, but the rhythms of the melodic line above the drum beat could be very complex indeed, with the application of pulsating accents at various points in the melody. Partch remarked on this as follows:

An example of a simple 13 rhythm – a strong impulse followed by twelve weaker pulsations, or an alternate 6-7 or 7-6 rhythm – is found in an old Edison cylinder record of the 'Stick Game Song' from the Hoopa (or Hupa) Indians of the north coast of California. This and other such records ... showed a wealth of rhythm more complex than anything Westeners have thus far attempted. (Partch 1979: 258)

Bearing in mind the hurdles that existed for composers when they tried to use Amerindian and Inuit material as a source in their compositions, we can begin to examine some of their approaches. Most composers in the pre-1910 period, and some after that time, never actually heard the music performed by indigenous peoples, either on recordings or in traditional context. Consequently, the most common approach was to take a melody transcribed into Western notation, but there are many deficiencies in trying to duplicate the essence of this music on paper in this way.

After selecting a melody, the composer took one of two directions – either to state the melody more or less as given in the printed or recorded form, or to use the original as a source of melodic motifs. Both of these possibilities are evident from the earliest stages of the 'Indianist' movement. For instance, *Lyrics of the Red Man*, op. 76, Book I, by Harvey Worthington Loomis, illustrates the first approach well since the original melodies are given with the score (Gillespie 1978: 206–15). This method has limitations when applied to the creation of a composition in the Western sense because of the major discrepancies between Native American and European musics outlined above. The composer accustomed to the phraseology based on the key and cadential principles of the diatonic system would normally try to force the Native material into that mould. Cadman articulated his approach as 'idealization' and stated:

Only one-fifth of all Indian thematic material is valuable in the hands of a composer ... (and) is suitable for harmonic investment. It becomes necessary to choose an Indian song or chant that is attractive in its simplicity, one that will stand alone by virtue of its inherent melodic line, and is fairly good in symmetry; otherwise the idealizer is confronted with a formidable problem. (1915: 391)

In the second approach, where the melody was used as a source for melodic motifs, the composer can work with the material in a manner more akin to his or her usual format. Although I cannot prove the assertion, since I cannot identify the original Iroquois melody, I suspect that in *Stadaconé* (see Example 1) Ernest Gagnon drew melodic motifs from the original (Keillor 1983: 105). Iroquois melodies tend to leap up at their openings, then descend in small intervals. The motif of bar three in *Stadaconé* illustrates this, while the leap of a fourth downwards in bar four is a common cadential feature of

Example 1 Opening of Gagnon's *Stadaconé*.

Iroquois melodies. The material of bar seven shows the pivoting around a pitch, as Gagnon was able to transfer that into a piano medium with tempered tuning.

MacDowell's use of the 'dirge' motif could be considered representative of this technique too, although he soon forgot its initial origin (probably through unfamiliarity with its original context) to judge by the type of surrounding material he used. Gilbert stated publicly that he did not wish his 'Indian compositions to be referred to as arrangements' because he had 'allowed himself freedom to depart from the original fragments of borrowed melody in every instance and ... provided all of the harmony, counterpoint, and form' (Longyear 1968: 123). Indeed one would suspect that his *Indian Sketches* were based on melodies which he worked on for the Curtis publications. A search of these melodies only reveals a slight resemblance in No. 3, 'Song of the Wolf,' to a tune on page 49 of volume 6 in the Curtis series, while No. 4, 'Camp Dance,' seems a bit closer to the 'Waqhli Dance – Song, No. 1 of the Wishham,' volume 8, page 177. Yet all of the melodic material seems genuinely 'Indian,' so perhaps Gilbert at this stage was so immersed in its sounds that he could manipulate motifs from various sources.

In Canada, as interest in Inuit and Amerindian materials increased, the melodic line as source for motifs has become the principal approach, particularly in purely instrumental settings. John Weinzweig's use of Inuit melodic motifs in *Edge of the World* is an early major work using this approach. Towards the mid-twentieth century, compositional techniques involving the use of intervallic motifs arose and this development accordingly encouraged composers to use First Nations material for these patterns.

In terms of rhythm, composers usually used a steady duple beat. To create an Amerindian atmosphere, a heavily accented duple metre occurs in these compositions again and again from Gagnon's *Stadaconé* and Gilbert's 'Camp Dance' of the *Indian Sketches* through to Mary Gardiner's *The Legend of the First Rabbit*. Some composers realized the complexities of Amerindian metric patterns as pointed out by Partch. In his 'Indian Music Talk' of 9 February 1909, Cadman remarked on the Amerindian's highly developed sense of rhythm as being not 'excelled by any other nationality in the world' (Perlson 1978: 84). To indicate these rhythmic complexities some composers consequently incorporated shifting metres as in the pieces by Loomis, Farwell's *Impressions of the Wa-Wan Ceremony* (Gillespie 1978: 69ff.), Talivaldis Kenins's *Ojibway Song*, and Violet Archer's *Ikpakhuaq* to name only a few.

Some of the more contemporary approaches in organizing rhythm have been used to advantage with this material. Paul Pedersen's *An Old Song of the Sun and the Moon and the Fear of Loneliness* has calibration in seconds, thus allowing the performers a degree of freedom within limits. This system permits an approach probably closer to the original, since Gilbert noted that 'although rhythmic values are fairly well preserved, he (the Indian singer) introduces ritards and accelerandos, and sometimes a long ritenuto' (Gilbert 1911: 166). Possibly because of these characteristics in the traditional contexts of certain examples, since 1950 many composers use a combination of metred and unmetred or aleatoric sections, as in Walter Buczynski's *The*

198 Elaine Keillor

Tales of Nanabozho, Diana McIntosh's *Kiviuq*, and Ruth Loman's *Five Ceremonial Masks*. In *Arctic Dances*, John Beckwith used two different tempos for oboe and piano (see Example 2). This could be an allusion to the fact that some North American Native songs seem to have two different tempos for voice and drum. Gilbert commented on this characteristic as follows:

When a song is accompanied by a drum-beat, it usually happens that the drummer keeps time in the most rigid and inflexible manner throughout the song. The singer,

Example 2 Portion of Beckwith's *Arctic Dances* II.

on the contrary, will introduce ritards, accelerandos, pauses of different length, and numerous variations of time. There consequently arises many complicated rhythmic relations between the drum-beat and the melody. (Gilbert 1911: 165)

If composers had to become more daring and innovative to deal with the complexity of rhythms, they faced another major challenge when placing Amerindian or Inuit material into a harmonic context. All North American indigenous music is basically monophonic, and if accompanied, the instruments would only be various types of rattles and/or drums. Fletcher wrote:

When two or more persons took part in a song, the voices were always in unison ... [T]hey moved along in a consonance of two and sometimes three octaves, thus bringing out harmonic effects, and making one aware of 'overtones.' (1898: 91)

One of the most common solutions used by composers providing harmony for Amerindian/Inuit melodies is to rely on open fifths and/or fourths. The opening of Gagnon's *Stadaconé* (see Example 1) has open fifths and MacDowell used drone fifths in *Indian Idyl*. It is an extremely rare occurence to hear Amerindians singing a fourth apart on recordings available today. When it does arise it presumably happens when a singer selects a more comfortable register for his voice. In the past this may have taken place more frequently than present recordings would suggest, as Farwell's statement about his *Navajo War Dance* indicates: 'I have employed bare fourths considerably in the work, as I have heard the Navajos sing the war dance in fourths' (Farwell 1972: 43). Since Amerindian tunes do not have an inherent major or minor tonality equivalent to the Western diatonic norm, open fifths and fourths have remained a frequent solution for composers using Native material. A more recent example can be found in John Beckwith's *The Sun Dance* (see Example 3).

Because North American art-music composers were so dominated by European harmonic practice around 1900, many of their attempts at 'harmonizing' Amerindian tunes are incongruous, if not disastrous. Within this essay the controversy over Fillmore's theory of 'latent harmonic sense' in Native Amerindian music will not be discussed, but its essentials can be found in McNutt (1984) and Pantaleoni (1985). Nor will I address the main points of contention between Cadman and Farwell – vocal versus non-vocal usage and retention of original milieu of the Native song (see Schuetze 1984: 57). Farwell wrote:

These melodies are all indissolubly linked to legends, myths, ceremonials, or reli-

Example 3 Portion of Beckwith's *The Sun Dance*.

gious rituals of the greatest poetic and dramatic beauty, and it is upon the suggestive power of these ... as much as upon the melodies themselves, that stress should be laid. (Farwell 1903: 276)

With regard to harmony he said:

Harmonies must be found which will not merely support the melody in a general way, but which will give a heightened expression to the feeling conveyed by that phase of life which gave birth to the melody ... The songs of the Indians are widely different from each other in their meaning, and therefore the spirit of each should lead to a keenly specialized harmonic presentation. (Farwell 1902: 212)

At times even Farwell tended to make the texture too thick with chromaticisms that were at odds with the original melody, as for example, in No. 1 of *Impressions of the Wa-Wan Ceremony* (Gillespie 1978: 69). Canadian composers often had the same problem, as Léo-Pol Morin's 'Weather Incantation' from *Three Eskimos* indicates.

Thoughtful composers discovered one solution to be the creation of ostinato patterns over which the Amerindian or Inuit tune could be placed. Such an approach frequently works very well and numerous examples can be found among the works listed in Tables 1 and 2. Examples 1 and 2 include ostinatos that are also present in other portions of the compositions concerned.

The breakdown of the hierarchical diatonic harmonic system in the twentieth century has freed composers to find new harmonizations for indigenous materials. Consequently works from 1940 on generally show a variety of quartal harmonies, polychords, modal, and bitonal combinations. All of these can be successful approaches as long as the texture remains relatively transparent. That in turn depends on the control over the medium which the composer has selected.

Tables 1 and 2 in the Appendix indicate that in the early years of the 'Indianist' movement, American and Canadian composers favoured the piano or voice and piano mediums. With the exception of Amerindian flute love songs, all the original indigenous melodies were sung, so the vocal setting was not as far removed as the piano – an instrument which has a wide register and can produce many sounds at once. If the composer gives regard to the matters of harmony and rhythms indicated above, a successful composition using indigenous material can be created for the piano or other keyboard instrument such as the organ. Where Preston Ware Orem's *American Indian Rhapsody* seems today to be 'stylistically conventional and eclectic, post-romantic and neo-Lisztian in its mannerisms and pretentiousness,' Farwell's *Navajo War Dance* impresses one with 'its finely controlled artistry' (Chase 1977: 2).

As composers selected chamber ensembles of various types, these too moved a considerable distance away from the context of the indigenous originals except in cases where flute and percussion were involved. When these are present, composers generally employ them extensively. For instance, when Gilbert made his orchestral version of *Indian Sketches* he appropriately gave solo lines to the flute in the 'Nocturne.' For the 'Camp Dance' he specified the use of an 'Indian drum,' but failed to give any details as to type. Was he not aware that there are many kinds of drums used by the Native cultures of North America? In the last *Sketch*, the 'Snake Dance,' an 'Indian gourd rattle' is specified, and it adds a distinctive colour to what I consider the most successful number of this orchestral set. Of course, it is not necessary to have instruments similar to the Native original to create an ambience of the Amerindian or Inuit soundscape. Many of the more contemporary compositions listed in Tables 1 and 2 manage to do this with whatever medium is at hand. Drum sounds can be created by hitting the bodies of various instruments and other expanded performance techniques can be introduced. For instance, in *Arctic Dances*, not only does Beckwith call upon the oboist to make microtonal glissandos similar to those heard in actual Inuit performances, but the pitchless reed squeaks remind this listener of the high pitchless vocal sounds to be found in recordings of some Amerindian and Inuit songs.

When composers included a voice or voices in their settings, they had to decide on a text. In many Amerindian songs, particularly those used for public social occasions, the text often has few meaningful words with the rest being vocables. The most common approach, accordingly, has been to translate what text there is and possibly elaborate on it in English, with perhaps some of the Amerindian and Inuit vocables being retained as a refrain-like section. This was the approach used by Ernest MacMillan in the effective settings of *Three Songs of the West Coast*. La Liberté followed a similar format in *Tenaouiche Tenaqa Ouicheka*, but of course employed a French text in the main part of the strophe (Poirier 1992: 29). This setting is distinctive in its inclusion of an octave leap up by the voice at the very end. During the nineteenth century, travellers in Canada, such as Elizabeth Simcoe, referred to the whoop which occurred in Amerindian song and was adopted by the voyageurs (McMillan 1983: 20). For instance, J.J. Bigsby described a parlour performance with piano of the voyageur song *Le premier jour de mai* finishing 'as is usual with the piercing Indian shriek' (Bigsby 1850/ 1969: 119). This seems to be the only aspect of indigenous music consciously influencing European-derived music prior to 1850, and La Liberté in his setting has continued that tradition.

Although most of the English or French texts are obtained by translations and expansions of meaningful text in the original, sometimes vocal settings have texts that have been written by non-Natives, more or less idealizing the 'Noble Savage' approach. This is the case in Cadman's *Four American Indian Songs*, which include the famous *From the Land of the Sky-Blue Water* and whose texts were written by Nelle Richmond Eberhart (Chase 1977: 2). In fact, the Omaha love song which Cadman used as a basis for this song was originally played by a flute, and Fletcher did not give a parallel vocal version, if it had been available.

More rarely, composers have retained the original language. Farwell followed this practice in the *Bird Dance Song of the Cahuilla Tribe* (Wa-Wan Press 1905). His effective choral setting of the *Navajo War Dance*, op. 102, no. 1, in which he incorporated the pulsations of the Native Southern Athapaskan vocal style, used the original text. A more recent example would be Kenins's *Ojibway Song*. When Harry Somers wrote *Kuyas*, the main solo of Riel's Cree wife in the opera *Louis Riel*, he utilized a Cree text. His *Shaman's Song* retained the Inuit text of Uvavnuk, a Netsilik woman, as told to Rasmussen, but with main phrases occurring intermittently in English translation.

Sensitivity to the text as well as the musical sound in organization and production remains for me a crucial point in determining how much a composer has striven to come to terms with indigenous music as a compositional source. Certain Canadian composers have displayed a fascination with the sounds of indigenous languages. After all, the name of their country, Canada, is a word from the language of the Iroquois. In *Keewaydin*, Harry Freedman chose Ontario place names of Ojibway origin as the text, and R. Murray Schafer used words for 'water' from several Native languages as the text for *Miniwanka*. Many of the Inuit-inspired works listed in Table 2 are named 'Anerca,' the Inuit word for 'soul' and the root of the verb 'to breathe' or 'to make poetry.' These composers have frequently selected their translations of Inuit texts or have been generally inspired by a collection called *Anerca*, prepared by Edmund Carpenter and first published in 1959 (Lefebvre 1986: 184).[5]

An Assessment of the 'Indianist' Movement

To try to determine how successful American and Canadian composers have been in utilizing indigenous materials, we need to remind ouselves of Temperley's second and third phases of musical nationalism as a reaction to domination by an alien musical culture. He has defined the second phase as follows:

Native subject-matter and recognizable native tunes and rhythms are introduced to provide superficial coloring on top of a style that fundamentally still belongs to the alien high-art culture. (Temperley 1990: 9)

His third phase 'involves radical innovations of style and form inspired by the native idioms' (Temperley 1990: 9).

Undoubtedly the 'Indianist' movement in Canada and the United States is largely a phenomenon that can be placed within Temperley's second phase. It can be dated as genuinely beginning in the 1850s in Canada, but not truly being in evidence in the United States until the early 1890s. Its importance in the United States then extended for approximately four decades, while in Canada the movement burst forth in earnest in the late 1920s and has remained vital to the present day.

Why should there be such a difference in its impact on American and Canadian composers? We have noted earlier how few American composers were involved in the 'Indianist' movement, even at its height. Peter Garland has written:

American culture begins with the Indian ... We Western composers have chosen to pay little attention to [it] ... in a continent peopled by spirits, natural forces, who were celebrated in the rites and music of these original Americans, but whose force and presence here have been almost totally forgotten. (Garland 1982: 16)

This statement seems to be more representative of the American composer than the Canadian, since proportionately a larger number of Canadian composers have turned to and found inspiration in indigenous music. Cultural critics and practitioners in other arts have noted the Canadian need for a mythology, often European in its roots but containing elements analogous to the culture of the Amerindians and Inuit. For instance, 'the dramatist John Coulter says of his play ... *Deidre of the Sorrows*: "The art of a Canadian remains ... the art of the country of his forebears and the old world heritage of myth and legend remains his heritage"' (Frye 1971: 238). Frye indicated that 'the kind of rapport with nature which the Indian symbolizes is central' to the Canadian pastoral myth in 'its sense of kinship with the animal and vegetable world' (Frye 1971: 239–40). Canadians have played a leading role in environmental causes and that has been expressed in particular compositions as well. The Prologue of Schafer's *Patria* is *The Princess of the Stars*, 'an eighty-minute ritual designed for a specific place and time: a wooded lake, in autumn, beginning exactly forty minutes before sunrise' (Adams 1983: 182).

Schafer's pageant enacts an original scenario patterned on Indian legends. It tells how the Princess ... fell from the sky into the lake. Wolf comes to find her, gets help from the Dawn Birds, but is prevented from rescuing her by The Three-Horned Enemy, who holds her captive beneath the lake. A battle develops on the water, interrupted finally by the Sun Disc (sunrise), who drives The Three-Horned Enemy away, sets tasks for Wolf before he can release the Princess, and exhorts the Dawn Birds to cover the lake with ice and desist from singing until Wolf succeeds. (Adams 1983: 182)

Table 2 lists a number of Canadian works which are settings of Amerindian or Inuit legends. This is a further exemplification of the importance of legend and also of the force of the pastoral myth within Canada, since most of the First Nations legends are animal stories. Because narrative poetry has been recognized as a predominant type of Canadian literature – being impersonal and a combination of tragic and ironic themes (Frye 1971: 242) – characteristics that are not pre-eminent in American literature, the settings of these legends in a musical context can be viewed as an extension of this Canadian proclivity.

Another contrast between the lists of Tables 1 and 2 is the fact that American composers rarely used Inuit material, in spite of having Alaska, with its Inupiaq-speaking Inuit in the north and the Yupik-speaking people of the south, as part of their country. Drawing on tunes transcribed in Boas's monograph *The Central Eskimo*, Amy Beach was apparently the first North American composer to use Inuit material. She accorded with MacDowell's statement that 'native folk-songs of the continent ... [were] those of the Indians or the Esquimaux,' not the blacks (Block 1990: 146). Cowell's use of Inuit material in *Animal Magic* may have been due to the interests of his wife, an ethnomusicologist. Since the publication of the Roberts/Jenness collection, Canadian composers have drawn on Inuit material extensively.

Canadians are fascinated with the Inuit culture not only because they are a northern people, but also because it is still possible to experience some very traditional musical practices of the Inuit through recordings, television, films, and personal contact. This is less true of the Amerindian nations. Although there have been some major studies on certain Amerindian musics in Canada – Kurath and Fenton on the Iroquois, Halpern on the Pacific West Coast – there is scant information about the musical practices of many other groups in Canada, and very few commercially available recordings (see Kallmann 1992: 923–35). Before I began fieldwork in 1984 among the Dene, with a population of some 13,000, one of the largest groupings in Canada, one commercial recording of one of their songs was available, plus a short article on some Slavey music, and one brief published discussion on the music of one group, the Dogrib.[6] On the other hand, a much more complete picture of the Inuit musical cultures has been done, and, as of this writing, there are three CDs of traditional Inuit music available plus a number of earlier commercial recordings.

In the United States, after the flurry of publications in the early part of the century, there was little research on Amerindian music. More recordings were done than in Canada, but they were often on obscure labels and difficult to procure. This situation probably led in part to American composers almost completely neglecting indigenous material after 1930, but another factor was the general change of view on Natives in American mythology.

Because Indians were on reservations separated from the rest of society, and because the frontier with which they were associated disappeared, they have until very recently vanished from the consciousness of most urban, industrial modern Americans. They have ceased in the twentieth-century to be the paradigm of otherness for Americans, and ceased to define the mythic boundaries of American community. (Robertson 1980: 111)

The situation in Canada was different to some degree since there was no Western frontier in the U.S. sense – law and order preceded settlement of western Canada and treaties were signed with various Amerindian bands (Berton 1982: 28). Amerindians in Canada were usually placed on reserves and denied a vote in a fashion similar to the situation in the United States, and thus non-Native Canadians tended to become indifferent to their situation during the twentieth century. On the other hand Canadians knew subconsciously that their ancestors had been very dependant on the Natives for survival in a hostile environment and that the furs provided by the Amerindian hunters produced the initial wealth of the country. Apart from the area some one hundred kilometres north of the U.S./Canada border, Canadians have been reminded constantly of the Amerindian presence because of their numbers in relation to the rest of the population.

The Inuit situation in Canada was different since it was not until around 1960 that the actions of the Canadian government had intruded into the life of practically every Inuit family. Because extensive contact occurred later, there has been the retention of more traditional types of music-making among the Inuit and composers have had a greater possibility of actually experiencing it, as mentioned above. Because of the fact that more recordings are available, composers have transcribed tunes directly from them for their compositions. A case in point is Harry Somers, who listened to the Folkways recordings to procure musical material for *A Midwinter Night's Dream*.

Murray Adaskin has written works based on both Amerindian and Inuit materials. The difference in the means of obtaining his tunes for these works underlines the contrast in the immediacy of contact generally possible with Amerindian and Inuit cultures in Canada. Adaskin's *Algonquin Symphony* includes the tunes 'Hiawatha's Farewell' and 'Omaha Tribal Prayer,' both originally sung for Adaskin by Taylor Statten, a white educator who had an interest in Amerindian lore (Lazarevich 1988: 222). In 1966 Adaskin travelled to Rankin Inlet, where 'he recorded the songs of two Inuit elders named Qalala and Nilaula' that became the basis of the orchestral work known by the same name (Lazarevich 1988: 224).

Because of the differences of history and circumstances vis-à-vis indigenous peoples and Canadians, it may be that the Canadian situation is more conducive to permitting composers to treat the indigenous material as in Temperley's third phase. Gaile McGregor has pointed out that

the prototypical Canadian 'fiction' ... juxtaposes unameliorated modal alternatives rather than pretending to reconcile them. This may be achieved by vertical layering of overt and covert possibilities, by semantic duplicity, by serial inversion, by compartmentalization – indeed, by any of the psycho-symbolic mechanisms by which myth achieves its formal ambivalence. The result ... is very often an extremely complex aesthetic object which is simultaneously despairing and affirmative. (McGregor 1985: 440)

There are compositional techniques somewhat analogous to these that can be found in various Canadian works, including Schafer's *The Princess of the Stars* and Kenins's *Naačnaača*.

This is not to say that an American composer has not succeeded in truly encompassing indigenous material within his own style. Garland has written eloquently about hearing Partch's *The Bewitched*:

It was an authentic indigenous expression – the hot desert afternoon outside merely seemed to confirm that Partch's music **belonged here**. And most of all, there was the **power** of that music, its sense of affirmation, of the magical force of sound, of the atavistic pull of rhythm, of the creative potential of **man**. It was as personal a music as I'd ever heard, and yet so timeless. The Cahuilla Indian melody, it seemed to me to sing in its bass profundity the ancient song of the land itself, this very place where I was at that moment, the southern California desert, a song of sorrow of the peoples whom our barbarous civilization had so ruthlessly displaced and destroyed. And *The Bewitched* was ART too, not that it cleverfully and successfully conformed to some stylistic precept or fad ... but in that it spoke so completely to all levels of my being, invoking the ancient past and yet being so completely in the present. (Garland 1982: 284)

Recently I have had similar experiences when listening to Raymond Luedeke's *Tales of the Netsilik* and Michael Colgrass's *Snow Walker*.[7] Both of these composers were born in the United States, but I doubt that they could have written these works without their experience of Canada, its mythology, and particularly the role of the North and the Inuit within that myth.

As yet very few Native musicians have created in concert genres. Job Nelson was a Native bandmaster and the leader of Nelson's Cornet Band in Metlakatla, British Columbia, but his *Imperial Native March* does not have as much Native musical influence as Emma Seymour's *Wahnotee*

(McIntosh 1989: 234). Louis W. Ballard (b. 1931), of Cherokee origin, claims that all of his compositions incorporate Native material. Since the 1960s, Native musicians on both sides of the Great Divide have been producing popular songs which blend characteristics of their traditional musics with country and rock-and-roll elements. For example, Buffy Sainte Marie's *Starwalker* (1985) incorporated Plains-style contour, and vocal characteristics of a tight, constricted sound and pulsations. The Canadian Innu (Montagnais) duo Kashtin (Claude McKenzie and Florent Vollant) have risen to the top of the Parisian hit parade with songs that use their original language and traits of their traditional music blended with elements of French cabaret and popular songs. Other examples are cited in Keillor (1988–9). John Kim Bell, originally from the Mohawk community of Kahnawake, received training in Italy and the United States as an orchestral conductor. In addition to composing the score for the PBS miniseries *The Trial of Standing Bear* (1988) and the soundtrack for the CTV drama *Divided Loyalties* (1990), he was the chief organizer of the classical ballet *In the Land of the Spirits* (1988), whose cast and orchestral members were all of Native background. In a recent interview he stated:

It was to be a melding of traditional with jazz, with modern, and with ballet – to make it truly based on a Native cultural aspect. The music was done the same way. I researched a number of traditional Native musics – not anything in particular – just Native music in general. One had to be inspired, then, to write an orchestral score based on this. In each and every case we tried to bring about an authentic Native component, but this was art, and so there was obviously a lot of license in it ... I bring a certain Native cultural tradition to it; I also bring a certain western cultural tradition to it, – the classical piano, the structure of the symphony ... I'm a melded product. (Cronk 1990: 74–5)

To truly reach a full blossoming of Temperley's third phase, we await further compositions by such 'melded products.' As commissions for works from Canadian composers often include requests to use Inuit and/or Amerindian material – Gary Kulesha's *Shaman Song* is a case in point – I expect that we will be able to look forward to more effective compositions where the composers have imbued their own style with the characteristics of the indigenous music of North America.

NOTES

1 This is an expanded and revised version of a paper read at the Sonneck Society Conference, Toronto, 22 April 1990. I wish to express my thanks to Mark Hand,

Indigenous Music as a Compositional Source   209

national librarian, and the staff of the Canadian Music Centre, and the interlibrary loan department of Carleton University's library for their assistance in obtaining data and scores.
2 Baker's dissertation contains forty-three musical examples.
3 Portions of Lavallée's *TIQ* and Clappé's masque are included in volume 10 of the Canadian Musical Heritage series, edited by Dorith Cooper.
4 Portions of Vézina's *La Fétiche* are included in the volume cited in note 3.
5 Garant was typical of Quebec composers of the past thirty years or so in not actually quoting any indigenous material, or in even consciously trying to invoke a northern soundscape. Nevertheless he and Micheline Coulombe Saint-Marcoux referred to indigenous textual sources based on a more intimate knowledge of the cultures involved than the creators of eighteenth- and early-nineteenth-century examples of pure exoticism. Accordingly I decided to include these works in Table 2. A part from Linda Bouchard, Quebec composers have not been involved recently in the 'Indianist' movement in Canada. This may be owing to their own strong sense of nationhood, and the fading in their collective subconscious of the role that the Natives played in the early history of New France.
6 In Helm and Lurie's *The Dogrib Hand Game* there are five pages of commentary on Dogrib music with transcriptions of twenty-six songs. Further information on the context of these songs and some transcriptions are given in Keillor 1986.
7 Colgrass lived with an Inuit family in Pangnirtung, Baffin Island, before composing *Snow Walker*. More recently Steven Gellman spent time with the Inuit in preparation for writing his *Arctic Symphony* (Mather 1992: 13).

REFERENCES

Adams, Stephen. 1983. *R. Murray Schafer*. Toronto: University of Toronto Press.
Baker, Theodore. 1882/1977. *Über die Musik der nordamerikanischen Wilden*, Leipzig: Breitkopf & Härtel; *On the Music of the North American Indians*, trans. Ann Buckley. New York: Da Capo.
Berton, Pierre. 1982. *Why We Act Like Canadians*. Toronto: McClelland and Stewart.
Bigsby, John J. 1850/1969. *The Shoe and Canoe, or Pictures of Travel in the Canadas*. London; reprint ed., New York: Paladin Press.
Blackstone, Tsianina. 1970. *Where Trails Have Led Me*. Santa Fe: Vergara Printing Co.
Block, Adrienne Fried. 1990. 'Amy Beach's Music on Native American Themes,' *American Music* 8/2, 141–66.
Boas, Franz. 1888. *The Central Eskimo, 6th Annual Report of the Bureau of*

American Ethnology. Washington, DC (reprinted Lincoln, Nebr., 1964; Toronto, 1974).
Brancaleone, Francis. 1982. 'The Short Piano Pieces of Edward MacDowell.' PhD diss., City University of New York.
– 1989. 'Edward MacDowell and Indian Motives,' *American Music* 7/4 (Winter 1989), 359–81.
Cadman, Charles Wakefield. 1915. 'The "Idealization" of Indian Music,' *Musical Quarterly* 1 (July 1915), 387–96.
Canadian Music Centre. 1980. *List of Canadian Music Inspired by the Music, Poetry, Art and Folklore of Native Peoples.*
Chase, Gilbert. 1977. 'The "Indianist" Movement in American Music.' Record notes of New World Records 213: Recorded Anthology of American Music.
– 1987. *America's Music: From the Pilgrims to the Present,* rev. 3rd ed. Urbana: University of Chicago Press.
Cooper, Dorith, ed. 1990. *Opera and Operetta Excerpts I,* Canadian Musical Heritage, 10. Ottawa: Canadian Musical Heritage.
Cringan, Alexander T. 1898 'Iroquois Music,' *Report of the Minister of Education of Ontario* (Appendix). Toronto.
[Cronk, Sam, ed.] 1990. *Sound of the Drum: A Resource Guide.* Brantford: Woodland Cultural Centre.
Curtis, Edward S. 1907–30/1970. *The North American Indian.* Cambridge: Harvard University Press; reprint ed., New York: Johnson Reprint.
Eastman, Sheila, and Timothy J. McGee. 1983. *Barbara Pentland.* Toronto: University of Toronto Press.
Farwell, Arthur. 1902. 'Aspects of Indian Music,' *Southern Workman* 31: 211–17.
– 1903. 'A Brief View of American Indian Music,' *Messenger* 4, 276–9.
Farwell, Bruce, ed. 1972. *Guide to the Music of Arthur Farwell and to the Microfilm Collection of His Work.* New York.
Fletcher, Alice Cunningham. 1893. *A Study of Omaha Indian Music.* Cambridge, Mass.: Archeological and Ethnological Papers of the Peabody Museum, Harvard University.
– 1898. 'Indian Songs and Music,' *Journal of American Folklore* 1 (April–June), 85–93.
– 1900. *Indian Story and Song from North America.* Boston: Small Maynard.
Frye, Northrop. 1971. *The Bush Garden.* Toronto: Anansi.
Garland, Hamlin. 1930. 'Roadside Meetings of a Literary Nomad,' *Bookman* 71 (March), 46.
Garland, Peter. 1982. *Americas: Essays on American Music and Culture, 1973–80.* Santa Fe: SOUNDINGS Press.

Gilbert, Henry F. 1911. 'Note on the Indian Music,' in Edward S. Curtis,' *The North American Indian*, vol. 6. New York: Johnson Reprint.
Gillespie, John. 1978. *Nineteenth-Century American Piano Music*. New York: Dover Publications.
Gleason, Harold, and Warren Becker. 1980. *20th-Century American Composers*. Bloomington: Frangipani Press.
Hallowell, A. Irving. 1965. 'The Backwash of the Frontier: The Impact of the Indian on American Culture,' in *The Frontier in Perspective*, Walter D. Wyman, Clifton B. Kroeber, eds. Madison: University of Wisconsin Press, 229–58.
Hamm, Charles. 1983. *Music in the New World*. New York: W.W. Norton.
Helm, June, and Nancy Oestreich Lurie. 1966. *The Dogrib Hand Game*, Bulletin 205, National Museum of Canada, Ottawa.
Hitchcock, H. Wiley. 1988. *Music in the United States*, 3rd ed., Englewood Cliffs, NJ: Prentice-Hall.
Jameson, Anna. 1838. *Winter Studies and Summer Rambles in Canada*. London.
Jezic, Diane P. 1988. *Women Composers: The Lost Tradition Found*. New York: The Feminist Press.
Kallmann, Helmut. 1960. *A History of Music in Canada 1534–1914*. Toronto: University of Toronto Press.
Kallmann, H. et al., ed. 1992. 'Native North Americans in Canada,' in *Encyclopedia of Music in Canada*, 2nd ed. Toronto: University of Toronto Press, 923–35.
Kassel, Richard. 1991. 'Harry Partch in the Field,' *Musicworks* 51 (Autumn 1991), 6-15.
Keillor, Elaine. 1983. *Piano Music I*, Canadian Musical Heritage I. Ottawa: Canadian Musical Heritage.
– 1986. 'The Role of Youth in the Continuation of Dogrib Musical Traditions,' *1986 Yearbook for Traditional Music* 18: 61–75.
– 1988–9. 'La naissance d'un genre musical nouveau: Fusion du traditionnel et du "country",' *Recherches amerindiennes au québec* 18/4, 65–74.
Lazarevich, Gordana. 1988. *The Musical World of Frances James and Murray Adaskin*. Toronto: University of Toronto Press.
Lefebvre, Marie-Thérèse. 1986. *Serge Garant et la révolution musicale au Québec*. Montreal: Louise Courteau.
Lieurance, Thurlow. 1936. 'Music of the American Indian,' in *Music on the Air*, ed. Hazel Gertrude Kinsella, New York: Viking Press, 148–57.
Longyear, Katherine Marie Eide. 1968. 'Henry F. Gilbert, His Life and Works,' PhD diss., University of Rochester, Eastman School of Music.
Lowens, Margery Morgan. 1971. *The New York Years of Edward MacDowell*. PhD diss., University of Michigan.

Marrocco, W. Thomas and Harold Gleason. 1964. *Music in America*. New York: W.W. Norton.
Mather, Jane. 1992. 'Composer Looks to Arctic as Inspiration for New Symphony,' *Classical Music Magazine* 15/3 (June), 13.
Maust, Wilbur R. 1973. The Symphonies of Anthony Philip Heinrich Based on American Themes. PhD diss., Indiana University.
– 1981. 'The American Indian in the Orchestral Music of Anthony Philip Heinrich,' in *Music East and West*, ed. Thomas Noblitt, Festschrift Series No. 3. New York: Pendragon Press.
McGregor, Gaile. 1985. *The Wacousta Syndrome*. Toronto: University of Toronto Press.
McIntosh, Dale. 1989. *History of Music in British Columbia 1850–1950*. Victoria, BC: Sono Nis Press.
McMillan, Barclay Francis Hanlon. 1983. 'Music in Canada, 1791–1867: A Travellers' Perspective.' MA thesis, Carleton University.
McNutt, James C. 1984. 'John Comfort Fillmore, A Student of Indian Music Reconsidered.' *American Music* 2: 61–70.
Pantaleoni, Hewitt. 1985. 'A Reconsideration of Fillmore Reconsidered,' *American Music* 3/2: 217–28.
Partch, Harry. 1979. *Genesis of a Music*, New York: Da Capo Press.
Perlson, Harry D. 1978. 'Charles Wakefield Cadman: His Life and Works.' PhD diss., University of Rochester, Eastman School of Music.
Poirier, Lucien, ed. 1992. *Chansons III sur des textes français*. Canadian Musical Heritage XII, Ottawa: Canadian Musical Heritage.
Roberts, Helen, and Diamond Jenness. 1925. *Songs of the Copper Eskimos*. Report of the Canadian Arctic Expedition, 1913–1916, vol. 14, Ottawa.
Robertson, James Oliver. 1980. *American Myth, American Reality*. New York: Hill & Wang.
Rogers, Delmer D. 1967. 'Nineteenth-Century Music in New York City as Reflected in the Career of George Frederick Bristow.' PhD diss., University of Michigan.
Salvatore, Ramon. 1990. Comments at Lecture/Recital, Sonneck Society Conference, Toronto, 21 April.
Schuetze, Frederick Edwin. 1984. 'The Idealization of American Indian Music as Exemplified in Two Indianist Song Cycles of Charles Wakefield Cadman: An Historical and Stylistic Analysis to Aid in Their Performance.' DMA diss., University of Missouri, Kansas City.
Skilton, Charles Sanford. 1938/1964. 'American Indian Music,' in *The International Cyclopedia of Music and Musicians*, ed. Nicolas Slonimsky. New York: Dodd, Mead & Company, 46–8.
Smith, Gordon. 1989. 'Ernest Gagnon on Nationalism and Canadian Music: Folk

and Native Sources,' *Canadian Folk Music Journal* 17: 32–9.
Temperley, Nicholas. 1990. 'The Great Musical Divide: Ocean or Channel?'
American Music 8/1, 1–11.

APPENDIX

Table 1
A Representative List of Compositions by American Composers Based on Amerindian or Inuit Material

Date	Composer	Title	Genre/Medium
1859	A.P. Heinrich	*Der Felsen von Plymouth*	orchestra(orch)
1891-5	E. MacDowell	*Indian Suite*	orch.
1893	C. Troyer	*Two Zuni Songs*	voice(vc) piano
1896	E. MacDowell	*From an Indian Lodge, op. 51, no. 5*	piano (pf)
1901	E. MacDowell	*Mid-Winter, op. 62, no. 3*	pf
	E. MacDowell	*In Deep Woods, op. 62, no. 5*	pf
	E. MacDowell	*Indian Idyl, op. 62, no. 6*	pf
	A. Farwell	*American Indian Melodies*	pf
1903	H.W. Loomis	*Lyrics of the Red Man: I*	pf
1904	C. Troyer	*Ghost Dance of the Zunis*	pf
1905	A. Farwell	*Cahuilla Bird Dance Song*	vc, pf
	A. Farwell	*From Mesa and Plain: Navajo War Dance, Pawnee Horses, Wa-Wan Chorus*	pf
1906	J.C. Fillmore	Harmonizations in A. Fletcher's *Indian Story and Song from North America*	vc, pf
	A. Beach	*Eskimos, op. 64*	pf
	F. Converse	*Pipe of Desire*	opera
	A. Farwell	*Impressions of the Wa-Wan Ceremony of the Omahas, op. 21*	pf
1908	A. Farwell	*Three Indian Songs, op. 32*	vc, pf
1909	C.W. Cadman	*Four American Indian Songs, op. 45*	vc, pf
1910	A. Nevin	*Poia*	opera
1911	H. Gilbert	*Indian Sketches*	orch/pf duet
	V. Herbert	*Natoma*	opera
	F. Converse	*The Sacrifice*	opera
1912	C.W. Cadman	*Idealized Indian Themes*	pf
		Daoma: The Land of the Misty Water	opera
	H. Gilbert	*Indian Scenes*	pf
	C. Ives	*The Indians*	chamber(ch) ensemble(en)
	H. Parker	*Mona*	opera

(continued)

Table 1 (continued)

1913	T.W. Lieurance	Nine Indian Songs	vc, pf
1914	C.W. Cadman	Thunderbird Suite	orch
		From Wigwam and Tepee	song cycle
1915	C.W. Cadman	Two Indian Dances	string quartet
1917	T.W. Lieurance	Indian Melodies for Violin and Piano	
	J.A. Carpenter	Little Indian	pf
1918	C.W. Cadman	Shanewis: The Robin Woman	opera
	P.W. Orem	American Indian Rhapsody	pf
	C. Troyer	Midnight Visit in the Sacred Shrines ...	clarinet, oboe, pf
	C.S. Skilton	Three Indian Sketches	pf
1920	C.S. Skilton	Sioux Flute Serenade	orch
		Suite Primeval	orch
	T.W. Lieurance	Songs of the American Indian	
1922	A. Farwell	The Hako	string quartet
	A. Beach	From Blackbird Hills: An Omaha Tribal Dance, op. 83	pf
1925	F. Jacobi	String Quartet on Indian Themes	
1926	C.S. Skilton	American Indian Fantasy	organ
1927	C.S. Skilton	Kalopin	opera
1929	C.S. Skilton	Shawnee Indian Hunting Dance	pf
	A. Beach	String Quartet, op. 79	
1930	C.S. Skilton	Bluefeather: The Sun Bride	opera
1932	E. Siegmeister	Theme and Variations No. 1	pf
	C.S. Skilton	American Indian Fantasie	cello, orch
1933	C.S. Skilton	Ticonderoga	cantata
1937	A. Farwell	Navajo War Dance, op. 102, no. 1	chorus
		The Old Man's Love Songs, op. 102, no. 2	chorus
1937	C.W. Cadman	The American Suite	orch
1938	H. Cowell	Amerind Suite	pf
	A. Beach	Piano Trio, op. 150	pf
1940	E. Carter	Pocohontas	ballet
1944	C. McPhee	Four Iroquois Dances	orch
	H. Cowell	Animal Magic	band
1950	H. Partch	Cloud Chamber Music: Intrusions #11	
	Louis W. Ballard	All works	pf, etc.
1955	H. Partch	The Bewitched – A Dance Satire	vc, ch, en
	L. Harrison	Four Strict Songs	8 vcs, orch
1960s?	J. Bojanowski	Indian Sketches	orch
1979	J. Zaimont	The Magic World: Ritual Music for Three (Amerindian)	
1980	R. Loman	Five Ceremonial Masks for the Yeibichai Night Chants	pf
1982	J. Zaimont	From the Great Land: Women's Songs (Inuit)	

Table 2
A Representative List of Compositions by Canadian Composers Based on
Amerindian/Inuit Material

Date	Composer	Title	Genre/Medium
1858	E. Gagnon	Stadaconé: Danse sauvage	pf
1865–6	C. Lavallée	TIQ: The Indian Question	opera
1879	A.A. Clappé	Canada's Welcome: A Masque	stage work
1891	C. Lavallée	Marche indienne: TIQ	band
1906	Emma Seymour	Wahnotee: March	pf
1907	Job Nelson	The Imperial Native March	pf/band
1912	J. Vézina	Le Fétiche	opera
1920s–50	L. Roy	47 Iroquois transcriptions arr.	pf, vc
1920s?	A. La Liberté	Deux Chansons indiennes	string quartet
1925	A. La Liberté	Tenaouiche Tenaga Ouicheka	pf, vc
1927	L.-P. Morin	Three Eskimos	pf
1928	E. MacMillan	Three Songs of the West Coast	pf, vc
1930s	L.-P. Morin	Chants du sacrifice	chorus 2 pf
1935	L. Smith	Indian Romance	cello(vcl.), pf
		Arrangements of West Coast Amerindian songs	
1939	L. Smith	An Indian Woman's Song	vc, pf
1942	J. Coulthard	Two Songs of the Haida Indians	vc, pf
	J. Weinzweig	Improvisation on an Indian Tune	organ
1945	J. Weinzweig	To the Lands Over Yonder	chorus
1940s	Q. Maclean	Algonquin Legend	orch
1944	J.-J. Gagnier	Journey	english horn, strings
1946	J. Weinzweig	Edge of the World	orch
1940s	R. Farnon	Canadian Impressions: Pow Wow	orch
1947	A. Brott	From Sea to Sea	orch
1948	W.H. Anderson	Indian Lullaby	chorus
1949	J. Weinzweig	Red Ear of Corn	ballet
1950	K. Peacock	Songs of the Cedar	vc, ch en
	F. Morrison	Tzinquaw: The Thunderbird and the Killer-Whale	musical drama
1952	M. Eisenstadt	Suite of Three Canadian Dances	
	B. Pentland	The Lake	opera
1954	U. Kasemets	Recitative and Rondino (Inuit)	strings
1955	S. Moisse	Variations sur un thème huron	pf
1958	M. Adaskin	Algonquin Symphony	orch
1959	C. Champagne	Altitude	orch, chorus
1960	M. Barnes	I Walked on Ice (Inuit)	chorus
1961	S. Garant	Anerca	ch en
	G. George	Songs of the Salish	orch
	V. Archer	Three Sketches for Orchestra	orch
	W. Bottenberg	Three Amerindian Songs	vc, chorus

(continued)

Table 2 (continued)

Year	Composer	Title	Forces
1962	P. McIntyre	*Fantasy on an Eskimo Song*	woodwinds
	T. Kenins	*Ojibway Song*	chorus
1966	H. Freedman	*Anerca*	vc, pf
	R. Fleming	*Fantasia No. 1 on Canadian Folk Themes*	saxophones, percussion
	A. Kunz	*The Sleeping Giant*	solo vc, chorus
1967	H. Somers	*Louis Riel*	opera
	R. Fleming	*Indian Legend*	ch en
	T. Kenins	*Fantasy Variations on an Eskimo Lullaby*	flute, viola
	T. Polgar	*The Last Words of Louis Riel*	cantata
1968	J. Beckwith	*The Sun Dance*	solo vc, chorus, organ
	M. Barnes	*Two Eskimo Poems*	Bass vc, TB chorus
1969	M. Adaskin	*Qalala and Nilaula of the North*	orch
	J. Beckwith	*Nass River Dance Song*	vc, pf
	V. Davies	*Anerca: Three Eskimo Chants*	vc, ch en
1970	M. Adaskin	*There Is My People Sleeping*	orch
	H. Freedman	*Klee Wyck*	orch
	T. Kenins	*Lagalaî*	chorus, ch en
1971	D. Healey	*Arctic Images*	orch
	K. Bissell	*How the Loon Got Its Necklace*	narr, ch en
	H. Freedman	*Keewaydin*	SAA chorus, tape
	R. M. Schafer	*Miniwanka*	SA or SATB chorus
	J. Tenney	*Hey when I sing ...*	chorus
1972	A. Brott	*How Thunder and Lightning Came To Be*	narr ch en
	I. Raminsh	*The Great Sea*	chorus, orch
1973	N. Beecroft	*Three Impressions*	chorus, pf
	D. Healey	*Salish Song*	chorus
		Eskimo Hunting Song	chorus
	T. Kenins	*Sawan-oong*	vc, chorus, orch
	P. Pedersen	*An Old Song of the Sun and the Moon and the Fear of Loneliness*	vc, elec. fl, pf
1974	K. Bissell	*Song for Fine Weather*	chorus
	M. Adaskin	*Nootka Ritual*	orch
	J. Coulthard	*Canada Mosaic*	orch
	D. Healey	*Three Quiet Pieces for Organ*	
	M.C. Saint-Marcoux	*Ishuma*	vc, ch en
	A. Rae	*Poems for Trio*	violin, cello, pf
1975	O. Morawetz	*The Song My Paddle Sings*	chorus
	K. Bissell	*A Song of Longing*	chorus
	T. Kenins	*Naačnaača: Trance*	orch
	T. Goldberg	*Songs of the Loon and the Raven*	orch, tape

(continued)

1976	D. Healey	*Seabird Island*	opera
	M. Forsyth	*Three Métis Songs from Saskatchewan*	vc, orch
	W. Buczynski	*Tales of Nanabozho*	narr, woodwind quintet
1977	M. Barnes	*Legend of the Wind*	guitar
	S.I. Glick	*Lullaby*	chorus
	L. Applebaum	*Inunit: from the Eskimo*	vc, ch en
	A. Fisher	*Cry Wolf*	Tenor vc, flute, violin, cello
	M. Surdin	*A Big Bear*	chorus
1978	E. Arteaga	*Echoes of the Land*	chorus
	T. Sullivan	*Five Indian Songs*	vc, flute, guitar
	P. Ware	*Tsankawi*	orch
	M. Colgrass	*Wolf*	cello
	C. Crawley	*Tyendinaga*	orch/band
1979	P. Crawford	*Six Canadian Folk Songs*	5 vc, pf
	M. Barnes	*Anerca for solo bassoon*	
1980	V. Archer	*Primeval*	Tenor vc, pf
	M. Adaskin	*Eskimo Melodies*	pf
	M. Barnes	*Anerca: The Raven and the Children*	narr, clarinet, bassoon
	E. Arteaga	*Echoes of the Land*	chorus
1981	S.I. Glick	*I Breathe a New Song*	chorus
	A. Pauk	*Legend of the Raven*	pf
	M. Barnes	*Anerca III*	narr, harp
	R.M. Schafer	*Patria: The Prologue – The Princess of the Stars*	environmental pageant
1982	C. Crawley	*Songs of Duke Redbird*	vc, pf
	A. Fisher	*Six Fantasy Pieces for piano*	
	I. Raminsh	*Along the Flower Trail*	chorus
	M. Barnes	*Indian Suite*	cello, guitar
1983	H. Somers	*Shaman's Song*	vc, pf
	I. Anhalt	*Winthrop (II:1)*	historical pageant
	M. Barnes	*Anerca for solo string bass*	
	R.W. Henderson	*Clear Sky and Thunder*	chorus, flute, percussion, pf
1984	J. Beckwith	*Arctic Dances*	oboe, pf
	V. Archer	*Ikpakhuaq* (Inuit)	piano trio
	M. Forsyth	*Atayoskewin*	orch
1985	I. Raminsh	*Song of the Stars: Song of the Lights*	SA, pf
	D. Schmidt	*Winter Songs of the Myth People*	vcs, ch en
1986	R. Deegan	*Death Song of Long Lance*	SAB, pf
	M. Gardiner	*A Long Time Ago in the Future*	pf
	W. Bottenberg	*Inook*	opera

(continued)

Table 2 (continued)

Year	Composer	Title	Instrumentation
	J. Tenney	*Three Indigenous Songs*	ch en
	S. Rickard	*Four Indian Songs*	soprano, ch en
	M. Barnes	*Themes from Maid of the Mist*	2 guitars
1987	M. Gardiner	*The Legend of the First Rabbit*	narr, flute, cello, pf
	D. McIntosh	*Kiviuq: An Inuit Legend*	narr, orch
	V. Archer	*Evocations for two pianos and orchestra*	
	I. Raminsh	*Copper Eskimo Song*	chorus
1988	P. Cardy	*Qilakitsoq: The Sky Hangs Low*	clarinet, bassoon, horn, pf
	H. Somers	*A Midwinter Night's Dream*	children's opera
	D. Healey	*Gabriola*	orch
	John Kim Bell	*In the Land of the Spirits*	ballet score
1989	R. Luedeke	*Tales of the Netsilik*	narr, orch
1990	G. Kulesha	*Shaman Song*	chorus, string quartet, clarinet, pf
	M. Colgrass	*Snow Walker*	organ, orch
	C.A. Weaver	*Algonquin Dream*	ch en
	D. Healey	*Salal*	orch
	V. Archer	*Improvisation for a Snare Drum*	
1991	D. Foley	*The Seventh Fire*	organ
1992	D. Patriquin	*Innoria: Huron Dance*	SSAA, pf
1993	L. Bouchard	*Ocamow (cree text)*	baritone, guitar, cello, percussion

PART FIVE

Canadian Popular Music, Past and Present

GORDON E. SMITH

The Genesis of Ernest Gagnon's *Chansons populaires du Canada*[1]

Ernest Gagnon (1834-1915) is remembered today for his folksong collection, the *Chansons populaires du Canada*, first published in 1865-7. The collection was one of the few in the nineteenth century to include integral renditions, musical and textual, of a sizeable folksong repertory (over one hundred songs). On a broad level, Gagnon's collection may be evaluated within the nineteenth-century European context in which folksong was considered by many as an effective means of nationalist expression;[2] in more specific terms, the collection may be considered within the framework of the spirit of French-Canadian nationalism which was the basis of the 'Mouvement littéraire de Québec.'[3] It was no coincidence that Gagnon's collection was published first concurrently with the culmination of the 'Mouvement littéraire de Québec' in the 1860s. The *Chansons populaires* was intended by Gagnon to be an integral part of that movement and, as such, it is appropriate to consider the work in its nationalist terms. In the following essay, the genesis of Gagnon's collection is traced. This genesis includes examinations of (1) the nationalist context in Quebec and a discussion of an important forerunner to Gagnon's work, Hubert LaRue's *Les Chansons populaires et historiques du Canada*; (2) publication details of the collection's two editions, and reaction to the collection, both in French Canada and in France; and (3) changes in the second edition and subsequent reprintings of the book. The thirteen reprintings (see Appendix) of Gagnon's *Chansons populaires* are testimony to the collection's continuing nationalist appeal to French Canadians.

The 'Mouvement littéraire de Québec,' of which Gagnon was a part in the 1860s, began around 1840. Following the 1837-8 rebellion, French Canadians felt conquered for a second time, and in a position of economic, political, and social inferiority vis-à-vis their anglophone counterparts. Faced with a closer prospect of assimilation and a need to cope with their sense of humiliation, French Canadians turned to their past. According to Monière:

The past assumed values that compensated for the powerlessness of the present ... Distress about what was to come found expression, in our young literature, in glorification of the colony's early days. Facing assimilation and fearing oblivion, we began to write our 'epic.' (*Ideologies in Quebec*, 129)

James Huston's *Répertoire national* (Montreal, 1982), a four-volume series including a variety of French-Canadian literary and historical works from the 1840s, represented an early attempt at establishing a nationalist canon. Another landmark nationalist work was François-Xavier Garneau's *Histoire du Canada*.[4] The works of Huston and Garneau fuelled nationalist aspirations and, as noted by Hayne, the 'Mouvement littéraire de Québec' reached a high point in the 1860s (1983: 535). The primary aim of the small group of intellectuals which made up this group was to create a nationalist literature which, although inspired by French Romantic models, was truly French-Canadian. The dichotomy between the 'Mouvement's' desire to establish its own nationalist identity and its links with literary trends in France was one of its distinguishing features.

An example was the citing of folk repertory as an effective means of creating a French-Canadian nationalist idiom in literature. Like their counterparts in France, nineteenth-century French-Canadian writers developed the technique of incorporating folksong texts in their works. Writers in both countries used excerpts and complete texts from folksongs to provide local colour; they described 'le peuple' as vividly and accurately as possible, albeit in an idealized manner. This technique became a characteristic of Romantic writers such as Chateaubriand, and subsequently of realists like Xavier Marmier. French-Canadian writers introduced 'chansons populaires' into their works in an effort to portray the French-Canadian people and their way of life. As Laforte asserts, it was French-Canadian writers who, simultaneously with their confrères in France, were the first to discover 'la chanson du peuple' (1973: 50). In fact, the first systematic collections of folk-song texts were provided by novelists such as Philippe Aubert de Gaspé. In *Les Anciens Canadiens* (1863) de Gaspé included seventeen songs, adding another ten in his *Mémoires* (1885). Other French-Canadian writers who cited folksong texts in this manner were Pierre-Joseph-Olivier Chauveau (*Charles Guérin*, 1852) and Joseph-Charles Taché (*Forestiers et voyageurs*, 1863).

As part of the 'Mouvement's drive to promote nationalism in literature, two journals were founded in the 1860s. The first of these, *Les Soirées* canadiennes, was founded by Joseph-Charles Taché, Alfred Garneau, and Hector Langevin, and ran for five years (1861–5). Les Soirées canadiennes became a vehicle for writers such as Taché (Forestiers et voyageurs, 1863). Le Foyer canadien was the second scholarly journal founded and published in the 1860s (1863–6) and another medium for 'Mouvement' writers. The statement of the founders' intentions in the introductory 'Prospectus' to the inaugural issue is a poignant assertion of the group's nationalist aspirations:

Ce recueil, destiné à réunir et à conserver nos essais de littérature indigène, sera consacré à la publication d'oeuvres inédites: – poésies – critiques littéraires – légendes – nouvelles, pourvu qu'elles soient fidèles aux moeurs et de la nature de notre pays. (Foyer canadien, 1863: 5).

[This collection is intended to contain and conserve our indigenous literature; it will be dedicated to the publication of previously unpublished works: – poetry, literary criticism, legends, short stories – as long as they are in accordance with the ways and nature of our country.][5]

Les Soirées canadiennes and Le Foyer canadien attracted the vanguard of the nationalist effort including such figures as Henri-Raymond Casgrain, Antoine-Gérin Lajoie, Hubert LaRue, Philippe Aubert de Gaspé, Louis Fréchette, Ernest Gagnon, and others.

The forerunner of Gagnon's song collection, Les Chansons populaires et historiques du Canada was completed by one of Gagnon's colleagues, Hubert LaRue (1830–1881).[6] Published in Le Foyer canadien in two parts, in 1863 and 1865 respectively, Les Chansons populaires et historiques du Canada is an essay and collection of folksong texts. The first, or 'chansons populaires' section of LaRue's work, which appeared in 1863, is structured on a division of the song repertory into categories pertaining to the origins of the individual songs as well as subject groups; in the nineteenth century this method of organization was not uncommon. This discussion is continued with the presentation of twelve song texts, of which some are fragmentary while others are complete with variants. The second, or 'chansons historiques' (1865), part of LaRue's work consists of songs associated with historical events from the seventeenth and eighteenth centuries such as battles and celebrations.

Apart from LaRue's strong interest in French-Canadian literature and history and his fervent belief in folksong as a vital means of documenting his country's national heritage, the impetus for his song collection came from two French sources: the first was the Instructions, a set of guidelines for folksong collecting published by Jean-Jacques Ampère, secretary of the organizing committee for the French governmental enquiry into folksong which took place in France in the 1850s; the second was the large collection of French folksongs compiled by the French writer Champfleury, with musical renditions (including accompaniments) by Jean-Jacques Weckerlin. LaRue also examined literature concerning folksong, such as Nerval's *La Bohème galante*, and Canadian songbooks such as John Lovell's *Recueil de chansons canadiennes et françaises* (1859) and the well-known *Chansonnier des collèges* (1860).[7] In spite of the French influences on LaRue's work, his position as a collector reflected a distinctly French-Canadian viewpoint paralleled and later expanded upon by Gagnon.

The reception of LaRue's *Chansons populaires* essay in France prompted a reply from Champfleury which forms a historic link with Gagnon's *Chansons populaires*. Extracts from Champfleury's letter to LaRue were published in *Le Foyer Canadien*:

Monsieur,
    Un de mes amis a bien voulu me communiquer le premier numéro de votre article si intéressant sur les Chansons populaires du Canada ...
    Les recherches que vous avez faites, Monsieur, sont d'une riche importance dans cette question encore si neuve en France ...
    Je n'ai regretté que la manque de musique, Monsieur, car les mélodies ont dû subir les mêmes modifications que les poésies ... (1864: 386–7).

[Dear Sir,
    A friend of mine was nice enough to send me the first publication of your very interesting article on the popular songs of Canada ...
    The research that you have done, Sir, is of great importance in this field of study which is still so new in France ...
    My only regret is the lack of music, Sir, as the melodies must have undergone the same modifications as the poetry ...]

The acknowledgment of LaRue's work by a well-known and respected French literary figure and folksong collector was indeed a strong endorsement of the French-Canadian folksong effort. At the conclusion of the 'historiques' section of his study, LaRue used the opportunity to answer Champfleury's remark concerning music:

... comme le dit si bien M. Champfleury, 'musiques et paroles sont inséparables, ce sont deux amis qui parent mutuellement ...'

J'ai donc été des plus heureux en apprenant que M. Ernest Gagnon voulait bien se charger de soin de publier ces chansons, avec paroles et musique ... Grâce à lui, ces chansons populaires du Canada ... les vieilles chansons de la France, seront désormais à l'abri des assauts du temps ... (*Le Foyer canadien* 1865: 69–70).

[... as Mr Champfleury so aptly remarked, 'music and lyrics are inseparable, they are two friends who embellish each other ...'
I was therefore among the happiest to learn that Mr Ernest Gagnon was willing to take the careful responsibility of publishing those songs, with words and music ... Thanks to him, these popular songs of Canada ... the old songs of France, will from now on be sheltered from the ravages of time ...]

In LaRue's opinion, Ernest Gagnon, as a musician, was eminently qualified to prepare the collection of folksongs with musical notation and commentaries.

Gagnon shared with LaRue a strong interest in French-Canadian literature and a fervent belief in folksong as a vital means of documenting Quebec's national heritage. Thus, the *Chansons populaires* may be understood as a continuation of LaRue's work, or as an effort to present the subscribers of *Le Foyer canadien* with musical as well as textual renditions of French-Canadian folksongs. Unlike the two parts of LaRue's *Chansons populaires et historiques du Canada*, which were published as integral contributions to *Le Foyer canadien*, Gagnon's *Chansons populaires* first appeared in a series of six instalments which were offered as an extra feature or bonus to *Foyer canadien* subscribers between 1865 and 1867. The fact that the collection first appeared in instalments also confirms Gagnon's initial intention, which was to provide a nationalist work along the lines of his colleagues.'[8]

A statement following the 1863 prospectus in the *Foyer canadien* reports that there were 2413 subscribers, and a count of the subscriber list from the same year reveals at least 2050 individual names and twenty-one newspapers in locations including Quebec, Montreal, Sorel, Trois-Rivières, and Ottawa.[9] Although this represents the *Foyer canadien*'s distribution a year ahead of the first instalment of the *Chansons populaires*, it is fair to assume that the number of subscribers remained approximately the same in 1865.

The dates of the six instalments of the *Chansons populaires* can be determined from announcements in *Le Courrier du Canada* for the first five and *Le Journal de Québec* for the sixth:
First instalment – 8 February 1865
Second instalment – 31 May 1865
Third instalment – 1 September 1865
Fourth instalment – 20 October 1865

Fifth instalment – 7 September 1866
Sixth instalment – January-February 1867[10]

For example, the first instalment reads:

Nous avons ... reçu la première livraison de la prime offerte aux abonnés par la direction du Foyer: Le titre de cette prime est: 'Chansons populaires du Canada' recueillies et publiées avec annotations, M. Ernest Gagnon (*Le Courrier du Canada*, 8 February 1865: [3]).

[We have received the first instalment of the free gift offered to the subscribers by the management of the *Foyer*: the title is 'Chansons populaires du Canada' collected and published with annotations by Mr Ernest Gagnon.]

The announcements for the remaining five instalments are similarly brief and do not contain specific information about the collection. An exception is the third announcement, which indicates that that instalment was larger than the first two (*Le Courrier*, 1 September 1865: [2]).

The first (1865) edition of Gagnon's *Chansons populaires* was indeed the six instalments which were issued consecutively between February 1865 and February 1867. The number of copies of the first edition can thereby be determined by the number of subscribers to the *Foyer canadien*, which, as previously indicated, was approximately 2500. The distribution of the first edition of the *Chansons populaires* was therefore both serial and limited. Indeed the only reason that libraries such as the Laval University Library, the Bibliothèque du Parlement (Quebec City), and the National Library in Ottawa possess bound copies of this edition is that some *Foyer canadien* subscribers had their respective six instalments bound into single volumes by the 'Bureaux du Foyer canadien.' These volumes, not the loose journal articles, found their way into libraries and other archival collections.[11]

Evidence that the *Chansons populaires* was also sent to Gagnon's French colleagues in instalments is confirmed in one review dating from April 1865, in which the French music critic Louis Roger mentions receiving the first instalment of the collection (*Le Courrier*, 28 April 1865: [3]). Similarly, Jean-Baptiste Weckerlin's request to the manager of the *Foyer canadien*, M. Darveau, for a copy of the *Chansons populaires* was also based on the examination of one instalment (*Le Foyer*, 1866: 330–1).

It has been suggested that the reason for the delay of nearly a year between the fourth and fifth instalments of the *Chansons populaires* was that Gagnon wished to make concordances with recently published French song collections (Laforte: 95). This suggestion is debatable, however, since

The Genesis of Ernest Gagnon's *Chansons Populaires*   227

Gagnon's specific references to French collections are spread almost evenly throughout his work. Another explanation for the delay is that, according to Gagnon's own account in a letter to Jean-Baptiste Weckerlin dated 18 March 1866, the printer, Georges Desbarats, had recently moved his operation to Ottawa from Quebec thereby temporarily stalling all activity (Gagnon, letter 18 March 1866).[12]

Reaction to the first edition of the *Chansons populaires* was positive in both France and French Canada. The French critic Louis Roger wrote:

Le recueil si éminemment intéressant des Chansons populaires du Canada, par M. Ernest Gagnon, n'a pas trouvé des admirateurs seulement au Canada ... Ne connaissant personne au Canada, nous avons surpris de recevoir de Québec, une brochure ... qui nous montre que les mers ne sont plus un obstacle à l'échange des idées ... bravo et merci. (*Le Courrier* 28 April 1865: [3])

[The very interesting collection entitled *Chansons populaires du Canada* by Mr Ernest Gagnon, has found admirers not only in Canada ... Not knowing anyone in Canada, we were surprised to receive from Quebec a booklet ... which shows us that the ocean is no longer an obstacle to the exchange of ideas ... bravo and thank you.]

It is understandable that both Gagnon and the *Foyer canadien* authorities felt prompted to forward the *Chansons populaires* to their French colleagues. The French Canadians evidently believed that, since many of the songs in the collection could be interpreted as variants of French songs, their colleagues in France would welcome this initiative.

Possibly the most important endorsement of Gagnon's work was from Jean-Baptiste Weckerlin, whose own research on French folksongs and collaboration on Champfleury's 1860 collection made him one of the leading authorities of the day. Evidence of Weckerlin's enthusiasm is found in the above-cited letter, dated Paris, 25 February 1866, which was a request to the *Foyer canadien* manager, M.C. Darveau, for a copy of the *Chansons populaires*. A letter dated Quebec, 18 March 1866, reveals that Gagnon had personally received a request from Weckerlin for a copy of the song collection. In his response to his French colleagues, Gagnon explains the most likely reason for the delay between the fourth and fifth instalments:

Cher Monsieur,
   J'ai reçu votre lettre il y a près de deux mois, et si j'ai tant tardé à vous répondre c'est que j'attendais un jour à l'autre l'apparition d'une 5e livraison des C-P qui

n'arrive pas: l'éditeur, M. Desbarats ... ayant un surcroit considérable en ce moment, par suite de transport de son imprimerie à Outaouais, notre nouvelle capitale.

Je suis d'autant plus heureux de vous offrir un exemplaire de mon travail ... [et] les quatre premières livraisons de mes *Chansons populaires du Canada* ... (Gagnon letter 1866)

[Dear Sir,
I received your letter nearly two months ago, and if I have waited so long to reply it is because I was waiting ... for the fifth instalment of the [*Chansons populaires*] to appear ... The editor, Mr Desbarats ... has had a considerable amount of work at this time following the move of his printing shop to Ottawa, our new capital.

I am very happy to present you with a copy of my work ... and I am sending you the first four instalments of my *Chansons populaires du Canada* ...]

Gagnon concludes the letter by writing that he is familiar with Weckerlin's work, and emphasizes the continuing affinity French Canadians have with 'la belle patrie.' Weckerlin was so impressed by the *Chansons populaires* that in 1868 he nominated Gagnon a corresponding member of the 'Société des Compositeurs de Paris,' an organization of which the French scholar was both librarian and archivist.

Gagnon's daughter, Blanche, wrote that Weckerlin, d'Ortigue, and Théodore Dubois all liked the *Chansons populaires* when it first appeared, in particular Gagnon's scholarly detail and precision and the plainchant–folksong thesis discussed in the song commentaries and the 'Remarques générales.'[13] An undated letter from Théodore Dubois to M. J.-Arthur Paquet, maître de chapelle at St-Sauveur Church in Quebec, further corroborates French support for Gagnon's views on the musical language of the 'chanson populaire':

Le volume des Chansons populaires est très intéressant, et les commentaires de l'auteur, M. Ernest Gagnon, sont d'un esprit très judicieux, très artiste, et très averti. Je vous serai obligé de le félciter sincèrement de ma part. Je partage ses idées en matière d'accompagnement de ces chants ... (Dubois, letter n.d.)

[The volume of popular songs is very interesting, and the comments by the author, Mr Ernest Gagnon, display a very judicious, artistic, and informed mind. I would be much obliged if you would congratulate him sincerely for me. I share his ideas in matters concerning the accompaniment of these songs ...]

Not surprisingly, the *Chansons populaires* was also received favourably in Quebec. For the subscribers of *Le Foyer canadien*, the song collection represented a unique contribution. An article in a Montreal publication aptly expressed appreciation of the *Chansons populaires* as an important affirmation of French-Canadian nationalism:

C'est une compilation intéressante et au point de vue des moeurs du peuple canadien et comme souvenir de vieilles traditions déjà passées. La notation seule suffrait pour rendre ce livre précieux ... Les 'Chansons populaires' sont un ouvrage précieux où ceux qui sont tant soit peu sceptiques à l'endroit de notre nationalité aimeront à aller retremper leur foi dans l'avenir. (*L'Echo de la France,* April 1867: 410)

[It (*Chansons populaires*) is an interesting ... compilation both from the point of view of the nature of the Canadian people and as a remembrance of old traditions of days gone by. The notation alone would suffice to make this book precious ... The *Chansons populaires* is a special work, and those who are a bit sceptical about our nationality will be able to rejuvenate their faith in the future.]

This review continues with a reproduction of several pages from the 'Remarques générales' and from Gagnon's commentaries for three songs from the collection: 'À la claire fontaine,' 'Par derrièr' chez mon père – Vive la Canadienne,' and 'Digue dindaine.' One of the most poignant endorsements of the *Chansons populaires* was from the French-Canadian writer Antoine Gérin-Lajoie, who maintained that, were he condemned to exile and allowed only one book, he would take Gagnon's song collection: 'Mieux que tout, disait-il, ce volume me rappellerai la patrie absente.'[14] ['More than anything else, this book will remind me of my distant homeland.']

The enthusiastic response to the first edition of Gagnon's song collection prompted the publication of the second edition of the work in 1880. Published by the Quebec City musician and music printer Robert Morgan, the second edition of the *Chansons populaires* was dedicated to the new governor general of Canada, the Marquis of Lorne and his wife, Princess Louise.[15] This dedication was evidently Gagnon's idea, since the page where the inscription is written is concluded with the words: 'Ce volume est respectuesement dédié par le compilateur et auteur: Ernest Gagnon.' ['This book is respectfully dedicated by its compiler and author: Ernest Gagnon.']

The publication of the second edition was also received favourably in France and in French Canada.[16] At first glance there does not appear to be a great deal of difference between the two editions. For the most part, the songs are presented in the same order with their respective commentaries, although Gagnon did use the opportunity of a second edition to make improvements. Referred to as 'la version définitive' by Blanche Gagnon (letter,

230 Gordon E. Smith

1946), notable changes include, for example, the absence of the twenty-page 'appendice.' As the title 'appendice' implies, this section of the collection is a list of some thirty-seven song annotations and/or variants which Gagnon seems to have added to the first edition as a kind of afterthought. With several small exceptions,[17] the information in the 'appendice' has been incorporated into the text of the 1880 edition.

With regard to the musical transcriptions, Gagnon made a number of small changes (pitches, rhythm, metre) in the second edition, the most important of which is the removal of the appoggiaturas which are found in one-third of the song renditions in the first version. In a few instances, he has incorporated the appoggiaturas, into the melody line, as in 'Un jour l'envi m'a pris de déserter de France' (1865: 168; 1880: 168), but for the most part he has simply eliminated them. It has been suggested that Gagnon was pressured into doing this by performers, who considered the ornaments a difficult intrusion in the melodies.[18] Patrice Coirault has used Gagnon's example of initially notating appoggiaturas and then removing them to validate the theory that such melodic embellishments were usually added at the whim of the individual informant, and did not constitute an integral part of the song melody (1941: 244-5). Contrary to Coirault's statement, some collectors of French-Canadian folksongs in this century have come to regard melodic embellishments, such as the appoggiaturas in Gagnon's work, as a vital part of the song melody.[19] The reason for the removal of the appoggiaturas from the 1880 edition of the Chansons populaires may, in fact, have been linked to the desire of Gagnon's publisher, Robert Morgan, to sell the collection as a useful songbook, rather than a scholarly volume. Gagnon does not refer to this question in the 'Préface' nor anywhere else in the 1880 edition, which further suggests that he had little say about the matter.

Gagnon also used the opportunity of the second edition to refine structurally the essays which begin and conclude the collection: the 'Préface' and the 'Remarques générales.' The opening pages of the latter are effectively transferred to the beginning of the former in the second edition. The second edition reflects the advantage of having given Gagnon more time to inspect French sources, and some of the revisions are indeed concordances or comparisons with French models. He emphasizes the French influence in the list of 'verbiages d'enfants' added to the 1880 'Préface,' and thereby indicates that most of these expressions came to Canada from France. In a footnote, he refers the reader to the French collections by Bujeaud, and Durieux and Bruyelle, respectively (Gagnon 1880: ix).

It appears that Gagnon did not work on the song collection again. This is indicated both in Blanche Gagnon's writings and in the 'Aux lecteurs' notice added by the Beauchemin editors on the occasion of the fourth reprinting ('5e édition') in 1905:

Nous avons demandé à M. Gagnon s'il désirait revoir son travail et y faire quelques retouches. Il nous a répondu que le mieux est parfois l'ennemi du bien et qu'il préférait ne pas même relire son ouvrage. (Gagnon, 1908)

[We asked Mr Gagnon whether he would like to re-examine his work and make some changes. His reply was that revisions would not make the collection any better and that he was not interested in even rereading the work.]

The Chansons populaires was so well received in French Canada that the second edition was reprinted thirteen times, beginning with 'troisième' and 'quatrième éditions' by Darveau in 1894 and 1900, and continuing with editions by Beauchemin, 'conforme à l'édition de 1880,' in 1900, 1908, 1913, 1918, 1925, 1935, 1940, 1947, 1952, and 1955. For the sake of clarification, a list of all the reprintings is provided in the appendix. Also indicated in the list are certain editorial changes in the various reprintings: (1) beginning in 1900 the 'Préface' was renamed 'Introduction'; (2) as noted above, beginning with the 1908 reprinting a new page, entitled 'Aux lecteurs,' was introduced before the 'Introduction'; (3) the reprintings from 1908 to 1925 included an autographed portrait of Gagnon; (4) the 1913 and 1925 reprintings used larger and clearer printing plates, and these two 'éditions' are designated on the respective title pages as being part of the 'Collection Jacques Cartier.'

In his folksong collection, Gagnon sought to provide a distinctively nationalist work by portraying the French-Canadian people through their folksongs. Like his colleagues in the 'Mouvement littéraire de Québec,' such as Aubert de Gaspé and LaRue, Gagnon emphasized the power of folksong as a means of establishing the French-Canadian identity. Gagnon's close intellectual ties with his colleagues in the 'Mouvement littéraire de Québec,' especially LaRue, inspired him to undertake the song collection. LaRue's scholarly approach was based partly on a preoccupation with France, and a desire to demonstrate French concordances wherever possible. Gagnon's approach was also determined partly by this influence, and he deliberately set out to compare songs in his collection with variants in French sources. These concordances are sometimes exact references, a fact that demonstrates both Gagnon's knowledge of French song collections of the day and his erudite

232 Gordon E. Smith

thoroughness. The importance which Gagnon attaches to both the music and the text in folksong is reflected in his inclusion of full song texts for each song, his thorough examination of musical details in the repertory, and notably, the plainchant–folksong thesis.[20]

The processes which govern the genesis of the *Chansons populaires* are rooted, in general, in the folksong collecting movement, which gained momentum during the nineteenth century. The view of folksong as an expression of nationalism, a view which captured the spirit of many European musicians and literary figures, is clearly identifiable in Gagnon's work. Of critical importance, however, is the fact that Gagnon also interpreted his work as a contribution to French-Canadian nationalist literature – 'Le Mouvement littéraire de Québec.' Rooted as it is in this historic movement, Gagnon's *Chansons populaires* may be interpreted as an important contribution to the spirit of nationalism that has become woven into the social, cultural, and political fabric of modern Quebec.

APPENDIX

Les Chansons populaires du Canada: Editions and Reprintings

Note that the use of the word 'édition' in the reprintings beginning in 1894 (which are all based on the 1880, or second, edition) refers simply to a new reprinting of the work, and does not imply any changes by Gagnon or the editors, other than the insertion of the autographed photo of Gagnon in several of the Beauchemin reprintings, the addition of the 'Aux lecteurs' notice in 1905, and the use of different typesetting in the reprintings from 1913 and 1925.

First edition – Quebec: Bureaux du Foyer Canadien, 1865. Six instalments
1st instalment: 'Préface' and p. 1 to p. 52 (including 'Digue dindaine') –
    8 February 1865
2nd instalment: 'Mon cri cra tir' la lirette' (p. 53) to 'J'ai cueilli la belle rose' (p. 97)
    – 31 May 1865
3rd instalment: 'Ah qui me passera le bois' (p. 101) to 'Adam et Eve' (p. 164) –
    1 September 1865
4th instalment: 'Adam et Eve' [conclusion] (p. 165) to 'Jamais je nourrirai de geai'
    (p. 236) – 20 October 1865
5th instalment: 'La Guignolée' (p. 237) to 'Dans tous les cantons' (p. 304) –
    7 September 1866

The Genesis of Ernest Gagnon's *Chansons Populaires* 233

6th instalment: 'Celle que mon coeur aime' (p. 305) to the end including the 'Remarques générales,' 'Appendice' and 'Errata' (p. 375) – January-February 1867

As indicated in the discussion of the 1865 edition, in some cases the instalments were bound together to make single volumes out of the collection. Besides the National Library, the following twelve Canadian librairies now possess bound copies of the 1865 edition: University of Ottawa, National Archives, Geological Survey of Canada, Queen's University, Victoria University, Metropolitan Public Library, Edmonton Public Library, Greater Victoria Library, Université de Montréal, Université Laval, Université du Québec à Trois-Rivières, and University of Toronto.

Second edition – Quebec: Robert Morgan, 1880. The title page reads 'Deuxième édition' and is followed by the dedication to the Marquis of Lorne and Princess Louise.

1st reprinting: Quebec: Darveau, 1894. The title page reads 'Troisième édition.'

2nd reprinting: Quebec: Darveau, 1900. The title page reads 'Quatrième édition' and 'conforme à l'édition de 1880.'

3rd reprinting: Montreal: Beauchemin, 1901. The title page reads 'Quatrième édition' ('conforme à l'édition de 1880').

4th reprinting: Montreal: Beauchemin, 1908. The title page reads 'Cinquième édition' ('conforme à l'édition de 1880') – autographed photo of Gagnon and 'Aux lecteurs' notice added.

5th reprinting: Montreal: Beauchemin, 1913. The title page reads 'Cinquième édition' ('conforme à l'édition de 1880') – 'Collection Jacques Cartier' – different plates.

6th reprinting: Montreal: Beauchemin, 1918. The title page reads 'Sixième édition' ('conforme à l'édition de 1880').

7th reprinting: Montreal: Beauchemin, 1925. The title page reads 'Sixième édition' ('conforme à l'édition') – 'Collection Jacques Cartier' – same plates as 5th printing above.

8th reprinting: Montreal: Beauchemin, 1930. The title page reads 'Septième édition' ('conforme à l'édition de 1880').

9th reprinting: Montreal: Beauchemin, 1935. The title page reads 'Septième édition' ('conforme à l'édition de 1880') – no photo.

10th reprinting: Montreal: Beauchemin, 1940. The title page reads 'Septième édition' ('conforme à l'édition de 1880').

11th reprinting: Montreal: Beauchemin, 1947. The title page reads 'Huitième édition' ('conforme à l'édition de 1880').

12th reprinting: Montreal: Beauchemin, 1952. The title page reads 'Neuvième édition' ('conforme à l'édition de 1880').
13th reprinting: Montreal: Beauchemin, 1955. The title page reads 'Dixième édition' ('conforme à l'édition de 1880').

NOTES

1 A French version of this article, 'La Genèse des *Chansons populaires du Canada* d'Ernest Gagnon,' is published in *Les Cahiers de l'ARMuQ*, no. 15 (May 1994), 38–53.
2 On this topic see the third chapter of my doctoral dissertation, 'Ernest Gagnon (1834–1915): Musician and Pioneer Folksong Scholar,' University of Toronto, 1989, 116–28.
3 For a detailed account of this nationalist movement, see the collection of essays entitled 'Mouvement littéraire de Québec 1860' in *Archives de Lettres canadiennes* 1 (1961), 7–167. See also Hayne, 'Le Mouvement littéraire de Quebéc' (1983), 534–5.
4 The third and most complete edition of this work was published by Augustin Côté in Quebec City in 1859. For more details on this source and Huston's work, see Réjean Robidoux, '*Les Soirées canadiennes* et *Le Foyer canadien* dans le mouvement littéraire québécoise de 1860,' Thesis, Diplôme d'études supérieures en littérature, Laval University, 1957, 7–10.
5 The Englich translations in this article are by the author.
6 LaRue was a medical doctor and professor at Laval University who was keenly interested in the oral traditions of his country. Gagnon and LaRue were close friends and during the 1860s lived on the same street, Saint-François in Upper Quebec. See the subscriber list at the conclusion of *Le Foyer canadien* (1863: iii), where Gagnon is listed as living at No. 5 Saint-François and LaRue at No. 12.
7 See Laforte, pp. 127–30, for a list of manuscript and printed collections prior to and concurrent with the first edition of Gagnon's *Chansons populaires*. These volumes include songs (usually text only) widely known and sung at educational institutions such as colleges and seminaries; rather than serious attempts to preserve oral tradition, they appear, generally, to have been intended for practical use.
8 Other nationalist works such as Philippe Aubert de Gaspé's *Les Anciens Canadiens* were also published serially in the 1860s. On this topic, see Robidoux, '*Les Soirées Canadiennes* et *Le Foyer Canadien*,' 72–80.
9 The reasons for the lower number is that some individuals and organizations, such as church parishes, received more than one copy, and also from the fact the

cited report is from October 1863, whereas the actual subscriber list is from February earlier in the same year. The list of individuals includes a number of names of Americans from states such as Maine, Illinois, Massachusetts, and New Hampshire, as well as a few subscribers from English Canada; for example, there is an R. Coleman listed from Toronto and an Aug. Cadotte from Lindsay, Ontario. The list of French Canadians from Quebec contains names of priests, educators, and government officials.

10 For the instalment announcements, see 'Le Foyer canadien,' *Le Courrier du Canada*, 8 February 1865, [3]; [no title], *Le Courrier du Canada*, 31 May 1865, [2]; 'Les chansons populaires du Canada,' *Le Courrier du Canada*, 1 September 1865, [2]; 'Publications,' *Le Courrier de Canada*, 20 October 1865, [3]; 'Les chansons populaires du Canada,' *Le Courrier du Canada*, 7 September 1866, [2]; [no title] *Le Journal de l'Instruction Publique*, January-February 1867.

11 There are two known exceptions to this statement: the Bibliothèque Gabrielle-Roy in Quebec City has a shelf copy of the sixth instalment, and the National Library in Ottawa has a copy of the fourth instalment.

12 I am grateful to Professor Conrad Laforte for showing me a copy of this letter and other manuscript documents pertaining to Gagnon's writings and correspondence.

13 This letter is part of a correspondence between Blanche Gagnon and Marius Barbeau contained in Conrad Laforte's private collection.

14 This quotation is found in several sources, including the 'Aux lecteurs' notice at the beginning of the *Chansons populaires* reprintings from 1908 on.

15 The second edition of the *Chansons populaires* was not the only musical dedicated to the arrival of the new governor general in Canada. See Kallmann, 137 and 239.

16 See, for example, 'Les chansons populaires du Canada,' *Le Courrier du Canada*, 12 July 1880: [2]. Reprint from *Le Globe*.

17 In the 1865 edition Gagnon provides an additional variant of 'Isabeau's s'y promène' (1865: 354), which he leaves out of the 1880 edition, probably because it is so similar. In addition, for no apparent reason, Gagnon leaves out provenance information in the second edition; see Gagnon (1865: 47, 355, 360, 361, 362, 366).

18 Laforte, 'Folk Music, Franco-Canadian,' in *Encyclopedia of Music in Canada* (Toronto: University of Toronto Press, 1992), 478. Professor Laforte has told me on several occasions that his statement regarding Gagnon's removal of the appoggiaturas in the second edition of the *Chansons populaires* is based on conversations with twentieth-century French-Canadian folklorists, such as Oscar O'Brien (1891–1958), and singers, such as Lionel Daunais (b. 1902), who

support the theory that Gagnon was pressured by singers and voice teachers who found the embellishments difficult to sing.
19 See Marguerite and Raoul d'Harcourt, *Chansons forkloriques françaises au Canada* (Quebec: Le Presses de l'Université Laval, 1956) and Dominque Gauthier and Roger Matton, *Chansons de Shippagan, Les Archives de Folklore 16* (Quebec: Les Presses de l'Université Laval, 1975). The ornamental figurations found in many of the songs in these collections are an important stylistic feature of these repertoires ('le style fleuri').
20 The providential mission of the French-Canadian people is central to Gagnon's plainchant–folk-song argument. At the time of Gagnon's collection in the 1860s, this theme was emphasized with particular vigour by certain literary figures as well as clergy; see Mgr L.-F.-R. Laflèche, 'The Providential Mission of the French Canadians' (1866), translated in *French-Canadian Nationalism*, ed. Ramsay Cook (Toronto: Macmillan, 1969), 92–106. In an unpublished article titled 'Ernest Gagnon's *Chansons populaires du Canada*: Processes of "Writing Culture,"' I explore the embedded meanings in Gagnon's text both in their historic context and against recent critical ethnographic approaches and notions of ethnic identity as articulated in, for example, *Writing Culture*, eds. James Clifford and George E. Marcus (Berkeley: University of California Press 1986), and Anya Peterson Royce's *Ethnic Identity: Strategies of Diversity* (Bloomington: Indiana Press, 1982).

REFERENCES

Champfleury. *Chansons populaires des provinces de France*. Paris: Bourdillat, 1860.
'Chansons populaires du Canada.' *L'Echo de la France*. Montreal, April 1867, 410.
Coirault, Patrice. *Notre Chanson folklorique*. Paris: Auguste Picard, 1941.
Dubois, Théodore. Letter to M. J.-Arthur Paquet, n.d. Collection Conrad Laforte.
Gagnon, Blanche. Letter to Marius Barbeau. Summer 1946. Collection Conrad Laforte.
Gagnon, Ernest. *Chansons populaires du Canada*. Quebec: Bureaux du Foyer Canadien, 1865–7.
– *Chansons populaires du Canada*. Quebec: Robert Morgan, 1880.
– *Chansons populaires du Canada*. Quebec: Beauchemin, 1908.
– Letter to Jean-Baptiste Weckerlin. 18 March 1866. Collection Conrad Laforte.
Hayne, David M. 'Le Mouvement littéraire de Québec,' in *The Oxford Companion to Canadian Literature*, ed. William Toye. Toronto: Oxford University Press, 1983, 534–5.
Kallmann, Helmut. *A History of Music in Canada 1534–1914*. Toronto: University of Toronto Press, 1960, 1987.

Laforte, Conrad. *La Chanson folklorique et les écrivains du XIX siècle (en France et au Québec)*. Montreal: Hurtubise, 1973.
LaRue, Hubert. 'Les chansons populaires et historiques du Canada.' *Le Foyer Canadien* 1 (1863): 321–84; *Le Foyer Canadien* 3 (1865): 5–72.
Monière, Denis. *Ideologies in Quebec: The Historical Development*, trans. Richard Howard. Toronto: University of Toronto Press, 1981.
'Mouvement littéraire de Québec,' *Archives littéraires de Québec* 1. Éditions de l'Université d'Ottawa, 1961, 7–16
Robidoux, Réjean. '*Les Soirées Canadiennes* et *Le Foyer Canadien* dans le mouvement littéraire québécois de 1860.' Thesis, Diplôme d'études supérieures en littérature, Laval University, 1957.
Roger, Louis. 'Chansons populaires du Canada.' *Le Courrier du Canada*, 28 April 1865, [3].
Smith, Gordon E., 'Ernest Gagnon (1834–1915): Musician and Pioneer Folksong Scholar.' PhD thesis, University of Toronto, 1989.
Smith, Gordon E. and François Brassard, 'Ernest Gagnon,' in *Encyclopedia of Music in Canada*, 2nd ed., eds. Helmut Kallmann and Gilles Potvin. Toronto: University of Toronto Press, 1992, 507–8.

TIMOTHY RICE with TAMMY GUTNIK

What's Canadian about Canadian Popular Music?: The Case of Bruce Cockburn

This paper asks the question, In what way is Bruce Cockburn an artist? And, moreover, how is he a specifically Canadian artist? Before attempting to answer these questions, however, I can perhaps be forgiven for beginning – in this most personal of collections, a festschrift – with some recollections of how I came to this topic and of John Beckwith's role in that process.[1]

Arriving at the University of Toronto in 1974, during Beckwith's tenure as dean of the Faculty of Music, I was as ignorant of *les affaires canadiennes* as most people from the United States. I had researched the music of Bulgaria and Yugoslavia, and consequently knew about the large communities of South Slavs living in Toronto. Beyond that I knew woefully little, and the next few years were an exciting time of learning about a new culture and its history – including how to spell words like colour properly, which my first class taught me with sardonic hisses as I recorded their comments on the blackboard. Their inarticulate but effective defence of Canadian identity in the face of an onslaught of U.S. products and culture – and professors – provided a wake-up call that I answered only years later in my teaching at the faculty.

In the meantime, John Beckwith acted as the very model of a modern Canadian composer, scholar, and musician: he was an active proselytizer for the work of Canadian composers, his own compositions contained references to Canadian customs and history, and he seemed as interested in nineteenth-century rural Ontario musical life as my other colleagues were in fifteenth-century European court music. He taught, by example, a general truism about many twentieth-century composers and musicians in the Americas: they tend to be fascinated by all kinds of music – sacred and secular, 'popular' and 'serious,' European and North and South American, and lately African and Asian – and ignore in the process the artificial boundaries of style and the arbitrary judgments of quality erected by musicologists, listeners, and performers to justify their particular taste. Beckwith's enthusiasm for the 'cultivated' and the 'vernacular,' the enormously complex and the pleasingly simple, matched my own democratic tendency, as an ethnomusicologist, to regard all music, or at least the music of all cultures, classes, and groups, as important for study.

Inspired by Beckwith's model, and inclined to a modest sense of social responsibility, I decided in the early 1980s that students at the Faculty of Music needed to know more about their own cultural patrimony, which was largely ignored in conventional surveys of music history. Accordingly, I revised the first semester of the two-year core sequence in music history to begin with Canadian music. Given what one faculty colleague called my 'sociological' proclivities, I could not limit myself to so-called art music, but examined, as ethnomusicologists usually do, 'all' the music of 'our time and place,' the place being English Canada with a decidedly Ontario bias in the time since the Second World War. Some of my choices of people and music probably did not please Beckwith, but I hope he applauded the spirit of the new curriculum.

I began with three so-called serious composers who, like Beckwith, seemed to possess nice senses of humour: John Weinzweig, Harry Somers, and R. Murray Schafer. The remaining four 'composers' came from the world of popular music and jazz, and perhaps challenged the sensibilities of those raised to exclude such music from serious consideration: Oscar Peterson, Leroy Sibbles, Carol Pope, and Bruce Cockburn.[2] Of these, Bruce Cockburn was recommended to me by my students within weeks of my arrival in Canada; to many of them he was the most interesting person in the Canadian folk music scene, and since they perceived me to be interested in teaching and learning more about folk music, they assumed I would be interested in him. In fact, popular or commercial music, even when labelled folk music, has been the last frontier for both historical musicologists and ethnomusicologists, both groups seeking the illusory solace of objectivity and scholarly distance by retreating to the distant past or faraway lands. The study of contemporary Canadian music constituted a new challenge for me, one I found enormously stimulating both musically and intellectually, and one for whom I have John Beckwith partially to thank.

What do the musicians I chose have in common, other than living and working in Canada? In my view, all are artists. Of course this ideologically loaded term begs defining. At least one colleague at the Faculty of Music, for example, judged only composers to be artists; performers were mere artisans. I suspect others might have rejected admitting musicians with commercial and popular appeal to the rank of 'true' artists. At the other extreme, some ethnomusicologists are probably uncomfortable with the prospect of trying to distinguish art from dross in an appropriately scholarly rather than personal manner, and might argue that virtually any musical making is an artistic act. While I have no sympathy for the first two views and a lot for the last, in this article I define musical artistry in the late-twentieth century as including three qualities that all seven musicians mentioned earlier share: they have all (1) contributed to the lexicon of devices within their traditions; (2) made unique personal statements rather than replicated existing frameworks; and (3) transcended the narrow definitions of the genres they inherited to create something new that challenged or blurred the boundaries between traditions (cf. Rockwell 1983). While a sociological study might find any commercially successful Canadian pop musician a potent subject for analysis and eschew making artistic judgments, this one, in a volume dedicated to one of Canada's premier musical artists, tries to integrate ethnomusicology's nonjudgmental respect for common music with the classical music world's devotion to artistry.

To understand Cockburn as an artist, this article examines his use of particular musical and textual devices in shaping personal statements that transcend the limits of particular genres. In order to understand Cockburn as a Canadian artist, the paper follows his development through three artistic periods and posits a relationship between his songs and albums and the evolving politics of Canada under the leadership of Pierre Trudeau. While this two factor approach downplays the many other complex factors shaping both Cockburn (his conversion to Christianity, for example) and Canada (the declining Canadian dollar and other economic woes, the rise of neoconservatism, and the election of Brian Mulroney), it provides a preliminary and provisional interpretation of one artist's work as a response to the society and world in which he lives.

The First Period, Bilingualism, and National Identity

Cockburn, born 27 May 1945 to a middle-class family in Ottawa, Ontario, studied in his youth a remarkable variety of instruments (clarinet, trumpet, piano, and drums) before beginning to play, at age fourteen, the *instrument de rigueur* of folk and popular music, the guitar. In high school he developed a literary sensibility, reading the poetry of Allen Ginsberg, William S. Burroughs, and Jack Kerouac. He also discovered the poetry of rock and folk, and with guitar performed the music of singers like Elvis Presley, Bob Dylan, and the Beatles. From 1964 to 1966 his musicianship expanded at the Berklee School of Music in Boston, where he studied jazz, classical, and non-Western music. As he describes the period:

I ended up getting sidetracked from pursuing straight jazz. It was the mid '60s, and half the students at Berklee were exploring Indian, Tibetan, and Arabic styles. That experimentation ... really appealed to me. (Ouellette 1988: 14)

Returning to Ottawa in 1966, he performed with several rock bands and soloed in coffee-houses before making his first major appearance at the Mariposa Folk Festival in 1967. He recorded his first album, *Bruce Cockburn*, for Bernie Finkelstein's new label, True North, in 1969, and since then has written a steady stream of new songs for some twenty additional records, all on True North. His work constitutes one of the most consistent records of musical production, development, and growth in the popular music field.

Cockburn began his career as a solo singer, songwriter, and guitarist, a combination that put him squarely in the 'folk music' category of 1960s popular music, probably the only type of popular music at the time available to a young anglophone with both musical and literary skills.[3] The folk revival emerged as an alternative to rock and roll in the late 1950s and early 1960s, precisely as the latter went through its 'dark age' of 'ice cream changes' and maudlin love songs before being revitalized by the Beatles and the 'British invasion.' Rock and roll, which had begun in the early 1950s as a rough-and-ready protest music for white youths in their perennial battle against parental authority, was thoroughly neutralized by the commercial recording business within a few years. Folk music gained popularity among young intellectuals reacting to the mindlessness, both musical and textual, of late-1950s and early-1960s rock and roll, and contrasted with it in nearly every way. Rock and roll of the period was electric, urban, loud, ensemble, collective, dance, incantational, love music; folk was acoustic, rural, soft, solo, individualistic, listening, wordy, topical music. Anyone alienated from the engulfing urban youth-culture pressures to conform, and desiring to imagine a new and better world, sought musical and poetic solace in the folk music of the period. For someone with Cockburn's musical and literary sensibilities, 'folk music' provided an appropriate and reasonably popular alternative to rock and roll. Folk music was also the perfect genre to symbolize Canadian national identity for at least three reasons. First, many Canadians feel marginalized within a larger North American culture dominated by the United States. Their rejection of its mainstream music, rock and roll, in favour of folk music was a subtle form of reaction against American hegemony in popular culture. Second, Canada lacks the large communities of descendants of former slaves that partially define the social fabric of the United States and, consequently, its popular culture and music. Folk music, with its strongest roots in the culture of British settlers in North America, more closely fits the English-Canadian experience than rock and roll, with its history of borrowing from African-American rhythm and blues and soul music.[4] Third, for many Canadians a sense of place and national identify is often associated with rural lifeways and vast wilderness. Cities, perhaps especially Toronto, and their fast-paced lifestyles often assume a negative valence. Unplugged music with texts about high winds and white sky may have spoken more powerfully to many Canadians than rock and roll songs about 'rockin' in Memphis' or 'dreamin' in Motown.'[5]

Cockburn's first two albums, *Bruce Cockburn* (1969) and *High Winds, White Sky* (1971), are dominated by solo acoustic guitar accompaniments to songs of his own composition, plus a few songs using a small set of acoustic instruments. Many of the guitar accompaniments use an American rural finger-picking style Cockburn says he learned from Fox Watson during his travels in the southern United States in the mid-1960s (see Example 1). The texts, elegiac and escapist, extol the virtues of the country as opposed to the city, but contain none of the angry protests against the Vietnam War heard in American folk music. In this sense his early songs speak a peculiarly Canadian message. The war was not Canada's war; the United States' problems are not Canada's problems. Many Canadians believe they have a distinctive, more peaceful life, perhaps more closely tied to nature, and Cockburn's early songs evoke a rural Canadian idealism far removed from the problems to the south, whether in Canadian or U.S. cities. The album

Example 1 Fox Watson's finger-picking style

notes capture the first hint of the correspondence between Cockburn's and Pierre Trudeau's vision of Canada: all Cockburn's song texts are published with French translations, putting into practice the Trudeau government's emphasis on bilingualism.

The Canadian response to these albums was outstanding. Cockburn was named folksinger of the year and received a Juno Aware in 1971, the first of six, and *High Winds, White Sky* 'went gold,' the first of six gold albums and two platinum albums in Canada.[6]

His early success as a distinctly Canadian musician was aided immensely by the establishment in 1970 of 'Canadian content' rules by the Canadian Radio-television and Telecommunications Commission (CRTC), specifically the requirement that 30 per cent of AM and most FM radio programs contain Canadian material.[7] Prior to this decision, Canadian playlists were chosen from American lists and charts such as those in Billboard Magazine. Canadian performers either were not heard on the radio or, like Paul Anka, Robert Goulet, Anne Murray, Hank Snow, and others, they sought their fortune by tapping into the U.S. market. In the process their identity as Canadians was largely submerged in order to fit in to the American market. Anne Murray became 'America's sweetheart' and Neil Young was canonized in a book called *All American Music* (Rockwell 1983). With the new rules, Cockburn's distinctively Canadian voice was not silenced, and he was able to combine his nationalistic idealism with commercial success. Cockburn stated that the ruling 'has definitely helped me. It's at least drawing ... attention to ... Canadian artists' (Yorke 1971: 58). Another writer commented:

When Cockburn started recording in the last 60s, he was determined to fight a perennial Canadian disease: the belief that to be successful in Canada, an artist had to start off by winning approval south of the border. (Guttman 1987)

Before the CRTC ruling, this was hardly a disease; it was a necessary, even healthy, step to success.

While Cockburn continues to enjoy commercial success, especially in Canada, he is interesting musically and culturally precisely because he has always refused to accept the boundaries of styles, particularly ones dictated by the American music industry. His independence from those strictures began as a personal commitment, but was aided by the new protective rules in Canada. Without them, his and True North Records self-imposed existence on the artistic margins of the popular music business might have been rather more silent.

Cockburn's poetry on the first two records may have had a subtly Canadian tinge, but his stylistic eclecticism can also be interpreted as referencing a Canadian musical world. In addition to Fox Watson's country fingerpicking, which might have typified dozens of 'folk singers' in this period, he uses a plethora of other styles: white gospel, English folk music, blues, and jazz. His music also employs classical guitar arpeggios, *musique-concrete*-like electronic sounds of waves, and aspects of North Indian and Persian classical music. A few other musicians and groups in popular music commanded such a range of styles (notably the Beatles, but also the Grateful Dead and others), but for most groups the demands of popularity usually meant hewing to the mainstream within rock or folk. As a Canadian trying to establish himself independent of American categories. Cockburn gave free rein to his musical instincts and background, and provided one of the richest tapestries of sounds in popular music of the day. Such stylistic eclecticism, and indeed any element of musical style, has to be interpreted in particular instances; its meanings are multivalent and not global. In Cockburn's case, I 'read' his eclecticism as at once a sign of his artistry, his independence, and his outsider status as a Canadian.

While musicians such as the Beatles added the sounds of Indian and other music into the mix, Cockburn integrates these styles into his underlying musical vocabulary. In 'Shining Mountain' (*High Winds, White Sky*, 1971), for example, he composes a striking evocation of a Persian *avaz*, an unmetred introduction he plays on the trapezoidal hammered dulcimer, the American cousin of the Persian *santur* (see Example 2). The song proper resembles a Persian metred song, or *tasnif*, but he plays with its normally regular metrical structure, combining groups of two and three beats, a subtle reference to neighbouring Turkish and Balkan music. Thus Cockburn does not simply use these styles; he composes with them, altering both the original and his own style in the process in order to create music that is distinctly his own, the act *par excellence* of an artist.

The next album, *Sunwheel Dance* (1972), contains new developments in both music and song texts. The latter become more critical. If the message of the previous two albums suggested that the world's problems could be escaped by ignoring or running from them, this record contains songs overtly critical of materialism and violence, but without yet naming the U.S. involvement in Vietnam. Whatever the source of his newly expressed anger and discontent, he makes an artistic decision when he selects a new musical style to represent them. While folk music was useful as a symbolic statement of protest against mainstream rock, it is not very good at capturing or expressing anger, even though it was used in that way by American protest singers. It is simply too quiet and wordy. Anger wants a loud, inarticulate

Example 2 Persian-style *avaz* from 'Shining Mountain' (*High Winds, White Sky*, 1971)

wail, precisely what screaming, distorted electric guitars provide. V.S. Naipaul, in his novel *A Bend in the River*, captures the irony of the link between gentle folk music and angry protest when he writes of hearing a Joan Beaz recording deep in the Central African forest and observes that such sweet songs of justice could only come from someone who expects to receive it. Anglo-American folk song, with its musically flat unexpressive character, only speaks about emotion; it doesn't evoke or represent it. The short lyric texts, sliding notes, changeable dynamics, and raspy timbres of African-American genres, on the other hand, contain powerful icons of emotion, and Cockburn, perhaps realizing this, turned to them as the themes of his songs changed. To match the new lyrics of, for example, 'It's Going Down Slow,' in which he damns the rhetorical power of lies and 'warlike pride' to cause the deaths of so many, Cockburn plays, for the first time in his recording career, the electric guitar, accompanied by electric bass, synthesizer, and drum kit in a 'folk rock' style. The distorted, bluesy guitar perfectly reflects the disdain for war expressed in the text. In addition to using an evocative, expressive style, he also uses chord choice as an expressive device, substituting a major triad on the sixth degree (VI) for the more usual minor triad (vi) during the most powerful section of his text. Cockburn's command of a variety of musical styles put in service of expressing his texts is particularly effective in this example.

The next two albums, Night Vision (1973) and Salt, Sun and Time (1974), expand into jazz. The first album uses a kind of jazz rock, where lengthy solos interrupt the normal strophic song structure; and the second contains acoustic jazz. In these recordings Cockburn plays violin as well as guitar and Jack Zaza joins him on clarinet. Instead of the triads and dominant sevenths of folk and rock music, he employs the more complex added chord structures of jazz: major seventh, ninth, eleventh and thirteenth chords. Here one senses that Cockburn was not content to pander to his audience; he was capable of more sophisticated musical expression and tried it on this album. The texts of Salt, Sun and Time refer, for the first time explicitly, to Canada and are critical of the United States, and are indicative of his evolution toward more political involvement. According to Gutnik (1990), these five albums constitute Cockburn's 'first period.'

The Second Period, Dance Music, and Multiculturalism

In 1975, Cockburn moved physically from the 'country' to the city (Toronto), lyrically from introspection and self-absorption to an outspoken worldliness, and musically from folk, folk rock, and acoustic jazz to electrified, harder-edged, closer-to-the-urban-mainstream popular styles. He tried to shed his image as a folk-singer 'and began in 1981 to call his music "rock"' (Gutnik 1990: 51). He continued, however, to evade easy labelling, both in his music and his comments, saying that he wanted 'to find a label that says the least' (Haynes 1981: 2).

In the late 1970s and early 1980s, dance music, in the form of disco, reggae, and new wave, replaced the spaced-out, psychedelic, 'head' music of the previous eight years or so, and Cockburn consciously tried to make his music more danceable while keeping his stylistic eclecticism alive. Speaking of the first album in the 'second period,' Joy Will Find a Way (1975), he said 'I wanted to get more of a feeling of freedom and happiness that the idea of dancing conjures up' (Bateman 1975: 8). Some of the happiness he felt came from his conversion to Christianity, and many of the songs are happy ones about love and the new joy he is experiencing. Again we find Cockburn responding both to the tenor of the times, with a sense of relief at the passing of an enormous social and political burden (the Vietnam War), and to newly awakened personal feelings with a new kind of musical expression:

What's Canadian about Canadian Popular Music   247

overtly danceable music. Dance music, which had seemed trivial to some in the 1960s, and was therefore rebelled against in folk music, was now a rehabilitated medium that brought people together. Imperialism and the racism associated with it became important issues on the world scene, and reggae, a dance music, bore the musical message of the world's oppressed, whether in the Caribbean, England, or Africa, much as folk music had ten years earlier. Rock and jazz rock provide Cockburn's stylistic basis throughout this period, much as folk music did in the 'first period,' but he adds the danceable Caribbean genres of calypso ('Burn,' *Joy Will Find a Way*, 1975) and reggae (for example, 'Rumours of Glory,' *Humans*, 1980) to his bag of stylistic tricks (see Example 3). Although they fit into his view that the world needs dance music and its attendant joys, they are also associated with the political message of protest that has figured, however subtly, in much of his work. Since calypso consists of improvised texts containing pointed social

Example 3 Calypso style from 'Burn' (*Joy Will Find a Way*, 1975)

commentary, Cockburn in effect appropriated both its function and its style. Caribbean music was also an important part of the musical life of Toronto, his new place of residence, with its large number of immigrants from Jamaica and Trinidad. Adopting reggae in this period was a gesture of solidarity with the aspirations of Africans at home and in the diaspora and a symbol of the gritty, urban reality he was experiencing. His adoption of Caribbean styles parallels his embrace of the electric guitar in order to express anger in the first period, as he damns American imperialism which crusades in the name of anti-Communism although its real purpose is to 'make the late news pay.'

Despite the change in underlying style and the use of new genres for their symbolic value, Cockburn's fascination with musical variety and non-Western forms in particular continues. He uses North Indian classical music for 'A Life Story' and 'Arrows of Light' (*Joy Will Find a Way*). About the title track on *Joy Will Find a Way* Cockburn said, 'With a few minor changes, I ripped off an Ethiopian thumb harp piece to make the guitar part' (McGregor 1986: 60).[8] In this period he refers occasionally to the plight of Native Canadians (in 'Gavin's Woodpile' from *In the Falling Dark*, 1976, and in 'Red Brother, Red Sister' from *Circles in the Stream*, 1977). The careful link between musical style and message is again evident. In the former he returns to folk music, as he sings, with acoustic guitar accompaniment, a plaintive lament for Indians in prison; in the latter, a lament for the death of Indian culture due to the onslaught of white culture, Christianity, and racism, he adds a refrain using 'vocables,' the non-lexical syllables that constitute the text in many Native songs. As in earlier borrowings, he doesn't merely copy them but evokes their spirit using repetitions of the syllable 'hey' in a manner vastly different from its use in African-American songs.

Cockburn's use of Caribbean styles and his references to Native Canadian problems can be interpreted as a response to a second cornerstone of the Trudeau government's evolving policies, namely, the move from biculturalism to multiculturalism, to the idea that every culture occupies an important and distinct place in the Canadian 'mosaic.' Cockburn's encounter with the multicultural reality of Toronto in this period, as well as with its articulation in government policy, seems to inform his work in this 'second period.' During this period many things change while others stay the same. He alters his underlying style from folk to rock, his texts and residency from rural to urban, and his mood from dreamy introspection to joyous engagement. At the same time his commitment to stylistic eclecticism, boundary blurring, musical complexity, and compositional integration of techniques continues. Cockburn's switch from folk to rock does not smell of the sellout. The artistic core remains intact as the stylistic skin moults.

The Third Period, World Travel, and North-South Relations

By 1983, after nine albums in eight years, Cockburn moved into a Beethovenian 'third style period' (Gutnik 1990). In fact it is difficult to sense a new musical approach, but there is a new concern in the texts with third-world issues. If Cockburn had formerly focused his anger on Canadian and, to a lesser extent, U.S. problems, his travels to Central America, during the period when the Reagan administration supported the contras' military opposition of the socialist government of Daniel Ortega in Nicaragua, infused his songs with a perspective that came from outside Canada. In a sense his work in this period is the musical embodiment of a third element of Trudeau's Liberalism, his recently articulated North-South vision, the notion that Canada's, and indeed the world's, future lay in the confrontation between the rich nations of the north and the poor nations of the south, rather than in the East-West relations that had dominated U.S. geopolitics for most of the century, particularly since the Second World War. On the title track of the first album of this 'third period,' *The Trouble with Normal* (1983), Cockburn articulates for the first time his concern for issues surrounding the relationships between industrialized and developing countries: businessmen 'play pinball with the third world,' encouraging countries to turn away from self-sufficiency in food production toward 'single crop starvation plans' that will keep the first world supplied 'normally' with its needs for sugar, tea, and coffee. 'But the trouble with normal is it always gets worse.' On *Stealing Fire* (1984) and *World of Wonders* (1986), his anti-American stance becomes most overt, as he openly champions, as many Canadians did, the Sandinista struggle against American imperialism, in songs with texts so strong some U.S. stations refused to play them (O'Connor 1987: 87). As one writer put it, Cockburn was 'Canada's musical conscience,' and had been for over a decade (MacDonald 1984: E1).

Predictably, the references to 'southern' musical styles increases during this period, but still within the framework of rock music. Four of nine songs on *Stealing Fire* use reggae, while other songs use Latin American devices: 'To Raise the Morning Star' uses *timbales*, a pair of tuned tenor drums used in Cuban and Puerto Rican popular styles; 'Nicaragua' contains guitar lines in parallel thirds, one of the most characteristic textures of Latin music (see Example 4). On 'Santiago Dawn' and two other songs from *World of Wonders*, Cockburn plays the *charango*, a small guitar-like instrument with four

Example 4 Latin-style parallel thirds from 'Nicaragua' (*Stealing Fire*, 1984)

double courses of strings and an armadillo shell for a body; this instrument has been used prominently by Chilean protest singers in the so-called *nueva canción* movement. On 'See How I Miss You,' from the same album, he evokes Trinidadian steel drum on the synthesizer. Speaking of *World of Wonders*, Cockburn said:

> It's true that the new songs have a more consciously internationalist sound, but that has less to do with those particular styles than with the fact that I come from a country with no musical tradition at all. When you travel around and see all this great stuff, why not use it. (Perry 1987: 12)[9]

During this period he also revisits Middle Eastern music with a love song, 'Sahara Gold' (*Stealing Fire*), and strikes out in an unexpected direction in 'Anything Can Happen' (*Big Circumstance*, 1989) with a reference to the 1920s pop schlock and *klezmer* music of Eastern European Ashkenazic Jews and their descendants in America, a style which enjoyed a modest revival in the 1980s spearheaded by young musicians in bands like Klezmorim, which appeared a number of times in Toronto, the New England Conservatory Klezmer Band, and Toronto's Flying Bulgar Klezmer Band.

Thus Cockburn, in his 'third period,' continues tendencies established earlier in his career, even as aspects of his approach change. His texts become ever more politically engaged at the same time that he draws back occasionally to write an introspective love song ('Making Contact,' *Stealing Fire*) or an evocation of a beautiful sight or moving experience ('Nicaragua,' *Stealing Fire*). His music remains thoroughly eclectic and continuously evolving, combining a variety of popular styles (country, folk, rock, jazz, reggae, new wave) with Middle Eastern music and Latin American and *klezmer* music. His artistic personality continued to develop at least partly in response to developments in Canadian and international politics while the core of that personality remained intact.

A review of Bruce Cockburn's career reveals a musician, working in popular music, who behaves as an artist while keeping in touch with the world around him. His artistry comes from his refusal to wear the strait-jacket of popular taste, his play with the boundaries of style, his continuous development as a musician and composer, and his use of all the musical resources at his command to create music that responds to his texts and is uniquely his own. It is not necessary to judge him a great artist or to measure him on a scale that in any case would be almost impossible to adumbrate. Rather, I claim that he belongs to a large category of composers and musicians who view their task as the creation of unique personal statements rather than popular or commercial ones. The medium or style they work in – classical, folk, popular, rock, jazz, ethnic – is immaterial; these categories are, after all, created by academics, journalists, and the music business. These musicians transcend the limitations of style and the demands of an audience with limited horizons. They answer to their own muse, not that of tradition or market success.[10]

Artists, including Bruce Cockburn, don't make what I have called their 'unique personal statements' in a social or cultural vacuum, however. Everything they create responds in one way or another to a historically created and received tradition and to the social conditions in which they live and work. Cockburn is important to his time and place and to the history of music in Canada because he made different decisions in the face of comparable traditions and circumstances than did his contemporaries and peers. Joni Mitchell and Neil Young, both interesting 'folk' artists, emigrated to the United States to cash in on their popularity there. Anne Murray stayed in Canada but moulded her career to the demands of popular American country music. (Another study might take up the question of whether and how these musicians' work continues to be interpreted as Canadian by their fans.) Cockburn, on the other hand, stayed in Canada, rejected the U.S. road to popular acceptance, and in the process endeared himself to a Canadian public in need of self-definition, and the articulation of Canadian perspectives, in the face of waves of media-channelled American culture washing over the country. As Cockburn says:

I love Canada. It's hard to pin down – it's not flag-waving ... Well, none of us has really figured out what Canada is, but nevertheless I have a very strong feeling for this country. (Oswald 1987: 23)

The easiest place to find Cockburn's devotion to a Canadian perspective is in his texts, beginning with his decision to publish them with French translations in his album notes, and continuing with his occasional singing of some of them in French as, for example, in 'Homme brulant' (*Circles in the Stream*, 1977). In fact, Cockburn's changing notion of Canada corresponds remarkably to Pierre Trudeau's changing vision of the same period: first, of a bilingual country treating both languages with respect; second, of a multicultural society with room for Native peoples and new immigrants who play reggae and *klezmer* music; and third, of a country sensitive to how rich, industrialized nations exploit the people and resources of poor, developing nations. Trudeau tried to give Canada a distinctive image of itself, although one that many in the country could not accept, and Cockburn fit that image, giving it musical and poetic expression and becoming in the process not only Canada's musical conscience but its unofficial poet laureate, a bard for Trudeau's Liberalism.[11]

Finding Canada in Cockburn's music is more difficult, as is the identification of nationalist traits in the work of many twentieth-century composers. Its essence may lie in his eclecticism, and Cockburn has said, 'Being from Canada, you're almost obliged to become a cultural pirate' (McGrath 1981: E7). If this refers to his borrowing of U.S. styles, then his statement would be true for anyone in popular music working outside of the United States, which, because of its history, has been the source for the dynamic mixture of European and African musical styles that has given us blues, jazz, rock and roll, gospel, and soul. Most Canadian musicians have not followed Cockburn's eclectic path, but have adopted wholeheartedly one of American popular music's genres, in the process losing their Canadian identity. Cockburn's eclecticism extends beyond styles that originated in the United States, and seems rooted first of all in his personal experience: of growing up hearing different kinds of music, playing many instruments, and then educating himself in a broader range of styles – including jazz, classical, and non-Western music – than those of most musicians, whether classical or popular. His nationalism and eclecticism complemented each other. By staying in Canada and rejecting the American market as a measure of success, he could remain true to his artistic instincts. His mastery of various styles could then be used symbolically to make musical statements representing a Canadian perspective.

His choice of folk music as his first style can be viewed as an outsider's protest against American cultural hegemony in music. Since Canadian folk music is largely devoid of the African and African-American influence so prevalent in popular music and culture, it represents a more English or European point of view, which is one of its distinguishing features.

His continued embrace of non-U.S. forms, and styles from India, Iran, Jamaica, Trinidad, and Latin America, teaches Canadians, and anyone who will listen, that the United States is not the sole source of interesting music. There is a whole world out there, and Canada must relate to it to reduce her dependence on the United States, both culturally and economically. Canada's relations with other nations must differ from those of the United States, according to Cockburn, and take on the character of a partner among nations rather than an exploiter of people, resources, and political and economic weakness.

Thus, Cockburn's eclecticism is not the source of his Canadianness, but rather a tool for making musical statements that speak symbolically to and for Canadians. With the variety of musical styles at his command, he expresses directly in music his independence from the strictures and demands of the American musical market, its tastes, and de facto cultural hegemony, and marks out a distinctly Canadian musical space for himself and his audience.

Discography

All of Cockburn's albums appear on the True North label.

Year	Cat.	Title
1969	TN–1	Bruce Cockburn
1971	TN–3	High Winds, White Sky
1972	TN–7	Sunwheel Dance
1973	TN–11	Night Vision
1974	TN–16	Salt, Sun and Time
1975	TN–23	Joy Will Find a Way
1976	TN–26	In the Falling Dark
1977	TN–30	Circles in the Stream
1978	TN–33	The Further Adventures of Bruce Cockburn
1979	TN–37	Dancing in the Dragon's Jaws
1980	TN–42	Humans
1981	TN–45	Mummy Dust
1981	TN–47	Inner City Front
1982	TN–51	Resume
1983	TN–53	The Trouble with Normal
1984	TN–57	Stealing Fire
1986	TN–66	World of Wonders
1987	TN–67	Waiting for a Miracle
1989	TN–70	Big Circumstance

NOTES

1 Rice, the 'I' of the paper, wrote the article and contributed its intellectual framework, cultural interpretation, and part of the musical analysis and library research. Gutnik, who wrote a master's thesis under Rice's supervision on Bruce Cockburn (Gutnik 1990), contributed the musical transcriptions, the research for some of the quoted references, and the periodization of Cockburn's career.
2 If, as I have suggested, the history of music should account for the music of 'our time and place,' the study of these seven individuals demonstrates that that history will not be exclusively the history of European art music, but will have to include the folk, tribal, and classical music of many people on many continents.
3 The use of the term 'folk music' in this paper refers to a genre of popular music that rose to prominence in the 1950s and retains a modest following to this day. Sometimes referred to as the 'folk revival,' it included American groups like the Kingston Trio, the Limelighters, and Peter, Paul and Mary, American singer-songwriters like Joan Baez and Judy Collins, and Canadian singers like Joni Mitchell and Ian and Sylvia Tyson. This usage of 'folk music' contrasts with its use by scholars of European and North American traditional music, who defined folk music in the late-nineteenth and early-twentieth centuries to comprise rural music passed on in oral tradition, which they believed played an important role in the preservation and formation of national consciousness. In Quebec, a somewhat analogous *chansonnier* movement paralleled the English-language folk revival, and influenced some anglophone songwriters, notably Leonard Cohen (see Giroux 1984). I am grateful to Beverley Diamond for this last point.
4 Although I argue that the aesthetics and most of the forms of folk music are primarily rooted in the British and other European traditions, the folk revival was not entirely immune to African and African-American influence: witness the talking blues, ragtime guitar and banjo styles, and songs such as 'Wimoway,' 'Michael Row Your Boat Ashore,' and so on.
5 I am grateful to James Robbins for this third 'reason.'
6 Gold albums include *High Winds, White Sky* (1971), *Night Vision* (1973), *Joy Will Find a Way* (1975), *In the Falling Dark* (1976), *Humans* (1980), and *World of Wonders* (1986). Platinum albums are *Dancing in the Dragon's Jaws* (1979) and *Stealing Fire* (1984). In Canada gold albums are those which have sold more than 50,000 copies, while platinum albums have sold more than 100,000 copies.
7 To qualify as Canadian, a song had to achieve at least two points out of four, with one point awarded for music, lyrics, artist, and production (LeBlanc 1992).
8 The 'thumb harp' is a metallophone with plucked metal tines or keys of

different length set on a box resonator. Widespread in Africa, its motoric, arpeggiated music has frequently been imitated on the guitar by contemporary African musicians.

9 Questions about the ethics of first-world musicians using third-world musical styles have increasingly been raised in the wake of the enormous commercial success of similar borrowings by Paul Simon, David Byrne, and Peter Gabriel. When eclectic appropriation turns into unethical misappropriation or expropriation at the expense of powerless third-world artists, then there may indeed be good reasons 'why not' to use it (see, for example, Meintjes 1990 and Feld 1988). While it is useful and appropriate to worry about these issues, they are complex, and the jury is still out. As ethnomusicologists in particular criticize musicians, we need to keep in mind the ways our own work involves ethically vexing acts of appropriation in uneven relationships of power. An examination of these issues in Cockburn's use of non-Western sources, or even better a comparative study of different musicians, would be interesting, but is beyond the scope of this paper.

10 John Rockwell makes a similar point in his book, All-American Music, which served as a text for the course mentioned in the introduction. His 'artists' include such disparate figures as Ernst Krenek, Philip Glass, Laurie Anderson, Ornette Coleman, Eddie Palmieri, and Talking Heads – and that all-American musician Neil Young.

11 I can imagine Cockburn being horrified at any implication that he was a shill for the Liberals. That is not my intention. Rather I intend simply to point out a connection between Cockburn's work and the world in which he and all Canadians lived, a world that Trudeau's political ideology helped to shape.

REFERENCES

Bateman, Jeff. 1975. 'Bruce Cockburn: In His Own Words,' *The Music Scene* 352: 8–10.
Feld, Steven. 1988. 'Notes on World Beat,' *Public Culture Bulletin* 1(1): 31–7.
Giroux, Robert, ed. 1984. *Les aires de la chanson québécoise*. Montreal: Triptique.
Gutnik, Tammy. 1990. 'Bruce Cockburn's Big Circumstance: An Ethnomusicology of Canadian Popular Music.' MA thesis, University of California, Los Angeles.
Guttman, Cynthia. 1987. 'Bruce Cockburn's Miracle,' *International Herald Tribune*, September 1.
Haynes, Dave. 1981. 'Cockburn Calls His Rock Music,' *Globe and Mail*, July 10: E1.
LeBlanc, Larry. 1992. '"Canadian-Content" Discontent: Quota Slots Seen Squeezing Domestic Acts,' *Billboard* 104(9): 40.

MacDonald, Peggy. 1984. 'Cockburn: Music with Conscience,' *Halifax Chronicle-Herald*, February 1: E1.
McGrath, Paul. 1981. 'Cockburn: Human Beings to Humans,' *Globe and Mail*, January 17: E7.
MacGregor, Arthur, ed. 1986. *All the Diamonds*. Ottawa: Ottawa Folklore Centre Publications.
Meintjes, Louise. 1990. 'Paul Simon's Graceland, South Africa, and the Mediation of Musical Meaning,' *Ethnomusicology* 34 (1): 37–73.
O'Connor, Tim. 1987. 'Political Activist Cockburn Still Waiting for a Miracle,' *Halifax Chronicle-Herald*, April 2: 11.
Oswald, Brad. 1987. 'Cockburn's Solo Concert Series Chance to Recharge Batteries,' *Winnipeg Free Press*, November 14: 23.
Ouellette, Dan. 1988. 'Bruce Cockburn,' *Downbeat* 55(5): 14.
Rockwell, John. 1983. *All American Music: Composition in the Late Twentieth Century*. New York: Vintage Books.
Yorke, Ritchie. 1971. *Axes, Chops and Hot Licks: The Canadian Rock Music Scene*. Edmonton: M.G. Hurtig.

PART SIX

A Canadian Looking-Glass

GORDANA LAZAREVICH

Aspects of Early Arts Patronage in Canada: From Rockefeller to Massey

The concept of patronage of the arts in Western Europe is as old as the arts themselves. From medieval times, when the church as patron provided the main impetus for the flourishing of the arts, to the Renaissance, the eighteenth century and beyond, when nobility and royalty constituted the predominant source of patronage, the history of the evolution of the arts is closely linked to the history of organizations, individuals, and – in more modern times – states, which have commissioned and supported creative activity.

Throughout the centuries there were varying motives for arts patronage. The church, which dominated medieval society, was responsible for the creation of cathedrals, magnificent edifices for the worship of the glory of God. Under the patronage of the church countless religious paintings, frescos, and other works were created. Later, royalty and nobility commissioned art, music, and plays, for aesthetic purposes and as symbols of the patrons' status and personal glory.

The famous Milanese Renaissance ducal Sforza family was known for its arts patronage, and today Lodovico Sforza is particularly remembered as the employer of Leonardo da Vinci.

Similarly, Prince Nicholas Eszterházy's name is inextricably bound with that of Joseph Haydn, as the patron and employer for whom the composer created a large number of his masterpieces. Prince Nicholas supported a full symphony orchestra, a complete cast of opera singers, and a marionette theatre. The lavishness and glitter of his court activities, which included over 100 operatic performances annually, earned his court an international reputation as one of Europe's leading operatic centres.

Another enlightened ruler of the eighteenth century, Frederick II or

Frederick the Great, was the patron and employer of C.P.E. Bach, J.J. Quantz, and others, who provided him with compositions for his own use. The many flute works written by Quantz were occasionally performed by Frederick in his music room at the Sans Souci summer palace, a large and lavish space, the walls and ceilings of which were covered by guilded ornaments and paintings by his court painter, Antoine Pesne, illustrating scenes from Ovid's *Metamorphoses*.

Despite the fact that the eighteenth and nineteenth centuries witnessed a democratization of the arts, whereby large numbers of the general population became its consumers (as both performers and audiences), the appreciation of art was still primarily a pastime of the educated segments of society, intended to fill their leisure hours.

This elitist stigma was very much in evidence in the New World. In Canada's early days settlers, concerned with cultivating the land and dealing with the harshness of the country's climate, considered art to be an unnecessary luxury. To a certain extent this attitude carried over into the first half of the twentieth century, and home-grown talent in particular felt affected by it.

Until the tabling in Parliament of the Massey Commission Report in 1951, and its subsequent repercussions throughout the 1950s and beyond, there was no direct government subsidy for the arts in Canada, and artists had the impression that they were working in a vacuum. In the absence of a national cultural policy, artists lacked a consistent source of material and spiritual support. They perceived the attitude of the Canadian public as one of colossal indifference towards the arts, and felt that foreign performers were more readily received than home-grown artists: a Canadian musician would only become interesting to Canadian audiences after having developed a reputation abroad.

The 1930s and 1940s marked the beginning of a growing awareness by artists of the country's cultural needs. Art was perceived as a form of communication, yet three factors seemed to threaten the dissemination of this type of communication: (1) the isolation of one region from another due to the country's vastness; (2) Canada's history and tradition of (what was perceived then as) two founding nations; and (3) the magnet of the giant culture to the south of the border, i.e. the United States.

In the first half of the twentieth century, art in Canada assumed functions particular to a society which was still searching for cultural self-definition: it was used for political propaganda, as a morale booster and a tool for the development of patriotic sentiments, as a publicity tool, and as a promoter of Canadian multiculturalism. Art was, of course, also practised for its own sake, and the freelance Canadian artist was the one who most intensely felt the sense of isolation from society.

Art as Political Propaganda

This was most evident during the years of the Second World War. The wartime radio dramas presented by the Canadian Broadcasting Corporation (CBC) romanticized the freedom of opportunity and the good life extended by Canada to its people. A phenomenon of the 1940s, hundreds of radio dramas were aired by the CBC, including such titles as 'New Homes for Old' (1941), 'The British Empire' (1942), and 'Our Canada' (1942–3). These dramas featured, among others, scriptwriters Alistair Grosart and Gerald Noxon, conductor Samuel Hersenhoren, composer John Weinzweig, producer Mavor Moore, and narrator Lorne Greene. Live music, which constituted an essential part of these programs, was provided by musicians from the Toronto area especially hired by the CBC, for whom the corporation represented a major source of income.

Art as Morale Booster

The war years also saw art used as a means of raising morale at home through the CBC's airing of musical programs which featured Canadian compositions. 'Canadian Snapshots,' inaugurated in December 1939, for example, was a series of fifty programs of music by fifty Canadian composers (including Louis Applebaum, Francean Campbell, Eldon Rathburn, and the thirteen-year-old Clermont Pépin), intermingling music with news and documentary stories.[1]

By stressing Canadian content the CBC not only elicited patriotic sentiments at home, but also became an active employer and promoter of artists. In that sense it was a patron of Canadian music. In its program schedule of 21 December 1941, the CBC stated:

To the serious young composer of concert or symphonic music, an auditorium, audience and orchestra of proportions suitable to the adequate performance of his works are rarely available ... The CBC has assumed as a duty the seeking out and encouraging of exceptional creative talent in the field of musical composition. A symphony orchestra and top-ranking conductor have been selected ... Samuel Hersenhoren is a prime mover in the systematic research, which has discovered outstanding ability among the younger composers of Canada: John Weinzweig, Godfrey Ridout ... Barbara Pentland.[2]

In keeping with this policy, throughout the 1940s and 1950s the corporation commissioned numerous works, including the first radio opera, Healey Willan's *Transit through Fire* (1942), with a libretto by John Coulter.

One government organization that was instrumental in boosting the morale of the Canadian armed forces overseas was the Department of National Defence (DND), which functioned as both promoter and patron of the arts. With the support of the National Gallery and such major corporations as Imperial Tobacco, Imperial Oil, and Neilson's, the DND, during the Second World War, provided funds for and commissioned silk-screen prints of Canadian landscapes to grace the walls of the military barracks, mess halls, recreation rooms, and huts of the Canadian armed forces overseas.

The DND also employed painters for service in the Canadian armed forces, an idea fostered by Vincent Massey, at that time High Commissioner for Canada in the United Kingdom. Such artists were first involved in field work, sketching scenes on the battlefield, followed by time in London to develop their sketches. Among these artists were (Major) Charles Comfort, (Major) Will Ogilvie, (Captain) Bruno Bobak, (Captain) Alex Colville, (Captain) Lawren Harris, (Lieutenant) Molly Lamb Bobak, and (F/L) Carl Schaefer, all of whom were or became significant names in the art world.[3]

A similar program had already been developed by the DND during the First World War with the help of Lord Beaverbrook, whose plan was to choose Canadian and other Commonwealth artists to paint war scenes as documentary evidence. The paintings created during that time by F.H. Varley, A.Y. Jackson, David Milne, and others are now in the National Gallery in Ottawa.

To help the Canadianization of the Second World War effort, Charles Matthews, from the eminent Toronto printing firm Samson Matthews, employer of A.J. Casson (the youngest member of the Group of Seven) for over twenty years, commissioned silk-screen prints from artists such as Walter Phillips, J.W.G. Macdonald, Yvonne McKague Housser, and Charles Comfort. Matthews also provided reproductions of masterpieces by the Group of Seven, as well as by Emily Carr.[4] The firm was heavily involved in the war effort through the design and printing of posters, as well as pamphlets and advertisements.

Art as a Publicity Tool

This function of art was particularly in evidence in the period between the two world wars when the Canadian Pacific Railway (CPR), originally built to create a link across the country and populate the West, developed the mandate early in the twentieth century of attracting tourists to the West in order to finance the company's operating expenses. Fulfilling this mandate involved an aggressive publicity campaign which included extolling the beauties of the Canadian Rocky Mountains. Painters and photographers were hired to capture, through their artwork, the flavour and beauty of the area. Wildlife artist Carl Rungius became especially known for his paintings of Rocky Mountain goats high up on the mountain ledges, while Walter Phillips and Charles Simpson specialized in nature scenes. The official CPR photographer was Nicholas Morant, whose works captured the interior elegance of the trains and of the Banff Springs Hotel, the CPR's pride and joy.

Between the 1880s and the late-1920s, the CPR had built a chain of chateau-type hotels, nine in all, ranging from the Château Frontenac in Quebec to the Empress Hotel in Victoria. The hotels, as well as the trains, offered the tourists the opportunity to travel in luxury and comfort. During their cross-country journey, tourists could relax in elegant train cars with embroidered upholstery, rugs, and mahogany panelling. They could break their westbound journey by overnighting in the CPR hotels, and once they reached the queen of the CPR line – the Banff Springs Hotel – they could spend their holidays in the resort-like atmosphere created for them by the CPR's management in the midst of the natural splendour of the Rocky Mountains.[5]

The CPR provided its guests with a lively cultural fare, and through its employment of artists, commissions of Canadian compositions, creation of massive multicultural festivals, and sponsorship of numerous concerts, particularly in the years prior to the Second World War, it functioned as employer, sponsor, and patron of music and the other arts.

Visitors to the Banff Springs Hotel, frequently consisting of the cultural elite from New York and Boston, as well as royalty from all over the world, had sophisticated musical tastes. Formal evening concerts and other types of musical offerings, therefore, assumed great significance in the CPR's plan to promote an aura of elegance and culture. The best talent in Canada was sought out to perform in Banff, resulting in musical events of a calibre otherwise found only in large Canadian cities.

Two types of concerts were offered between 1927 and 1941: formal after-dinner recitals of vocal music starting at 9 p.m., and less formal pre-dinner chamber music recitals, both given in Mt Stephen Hall. The star attraction at Banff over a period of fifteen years was young soprano Frances James, whose evening recitals were presented in an atmosphere of formality and elegance. The pre-dinner recitals were provided by the Banff Springs Hotel Trio, later known as the Toronto Trio, whose leader was the young Toronto violinist Murray Adaskin, who later became one of Canada's most important composers. It was only fitting that the leading soprano and the leading violinist decided to cement their relationship through marriage in 1931.

Up to the Second World War, the CPR supported an active publicity department with its own music subsection responsible for publicizing the large number of cultural events sponsored by the corporation. The publicity office produced brochures and booklets, and distributed press releases both nationally and internationally. These events were reviewed by media especially employed by the CPR for that purpose. Even the *New York Times* carried notices from Banff through its correspondent Paul Standard.

The manager of the publicity office in the CPR's headquarters in Montreal was John Murray Gibbon, a remarkable Scot who had emigrated to Canada. A man of vision, enterprise, and energy, he combined his extensive knowledge of languages, literature, and music with his business abilities in order to create an atmosphere of cultural nationalism not to be encountered in Canada again until the centennial celebrations of 1967.

Gibbon's good fortune was to enjoy the full support of the CPR management, especially its president Sir Edward W. Beatty, who enabled him to carry out his many original ideas. Gibbon functioned as an impresario, engaging the country's leading artists in concerts; he conceptualized and organized all of the musical events sponsored by the CPR over the fifteen year period; he created massive folk-art and folk-music festivals; and he wrote elaborate program notes for these festivals which he used as publicity tools. Through Gibbon's creative efforts the CPR also commissioned Canadian compositions for the music festival held in Quebec in 1927, and sponsored a cross-country tour of British and Canadian music in 1929–30. Gibbon particularly felt that folksongs provided the means of unifying the country and a platform for promoting better understanding between francophones and anglophones.

Throughout the 1930s the CPR was involved in radio broadcasting. It also sponsored lecture/travelogues across the country, which consisted of concerts of folk-songs interspersed with narrative, with background projections of paintings of Canadian scenes by artists whose works were on display at the National Gallery of Ottawa.

Art as Promoter of Multiculturalism

The CPR hotels served as venues for a variety of company-sponsored musical and cultural events. The sixteen remarkable folk-art and folk-music festivals held between 1927 and 1931 constituted a fourth function assumed by art in early-twentieth-century Canada. They were intended to attract tourists from all over the world and to present a comprehensive picture of the living traditions of the various provinces, in the process highlighting the historical roots of these traditions.

The festivals were three to five days in duration and were held in Quebec's Château Frontenac, Toronto's Royal York Hotel, Winnipeg's Royal Alexandra, Calgary's Palliser Hotel, the Banff Springs Hotel, the Hotel Vancouver, and Victoria's Empress Hotel. The themes of the festivals for the most part reflected their geographic location. Quebec had the Canadian Folk-Song and Handicraft Festival; Toronto, the English Music Festival; the Prairies, the Great West Canadian Folk-Song, Folk-Dance, and Handicrafts Festival; Banff, the Banff Highland Gatherings and the Scottish Music Festivals; Vancouver, the Sea Music Festivals; and Victoria, the Old English Yuletide Festivals.[6]

One of the brochures outlines the scope of these ideas:

In order to visualize the close association between the folk song and handicraft in the Province of Quebec, arrangements have been made to hold a Folk-song and Handicraft festival at the Château Frontenac, Quebec, May 20–22, under the auspices of the National Museum of Canada, which is co-operating with the CPR in organizing this festival on a very comprehensive scale. Dr. Marius Barbeau of the National Museum ... is in charge. A number of skilled weavers and spinners from the country districts will demonstrate the complete process of making the flax into thread and spinning of weaving homespun clothes, hookrugs, etc. The ancient method of making the coloured sashes ... will also be demonstrated. All such work is done to the accompaniment of folksong, and the workers engaged are either accomplished singers themselves, or are accompanied by such singers.

Specimens of fine homespuns, hookrugs, etc. lent by the National Museum of Canada and other distinctive collections, will be on exhibition at the Château Frontenac during this festival. An exhibition of pictures illustrating the landscape and the life of Quebec – lent by the National Gallery of Canada – will be on display at the Château Frontenac during this festival.[7]

These paintings included works by artists such as André Bieler, Clarence Gagnon, A.Y. Jackson, Arthur Lismer, Cornelius Krieghoff, Mabel May, Kathleen Morris, Anne Savage, and Sarah Robertson.

Huron Indians made snowshoes, moccasins, canoes, and baskets, and sang what little they remembered of their tribal songs. The popular By-Town Troubadours of Ottawa, a quartet of gifted chansonniers, wandered through the halls in colourful lumberman garb singing 'chansons populaires.'

Each of the festivals was a spectacular manifestation of folk traditions particular to the region in which it was held. The musical fare provided by the CPR for the occasion was rich and varied. Folk-music was skilfully worked into many of the ballad operas performed during the five-year period of the CPR festivals. The concept of ballad opera dates from eighteenth-century England, where one of the most famous examples of the genre, *The Beggar's Opera,* was created. Gibbon translated this concept to Canada by commissioning ballad operas from such Canadian musicians and folk-song arrangers as Harold Eustace Key, J. Campbell McInnes, and Healey Willan.

Historical topics were the basis for *L'Ordre de bon temps* (also performed in Vancouver as *Order of Good Cheer*), *Prince Charlie and Flora, The Ayrshire Plowman, Bound for the Rio Grande, The Chester Mysteries,* and *The Jolly Beggars.* Gibbon was also instrumental in producing the North America première of Vaughan-Williams's *Hugh the Drover* on the occasion of the opening of the CPR's Royal York Hotel in Toronto in 1929.

Healey Willan arranged folk-songs for many of the ballad operas, while Gibbon himself was responsible for choosing and occasionally even writing the texts. Painter's Charles Simpson and Arthur Lismer were involved in designing stage sets for at least two of the ballad operas.

Throughout his years as director of the CPR's publicity office, Gibbon engaged prominent Canadian musicians, folk-song collectors, arrangers, composers, and performers to participate in the festivals and other CPR-sponsored events. Sir Ernest MacMillan, Marius Barbeau, Alfred Whitehead, Claude Champagne, Oscar O'Brien, Toronto's Hart House String Quartet, the By-Town Troubadours, Alfred Heather's Light Opera Company, and singers J. Campbell McInnes, Jeanne Dusseau, and Frances James were some of the Canadian artists sponsored by the CPR.

One of the earliest commissions of Canadian music occurred under the sponsorship of the CPR. The president of the corporation, Sir Edward Beatty, donated three thousand dollars in prize money for orchestral and vocal compositions based on French-Canadian folk music. An international jury chose the winning compositions, which included Claude Champagne's *Suite Canadienne* and Ernest MacMillan's *Six Bergerettes du bas Canada.* Both were premièred at the 1928 Quebec festival.

While the primary purpose of the CPR concerts was promotional – using art to promote tourism and multiculturalism – there was also an educational aspect: they hoped to create an awareness among Canadian audiences about Canadian and British contemporary music.

As demonstrated, support for the arts came from a number of different sectors – the CBC, DND, and CPR. State support, therefore, was indirect, through government departments, companies, and corporations which had jurisdiction over their budget and could make independent budgetary decisions. There was as yet no central government granting agency, nor was there a government policy on the arts.

Support also came from the public sector. Canadian artists in the first half of the twentieth century received much assistance from the efforts of dedicated groups of volunteers – to a great extent, although not exclusively, women – who donated time to their local organizations for the purpose of raising money through ticket and other types of sales, in order to sponsor theatrical and musical events. These individuals usually worked at the grass roots level within small communities in the interior, as well as in larger cities.

Canada-wide networks of Womens' Musical Clubs from Halifax to Vancouver sponsored domestic and international artists. These clubs, consisting of amateur musicians and music lovers, were dedicated to enriching their own members' knowledge and appreciation of music, in the process contributing to the artistic and cultural life of their communities. Although some clubs were formed as early as the 1890s, they were particularly active throughout the first half of this century. For example, the Montreal Ladies' Morning Musical Club during its 1946–7 season sponsored fourteen concerts, which featured artists such as violinists Joseph Fuchs and Isaac Stern, violist William Primrose, the Griller String Quartet, Canadian tenor Léopold Simoneau, and Canadian soprano Frances James with Bernard Naylor at the piano.

Although a cross-country tour organized by these groups was not profitable, it nevertheless enabled an artist to be heard outside of the main cultural centres, supplying just enough revenue to cover his or her expenses.

The involvement of a large number of women, who functioned as playwrights, directors, actors, designers, teachers, critics, historians, and administrators, allowed amateur theatre groups to flourish nationally from the 1930s to the 1960s. Two of the major names involved in the theatrical world were Elizabeth Sterling Hayes and Dora Mavor Moore.[8] Community organizations such as Womens' Musical Clubs and the amateur theatre groups, therefore, may also be viewed as early patrons and promoters of art in this country.

Although Canada has never had the tradition of philanthropy enjoyed by the United States, the arts in the early part of the century were enhanced through the generosity of such people as Lord Strathcona, Vincent Massey, and J.S. McLean, president of Canada Packers. Lord Strathcona, or Donald Alexander Smith, a Montreal statesman, financier, and philanthropist, created the Lord Strathcona scholarships in music for gifted young artists in the early decades of the century. Vincent Massey was one of Canada's greatest philanthropists during the first half of the century; a diplomat (he was Canada's High Commissioner in Great Britain) and later governor general, he was influential in the cultural and political life of this country. Through the Massey Foundation, Vincent Massey provided full financial support for the Hart House String Quartet, the first fully professional chamber group in Canada. Formed in 1925, the quartet received full salaries and benefits to perform six to eight annual concerts at Hart House, tour the United States and Europe – which it did even during the Depression – and visit Canada's interior communities.

In addition to his role in the building of Hart House on the University of Toronto campus, Massey was also a strong supporter of the Group of Seven painters. In the 1920s he purchased some Tom Thomson oil sketches for display at the Arts and Letters Club in Toronto. In 1934 he purchased the entire collection of 250 paintings of David Milne – at that time a virtually unknown artist. Some of the canvasses acquired by the Masseys were offered for resale, with a proportion of the proceeds used to establish a David Milne trust fund. Massey was also involved in the theatrical world; in 1933 he launched the Dominion Drama Festival, later known as Theatre Canada.

A number of distinguished citizens in communities across Canada helped artistic endeavours within their community. During the 1950's in Saskatoon, for example, Fred Mendel, founder and chairman of the board of Intercontinental Packers, Ltd, was instrumental in the creation of the Saskatoon Art Gallery (now known as the Mendel Art Gallery). The Montreal financier Izzac Walton Killam, born into a Maritime family of merchants and shipowners, left a forty million dollar estate for the support of the arts, education, and science. The Canada Council was established in part with funds from taxes on his estate.

Other benefactors dot the Canadian cultural horizon. The Koerner Foundation was established in 1955 with a capital grant of one million dollars to support projects by music schools and performing groups, as well as individuals and institutions such as libraries, universities, and other organizations devoted to the fine arts.

Despite this considerable generosity toward the arts on the part of philanthropists, no Canadian foundation in the early part of the century could measure up to the Carnegie, the Rockefeller, and more recently, the Ford foundations.[9]

Historically, American philanthropy reached out to Canada at a time when cultural activities received low priority on the part of the Canadian government. The Massey Commission Report was one of the earliest sources to document the vast cultural importations from the United States, and Canadian dependence on U.S. charity. Monetary gifts included $7,346,188 in the period between 1911 and 1949 from the Carnegie Corporation, and $11,817,707 between 1914 and 1949 from the Rockefeller Foundation. For that period in time, these were considerable sums.[10] The money, largely granted to universities, was used for endowment, for the purchase of equipment, and to facilitate development, research, study, and publication.

University recipients of the larger grants included Dalhousie (with over $1 million, including $70,626 for a new building); McGill (to a total of $1,249,900); Queen's ($308,350); the University of Alberta ($241,500, of which $100,000 was earmarked for a new building); and the University of Saskatchewan ($121,500). At the request of Walter Murray, the first president of the University of Saskatchewan, the Carnegie Foundation provided funds for the establishment of a chair in music because the province claimed that it was not in a position to provide funds for music. Arthur Collingwood became the first holder of the chair at the university. Additional funds requested by Collingwood for equipment, pianos, and so on, were used by President Murray to help establish a music reference library and to re-establish the Saskatoon Symphony Orchestra, which was conducted by Collingwood.[11]

The Banff Centre School of Fine Arts began in 1933 as an experimental theatre with a grant of thirty thousand dollars over three years from the Carnegie Foundation to the University of Alberta. At first it was a training centre for theatre, and then classes were added in creative writing, painting, and piano performance.

Similarly, the Conference of Canadian Artists, or 'the Kingston Conference,' held in June 1941 in Kingston and organized by André Bieler, was also supported in part by the Carnegie Corporation of New York. The president of the corporation paid Bieler a visit the previous year in order to study the plans for the conference, and gave $3000 to meet the travel expenses of artists attending the conference. This was the first time that a meeting of artists from across Canada was organized, and it led to the creation of the Federation of Canadian Artists. The Carnegie Corporation continued to support the newly formed federation during its first two years by helping with secretarial and travel costs.[12]

Another American organization, the Rockefeller Foundation, supported public health, medical science, natural sciences, social studies, and cultural studies in Canada. In the category of cultural studies the beneficiaries included the National Film Society of Canada and the Royal Ontario Museum of Archaeology. McGill University and the universities of Alberta, British Columbia, Manitoba, Montreal, New Brunswick, Saskatchewan, and Toronto each received grants for cultural studies.

Centres in the United States offered training not available in Canada in the areas of town planning, industrial design, library science, dramatic art, ballet, pictorial arts, and journalism. Canadian scholars belonged to American learned societies. Fellowships were awarded to Canadian students to study at American universities. Between 1940 and 1950, fifty-three Guggenheim Memorial Foundation Fellowships were awarded to Canadians. Recipients in the arts included Carl Schaefer for creative work in painting, Quebec novelist Roger Lemelin, Jack Nichols for creative work in painting, and Northrop Frye and Hugh MacLennan.

Importations of U.S. culture dominated the Canadian market. These included periodicals, books, Sunday symphony and opera concerts on the radio, the American Book-of-the-Month Club, maps, school textbooks, and Hollywood films. This generosity on the part of the United States toward Canada also contained some inherent problems. In addressing the issue of American philanthropy in Canada, the Massey Commission remarked:

Cultural exchanges are excellent in themselves. They widen the choice for the consumer and produce stimulating competition for the producer. It cannot be denied, however, that a vast and disproportionate amount of material coming from a single alien source may stifle rather than stimulate our own creative efforts; and, passively accepted without any standard of comparison, this may weaken critical faculties. We are now spending millions to maintain national independence which would be nothing but an empty shell without a vigorous and distinctive cultural life ... We have made important progress, often aided by American generosity. We must not be blind, however, to the very present danger of permanent dependence.[13]

Despite the extent of American influence on our cultural life in the first half of this century and its potential dangers to our cultural identity, we must not underestimate our indebtedness to the United States for providing financial support for Canadian cultural endeavours at a time when our own government was less than forthcoming in these areas. In its eloquently written 505-page report, the Massey Commission aptly identified the problems that faced Canadian culture up to 1951. Despite the sponsors, employers, patrons, promoters, and supporters without whose assistance art in this country would not have been able to survive, the Commission offered the following observations:

No novelist, poet, short story writer, historian, biographer, or other writer of non-technical books can make even a modestly comfortable living by selling his works in Canada. No composer of music can live at all on what Canada pays him for his compositions. Apart from radio drama, no playwright, and only a few actors and producers, can live by working in the theatre in Canada. Few painters and sculptors, outside the field of commercial art and teaching, can live by sale of their work in Canada.[14]

The commissioners made a strong statement that the arts and letters 'lie at the roots of our life as a nation' and that 'they are the foundations of national unity.' They recommended to the government of Canada that in order to foster this intellectual and cultural endeavour, federal, provincial, and local governments will have to provide financial support. An active cultural life was essential to national independence. The commissioners stressed that some countries have ministries of fine arts and cultural affairs, where governments take considerable measures of official responsibility for cultural support.

As a result of the Massey Commission recommendations, the Canada Council was created in 1957. Two decades later the newly established Social Sciences and Humanities Research Council took over the humanities and social sciences division originally administered by the Canada Council.

The resultant explosion of cultural activities over the last four decades constitutes a remarkable chapter in this young country's history. Canada has witnessed greatly increased artistic activity, the establishment of such institutions for the study and performance of the arts as concert halls, theatres, museums, art galleries, university fine arts faculties, and national organizations for the protection of the arts, as well as the establishment of provincial arts councils.

Although the problems of the position and survival of the arts in Canadian society are by no means resolved, in order to facilitate their resolution it is important to be aware of the historical position of the arts in our society in the first half of this century. Canada's culture is defined by its geographic parameters, its youth as a country, and its history, shaped by its first peoples, its founding nations, and its multicultural influx. In order to ensure the continuing development of our country's culture, it is imperative that we understand the circumstances that have shaped and supported this country's artistic endeavours and the means by which the arts survived up to the present age.

NOTES

1 Gordana Lazarevich, *The Musical World of Frances James and Murray Adaskin* (Toronto: University of Toronto Press, 1988), 28.
2 Lazarevich, *Musical World*, 78.
3 Graham McInnes, *Canadian Art* (Toronto: MacMillan, 1950), 81.
4 Paul Duval, *A.J. Casson, His Life and Works: A Tribute* (Toronto: Cerebrus/Prentice Hall, 1980), 150.
5 For more information on the cultural activities fostered by the CPR, and its music and folk-art festivals, see Lazarevich, *Musical World*, 6–18.
6 Lazarevich, *Musical World*, 10–15.
7 CPR Festival programs, Canadian Pacific Corporation archives, Montreal.
8 Ann Saddlemyer, 'Women of the Canadian Theatre,' in *A Celebration of Canada's Arts, 1930–1970*, ed. Gordana Lazarevich and Glen Carruthers, (Canadian Scholars' Press) in press.
9 Even today philanthropy in Canada leaves something to be desired. According to an article in *Musicanada* (January 1988) by Robert Landry, vice-president of Imperial Oil, 90 per cent of Canadian corporations do not make charitable contributions of any kind. Of those who do, only 11 percent of their donations go towards arts and culture.
10 All the figures, and those that follow are derived from: Royal Commission on National Development in the Arts, Letters, and Sciences, 1949–1951, *Report*, Appendix VA, 436–9, and Appendix VB.
11 Gordana Lazarevich, *Musical World*, 176.
12 Frances K. Smith, *André Bieler: An Artist's Life and Times* (Toronto: Merritt, 1980), 35.
13 *Report*, 18.
14 *Report*, 182.

BEVERLEY DIAMOND

Narratives in Canadian Music History

Preface

John Beckwith's teaching and research of Canadian music history have played a major role among the forces which led me to write the present article. I speak here not just of the priority which he gives to Canadian subjects, although his enthusiasm in this regard is compelling, but also of his insistence that we look carefully at social realities, both for the shape of our value systems and for the direction of our action as human beings. How could musicians regard hymns as unimportant – he has been known to ask – when millions of people find them deeply moving? By looking to social realities for 'culture,' he acknowledges, as I read it, that the anthropological definitions, rather than the more narrowly-framed ones of the concert-goer, constitute an appropriate intellectual basis for the study of Canadian or any other music cultures.

His interests are not dispassionate ivory tower pursuits but intersect with decisive action. A good case in point is his often-quoted article, 'About Canadian Music: The P.R. Failure,' (*Musicanada*, 1969),[1] where he articulated the problems of the avant-garde compositional community of his peers in a way which contributed to the considerable improvement of their situation in the ensuing twenty years. In his identification of the critical problems of 'PR' for new music, he articulated the hegemonic situation of the arts in relation to other national priorities, and of Canadian culture in relation to American or European – in short he anticipated the critical discourse and 'reflexive' scholarship which have had a striking impact in the humanities and social sciences in the last two decades.

While my work has departed in radically different directions from that of Beckwith, these lessons which I learned from him were profoundly important ones. This paper is informed, not by his subjects or issues, but by the spirit in which he engages in research. For both his inspiration and direction, I am deeply grateful.

Historiographic Issues and Boundaries

My aim is to deconstruct the values and assumptions of the 'narrative' which was created about Canadian music during that post-1960 period in which Beckwith played such an important role. In my view, the problems he articulated in 1969, in particular the need to create, for international consumption, an image of a group of Canadian composers who were at the forefront of compositional developments, helped to shape the way our music history was written around that time and subsequently. The intent of my deconstruction is not to evaluate the rightness or wrongness of that narrative, but rather to give us the option to choose whether the narrative of the next thirty years ought to be the same one. I recognize that my scrutiny of the structures which led a particular author to say one thing at a certain time and place is fascinating but also disturbing. As Leo Treitler has written in *Music and the Historical Imagination*, 'We do not like to acknowledge that, as historians, we are within history. We do not like to think that our choice of problems or our ways of identifying and evaluating evidence serve any particular ideologies or that they reflect the ways in which our worlds are structured, or that they would respond to change in the circumstances around us' (1989: 4).

'Narrative,' in this context, does not imply that scholarly writing is 'fictitious' but rather acknowledges what has become widely accepted in postmodernist textual criticism: that scholarly writing, like creative writing, is reflective of its historical and cultural situation. On one hand, this approach recognizes the 'literariness' of any written text since, as James Clifford has observed, '[l]iterary processes – metaphor, figuration, narrative – affect the ways cultural phenomena are registered, from the first jotted "observations," to the completed book, to the ways these configurations "make sense" in determined acts of reading' (1986: 4). On the other hand, the approach considers the 'political' or power-related dynamics involved in the relations of production of texts by examining their 'systematic and exclusive' (Clifford 1986: 6) aspects.

This approach to historiography, then, is influenced by the work of a number of critical theorists. Some of those works are social scientific studies which point to fundamental intra-cultural or cross-cultural 'themes' which are played out in scholarly texts (e.g., Boon 1983, Clifford 1988, or Bruner

1986). Others explore the impact of colonial power relations or indeed, concepts of 'nation' in relation to our constructions of self and 'other' (Spivak 1990, Waterman 1990, Grenier and Guilbault 1990). Still others (Trigger 1985) challenge the traditional Western disciplinary boundaries – between history and anthropology for example. In part, I am attempting to do a small-scale exercise in what Michel Foucault (see Rabinow 1984: 76–100) calls a 'genealogy' of ideas and interpretive strategies, in this case ideas and interpretive strategies about Canadian music history of the past thirty years.

My genealogy begins with a textual analysis of three well-known English-language monographs which survey a fairly broad spectrum of Canadian music, which often serve as texts – hence first introductions to our music culture for many students – and which reach a public market outside of the university context. The monographs are Kallmann's *A History of Music in Canada, 1534–1914* (1960, 2nd edition 1987), Ford's *Canada's Music: An Historical Survey* (1982), and McGee's *The Music of Canada* (1985). They are, clearly, important documents in the imaging of who we are and in the definition of a sort of canon of knowledge about our music culture. I will look at the representation of this image and the structure of this canon. In footnoted references the themes which reveal themselves in the textbook analysis are compared to other writing, mostly scholarly in intent and style, on more narrowly focused Canadian music research. I also make a comparison with textbooks on American (i.e., United States) music in order to explore how the narratives have been constructed differently within each nation. It is obvious that neither of these comparative exercises approaches comprehensiveness but rather they serve to contextualize the analysis of the three Canadian textbooks.

Narratives in Canadian Music Textbooks

The three aforementioned textbooks on Canadian music are not entirely comparable in scope: Kallmann ends his history at 1914, while Ford and McGee cover the twentieth century; McGee includes sub-sections on popular musics and a chapter on Native musics, while Ford and Kallmann focus on the 'classical' tradition with some mention of folk and Native musics. There are some overt differences between these three and other types of surveys of Canadian musics. Jazz studies such as those by John Gilmore (1988) or Mark Miller (1982, 1987) for example, and rock or other popular music music studies (e.g., Yorke 1971, Melhuish 1983, or Fetherling 1991) contrast notably through their focus on individual biography and their more limited chronological or geographical scope.[2] Earlier anthologies (e.g., Walter

1969 or MacMillan 1955) contrast by their report-like presentation of certain domains of *contemporaneous* activity, and other later monographs (e.g., Proctor 1980) by an emphasis on specific *domains* (e.g., composition). Several newer collections of writing – e.g., the Canadian Music Centre's *Celebration* (n.d.) or Beckwith and Hall's *Musical Canada* (1988) – are more diverse but they do not intend a comprehensive representation of any sort. Hence, Kallmann, Ford, and McGee are perhaps comparable in a way which other publications are not through their commitment to greater chronological and subject comprehensiveness. Notwithstanding the differences in scope and in research material on which to draw, a close reading is engaging because it permits us to examine the historiographic continuities and discontinuities established by three writers over a twenty-five year period.

Narratives of Intent

The obvious starting point for my researching of these texts was the examination of what the authors made explicit about their objectives. In this respect, Kallmann and Ford offer us quite a lot while McGee makes few explicit statements about his perspective. Both Kallmann and Ford emphasize their sociological orientation. Kallmann describes the aim of his book as 'the description of music at various stages of Canadian history and of the meaning it held in the life of the Canadian people' and stresses the 'continuity and cohesion of musical effort' as the 'musical pastimes and aspirations of the many' (3). He introduces at least two pervasive metaphors: 'the planting of seeds rather than the harvesting of the fruits' and the 'ever-present themes of transplantation, assimilation and search for identity' (5). Ford defines his sociological approach as one which subjects 'other aspects of music – music production, performance, education, and economics – to a socio-musical cosmology which can be constructed from historical data' (2). He contrasts this with a musico-historical approach, which he sees as one which traces the 'stylistic development of Canadian composition.' Ford quotes Kallmann on the planting of seeds and states that it is not his intention to show what is Canadian but to understand 'why the Canadian musical community developed as it did' (7). In this regard, he sees a tension between a 'natural evolutionary regionalism' and the 'aspirations of a national consciousness' (7) – the latter more positive in his view than the former. McGee describes his intent to write 'a general narrative that can be understood by the layman, while at the same time including some technical details for those who are interested in that kind of information' (xi). Implicit in this is the clear pedagogical intent of his book.

Narratives in Canadian Music History 277

These statements were hardly intended as political flags. But believing that language is never neutral, I find several aspects of these stated objectives worthy of reflection. What is the pre-text of Kallmann's commendable commitment to a 'social' history at a time when such a perspective was not popular in historical musicological writing?[3] Further, why would Ford actually strengthen his commitment to this perspective a decade later? What are the implications of the organic imagery (planting, seeding, harvesting)? How does the tension that Ford feels between 'regionalism' and 'national significance' play itself out? Is it significant that Kallmann states his objectives in terms of his subjects, that Ford seems more ready to make his own ideology overt, and that McGee chooses to be almost self-effacing in his statement of intent in terms of his prospective audience? Realizing that there may be simple answers to these questions (e.g., a publisher wanted it that way), I offer no further comment at this point but rather look at the content of the books.

Narratives of Proportion

Although a quantitative analysis of how much space is relegated to certain subjects might seem less significant than qualitative explorations, the proportioning of space within Canadian music textbooks indicates a number of priorities and deeply ingrained notions. First, with regard to the allocation of space for different chronological periods and with regard to the boundaries of those periods, few shifts have occurred since Kallmann's book was first published. If we may use the chapter boundaries as some sort of chronological markers, it is interesting that the dividing points are consistent from Ford to McGee and only marginally different in Kallmann. Have we, then, arrived at a comfortable periodization of our cultural history? Furthermore, the dates used to demarcate 'eras' are ones chosen for convenience (the end of a century) or with reference to major political events (confederation and world wars), unlike European classical music history which has generally attempted to demarcate historical eras according to major changes in musical style or in relation to other creative domains (e.g., art, literature.)

The proportion of space (see Figure 1) devoted to historical periods is consistent with the organic metaphor alluded to in two of the three introductions. The coverage of each successive period 'grows' to fill more pages than the last; while the Kallmann graph appears to contradict this in the last column, note that the last two columns combined are the equivalent of column four on the Ford and McGee graphs. McGee seems to have tried to give equal space to each 'period' although the twentieth-century periods are

278 Beverley Diamond

Figure 1 Number of Pages Per Chronological Period

Kallmann:

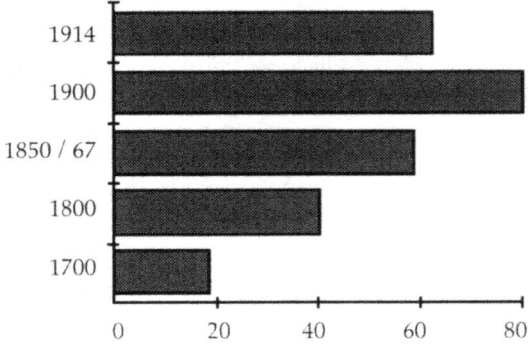

Ford:

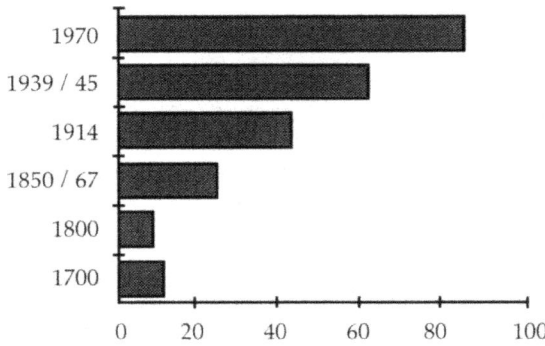

McGee:

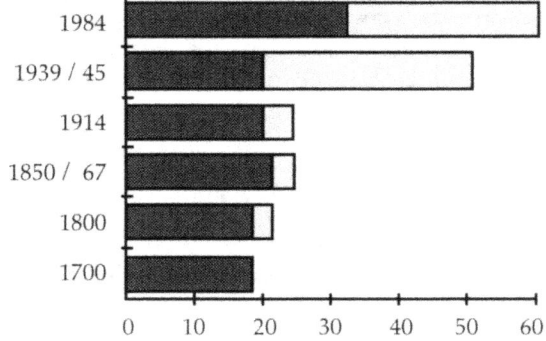

of course shorter than the earlier ones. But even here, the inclusion of musical examples produces the 'growth' phenomenon. It might seem obvious and natural to see our music history as a slow expansion culminating in the twentieth century. There are fewer materials for the earlier periods and a huge wealth of activity and creativity to discuss at present. But the same argument applied to European or Latin American music history does not seem to hold. Is it obvious and natural that so many musicologists study Medieval and Renaissance European music but few Canadian musicologists (Amtmann is an exception) have found it compelling to expand the data for the seventeenth and eighteenth centuries in survey-type works?[4] Perhaps separate monographs on these periods are now in order. But then, my suggestion presumes a different narrative – that proportional balance is somehow a truer story – and that merits considerable debate.

In addition to the proportioning of pages for different time periods, I tabulated the space devoted to specific places. Have we regarded cities as the cultural hubs of the nation? If so, does this constitute an adequate representation of the musical culture of our country? Or, if we regard small cities as pale reflections of larger ones, are we extending the injustices of a colonial perspective to our own traditions? I should acknowledge here that my own bias, stemming no doubt from the fact that I have lived approximately equal parts of my life in small, medium, and large communities, is that I find the *quality* of cultural life to be different in places of different size, different environment, and different social constitution but that difference has never been quantifiably proportional to the size of the community. Hence, I think we do colonize ourselves if we regard small cities as pale reflections of larger ones. To what extent is the qualitative variety of different places represented in our music history textbooks?

The next series of graphs (Figure 2) may at least provide a point of entry for answers to these questions about regional representation. First, both Kallmann and Ford clearly state that they regard major cities as representative. Kallmann (6) says 'the example of a few cities or careers usually serves to illustrate the essential features in many others' and he proceeds to use major cities as sub-headings in most chapters. Ford states his opinion with less neutrality, equating the development of cities directly with increasing cultural sophistication and 'progress toward a national consciousness' (104). I note statements such as the following: 'Naturally the most sophisticated towns in Canada would attract most of the talent, those towns being Halifax, Quebec, Montreal and Toronto' (34). In attempting to graph the coverage of urban musical life in these three books, I expanded Ford's list from four to nine: Halifax, Quebec, Montreal, Toronto, Winnipeg, Calgary, Edmonton,

Figure 2 Regional Representation

Kallmann

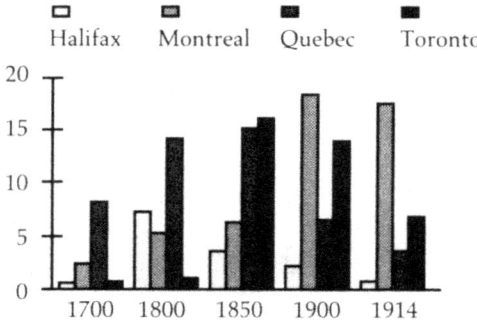

Notes difference in the scale of the two graphs.

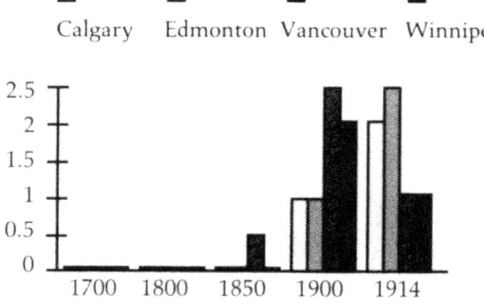

and Vancouver. The graphs demonstrate the obvious in many cases. That Halifax and Quebec were proportionately dominant in early periods and superseded by Toronto and Montreal in later ones is no surprise, although the extent of the gap by 1918 is, perhaps, greater than the population growth would lead one to anticipate. In spite of their consistent description of the rapid growth in Western Canada in the nineteenth century, the scant coverage of Western cities in not only the nineteenth century but also the twentieth century is striking when laid out in this graphic format. Perhaps we need a history of Canadian music authored by a Westerner to rectify the balance.[5] Certain anomalies are positive advantages to us. Ford's more extensive attention to Halifax in the nineteenth century, logical since he taught at

Figure 2 Regional Representation (continued)

Ford:

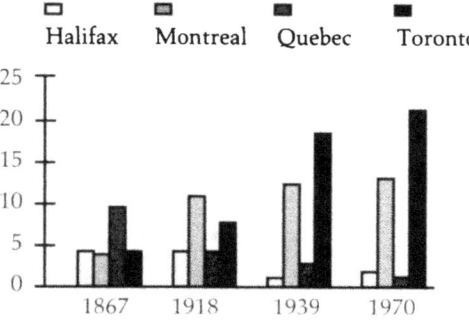

Notes difference in the scale of the two graphs.

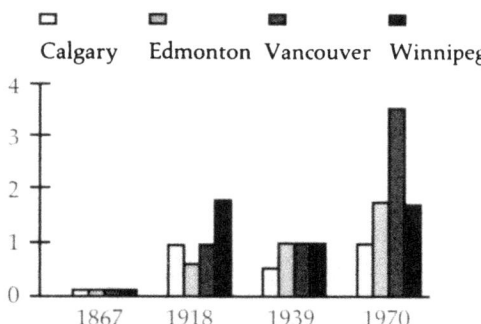

Dalhousie during at least part of the preparation period for this book, is welcome. McGee similarly provides some new data about Niagara. Nevertheless, the amount of ink accorded to different cities is, in my view, politically loaded.

If one accepts that major centres reflect the most important cultural developments, surely the demographic profile of the Canadian population should, at least, be considered within specific historical frameworks. The largest cities of today are not the same as those of the mid-nineteenth century, of course. The *Canadian Encyclopedia* lists the 9 largest cities in 1851 as Montreal, Quebec City, Saint John, Toronto, Halifax, Hamilton, Kingston, Ottawa, and London. Guelph, St Catharines, Brantford, and

Figure 2 Regional Representation (continued)

McGee:

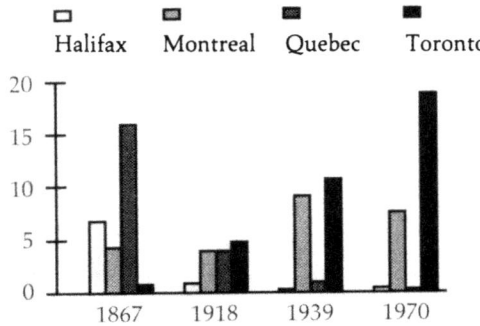

Notes difference in the scale of the two graphs.

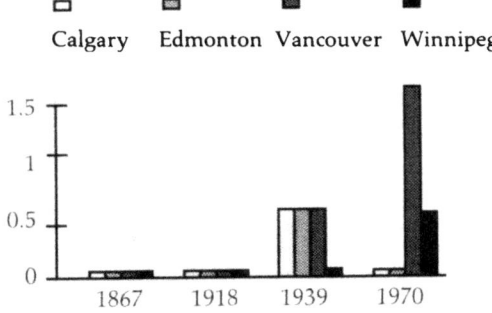

Belleville are described as 'a second tier' (article on 'City,' 1: 346) with populations close to 10,000. While Saint John is accorded considerable space in Kallmann, and more recent research published in other venues has redressed the balance to some extent, we should consider the extent to which we bias our music history narrative by relying on contemporary, rather than historically specific, demographics.[6]

If, on the other hand, cultures are qualitatively different, not only in different locales but different sizes of locale, we might ask, what of the smaller centres? Perhaps reflecting his aforementioned objective of describing the 'musical pastimes and aspirations of the many,' Kallmann presents a rich array of data (necessarily *in passim* most of the time) about smaller centres. Sixty-nine places other than the big nine are cited. The tendency in both later books reduces this number drastically. (Of the twenty-two smaller places mentioned in Ford, five are in Nova Scotia). I counted nineteen in McGee, of which about half are not listed in the index (see Figure 3).

The regional biases of the three texts have implications regarding the coverage of different ethnic groups, of course, since, until the post-1945 period, the east had a larger proportion of English/Scottish/Irish and French than the Western regions, which were populated extensively by Eastern and Northern European peoples. In addition, prior to the restrictive immigration law of 1923, sizeable communities of Chinese and other Asian and mid-Eastern groups were established. Ethnic diversity is not emphasized as a theme in any of the textbooks. Kallmann makes several references to cultural demography (see, for example, page 29) and includes biographical sketches of a paragraph or more about five German musicians (Glackemeyer, Brauneis Sr and Jr, S.W. Sabatier, T. Molt and A. Zoellner) and two Belgians (F. Jehin Prume and Jules Hone). In later chapters, Vogt and von Kunits are profiled. He also describes German traditions such as the *Sängerfest* and *Singverein* organizations. While the individuals appear prominently in the succeeding books, the culturally specific traditions are not profiled. McGee does write about multiculturalism in his chapter 'Recent Developments,' although his slant on retention (stressing religious minorities such as the Doukhobors, Mennonites, and Hutterites) and integration (a section in which Ukrainians, Asians, and Caribbeans are briefly discussed) is idiosyncratic. A small, perhaps insignificant, change in the manner of presenting biographical information was made by McGee. Although, in parentheses, he carefully notes the birthplace of musicians for whom he writes biographical information, the first sentence of most biographies describes their training in the institutions of European concert music. Hence, cultural 'roots' are reduced

Figure 3 Representation of Small Communities

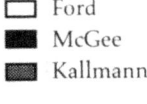

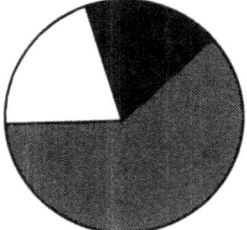

Figure 4 Subject Representation

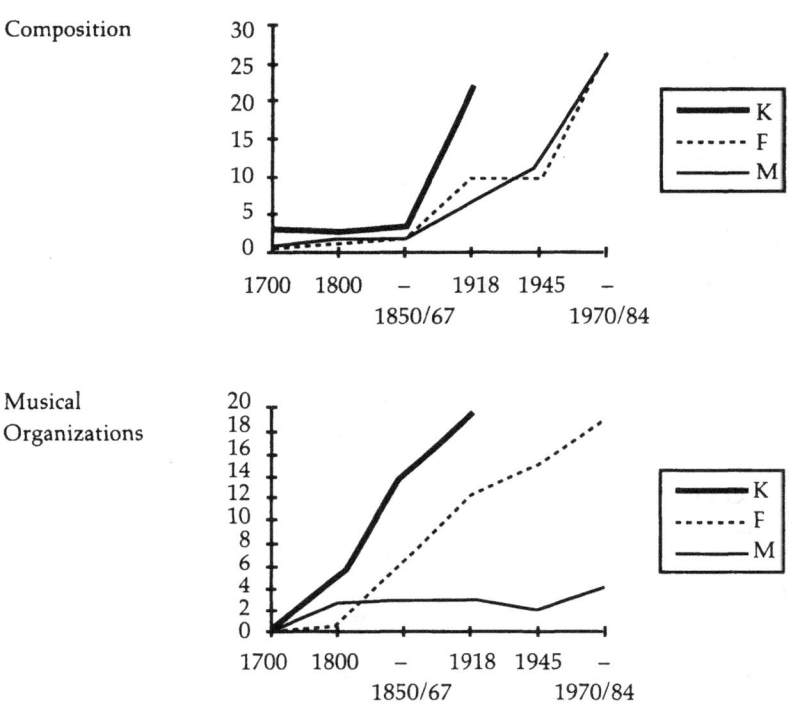

and parenthesized, so that the 'real' biography can start with initiation into the institutional realm. Coupled with the separation of information on 'multiculturalism,' this subtle manner of writing biography (done, no doubt, for reasons of efficiency) implies that the concert music tradition is outside of issues of ethnicity or specific cultural background. Hence a notion of mainstream and periphery is perhaps more overt in McGee's text than in those of his predecessor. For the most part, however, the ethnic heritage of musicians who contributed to the development of Canadian concert life is not a significant part of the story. The profile of those musicians who are given biographical consideration is a balance of French and English (and to some extent German in Kallmann's account). Other groups are paid little attention.[7] None of the histories explore the manner in which specific musical genres and styles were used to articulate the critical intersections of class, gender, and ethnicity within Canadian society.[8]

Figure 4 Subject Representation (continued)

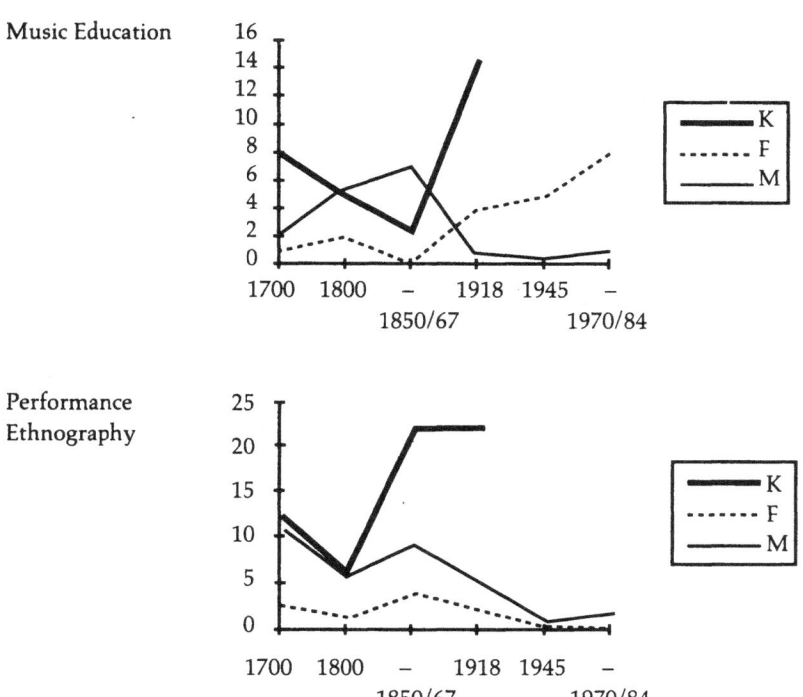

Music Education

Performance Ethnography

The plotting of subject matter through the same sort of statistical structural analysis was a more difficult matter. A rough distinction was made between comments which comprised most of a page (over half) and those which were passing references (under half). The distinctions among subject categories are not always clear. A single sentence might contain biographical information, style description, and historical data. Hence, the exact statistics produced by my close reading for subject matter are probably neither verifiable nor replicable by either me or anyone else. Notwithstanding these difficulties, the series of graphs in Figure 4 are probably accurate reflections of tendencies.

Kallmann's narrative of growth is reflected consistently on all graphs. He attends with amazing consistency to how we learn music, to performance events, and to pieces. In each case, the late-nineteenth and early-twentieth century is quantitatively larger, defining a rapid cultural blossoming. The two later histories, however, do not present the same story. Rapid blossoming is clearly indicated by the composition graph, but for a much later period than in Kallmann. Other aspects of our socio-musical life, however, are not represented in the same way. Performance ethnography or issues of education have gradually been factored out in the chapters concerning the twentieth century. Hence, the privileging of composition as the aspect of musical life most worthy of study is strong in Ford and McGee. A consequence of this is the emphasis on a relatively small number of individuals and their work.

Narratives of Organization

How much is written about specific eras, regions, social groups, or subjects provides some superficial indications of underlying values and assumptions but, as has been noted in several instances, there are other explanations such as the availability of data. How we organize what we talk about, on the other hand, almost invariably reflects 'prior texts' or, indeed, attempts to avoid prior texts. The aforementioned periodization in all three books, which uses century changes or major political events, may be a way of structuring that seeks *not* to impose values. On the other hand, Kallmann's chapter titles overtly present an evolutionist perspective: for example, 'The Dark Age,' or 'The Dawn of Urban Musical Life.' Ford retains hints of this only in his first chapter, 'The Planting of Seeds,' while McGee uses chapter headings with no overt value connotations.

A different 'narrative' is represented by the switches in 'ethnic' emphasis from one time period to another. The move from French to British society with the advent of the eighteenth century would bear comparison with French-language histories. The placement of Native music cultures in the first chapter(s) but not in later ones is a further, perhaps more striking example of a culture depicted as frozen in time. McGee attempted to avoid this very problem by writing a separate chapter on Native culture at the end of his survey and by including reference to contemporary events. Unfortunately, for me, this chapter still seems to be outside of history by its very placement. Cultural historians, to date, are perhaps still reluctant to view Native and European cultures in interaction in any century. Further, the move from generic groups of people (Missionaries, the aristocracy, the 'people') in the seventeenth century to individuals and the institutions of the dominant society is striking in all three.[9]

The gradual imposition of the contemporary subdivisions for music activity (composition, performance, music education, and, predictably, the increased emphasis on composition) seem to be structural markers for twentieth-century musical life. In fact, the change of the narrative at 1914 in the two later books is striking. Does the very fact that Kallmann ended his survey at the First World War actually facilitate this change of narrative?

A further way of looking at the structure of these books is to examine how the essentially linear format of page-after-page collapses multiple dimensions of our experience. What I mean by this is that the very structure of any book forces every author to line up a number of themes or narratives which are not otherwise logically aligned. If a book moves chronologically, as these do, and if there is an overt or subtle progression of images from the planting of seeds to the harvesting of fruits, the images of growth and fruition are automatically aligned with the historical sequence. Every author has to struggle with this and live with the distortion which may be inherent in the progression from beginning to end of a book. The following chart (see Figure 5) attempts to represent the collapsing of time, space, and value in the three books. These charts are unabashedly reductionist but, at the same time, indicative of underlying value systems.

The reader is invited to assume, for the moment, that none of these alignments is inherently logical or necessarily true. That is, a development from rural to urban need not equate with a trend from communal to individual music-making or with a change from regional to international styles. The institutionalization of music making, largely hailed as a positive thing in these books, is not necessarily a mark of increasing sophistication. Many of the continua alignments are, of course, politically loaded, for example, the subtle equation of a move toward Toronto and Montreal with a move toward greater sophistication, individuality, or professionalism.

These charts allow us to examine what we miss in our scholarly recognition of contemporary musical life by buying into certain narrative lines. For example, musicologists have perhaps not paid sufficient attention to amateur music making or to the interface between amateur and professional. By emphasizing the individual, especially the individual composers – but only of serious music – in twentieth-century textbooks, have we failed to pay attention to the rest of the socio-cultural network, perhaps thereby losing touch with the values which performers and listeners bring to their experience of Canadian music and simultaneously reinforcing stereotypic notions that 'serious' contemporary Canadian music is inaccessible? Furthermore, have we so isolated the different kinds of music making in our society that we may not have a grasp of what is happening in complex urban contexts, where jazzers play salsa, youth rap to pre-recorded musics of varying types, and multinationals tap the Third World to satisfy our voracious musical appetites for new sounds.

Figure 5 Collapsing Time-space-value

	1534	1800	1918	1984
Kallmann	East..................................... primitive .... rural .... communal.... amateur	institutional	(+West) ...	Ontario/Quebec sophisticated urban individual (composers) professional
Ford	amateur .... (professional conductors) aperiodic performance .... series miscellaneous .... choral dominant .... portable instruments .... pianos, organs .... rural .... local, regional .... composer utilitarian .... composer-performs/teaches ... -organizer inheritance .... happenstance	amateur societies		professional instruments dominant (orchestras) electr. media urban international university composer evolution planning
McGee	amateur ....professional .... colonial culture .... rural .... music consumer .... music making			Canadian identity urban music producer composition

A second potential stimulus from these charts is the possibility, after Derrida, of writing history with different narratives. What if some of the continua were reversed? If, for example, we moved from individuals to communal music making as we simultaneously described musics in the seventeenth through the twentieth centuries, we might then begin with a story of individual Ojibwe and Iroquoian and Kwakiutl singers, who taught the newcomers as much as they could about survival skills at the same time as they shared cultural traditions. At the other end of the historical spectrum, we might have a story about cultures in contact or about the influence of popular music technology in all our lives in the cities of the 1990s. Such historical writing need be no less 'true' than what we already have. On the other hand, there are undoubtedly some ways of collapsing time, space and value which are 'truer' than others – especially for a particular point in time. The narrative structures of the past undoubtedly revealed some deeper truth for the time in which they were written. But which narratives reflect something essential about our current vision of past, present, and future?

Narratives of Metaphor

My quantitative analyses above and, particularly, the value-laden continua represented in Figure 5, beg for an assessment of more 'qualitative' aspects of the discourse of Canadian music history. Writing style is one such aspect. If, as I suggest, we have privileged the urban, the institutional, and the compositional product, and if, furthermore, we have equated aspects of these with values such as sophistication, is this privileging evident in language as well as structure? Furthermore, what aesthetic values are associated with this particular construction of 'sophistication'? Have we written about musical *style* using language which is consistent with the *social* values implicit in the structuring of the text books?

It is more difficult to find definitive answers to these questions than to the previous ones. In part, this relates to the polysemic quality of language and the multiplicity of readers' interpretations. In part, it relates to the tendency of recent musicologists to avoid value-laden aesthetic descriptors in their writing about musical style. In part, it simply reflects the impracticability of examining the aesthetic nuance of each textual phrase. Hence, the following comments are necessarily more impressionistic than those in the preceding sections.

In an attempt to delimit the task, I decided to make a comparative examination of descriptive phrases used by the three authors in relation to specific genres (and pieces where possible) of music from different time periods. I selected two voyageur songs, Calixa Lavallée's *The Widow* and Somers's *Louis Riel*, as points of comparison. Endemic to introductory music history textbooks is the challenge of presenting the 'norms' of a composer's style or of a specific genre without violating the uniqueness of specific works. In most cases, however, authors rarely have the luxury of words to describe why specific works may 'work' artistically and aesthetically; rather they must encapsulate a few features in a compromisingly efficient manner. The

290   Beverley Diamond

need to select detail in this compromise, however, is often revealing of underlying value systems, which we may fail to articulate to our students. Such is the case with the excerpts from the three textbooks in Figure 6.

Figure 6 Discourse about Three Genres/Pieces of Canadian Music

Voyageur Songs

19th-century sources   *Music histories*

'easy, extemporaneous songs, somewhat smutty but   'uniquely romantic
never intolerant. Many of their canoe songs are   setting' [K: 32]
exquisite; more particularly the air they give them.'
[John MacTaggart, 1829; cited K: 32–3]   'not always equal to
                                                                                                drawing-room standards'
'diversity of taste and skill'   [K: 34]
[Anna Jameson, 1839; cited K: 33]
                                                                                                'glorious period of
'They kept time to those songs as they rowed; and the   voyageur songs' [K: 35]
splashing of the oars in the water, combined with the
wildness of their cadences, gave a romantic character
to our darksome voyage ... Their music might not
have been esteemed fine, by those whose skill in
concords and chromatics, forbids them to be gratified
but on scientific principles ... singularly plaintive and
pleasing.' [John Glasgow, 1823: cited K: 33]

'wild, romantic song ... [The men] sang with all the   'a picture of adventure
force of three hundred manly voices, one of their   and romance' [F: 25]
lively airs, which, rising and falling faintly in the
distance as it was borne, first lightly on the breeze,
and then more steadily as they approached, swelled
out in the rich tones of many a mellow voice, and
burst into a long enthusiastic shout of joy! Alas! the
forests no longer echo to such sounds.'
[R.M. Ballantyne, 1848; cited in K: 36 and F: 25]

'The song is of great use: they keep time with their   'Tales of the Voyageurs
paddles to its measured cadence.'   conjure up romantic
[Hugh Gray, 1809; cited M: 7]   visions of the rugged
                                                                                                frontier life' [M: 6]

'They sang their gay French songs, the
other canoe joining in the chorus. This
peculiar singing has often been described;
it is very animated on the water and in
the open air,
but not very harmonious.'
[Jameson, 1839; cited in M: 7 and K: 33]

Lavallée – The Widow

19th-early 20th-century sources

'not merely ... an adroit deviser of
pretty melodies and sensuous harmonies, but (as) a genuinely creative
artist, a pure musical genius.'
[A.S. Vogt, 1913; cited in K: 143]

'I would rather devote my time to
compositions which, if less profitable,
are more artistic.'
[C. Lavallée, cited 1891; cited in K: 241]

Music histories

'[his importance] lies in attitude rather
than achievement.' [K: 141]

'an inexhaustible gift for melody –
facile and trivial at times, but always
spontaneous and musical. This music is
not overburdened with complexity or
originality, but it has great vitality and
is popular in appeal without being
vulgar.' [K: 239]

[Arias in *The Widow*] 'pulse and
sparkle ...'

'It is a pity that the surviving works
represent only the lighter aspect of
Lavallée's style for his skill in combining 3 songs contrapuntally in the
cantata for the Marquis of Lorne would
seem to indicate that the symphonies
and chamber works probably contained
passages of greater contrapuntal and
harmonic interest than *The Widow* or
the "Bridal Rose" Overture.' [K: 240–1]

'... melodically inventive mind. In
particular, the marches and dance
music for the piano show a rhythmical
clarity and vitality with a harmonic

292   Beverley Diamond

> language clearly derivative of the French salon composers of the mid-nineteenth century.' [F: 64]

> 'That Lavallée's music was more than a cut above the average salon music written at the time can be seen in his "Mouvement à la Pavane" ... many were composed for amateur keyboard players throughout the century. But Lavallée's work must have given more than a few of them a bit of a start. The phrases are heavily chromatic, and although it is a simple, short dance, the harmonies move through several keys, making surprising chromatic turns.' [M: 77]

> [Re The Widow]: 'The solos and duos are rather demanding, but the choruses have simple rhythms with easily sung intervals that could be performed by amateurs. Typically, the plot is one of silly amorous intrigue, intentionally lighthearted ... [In "Single I will never be"] Lavallée has written an attractive and melodically creative song, with interesting and unexpected harmonic changes.' [M: 77]

Somers – Louis Riel

'In his opera *Louis Riel* (1967), Somers incorporated semi-improvisatory sections, electronic music, tonal (folk song) and atonal material, and an array of new vocal techniques which evolved from his use of Indian material ("Kuyas," from the beginning of Act III). Perhaps the most important development from his work on the opera, vocal techniques such as glissandi, whispering, timbral inflections, etc. occupied Somers' compositional thinking right into the 1970's.' [F: 232]

'In setting the text, Somers employed a wide range of techniques and styles. He used actual native song, and created his own folk and popular songs modeled on

Narratives in Canadian Music History 293

those of the period. There is dissonant atonal writing in dramatically intense scenes and diatonic writing in the relaxed and lighthearted scenes.' [M: 135]

'When the orchestra is playing alone, the music is emotionally evocative, sometimes emphasizing conflict through strongly dissonant and clashing passages, or suggesting the simplemindedness of government officials through simple melody set to diatonic harmonies.' [M: 136]

All three make use of nineteenth-century descriptions in their unabashedly romanticized presentation of voyageur songs. These contemporaneous quotations can serve as a fourth point in the historiographic spectrum, a point where the focus on beautiful, vigorous, and engaging melody is particularly striking, and a point where the class connotations of specific musical genres were already clearly delineated.

While some contemporaneous quotes are used for Lavallée, the authors create their own musical assessments here and, in doing so, reveal a critical aesthetic dilemma about this particular repertoire. Lavallée's melodic facility is now something of a problem, praised in some contexts but serving as a means of dismissal in others. The features which are consistently looked to as marks of sophistication are chromatic harmony, counterpoint, and large-scale 'organic' form. While these parameters might seem obvious and natural measures of compositional craft, it seems to be no accident that they are the same aspects which are the most easily controlled within the framework of institutional training. The social implications of the emergent aesthetic are clarified by references to the salon or drawing room, now clearly associated with the trivial. Stylistic elements, then, again serve as class markers.

The aesthetic which seems to emerge here is confirmed in the descriptions of Somers's *Louis Riel* where 'simple, diatonic' harmony is now dramatically associated with the simple-minded characters or situations. A new mark of sophistication here is the command of various modes of sound production (ranging from early-twentieth-century innovations in vocal style, such as *Sprechtstimme*, to electronic sounds in battle scenes) and disparate styles. Is this a departure from the aesthetic of organicism, evident in the Lavallée descriptions?

While it would be dangerous to over-interpret fragmentary descriptions of selected moments in expressive culture, the consistencies of the descriptions of musical style and the way in which they reinforce the alignments in Figure 5 are, in my view, significant. If the poles are 'simple, rural, unsophisticated' on one hand and 'complex, urban, sophisticated' on the other, the musical styles paralleling these poles might be configured as follows:

SIMPLE, RURAL, UNSOPHISTICATED / COMPLEX, URBAN,
SOPHISTICATED
monophony / counterpoint
diatonic melody / chromatic harmony
short or sectional works / large-scale, organic forms

If these poles are not accepted as adequate representations, however, the challenge is to find alternatives to the musical style code. On one hand, the stylistic features associated with each pole could be reconsidered. We might, for example, try associating the following with 'sophisticated':

SOPHISTICATED
- rhythmic vigour and energy
- ingenuity of melodic ideas
- phrase balance but variety
- command of a range of disparate styles

In this case, a number of voyageur songs would be celebrated because of their sophistication with regard to the first three style features. Lavallée would be commended for his command of both parlour and concert repertoires, not condemned for his 'light' works. Somers would fare none the worse. None of these style aspects is arbitrary; as musicians, we learn to value such aspects but as historians we select which ones to reify and thereby, knowingly or inadvertently, construct a value-laden narrative.

Narratives in U.S. Music Textbooks

In order to assess some of the reasons for the creation of the narratives defined in the sections above, I undertook an analogous, though less detailed study, of comparable textbooks on the music of the United States: Charles Hamm's *Music in the New World* (1983) and Daniel Kingman's *American Music: A Panorama* (1979, revised 1989). The close association of our two populations, the intertwining of their immigration histories, and the much mythologized ease with which we pass across our long undefended border might lead one to expect the Canadian and American music histories would be framed similarly.

There are, indeed, some similarities. Native music cultures are consistently treated without historical specificity and are isolated from the rest of the story. Folk musics are similarly ahistoicized, though the separation of information is less severe. Both Canadian and American music histories exclude most immigrant musics from the story, an exclusion justified (with regret) by Charles Hamm as follows:

I have dealt with music which has changed in style and form after being brought to the New World, music which has eventually taken on a different character in America, music which has been subjected to acculturation, or, if you will, 'contaminated' music.

I have not dealt with music which did not change in significant ways in the New World, music which remained identified with the national and ethnic groups who brought it to America, music which did not interact with other forms of music. (1983: 656)

Underlying this comment are several fascinating assumptions. For one thing, the 'text' of music, for Hamm is clearly the 'style and form' of the sounds, not the performance, the event, the social framing, or any of the other constructs used widely within ethnomusicological study (among others). Further, the notion of cultural interaction is thus tied to the very core of what is authentically 'American.' This, in itself, merits careful scrutiny in relation to the Canadian parallel – the virtual exclusion of histories other than those of the English and French in Canada.

While the exclusions of the majority of immigrant traditions is evident in the textbooks of both nations, this last issue, the attitude toward 'interaction' and 'acculturation' as markers of 'authenticity' differ. This is not the only difference.

In fact, the differences between the Canadian and American narratives of music history may be even more striking than the similarities. In the texts by Kingman and Hamm, the historical proportioning and organizational frames for the subject matter are distinctive. Kingmans' own content analysis is printed on the inside cover of his book. Duplicated below is a parallel chart to show the chronological range and order of the twenty chapters in Hamm's *Music in the New World* (see Figure 7). Neither book adopts a chronological framework; both organize the content of American music into 'streams' of variable duration. The 'stream' metaphor is an important one for American music since the merging of bodies of water is homologous with the 'melting pot' ideology alluded to above. It is further significant that Native American culture is regarded as outside of any other stream.

Neither author attempts a periodization of American music; in fact, the stream concept probably deliberately avoids it. Nonetheless, two events emerge as dividing points within the narrative: the first is the Civil War (e.g., the ending point for chapters 3, 5, 6, 7, 8, and 11 in Hamm) and the second, the beginning of commercial recordings circa 1920 (the ending point for chapters 12 and 14, as well as the beginning point for chapters 17, 18, and 19 in Hamm). The former, like the chapter frames of the Canadian textbooks, is framed by a socio-political event, but the latter, unlike the Canadian monographs, uses a technological/cultural boundary.

Furthermore, proportionally less attention is paid to pre-eighteenth-century music in the American music books. This proportioning suggests to me that American music history is more integrated with the political history of the nation, a story which begins with the American Revolution, while that of Canada is closer to a history of people who have lived in the geographical area now known as Canada.

Our propensity to use a more rigid chronological frame (which, I implied above, almost amounts to a periodization) may be a matter of convenience in a history which remains fragmentary, but it does suggest a closer alliance with European music history, the periodization of which is used as a frame for textbooks and curricula alike in both countries. The American textbooks pay homage to history, chronology, and 'development' more consistently in the chapters about the European classical traditions. See, for example, such historically-referenced chapter titles in Hamm as 'The Dawning of Classical Music in America (1825–65)' or 'The Rise of Classical Composition in America: the Years after the Civil War.'

A second fundamental difference in the two national music history narratives is the relative attention paid to popular[10] music. In Hamm, it proportionately outweighs every other subject traced on Figure 7, though the European-based classical tradition is a close second. The importance of the vernacular, and of popular culture, has been celebrated in the United States but virtually masked in Canadian academic studies.[11] Nevertheless, the distinct separation of musics into highbrow and lowbrow is perpetuated by both historiographic strategies. Hence, the highbrow/lowbrow distinction which emerged in the nineteenth century (though the date of its emergence continues to be debated)[12] is securely entrenched in present-day historical writing.

A third difference lies in the treatment of locale and region. As described above, Kallmann used urban centres as sub-headings in nineteenth- and twentieth-century chapters, while Ford and McGee intensified the trend of concentrating attention on musical life in a limited number of urban centres. While cities do emerge in the sub-headings of certain streams of American music history (Billings of Boston, Chicago blues, etc.), they are not consistently indexed in either Hamm or Kingman. Regions, on the other hand, are given more prominence though generalized identities (the South, New

Narratives in Canadian Music History 297

Figure 7 Hamm's *Music in the New World* (1983)

The proportion of space devoted to specific historical periods

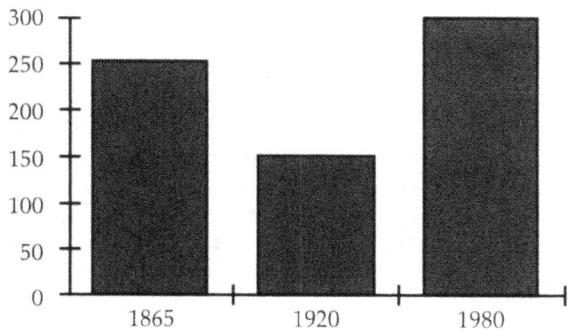

The proportion of space devoted to specific musical 'streams'

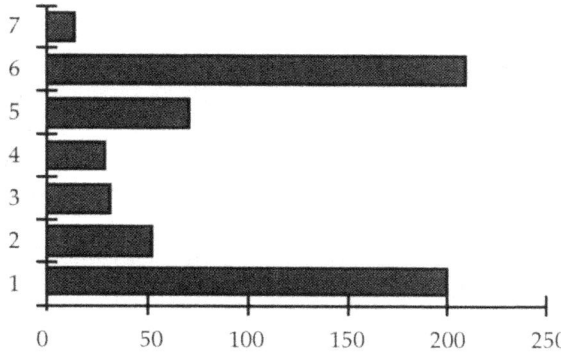

1. European 'Classical' – chapters 4, 8, 12, 15, 18, 19
2. Sacred – chapters 2, 6, 10
3. Anglo folk – chapter 13
4. Afro-American – chapter 5
5. Pre-jazz and jazz – chapters 14, 17
6. Pop – chapters 7, 9, 11*, 13, 16, 20
7. Native – chapter 1

*Marching and Dancing – could justifiably have a separate category.

England etc.). While we clearly have comparable regional 'identities' in Canada (the Maritimes, the West, French Canada), cities rather than regions emerge more frequently as the identity boundaries in our music history. Thus the urban/rural divide is written with more severity in Canada and the denigration of the latter is more consistent.

The fundamental nature of these differences in the national narratives of American and Canadian scholars may be instructive on several counts. In my experience, Canadian music is most often either segregated into a separate course (or a separate section within a course) in our university curricula or paid slight attention in the context of courses on 'North America.' Both approaches are problematic, in my view. The differences in narrative noted above may indeed explain, in part, why it has been difficult to teach the interaction of our music histories. The differences may also stimulate some creative thought about alternative models which might be more effective framing formats.

Conclusions: Toward Future Books on Canadian Music?

Clearly I have extended a number of invitations to reflect on certain matters in the course of this paper. Do many of the old narratives still reflect fundamental attitudes which have meaning for us? Do we still feel the need to describe history as a process of growth or, having perhaps seen the 'fruition' of composers with international status, independent and autonomous styles of composition, and numerous world-class performers, do we now want to look at our history with different lens? Do we still hold to the discrete categories of the past: whether composers and performers, or popular and formal, or Native, English, French, and Ukrainian? Or is there a new richness to be derived from careful scholarship which attends to the interaction among these categories? Are we aware of the vestiges of colonialism which may manifest themselves in city-centred histories among other things? How do the exigencies of 'science' shape how we write about Canada's music culture? Can we learn from a comparison with the American narrative, if only to open our minds to the ways in which national interests have played themselves out in scholarship, if only to learn that there are alternatives?

I have no conclusions.

As a final note, however, I should mention one word which has been conspicuously absent from the previous discussion: power. What are the hegemonic dynamics of all of the aforementioned narratives? Who gets advantaged? Who gets legitimized? And conversely, who gets disadvantaged or ignored? These are hard and often uncomfortable questions but, in my

Narratives in Canadian Music History 299

opinion, we should address them if the next twenty-five years of historical writing are to produce anything with the vigour and insight of the work of the generation of Kallmann and Beckwith.

NOTES

1 See also his update, 'A "Failure" Re-visited: New Canadian Music in Recent Studies and Reference Works,' in *Hello Out There*, ed. John Beckwith and Dorith Cooper, CanMus Documents 2: 114–23, 1988.
2 This is not to say that these authors do not offer substantial comment on 'cultural constructions,' which are discussed in the course of this paper. Miller's introductions, especially in *Boogie, Pete and the Senator*, 1987, for example, contain fascinating comments about regional styles while Fetherling (1991) identifies the 'nationalism' of several internationally prominent songwriters.

It should also not imply that biographical accounts are absent in the concert music domain. From the early CBC sketches (e.g., the Canadian Broadcasting Corporation's *Thirty-four Biographies of Canadian Composers*, 1964), through Beckwith and MacMillan's *Contemporary Canadian Composers* (1975), the *Encyclopedia of Music in Canada* (2nd edition, 1992), and the growing number of recent biographical monographs (e.g., Sheila Eastman and Timothy McGee's *Barbara Pentland*, 1983; Brian Cherney's *Harry Somers*, 1975; Louise Bail Milot's *Jean Papineau-Couture*, 1986; Marie-Thérèse Lefebvre's *Serge Garant et la révolution musical au Québec*, 1988), individual composers have been documented and celebrated.

Furthermore, academic studies of diverse aspects of Canadian popular musics do, of course, exist, although often in disciplines other than music: history, folklore, cultural studies, communications. The publication venues (see, for example, the *Canadian Historical Review*, the *Journal of Canadian Studies*, or *Canadian Issues*) are, consequently, also separated and hence often missed by music students.
3 In a letter to the author (14 October 1989) responding to an earlier version of this paper, Kallmann outlined a number of the influences on his own scholarly development which led him to write with an emphasis on an expansive range of socio-cultural data. He cites his father's humanistic education, his mother's social worker background, the very pace of social change during his 1920s childhood, his propensity for mapmaking and his belief in the 'Golden Age' theory as general influences. 'Educational' influences include what he describes as 'conventional music writing' (he cites the Jahns, the Bekkers, the Nohls, and P.H. Lang), the experience of the war years and their emphasis on the explanation of the causes of evil through ideology and Marxist theory, 'reinforced by

Friedrich Blume,' Arnold Walter, W. Dwight Allen, Edwin H. Carr, Erich Doflein, and Joseph Kerman.
4 My chosen emphasis on 'surveys' here distorts the picture somewhat since many Canadian musicologists have presented the results of their historical research in scholarly articles. Even here, however, the relatively undeveloped state of research is perhaps reflected in the large number of articles which focus on the documentation of sources or which serve to make sources accessible in modern editions. While a complete survey of this literature is beyond the scope of this paper, I might mention *Le Catalogue collectif des archives musicales au Québec*, in *les Cahiers de l'ARMuQ*, 9, 1988, as well as work by Claude Beaudry ('Catalogue des imprimés musicaux d'avant 1800 conservés à la bibliothèque de l'Université Laval,' Beckwith and Hall, 1988: 29–49), Eric Schwandt ('The motet in New France: some 17th- and 18th-century manuscripts,' in *Fontes Artis Musicae* 28/3 1984: 194–219), Élisabeth Gallat-Morin and Antoine Bouchard (*Témoins de la vie musicale en Nouvelle-France*, Quebec: Archives Nationale du Québec, 1981), and Juliette Bourassa-Trépanier and Lucien Poirier (*Répertoire des données musicales de la presse québécoise*, vol. 1, Quebec: Les Presses de l'Université Laval, 1990). In addition, the work of the Canadian Music Heritage Society, whose fully annotated facsimile editions of early music are invaluable resources, must be mentioned. While the musical life of these periods has not been ignored – see, e.g., Timothy J. McGee, 'Music in Halifax, 1749–1799,' *Dalhousie Review* 49 (1969): 377–81 and Frederick A. Hall, 'Musical Life in Eighteenth-Century Halifax,' *Canadian University Music Review* 4 (1983): 278–307 – the socio-historical picture is, at best, fragmentary.
5 Again, the periodical and monograph literature changes the picture somewhat. Among the rare monographs on the music culture of a specific region is Dale McIntosh's *History of Music in British Columbia, 1850–1950*, (Victoria: Sono Nis Press, 1989), and Gordana Lazarevich's *The Musical World of Frances James and Murray Adaskin* (Toronto: University of Toronto Press, 1988) presents a rich array of socio-cultural and historical information. Articles on musical life in Western Canada include Wesley Berg's 'Music in Edmonton, 1880–1905,' in *Canadian University Music Review* 7 (1986): 141–70 and Russell E. Chester's 'Music in Winnipeg 1900–1907,' in *Canada Music Book* 8 (1974): 109–16.
6 City-centred music research has been conducted in a few of these and other places. See, for example, F.A. Hall's 'Hamilton, 1846–1946: A Century of Music,' (*C.A.U.S.M. Journal*, IV, 1/2 [1974]: 98–114) or his 'Musical Life in Windsor, 1875–1901,' in *Canada Music Book* 6 (1973): 111–24; Elaine Keillor's 'Musical Activity in Canada's New Capital City in the 1870s,' in Beckwith and Hall, 1988: 115–33.

7 The growth in ethnomusicological research and publication as evidenced in Robert Witmer, ed. *Ethnomusicology in Canada* (Toronto: Institute for Canadian Music, 1990) is some indication that a wide number of music scholars currently research many other musical traditions.
8 Recent studies in folklore, ethnomusicology, and feminist musicology have begun to research these intersections. An early analysis of this sort was Carole H. Carpenter's 'The Ethnicity Factor in Anglo-Canadian Folkloristics,' in *Canadian Ethnic Studies* 7/2 (1975): 7–18. Neil Rosenberg's 'Ethnicity and Class: Black Country Musicians in the Maritimes,' in *Journal of Canadian Studies* 23/1 & 2 (1988): 138–56 is one of the few examples of particularized research which factors in several hegemonic dimensions.
9 In this regard, we may be behind other historians. Carl Berger (1986: 298), for example, cites a tendency of post–1960 Canadian history to represent 'competing claims that history had to be re-interpreted in terms of class, gender, and ethnicity as basic units of analysis.' And Bruce Trigger (1986: 4–5) has challenged scholars to break down the wall between history which, in Canada, usually treats of the English and French, and anthropology which has traditionally had more to say about Native cultures on one hand and newer immigrant cultures on the other. Both historians imply that the historical record looks different depending on the perspective of the narrator. Conversely, the historical record does not adequately represent the strength of 'minority' cultures without an analysis of the power relationships among various groups.

Nevertheless, more critical looks at the power structures implicit in the arts institutions of specific historical periods have begun to appear. See, for example, John Beckwith and Dorith Cooper's *Hello Out There! Canada's New Music in the World, 1950–85* (Toronto: Institute for Canadian Music, 1988), Maria Tippett's *Making Culture: English-Canadian Institutions and the Arts before the Massey Commission* (Toronto: University of Toronto Press, 1990), or J.L. Granatstein's 'Culture and Scholarship: The First 10 Years of the Canada Council,' *Canadian Historical Review* 65/4 (1984): 441–74. Future research will, perhaps, expand the boundaries to incorporate not just Eurocentric institutions, but vernacular traditions as well.
10 'Popular' is used here to represent a broad range of musics intended for widespread consumption, not just those which have been commodified for commercial gain. While Hitchcock prefers the term 'vernacular,' 'popular' is advantageous in that it recognizes that not all 'vernacular' musics are intended for widespread popular consumption; many, in fact, are highly esoteric. Hamm uses popular in the broad sense that I use it here. Kingman generally avoids it wherever possible, preferring more specific generic terms where possible.
11 A noteworthy statement about this division of the 'classical' and 'vernacular'

traditions appears in George Proctor's *Canadian Music of the Twentieth Century* (Toronto: University of Toronto Press, 1980). He excludes 'popular, jazz, folk, and rock music' because 'they have their own promotional and critical avenues and are constantly before the public in some form or other' (p. ix). Furthermore, he defines the first aim of his book as follows:

'to help bring about such an understanding between the composer and his [sic] audience and to bridge the sizeable gap which at present exists between the producer and the consumer of Canadian music' (ix).

In this honest statement about his political motivation, he implies that the historian's job is to educate, to introduce what is not known. Although unfortunately not all musicologists present their social agendas so clearly, I suspect that Proctor's motives were shared by the many scholars who have undertaken research on little known repertoires. Recently, however, there has been a resurgence of interest in the interpretation of what we don't yet understand about widely known forms of music as well as little known ones.

12 The point in the nineteenth century at which a clear highbrow/lowbrow distinction emerged in the public consciousness continues to be debated. See, for example, John Spitzer's review of Lawrence H. Levine's *Highbrow/Lowbrow: The Emergence of Cultural Hierarchy in America* (Harvard University Press, 1988) in *American Music* 8/2 (1990): 233–6, for citations of several different opinions about this subject. The historical debate may be masking a more critical point: namely, the identification of the perspective reflected in the labelling of the distinction. In other words, is the highbrow/lowbrow distinction made only by those who regard themselves as part of the 'highbrow' community? Is there a parallel labelling system operative among those who situate themselves differently (e.g., 'arrogant/real'). In other words, the analysis of a class distinction must take care to lay open the perspective within the asymmetrical power structure which is reflected by the label.

REFERENCES

Amtmann, Willy. 1975. *Music in Canada, 1600–1800*. Quebec: Habitex.
Bail Milot, Louise. 1986. *Jean Papineau-Couture: La vie, la carrière et l'oeuvre*. Quebec: Hurtubise HMH.
Beaudry, Claude. See Beckwith and Hall, 1988.
Beckwith, John. 1969. 'About Canadian Music: The P.R. Failure,' *Musicanada* 21: 4–7, 10–13.

Beckwith, John & Dorith Cooper, eds. 1988. *Hello Out There! Canada's New Music in the World 1950–1985.* CanMus Documents 2, Toronto: Institute for Canadian Music.
Beckwith, John & Frederick A. Hall, eds. 1988. *Musical Canada. Words and Music Honouring Helmut Kallmann.* Toronto: University of Toronto Press.
Berg, Wesley. 1986. 'Music in Edmonton, 1880–1905,' *Canadian University Music Review* 7: 141–70.
Berger, Carl. 1986. *The Writing of Canadian History: Aspects of English-Canadian Historical Writing Since 1900.* 2d ed. Toronto: University of Toronto Press.
Boon, James. 1983. *Other Tribes, Other Scribes: Symbolic Anthropology in the Comparative Study of Cultures, Histories, Religions, and Texts.* New York: Cambridge University Press.
Bruner, Edward M. 1986. 'Ethnography as Narrative,' in Victor W. Turner and Edward M. Bruner, eds. *The Anthropology of Experience.* Urbana and Chicago: University of Illinois Press, pp. 139–58.
Canadian Broadcasting Corporation. 1964. *Thirty-four Biographies of Canadian Composers.* ed. V.I. Rajewsky, Toronto: CBC.
Carpenter, Carole H. 1975. 'The Ethnicity Factor in Anglo-Canadian Folkloristics,' *Canadian Ethnic Studies* 7/2: 7–18.
Cherney, Brian. 1975. *Harry Somers.* Toronto: University of Toronto Press.
Chester, Russell E. 1974. 'Music in Winnipeg 1900–1907,' *Canada Music Book* 8: 109–16.
Clifford James. 1988. *The Predicament of Culture. 20th-Century Ethnography, Literature, and Art.* Cambridge: Harvard University Press.
Clifford, James and George Marcus, eds. 1986. *Writing Culture: the Poetics and Politics of Ethnography.* Berkeley: University of California Press.
Eastman, Sheila and T.J. McGee. 1983. *Barbara Pentland.* Canadian Composers 3. Toronto: University of Toronto Press.
Fetherling, Douglas. 1991. *Some Day Soon: Essays on Canadian Songwriters.* Kingston: Quarry Press.
Ford, Clifford. 1982. *Canada's Music: An Historical Survey.* Agincourt: GLC Publishers.
Gallat-Morin, Élisabeth & Antoine Bouchard. 1981. *Témoins de la vie musicale en Nouvelle-France.* Quebec: Archives Nationale du Québec.
Gilmore, John. 1988. *Swinging in Paradise: The Story of Jazz in Montreal.* Montreal: Vehicule Press.
Granatstein, J.L. 1984. 'Culture and Scholarship: The First 10 Years of the Canada Council,' *Canadian Historical Review* 65/4: 441–74.
Grenier, Line & J. Guilbault. 1990. '"Authority" Revisited: The "Other" in Anthropology and Popular Music Studies,' *Ethnomusicology* 34/4: 381–99.

Hall, Frederick A. 1974. 'Hamilton, 1846-1946: A Century of Music,' *C.A.U.S.M. Journal* IV (1/2): 98–114.
Hall, Frederick A. 1983. 'Musical life in Eighteenth-Century Halifax,' *Canadian University Music Review* 4: 278–307.
Hall, Frederick A. 1973. Musical Life in Windsor 1875–1901,' *Canada Music Book* 6: 111–24.
Hamm, Charles. 1983. *Music in the New World.* New York: Norton.
Hutcheon, Linda. 1988. *The Politics of Representation in Canadian Art and Literature.* Toronto: York University. Robarts Centre for Canadian Studies, Working Paper Series, 88–101.
Kallmann, Helmut. 1960, 1987. *A History of Music in Canada, 1534–1914.* Toronto: University of Toronto Press.
Kallmann, Helmut et al, eds. 1992. *Encyclopedia of Music in Canada,* 2nd edition. Toronto: University of Toronto Press.
Keillor, Elaine. See Beckwith and Hall, 1988.
Kellogg, Patricia. See Beckwith and Hall, 1988.
Kingman, Daniel. 1989. *American Music: A Panorama,* rev. ed. New York: Schirmer.
Lazarevich, Gordana. 1988. *The Musical World of Frances James and Murray Adaskin.* Toronto: University of Toronto Press.
Lefebvre, Marie-Thérèse. 1988. *Serge Garant et la révolution musicale au Québec.* Montreal: L. Courteau.
McGee, Timothy J. 1969. 'Music in Halifax, 1749–1799,' *Dalhousie Review* 49: 377–81.
– 1985. *The Music of Canada.* New York: Norton.
McIntosh, Dale. 1989. *History of Music in British Columbia, 1850-1950.* Victoria: Sono Nis Press.
MacMillan, Ernest, ed. 1955. *Music in Canada.* Toronto: University of Toronto Press.
MacMillan, Keith and J. Beckwith, eds. 1975. *Contemporary Canadian Composers.* Toronto: Oxford University Press.
Melhuish, Martin. 1983. *Heart of Gold: 30 Years of Canadian Pop Music.* Toronto: CBC Enterprises.
Miller, Mark. 1982. *Jazz in Canada: Fourteen Lives.* Toronto: University of Toronto Press.
– 1987. *Boogie, Pete and the Senator: Canadian Musicians in Jazz: the Eighties.* Toronto: Nightwood Editions.
Napier, Ronald. See Beckwith and Hall, 1988.
Proctor, George. 1980. *Canadian Music of the Twentieth Century.* Toronto: University of Toronto Press.

Rabinow, Paul, ed. 1984. *The Foucault Reader.* New York: Pantheon.
Rosenberg, Neil. 1988. 'Ethnicity and Class: Black Country Musicians in the Maritimes,' *Journal of Canadian Studies* 23/1&2: 138-156.
Schwandt, Eric. 1984. 'The Motet in New France: Some 17th- and 18th-Century Manuscripts,' *Fontes Artis Musicae* 28/3: 194-219.
Spivak, Gayatri Chakravorty. 1990. *The Post-Colonial Critic. Interviews, Strategies, Dialogues.* ed. Sarah Harasym, New York: Routledge.
Tippett, Maria. 1990. *Making Culture. English-Canadian Institutions and the Arts before the Massey Commission.* Toronto: University of Toronto Press.
Treitler, Leo. 1989. *Music and the Historical Imagination.* Cambridge: Harvard University Press.
Trigger, Bruce. 1985. *Natives and Newcomers.* Kingston and Montreal: McGill-Queen's University Press.
Van Maanen, John. 1988. *Tales of the Field: On Writing Ethnography.* Chicago: University of Chicago Press.
Walter, Arnold. 1969. *Aspects of Music in Canada.* Toronto: University of Toronto Press.
Waterman, Christopher. 1990. '"Our Tradition is a Very Modern Tradition": Popular Music and the Construction of Pan-Yoruba Identity,' *Ethnomusicology* 34/4: 367-79.
Witmer, Robert, ed. 1990. *Ethnomusicology in Canada.* Toronto: Institute for Canadian Music.
Yorke, Ritchie. 1971. *Axes, Chops, and Hot Licks: The Canadian Rock Music Scene.* Edmonton: Hurtig.

LAWRENCE BECKWITH

John Beckwith's Principal Compositions and Writings to 1994

Abbreviations

Publishers
Ber   Berandol Music Limited, Toronto
Harris   Frederick Harris Music, Oakville
Jay   Jaymar Music, London
Wat   Waterloo Music, Waterloo
(unpublished scores available from Canadian Music Centre)

Recordings
Cap   Capitol
Cen   Centrediscs
Phil   Philips
RCI-ACM   Radio Canada International, Anthology of Canadian Music

COMPOSITIONS

Stage

1953–8   *Night Blooming Cereus*, opera, 8 singers, 14 instrumentalists (J. Reaney)
1960   *The Killdeer*, incidental music, prepared pianoforte (J. Reaney)
1965–82   *The Shivaree*, opera, 12 singers, 20 instrumentalists (J. Reaney)
1987–8   *Crazy to Kill*, opera, 3 singers, 2 speakers, 2 instrumentalists, tape (J. Reaney, after A. Cardwell)
1989–91   *Lucas et Cécile* (restoration of J. Quesnel opera, c. 1808) Pub: Doberman/Yppan

1993–4	*Taptoo*, opera, 18 singers, 18 instrumentalists (J. Reaney)

Chorus

1963	*Jonah*, 4 soloists, choir, small orch. (Bible, J. MacPherson). Pub: Wat
1964	*The Trumpets of Summer*, 5 soloists, choir, 6 instrumentalists (M. Atwood). Rec: RCI-ACM
1966	*Sharon Fragments*, choir (D. Willson). Pub: Wat; Rec: Cap, Seraphim
1966–7	*Place of Meeting*, 3 soloists, choir, orchestra (D. Lee)
1968	*Three Blessings*, choir (Fisher, Burns, Wesley). Pub: Ber; Rec: Cap, RCI-ACM
	The Sun Dance, speaker, 6 soloists, 2 choirs, percussion (E. Smart, Cree, ancient Chinese)
1969	*Gas!*, 20 speaking voices (Ontario street and traffic signs). Pub: Ber
1970	*1838*, choir (D. Lee). Pub: Novello
1980–1	*Three Motets on Swan's 'China'*, choir (Bible, D. Willson). Pub: Wat; Rec: Melbourne, RCI-ACM
1981–2	*Mating Time*, 20 soloists, electric pianoforte, percussion (bp Nichol)
1982	*A Little Organ Concert*, choir, organ, brass quintet (vocables)
1984	*Earlier Voices* (arr.), choir, pianoforte (Canadian trad.)
1984–5	*Harp of David*, choir (Bible). Pub: Jay; Rec: Cen
1990	*beep*, 2 soloists, choir, percussion (bp Nichol)

Voice(s)

1947	*Five Lyrics of the T'ang Dynasty*, high voice, pianoforte (ancient Chinese, trans. W. Bynner). Pub: Ber; Rec: Cen, Phil, RCI-ACM
1949	*The Great Lakes Suite*, soprano, baritone, clarinet, violoncello, pianoforte (J. Reaney)
1950	*Two Songs to Poems by Colleen Thibaudeau*, baritone, pianoforte (C. Thibaudeau)
	Four Songs to Poems by e.e. cummings, soprano, pianoforte (e.e. cummings). Pub: Wat
1961	*Four Songs from 'Volpone'*, baritone, guitar (B. Jonson). Pub: Ber
1962	*A Chaucer Suite*, alto, tenor, baritone (Chaucer)
	Wednesday's Child, 2 singers, 4 instrumentalists (J. Reaney)

1963	*Ten English Rhymes*, children's voices, pianoforte (anon.). Pub: Ber
1969	*Four Love Songs* (arr.), baritone, pianoforte (Canadian Trad.). Pub: Ber; Rec: RCI-ACM
1971	*Five Songs* (arr.), alto, pianoforte (Canadian trad.) Pub: Ber; Rec: Select, RCI-ACM
1980–2	*Six Songs to Poems by e.e. cummings*, baritone, pianoforte (e.e. cummings)
1985	*Avowals*, tenor, keyboard (bp Nichol)
1986	*Les Premiers hivernements*, soprano, tenor, early instrument ensemble (Lescarbot, Champlain)
1987	*Synthetic Tales*, soprano, clarinet, pianoforte (vocables)
1988	*Old Meg Merrilies*, mezzo-soprano, pianoforte (Keats) Pub: Jay
1990	*The Hector: A Documentary Cantata*, soprano/narrator, early instrument ensemble (various historical sources)
1992	*A Birthday Greeting For H.A.R.R. (y) F.R.E.E.D. (m)A. (n)*, soprano, pianoforte

Orchestra

1949	*Music for Dancing* (reorchestrated 1959). Pub: Ber; Rec: RCI-ACM
1953	*Montage* (reorchestrated 1955)
1956	*Fall Scene and Fair Dance*, clarinet, violin, string orchestra. Pub: Ber
1958–60	*Concerto Fantasy*, pianoforte, orchestra
1962	*Flower Variations and Wheels*
1963	*Concertino*, horn, orchestra
1969	*Elastic Band Studies*, concert band (revised 1975)
1972–3	*All the Bees and All the Keys*, speaker, orchestra (reorchestrated 1987)
1982–3	*A Concert of Myths*, flute, orchestra
1989	*Peregrine*, viola, percussion, orchestra
1991	*Fifteen Figural Chorales* from J.S. Bach, Orgelbüchlein)
1991–2	*Round and Round*
1993	*Fourteen Figural Chorales (Second Set)* from J.S. Bach, Orgelbüchlein)

Chamber

1955–6	*Three Studies for String Trio*, violin, viola, violoncello

John Beckwith's Principal Compositions and Writings 309

1967	*Circle, with Tangents*, harpsichord, 13 solo strings. Pub: Ber
1969	*Fanfare*, brass sextet
1972	*Taking a Stand*, brass quintet. Pub: Ber
1973	*Musical Chairs*, string quartet, double bass. Pub: Ber
1977	*Quartet*, string quartet. Rec: Melbourne, RCI-ACM
1980	*Case Study*, any 5 instruments
1981	*Eight Miniatures* (arr.), violin, pianoforte. Pub: Harris
	Sonatina in Two Movements, trumpet, pianoforte
1984	*Arctic Dances*, oboe, pianoforte. Rec: McGill
	For Starters, 11 brass instruments
1990	*College Airs*, string quartet
1991	*Scene*, clarinet, trumpet, 2 percussion, pianoforte, double bass
1994	*After-images, after Webern*, guitar, violoncello
	Blue Continuum, trumpet, pianoforte, violin, viola, violoncello

Keyboards(s)

1948	*Music for Dancing*, piano 4 hands
1951	*Novelette*, piano. Pub: Ber; Rec: Cen
1976–7	*Upper Canadian Hymn Preludes*, organ, tape. Rec: Cen, RCI-ACM
1979	*Keyboard Practice*, 10 keyboards, 4 players. Rec: RCI-ACM
1983	*Etudes*, piano Rec: RCI-ACM

Collage

1960	*A Message to Winnipeg*, 3 speakers, 4 instrumentalists (J. Reaney)
1961	*Twelve Letters to a Small Town*, 4 speakers, 4 instrumentalists (J. Reaney)
1962	*Wednesday's Child*, 3 speakers, 2 singers, 4 instrumentalists (J. Reaney)
1965–7	*Canada Dash – Canada Dot*, 5 speakers, 5 singers, 9 instrumentalists (J. Reaney)
1972	*The Journals of Susanna Moodie*, 2 keyboards, percussion (M. Atwood) (revised 1990)
1992	*'In the middle of ordinary noise ...': An Auditory Masque*, speaker, 2 singers, 3 instrumentalists, tape (J. Reaney)

WRITINGS

Books

1961	*The Modern Composer and His World*, co-editor with Udo Kasemets, conference proceedings (Toronto: University of Toronto Press)
1975	*Contemporary Canadian Composers*, co-editor with Keith MacMillan (Toronto: Oxford University Press)
1986	*The Canadian Musical Heritage, vol. 5* (Hymn tunes/ Cantiques), editor (Ottawa: Canadian Musical Heritage Society)
1987	*Sing Out the Glad News: Hymn Tunes in Canada*, editor, conference proceedings (CanMus Documents 1), (Toronto: Institute for Canadian Music)
1988	*Hello Out There! Canada's New Music in the World, 1950 – 85* co-editor with Dorith R. Cooper, conference proceedings (CanMus Documents 2), (Toronto: Institute for Canadian Music)
	Musical Canada: Words and Music Honouring Helmut Kallman, co-editor with Frederick A. Hall (Toronto: University of Toronto Press)

Chapters in books

1976	'Satisfaction Mingles with Frustration in the Composer's Life' in *The Arts in Canada: Today and Tomorrow*, Dean Walker ed. (Toronto: MacMillan Press)
1977	'Reflections on Ives' in *An Ives Celebration*, H. Wiley Hitchcock and Vivian Perlis ed. (Urbana, Ill: University of Illinois Press)
1982	'Kolinski: An Appreciation and List of Works' in *Cross-Cultural Perspectives on Music*, Robert Falck and Timothy Rice ed. (Toronto: University of Toronto Press)
1983	'Shattering a Few Myths' in *Glenn Gould*, John McGreevy ed. (New York: Doubleday)

Dictionary Entries

1974	'Canada,' 'Harry Somers' in *Dictionary of Contemporary Music*, John Vinton ed. (New York: Dutton)
1980	'Istvan Anhalt,' 'Glenn Gould,' 'Udo Kasemets,' 'Mieczyslaw

John Beckwith's Principal Compositions and Writings 311

	Kolinski,' 'Ernest MacMillan,' 'Lois Marshall,' 'Leo Smith' in *The New Grove Dictionary of Music and Musicians*, Stanley Sadie ed. (London: Macmillan)
1981	'Chamber Music Composition,' 'Concertos and Concertante Music,' 'Criticism,' 'Hymnbooks,' 'Toronto Symphony' and others in *Encyclopedia of Music in Canada*, Helmut Kallmann, Gilles Potvin and Kenneth Winters ed. (Toronto: University of Toronto Press)
1985	'Hymns,' 'Ernest MacMillan' in *The Canadian Encyclopedia*, James H. Marsh ed. (Edmonton: Hurtig Publishers)
1988	'Music – Composition,' 'Singing Schools' in *The Canadian Encyclopedia*, James H. Marsh ed. 2d. (Edmonton: Hurtig Publishers)
1989	'Gabriel Charpentier' in *Oxford Companion to Canadian Theatre*, L.W. Conolly and Eugene Benson eds. (Toronto: Oxford University Press)
1992	'Chamber music performance,' 'Gospel music' and others in *Encyclopedia of Music in Canada*, Helmut Kallmann and Gilles Potvin eds. (Toronto: University of Toronto Press)

Articles

1960	'Let's Seek a Recipe for Canadian Opera,' *Opera in Canada*, i/2, May–June
1961	'Notes on a Recording Career [Glenn Gould],' *Canadian Forum*, January
	'Schoenberg Ten Years After,' *Canadian Forum*, November
1962	'A Stravinsky Triptych,' *Canadian Music Journal*, vi/4, Summer
1964	'The Berstein Experiment,' *Canadian Forum*, April
1969	'About Canadian Music: The PR Failure,' *Musicanada*, xxi, July-August [reprinted with postscript, *Music*, (AGO/RCCO magazine), v, March 1971]
1970	'What Every U.S. Musician Should Know about Contemporary Canadian Music,' *Musicanada*, xxix
	'Music in Canada,' *Musical Times*, cxi, December
1972	'Teaching New Music: What? How? Why?,' *The Recorder*, xv/1, September [reprinted in *The Music Scene*, March–April 1973]
	'Healey Willan,' *Canadian Forum*, December

1973	'Sir Ernest MacMillan (1893–1973),' *Music* (AGO/RCCO magazine), August
1977	'A Big Song-and-Dance,' *The Canadian Music Educator*, viii/3, Spring
1979	'Music: The Search for Universals,' *ISME Yearbook*, vi
1981	'Composing in the Eighties,' *Australian Journal of Music Education*, xxviii, April
1985	'Notes on Canadian Choral Repertoire,' *Anacrusis*, iv/3, spring
1988	'Canadian Tunebooks and Hymnals, 1801–1939,' *American Music*, vi/2, Summer
	'Réalisations et projets de l'Institut de musique canadienne,' *Les Cahiers de l'ARMuQ*, x, juin
1989	'Colloquy: From Composer to Audience: The Production of Serious Music in Canada,' *Canadian University Music Review*, 9/2
1991	'Keith MacMillan (1920–91): An Appreciation,' *Notations*, iii/3, July
	'Restoring Joseph Quesnel's *Other* Operetta, *Lucas et Cécile*,' *Notations*, iii/4, October
1992	'Memories and a Few Redneck Opinions,' *SoundNotes*, ii, Spring–Summer
1993	'Samurai Warriors? Ah, That Must Be *Macbeth*,' *The Globe and Mail*, 23 November
1994	'Sir Ernest MacMillan,' *Notations*, vi/1, Winter–Spring
	'Choral Music in Montreal ca. 1900: Three Composers,' *University of Toronto Quarterly*, lxiii/4, Summer

Reviews and Review-Articles

1957	Pearl McCarthy: *Leo Smith: A Biographical Sketch*, *University of Toronto quarterly*, xxvi/3, April
1958	'The Vancouver International Festival, 1958,' *Canadian Music Journal*, iii/1, Autumn
1959	'The Toronto Bach Society,' *Canadian Music Journal*, iv/1, Autumn
1961	Helmut Kallmann: *A History of Music in Canada, 1534–1914*, *University of Toronto Quarterly*, xxx/4, July
	'The Summer Season; Stratford,' *Canadian Music Journal*, vi/1, Autumn

John Beckwith's Principal Compositions and Writings 313

1964	R. Murray Schafer, ed: *British Composers in Interview*, *University of Toronto Quarterly*, xxxiii/4, July
	Igor Stravinsky and Robert Craft: *Dialogues and a Diary*, *Canadian Forum*, July
1965	'Wanda Landowska,' *The Tamarack Review*, xxvii, Autumn
1971	Iannis Xenakis: *Syrmos* and other works (5-LP album), *Les Cahiers canadiens de musique/Canada Music Book*, ii, Spring
1975	Wilhelm Amtmann: *Music in Canada, 1600–1800*, *The Globe and Mail*, 10 May
1977	Leonard Bernstein: *The Unanswered Question*, *The Globe and Mail*, 17 January
1984	Stan Rogers: *From Fresh Water* (LP), *Canadian Folk Music Bulletin*, xviii/4, December
1989	H. Wiley Hitchcock and Stanley Sadie ed: *The New Grove Dictionary of American Music*; Gilbert Chase: *America's Music*, 3d ed; H. Wiley Hitchcock: *Music in the United States: A Historical Introduction*, 3d ed, *Canadian University Music Review*, ix/2
	Otto Friedrich: *Glenn Gould: A Life and Variations*, *Books in Canada*, June–July
1991	Dale McIntosh: *History of Music in British Columbia, 1850–1950*, Music Library Association *Notes*, xlviii/2, December
1992	Carol Oja: *Colin McPhee: Composer in Two Worlds*, *American Music*, x/2, Summer

List of Contributors

Lee R. Bartel	University of Toronto
Lawrence Beckwith	Canadian Broadcasting Corporation
Beverley Diamond	York University
Gail Dixon	University of Western Ontario
Alan M. Gillmor	Carleton University
Tammy Gutnik	University of California, Los Angeles
Elaine Keillor	Carleton University
Gordana Lazarevich	University of Victoria
John Mayo	Scarborough College, University of Toronto
Timothy J. McGee	University of Toronto
Don McLean	McGill University
Carl Morey	Institute for Canadian Music, University of Toronto
James Reaney	University of Guelph
Timothy Rice	University of California, Los Angeles
Patricia Martin Shand	University of Toronto
Marilynn J. Smiley	State University of New York, Oswego
Gordon E. Smith	Queen's University
Nicholas Temperley	University of Illinois

www.ingramcontent.com/pod-product-compliance
Lightning Source LLC
Chambersburg PA
CBHW071149070526
44584CB00019B/2719